First Course in
Applied Behavior Analysis

Also of interest from Brooks/Cole

Learning

Learning and Behavior, Third Edition by Paul Chance

Sniffy, the Virtual Rat, Version 4.5 for Macintosh and Windows
by Lester Krames, Jeff Graham, and Tom Alloway

Behavior Therapy/Behavior Modification

Self-Directed Behavior: Self-Modification for Personal Adjustment, Sixth Edition
by David L. Watson and Roland G. Tharp

Contemporary Behavior Therapy, Third Edition by Michael L. Spiegler and
David C. Guevremont

First Course in
Applied Behavior Analysis

Paul Chance

Salisbury State University

Brooks/Cole Publishing Company

I(T)P® An International Thomson Publishing Company

Pacific Grove • Albany • Belmont • Bonn • Boston • Cincinnati • Detroit • Johannesburg • London • Madrid
Melbourne • Mexico City • New York • Paris • Singapore • Tokyo • Toronto • Washington

Sponsoring Editor: *Marianne Taflinger*
Marketing Team: *Lauren Harp, Christine Davis,*
 and Alicia Barelli
Editorial Assistant: *Scott Brearton*
Production Editor: *Jamie Sue Brooks*
Production Service: *Penna Design and Production*
Manuscript Editor: *Barbara Kimmel*
Permissions Editor: *Elaine Jones*

Interior Design: *Katherine Tillotson*
Illustrations: *Diane Chance*
Cover Design: *Lisa Thompson*
Cover Illustration: *Harry Briggs*
Typesetting: *TBH/Typecast, Inc.*
Cover Printing: *Phoenix Color Corp.*
Printing and Binding: *Maple-Vail Book*
 Manufacturing Group

For more information, contact:

BROOKS/COLE PUBLISHING COMPANY
511 Forest Lodge Road
Pacific Grove, CA 93950
USA

International Thomson Publishing Europe
Berkshire House 168–173
High Holborn
London WC1V 7AA
England

Thomas Nelson Australia
102 Dodds Street
South Melbourne, 3205
Victoria, Australia

Nelson Canada
1120 Birchmount Road
Scarborough, Ontario
Canada M1K 5G4

International Thomson Editores
Seneca 53
Col. Polanco
11560 México, D. F., México

International Thomson Publishing GmbH
Königswinterer Strasse 418
53227 Bonn
Germany

International Thomson Publishing Asia
221 Henderson Road
#05–10 Henderson Building
Singapore 0315

International Thomson Publishing Japan
Hirakawacho Kyowa Building, 3F
2-2-1 Hirakawacho
Chiyoda-ku, Tokyo 102
Japan

Printed in the United States of America.

10 9 8 7 6 5 4 3 2 1

Library of Congress Cataloging-in-Publication Data

Chance, Paul.
    First course in applied behavior analysis / by Paul Chance.
        p.   cm.
    Includes bibliographical references and index.
    ISBN 0-534-33936-0 (pbk.)
    1. Behavior modification.   I. Title.
BF637.B4C43   1997
153.8'5 — dc21   97-25987
                                                  CIP

To the students of Salisbury State University
and Mary Baldwin College
who helped make this book better

Preface

*F*IRST *COURSE*, as its title implies, is intended for students taking an introductory course in applied behavior analysis or related subject, such as behavior modification, behavior theory, or applications of learning. The emphasis of the text is on practical solutions to behavior problems, including problems encountered by parents, teachers, managers, guidance counselors, school psychologists, clinical psychologists, psychiatrists, speech therapists, nurses, physical and occupational therapists, and social workers. Any student whose work or daily activities will require interacting with people whose behavior is problematic should benefit from reading this text.

The text is divided into the following eight sections:

Introduction. The introductory section includes a chapter on the basic theory behind applied behavior analysis and a chapter on methods. The latter chapter introduces the student to behavioral assessment, single case research design, measures of behavior change, inter-observer reliability, graphing, and other topics basic to behavioral research. For students who are already familiar with these concepts, the chapter provides a good review; for students who are unfamiliar with behavioral methods, the chapter provides essential background for understanding studies described in later chapters.

Increasing the Frequency of Behavior. This section includes chapters on reinforcement, prompting and fading, and shaping and chaining—all useful procedures when the problem is that a behavior does not occur as often as desired.

Decreasing the Frequency of Behavior. This section includes two chapters covering extinction, differential reinforcement, and punishment—procedures for dealing with problems in which a behavior occurs too often. Punishment is covered last to emphasize that, in general, other procedures should be tried first.

Establishing Discriminations. This section includes a chapter on discrimination training and introduces the concept of stimulus control. Discrimination is covered at this point because sometimes the problem is to increase the frequency of a behavior in one situation and decrease it in others.

Generalization and Maintenance. Once a behavior problem has been successfully treated, steps must be taken to ensure that the changes occur in natural settings and that the changes persist after the intervention has ended. The chapter on maintenance includes both maintenance schedules and maintenance training.

Modifying Respondent Behavior. All of the problem-solving procedures covered thus far apply primarily to operant behavior. This section deals with procedures for modifying respondent behavior.

Ethics and the Future of Applied Behavior Analysis. The chapter in this section discusses ethical problems faced by those who attempt to change behavior. It also discusses the current status of applied behavior analysis and the prospects for its future.

Review and Sham Exam. The chapter in this section provides a brief review of the entire text. It also provides a practice (sham) exam. No new material is covered in this chapter; its sole purpose is to help the student prepare for the instructor's final examination.

Features of the Text

Most chapters of the book follow a standard format: a very brief review of the topic covered in the previous chapter, followed by coverage of the new topic, followed by a chapter review. After this the reader finds a number of "handouts"— items similar to those instructors typically provide to students. Handouts include a set of exercises, a reprint (in most cases, an excerpt from a journal; some of these are classics), a reading list, and a set of endnotes. The endnotes provide sources for material covered in the chapter as well as supplementary discussion. Some chapters also include a mini-essay on a topic related to the chapter.

First Course assumes no background in behavior analysis, learning principles, or research methods. It is meant to be easy to understand and fun to read. The assumption is that the challenge in a course on applied behavior analysis should come from figuring out how to apply scientific method to behavior problems, not from struggling with the turgid prose of a text. Toward this end I have tried to use a minimum of jargon and to write in simple declarative sentences. I have also used lots of examples and have exemplified each procedure (reinforcement, extinction, etc.) with research and case studies usually covered in some detail under the heading "illustrative studies."

A Simulated Classroom

The text is unusual in several ways, but by far the most striking difference between it and other texts is that it creates a simulated classroom. The course content is presented by a fictitious instructor, Dr. Cee, to a small group of equally fictitious students. (This requires a certain amount of what the poets call "suspension of disbelief.") The purpose of the simulation is not merely to entertain the reader; it is to prompt the reader to answer questions raised in the course of a "lesson" and provide feedback about those answers.

I was unsure of my ability to create convincing dialogue. But when an instructor who read an early draft of the book first accused me of taping my classes and transcribing the tapes to produce a manuscript (something it did not occur to me to do), and then complained about the students "interrupting" Dr. Cee "just when he was about to say something important," I took this as evidence that my effort at creating a believable classroom had been at least moderately successful.

Another unusual feature of *First Course* is the inclusion of studies in which the intervention failed or was not entirely successful. The challenge for the instructor (and the textbook writer) is to make the fundamentals of applied behavior analysis as simple as possible without giving the impression that solving behavior problems is child's play. We must convey to our students that the great thing about scientific method is not that with it we are always successful; the great thing is that with it we always know *whether* we have been successful.

Presents Original Research Articles

A third unusual feature of the text is the reprinting of previously published material. Most of the reprinted material is excerpted from journal articles and illustrates the application of behavioral procedures. These excerpts should help to give the student a clearer idea of how behaviorists go about solving behavior problems, and of the difficulties they encounter along the way.

Instructor's Manual and Test Bank

The Instructor's Manual for *First Course in Applied Behavior Analysis* includes suggestions for teaching behavioral principles. The chapters parallel the text; each includes an outline, classroom activities, solutions to text exercises, and a chapter quiz. The chapter quiz is similar to the practice quiz in the text, and is printed on one page so that it can be photocopied for class use. A key is provided on a separate page. The manual also includes a test bank organized by chapter. Test items include completion, true-false, multiple choice, short answer, and short essay, with at least 35 items per chapter. The 465 test items are also available in a computerized format that allows selection and printing of items in a variety of ways. Items may be edited and new items can easily be added.

Acknowledgments

Many people helped make this book better than it would otherwise have been. Several people reviewed earlier drafts of the book and made useful comments and suggestions. I wish to express my appreciation to: Carl D. Cheney, Utah State University; Samuel H. Clark, North Adams State College; Douglas P. Field, Temple University; Jeannie Golden, East Carolina University; Janel K. Harris, Minnesota Department of Health; Timothy D. Ludwig, Appalachian State University; Cam L. Melville, McNeese State University; Joseph J. Plaud, University of North Dakota; Elizabeth M. Street, Central Washington University; Steven Taylor, Florida State University; Frans van Haaren, University of Florida; Jerry Venn, Mary Baldwin College; and Todd Zakrajsek, Southern Oregon State College.

I am grateful to Jamie Sue Brooks, Lisa Torri, and Elaine Jones of Brooks/ Cole. I owe a special debt to Marianne Taflinger, acquisitions editor at Brooks/ Cole, for supporting a project that undoubtedly would have scared off many other editors. I hope her faith in the project—and in me—proves justified.

Detta Penna, of Penna Design and Production, saw the project through the production stage with the help of designer Katherine Tillotson and editor Barbara Kimmel. My thanks to them all.

I would also like to offer my thanks to several people who provided information, suggestions, or especially useful comments concerning specific topics or problems: Teodoro Ayllon, Georgia State University; John E. Calamari, Chicago Medical School; E. G. Carr, State University of New York at Stony Brook; Carl D. Cheney, Utah State University; Alyce Dickinson, Western Michigan University; Robert Eisenberger, University of Delaware; John Eshleman, Aubrey Daniels Associates; Julien Guillaumot, Virginia Tech; Robert Koegel, University of California at Santa Barbara; K. A. Lattal, University of West Virginia; Jack Michael, Western Michigan University; E. K. Morris, University of Kansas; John Nevin, University of New Hampshire; J. Grayson Osborne, Utah State University; Curt Reed, University of Nevada at Reno; Bruce Thyer, University of Georgia; Jerry Venn, Mary Baldwin College; W. Joseph Wyatt, Marshall University; and Sylvia Wallace, Los Angeles.

I also want to thank Diane Chance, who created the figures and tables, and offered moral support throughout the project.

Finally, a special thanks to Jerry Venn and his students at Mary Baldwin College and to my students at Salisbury State University for serving as "guinea pigs" in the testing of early drafts of this book in courses on applied behavior analysis. Their suggestions and support are much appreciated.

All of these people helped immeasurably to improve this book. Whatever flaws remain are entirely my responsibility.

Student response to *First Course* has thus far been remarkably consistent: Although at first students are taken aback by the classroom simulation, nearly all come to like it. Most report that they find the book easier and more enjoyable than other texts they have used, yet they complete the course feeling that they have learned a good deal.

I have three main goals in teaching courses in this area: I want my students to learn the language of behavior analysis; to become acquainted with the most important procedures for changing behavior; and to learn to think differently about behavior—to recognize that scientific method can be used successfully to solve behavior problems. These were also my objectives in writing this text. I hope *First Course* will prove useful to those instructors who have similar goals.

Paul Chance

A Word to the Student

THIS TEXT IS UNLIKE any you have ever used. My hope is that it will also prove to be both more enjoyable and more helpful.

I have attempted to create a simulated classroom. There is an instructor, Dr. Cee, and eight college students fairly typical of those taking an introductory course in applied behavior analysis or a related subject. (You will find their names and a few biographical facts in the class roster that follows.) Each chapter is a "lesson" on a given topic, followed by "handouts" that include exercises, a recommended reading list, one or two reprints, endnotes (references to material covered in the lesson), and sometimes a mini-essay by Dr. Cee.

Dr. Cee's teaching style consists of a lecture punctuated by frequent questions. The questions are designed both to keep his students on their toes and to induce them to think critically about the day's topic. (More than anything else, Dr. Cee wants his students to come out of his course thinking differently about behavior.) Students also ask questions and offer comments of their own during the lessons, and Dr. Cee responds to these remarks.

As with any class, not everything that is said is worth committing to memory. This may cause you some problems. If Dr. Cee were to ask, "Jamal, what is 8 times 7?" Jamal might answer, "Fifty-six"—or he might say, "Forty-two." When Jamal answers our hypothetical question, Dr. Cee is likely to say, "That's right" or, "No, try again." But he might instead turn to another student and ask, "Maya, what do you think? Is Jamal right?"

This approach can get confusing for the student who is not reading carefully. You might be tempted to say, "Why doesn't the author simply say, 'Eight times seven is 56' and be done with it?"

The reason is that the interactions between Dr. Cee and the students provide a mechanism for involving you

Science is . . . an attempt to discover order, to show that certain events stand in lawful relations to other events.

B. F. Skinner

personally in the simulated classroom. If Dr. Cee asks, "Belinda, what is an octagon?" I want you to attempt to answer before reading further. When you then read Belinda's reply ("An octagon is a kind of poisonous snake"), I want you to make a judgment about her answer before reading Dr. Cee's reaction. In some ways, *First Course* resembles programmed texts, since students are asked to participate in an active way; the difference is that the programming is in a "softer" form. I hope the simulation will make the book both interesting and effective.

The fulfillment of that hope depends partly on how you use the text. If you attempt to answer questions asked by Dr. Cee or his students, if you think critically about the answers given and comments made *before* you read on, then I believe you will get a great deal from the text. If, on the other hand, you attempt to read this text as you would any other, then there is little reason to believe that the simulation will provide any advantage.

I strongly recommend that you use a bookmark to cover the material you haven't read so that you won't see the answers to questions before you've attempted to answer them. (*A bookmark is provided for that purpose.*) I also recommend that you read each chapter at least twice; your ability to answer the questions raised in the text during a second reading should give you a pretty fair idea of how well you know the material covered.

This book is an experiment, and I hope you will help me make it a successful one. If there are things about the book you love or hate, or if you have ideas for exercises or other "handouts," please share them with me so that I can make the next edition of the book better. You can write to me c/o Brooks/Cole Publishing, 511 Forest Lodge Rd., Pacific Grove, CA 93950–5098. Better yet, send your thoughts by e-mail to Paul_Chance@CompuServe.com. Barring an unexpected flood of correspondence, I will get back to you by e-mail or snailmail.

Good luck with the book, and good luck with your first course in applied behavior analysis.

First Course in Applied Behavior Analysis

Paul Chance • Brooks\Cole Publishing Company

‹ *Class Roster* ›

Alfred   Major: General studies. Minor: None.
Plans to work in his uncle's feed store after graduating.

Belinda   Major: Education. Minor: Art.
Intends to teach in an elementary school.

Brian   Major: Psychology. Minor: Biology.
Plans to do graduate work and then specialize in basic research.

Carlotta   Major: Psychology. Minor: Mathematics.
Wants to go to graduate school and then be a consultant or
therapist.

Jamal   Major: History. Minor: Psychology.
Plans to teach history in high school, then do graduate work in
archaeology.

John   Major: Psychology. Minor: Business.
Hopes to work in the human resources department of a large
corporation.

Maya   Major: English. Minor: Journalism.
Wants to be a novelist; expects to work in public relations first.

Midori   Major: Special education. Minor: Psychology.
Plans to teach special education or work with autistic children in
a clinic.

Contents

First Course in
Applied Behavior Analysis

The ABC's of Applied Behavior Analysis

HELLO. I AM DR. CEE, and I am your instructor for this course.

Before we actually begin our study of behavior analysis, I want to say a few words about the way the course will be conducted. It is a rather unconventional approach, so please pay careful attention.

To begin with, none of you is actually a real person; you are all merely characters in a book. I have created you out of dreams and stardust, as the poet says. You are what is known as a literary device, a mechanism for accomplishing some purpose. In this case, the purpose is to convey to my readers the central ideas of behavior analysis in an effective and engaging way. That is why you are here, and I hope you are up to the task.

"Dr. Bee?"

That's *Cee,* as in the third letter of the alphabet, John. Here, I'll write it on the board:

Cee

"Oh. Sorry. Dr. Cee, I'm a bit confused."

Inevitably, John. So are some readers.

"Some what?"

Never mind. You had a question?

"Right. I'm confused. Are you actually saying that we are all just characters in a book?"

Exactly.

"But that's crazy. I mean, I'm *real*! I can see you and the classroom and the other students. I can feel the chair I'm sitting on. You're even talking to us. How can you say we're not real?"

I didn't say you weren't real, John. I said you weren't real *people*. You have a kind of reality. You exist within the realm of these pages. This book is your world, and, although it isn't perfect, it's a pretty good world as worlds go. You come to life whenever any character in a book comes to life—when someone reads the book.

"I agree with John, Dr. Cee. This sounds like a class in existential philosophy. I mean, I *know* I'm not just a figment of somebody's imagination."

Well, Carlotta, you are free to believe that you are a real person; it does no harm. And we haven't time to pursue the philosophical problem of proving one's existence. Let's get on with the matter at hand, which is to introduce this course.

Each class period (which is, from the reader's standpoint, a chapter) will follow the same basic structure. Each day will focus on a new topic. I don't usually lecture for very long at a time. I generally use a sort of Socratic technique that involves asking you a lot of questions. I also hope that you will ask me questions or make comments about the day's topic.

Of course, I hope that the reader will attempt to answer these questions—yours and mine—before reading further. In fact, that's the whole point of the questions—to get readers actively involved in the "class" I'm conducting. That way, this text becomes a kind of tutorial: The reader attempts to answer a question raised by one of us, and then reads the answer. Instead of just reading about the subject, the reader becomes an active member of our class.

At the end of the day's lesson, I will give you a number of handouts. Some of these will be exercises of various sorts, at least some of which I think you will enjoy. They are intended to help you (and the reader, of course) learn the concepts covered in the lesson.

For instance, one of today's handouts is an exercise I call "Feed the Skeleton." This is a skeletal outline of the day's lesson. Your task is to fill in the missing information—to put some meat on the bones—by providing missing information. This exercise will help you review, and it will help you understand how the various points covered in the lesson are related to one another. At least, I hope it will.

Other handouts are meant to encourage you to think critically about a specific problem related to the day's lesson. For instance, you might be asked to suggest how you would apply a particular procedure to a hypothetical problem.

Some handouts are outside reading materials. I wrote a few of these myself, but most are by other people and have been published before. They cover topics not covered in the day's lesson.

Another handout is a list of suggested readings. These items are all relatively short, and most are easy to read. If you are seriously interested in behavior analysis, or if you contemplate a career in psychology, social work, or some other area dealing with human behavior, you should read at least a few of the items on these lists. Many of them are classics.

The last handout is always a set of endnotes concerning points covered in the day's lesson. They include references for research studies mentioned, discussion of some of the finer points of behavior analysis, and, once in a while, one of my quips.

"One of your whips! Wow, this class is beginning to sound kinky."

Quips, Alfred! Quips! A little joke. A bon mot. A pun. A funny remark. A—

"Are these handouts just for our entertainment, or do we actually have to read all this stuff and do all the exercises?"

Well, if you are a student in my class, you have to read every word of the handouts and do all the exercises. However, if you are a student in someone else's class and you're reading this book, then you'll have to ask your instructor about that. Some instructors may assign only some of the handouts.

If you pay careful attention in class, attempt to answer all the questions that come up (whether from me or another student), and do the exercises and some outside readings, you will learn a great deal and should even ace the course. Any questions? Yes, Alfred?

"You didn't mention our text. Isn't there a text for the course?"

We are the text, Alfred. That's what we've just been talking about. You and your classmates and I are the text. And, of course, the exercises and reading assignments I mentioned. Really, Alfred, you must pay closer attention.

"Sorry. I forgot."

Now, let's talk about behavior analysis.

Behavior Analysis

Behavior analysis is such a young field—it's only about 50 years old—that people are still arguing about how to define it.[1] I'd like the field to come up with a definition that is short and simple, something like the definition biologists use for their field: the study of life.

One short, simple definition of behavior analysis that I have proposed is:

> **Behavior analysis:**
> **The science of behavior change.**

I like that definition because it seems to me that the unique focus of behavior analysis is how and why behavior changes. People in other fields—cognitive psychology, social psychology, anthropology, and sociology, to name a few—are interested in behavior, but they are not especially interested in understanding how and why behavior changes; behavior analysts are.

Perhaps this definition will catch on eventually, but until then I have to ask you to learn a more conventional definition. So, I'm going to give you a definition that most behavior analysts would probably find reasonably satisfactory. I'll put it on the board, and then we'll discuss it:

> **Behavior analysis:**
> **The study of the functional relations**
> **between behavior and environmental events.**

Now, this definition—

"I like the first definition better."

Well, thank you, Belinda. So do I. But this more formal definition is closer to the way most behavior analysts define the field.[2] Now, this definition, the more formal one, requires that you understand three concepts: functional relations, behavior, and environmental events. Let's take each in turn.

Functional Relations

A functional relation is one in which one event varies dependably with another:

Functional relation:
The tendency of one event to vary in a regular
way with one or more other events.

The simplest sort of functional relation is the one that is stated, "If X, then Y." This means that if event X occurs, then event Y occurs. They are connected, at least in the mathematical sense, so that you can reliably predict that whenever X occurs, Y occurs. For example, if I throw the switch on the wall over there, the ceiling lights go off. If the switch is down, the lights are off. If X, then Y. See?

Science can be defined as the search for functional relations among events. Maybe the best way to illustrate this is with an example. Imagine that you have a music box. You lift the lid, and suddenly you hear the melody, "Pop Goes the Weasel." You close the lid, and the melody stops. Someone tell me what's going on. Yes, Belinda?

> "Well, when you lift the lid, it releases a latch, and that allows a wheel to turn. The wheel is operated by a spring, and when the wheel turns, little burrs on the wheel hit different bars. Each bar sounds a different note. The burrs are arranged on the wheel so that the notes for "Pop Goes the Weasel" sound."

That's amazing! You can tell all that just from what I said?

> "Well, no, not really. But I had a music box and that's how it worked."

I see. Well, that's very interesting. So you're saying that there is a functional relation between the position of the lid and the music. Suppose I lift the lid again, and there's no melody?

> "Well, like I said, it's powered by a spring. The spring has wound down, so the wheel isn't turning."

Remarkable. Well, if I ever have a broken music box, I'll bring it to you. Now, suppose the box is sitting there, with the lid up, and I hear the melody again?

> "Maybe the wheel was just sort of gummed up by dirt and it got loose."

Suppose I walk over to my window, which was open, and I close it, and the music abruptly stops?

"Hmm. I don't see how that could affect the box."

I open the window, and now I hear the melody again. I close the window, and the melody abruptly stops; I open the window, and the melody starts; close it, and the music stops; open—

"The music is coming from outside! That's not fair: I thought you meant the music was coming from the *box*."

I know. I tricked you. The point is that identifying functional relations between events seems very simple once the relations have been pointed out, but they're not always so easy to see before that. And most functional relations are more complicated than a simple, "If X, then Y." The relation might be more like, "If V, W, and X, then Y." Or, perhaps, "If V, W, and X, then Y and Z." You have a question, Jamal?

"Yes. If you find a functional relation, like 'If X, then Y,' does that mean that X causes Y?"

Not necessarily. Usually cause-effect relations are more complicated than that, so scientists generally talk about functional relations, rather than causal relations. It is often difficult to say, "X causes Y," but you can say that X and Y vary together in some regular way. You can say, for example, that if the earth is in a certain position with respect to the sun, then a certain hemisphere will have summer weather. Or, you can say that if a person is exposed to bacteria X, it's likely that he will get disease Y.

I've said that science is the search for functional relations among events. Behavior analysis is the search for functional relations among behavioral events and environmental events. So, next you have to understand what is meant by behavior.

Behavior

What is behavior? Yes, John?

"It's whatever people do."

That's the way behavior is often defined, but in this course our definition will be a little different:

Behavior:
Anything a person does
that can be observed.[3]

This definition suggests that it is not enough to say that behavior is what someone does; we must also specify that it can be observed by someone. What do you think of that? Yes, Midori?

"I don't see why you have to be able to observe it. If somebody does something that can't be observed, it's still behavior."

Perhaps, but you can't have a science of things that can't be observed in some way.[4] It's rather like the philosopher's question about a tree falling in a forest—you know the one I mean?

"If a tree falls in the forest, and there's no one there, does it make a sound when it hits the ground?"

Yes, that's the one. I don't know what the philosophers say about that, but from the perspective of *science,* if we can't observe an event, it doesn't exist.

"What about thinking and feeling? Do they count as behavior?"

Are thinking and feeling things that you do?

"Yes."

Can you observe them?

"Well, I usually know what *I'm* thinking and feeling."

Then they qualify as behavior. But you're right in suggesting that thoughts and feelings are different from other sorts of behavior. For example, you can walk across a room and get a banana, or you can *think* about walking across the room and getting a banana. They're both behavior, but there's a big difference. Does anyone see what it is? Yes, Alfred?

"In one case, you get to eat the banana!"

Exactly. Thoughts and feelings don't have the same sort of effects on the environment that actions have. Actions usually have measurable effects on the environment—such as picking up a banana—and this makes it possible for other people to observe them; thoughts and feelings don't, which means they can be observed only by the person performing them. Behavior analysts use this difference to distinguish between overt and covert behavior. I'll put the definitions on the board:

Overt behavior:
Behavior that can be observed by someone other than the person performing it.

Covert behavior:
Behavior that can be observed only by the person performing it.[5]

Now, these terms imply a clear dichotomy. In fact, however, it's more of a continuum. Walking is very clearly an overt behavior, and thinking about walking is clearly covert.[6] But what about the beating of your heart? Is that overt or covert? Jamal?

"I'd say it's covert, because other people can't see it. Even the person himself can't tell his heart is beating unless it's beating really fast or hard."

So you think it's covert. Yes, Midori?

"With a stethoscope, you can hear a person's heart."

Good point. That means that, with the right equipment, it can be observed. And that illustrates the difficulty with the distinction between overt and covert behavior. Sometimes it depends on the technology available to us. Thinking provides another example. Sometimes we think "out loud." In other words, our thoughts are audible speech. In that case, anyone can observe our thinking, or at least part of it, so it's overt behavior. When people think aloud, their thinking is overt, but if they remain silent, they can keep their thoughts to themselves; then the behavior is covert. Yes, Belinda?

"Sometimes you can see people's lips move. You can't hear what they're saying, but their thoughts are observable, in a sense. I mean, if you videotaped them and showed the tape to someone who reads lips, the lipreader might be able to tell you what the person was thinking."

That's true. We could also record muscular activity in the area of the larynx, and (theoretically, at least) we might be able to translate those recordings into words. So again we see that behavior falls on a continuum from overt to covert, and how we classify a particular behavior depends not only on who observes the behavior but also on the technology available to the observer. The important thing to remember is that behavior includes only things that people do that can be observed by someone. Yes, John?

"What about unconscious thoughts? Do they count as behavior?"

In order to qualify as behavior, an act has to be observable. Unconscious thoughts and feelings (if they exist at all) are, by definition, unobservable, so they fall outside the realm of behavior analysis.

"What about dreams? I'm unconscious when I dream, but if I'm awakened during a dream, I can describe it."

A good point, Midori. Dreaming is something we do, and if you can report a dream, then it counts as behavior. Dreaming also qualifies as behavior if someone else observes it. Dreaming is associated with rapid eye movements and with certain electrical patterns, or brain waves, on an electroencephalograph or EEG. If you are asleep, and I observe rapid eye movements and certain brain waves, I can't say that I have observed your dream, but I can say that I have observed you dreaming.

Okay. So behavior is overt or covert. There's another way of classifying behavior that also divides behavior into two kinds. One type is called respondent:

**Respondent behavior:
Behavior that is most readily influenced by
events that precede it; reflexive behavior.[7]**

Respondent behavior is the kind of behavior people usually describe as involuntary or reflexive. It is behavior that is preceded and readily produced by a specific environmental event. For instance, if you're sitting quietly and a jet plane flies over and breaks the sound barrier, causing a sudden loud noise—the sonic boom—you're likely to jump, and there will be some physiological changes, including a sudden increase in heartbeat. That's the startle response. The startle response is an example of respondent behavior. Other examples are the flow of acids into the stomach in response to food; inhaling and exhaling in response to changes in the levels of oxygen in the blood; and blinking an eye when a speck of dust hits it. Other examples include emotions, such as anger, fear, and love. These feelings are associated with reflexive physiological responses, such as changes in heart rate, breathing patterns, sweating—

"Knocking knees."

Quite right, Alfred. When you are very frightened, such as you might be if you had to give a talk before a large audience, your palms would sweat, you'd feel hot and maybe a little dizzy, your stomach might feel upset, your hands might get a little shaky and your knees might literally knock together.

"Is the fear the feeling of being afraid, or is it all those physiological things that are happening?"

That's an excellent question, Carlotta. I can probably say, without too much fear of contradiction, that most behaviorists would say the physiological changes *are* the feeling of fear. In other words, when you say you feel afraid, what you are doing is commenting on the physiological changes that are happening. Social psychologists have done some interesting work on emotions and physiological reactions that supports this view.[8] But this—

"But you don't just feel your heart beating faster and sweating and all that stuff when you're afraid; you feel fear."

To say that a feeling is physiology is not to demean the feeling in any way, Midori. The feeling is just as real and just as important however you view it. But the behaviorist is saying that when you feel afraid, what that means is that you are feeling various physiological reactions. . . . I can see I'm not making this very clear; can anybody say it more clearly than I have? Yes, Brian?

"I think an example might help. Suppose two guys see a rattlesnake while they're hiking. One of them reacts very little physiologically, while the other one's body goes ballistic. It's the second one who's going to say he's really scared. They both know rattlesnakes are dangerous and that they have to be careful, but one of them is feeling all these things going on in his body and calls it fear, while the other doesn't."

Well said, Brian. Does that help, Midori?

"I don't know. Maybe. I'll have to live with it for a while."

That's fair enough. One of today's handouts is an essay on feelings by B. F. Skinner; perhaps that will help.

Now, respondent behavior is a very important part of our lives. Feelings such as fear, anger, love, hate, and disgust are among the things that make humans different from machines. These emotions are also sometimes the source of considerable trouble to us, particularly when they are inappropriate. For example, it's very helpful to be a little afraid of a rattlesnake, but it's not helpful to be so afraid of them that you leap off the edge of a cliff to get away from one. One of the things behavior analysts do is help people get control over emotions that are making them miserable.

Okay, so respondent behavior is one kind of behavior, and it's very important. But it's obvious that we do a lot of things that are not respondent. This other kind of behavior is called operant:

**Operant behavior:
Behavior that is readily influenced
by events that follow it.[9]**

Examples of operant behavior include walking, talking, picking up a telephone, writing a letter, and telling a story. Most of the things we think of when we think of behavior are examples of operant behavior.

Operant behavior, unlike respondent behavior, is *not* a reflex reaction to some event. In overt operant behavior, the person is acting on the environment every bit as much as the environment is acting on the person.[10] Behaviorists often talk about—

"Wait a minute."

Yes, Jamal?

"How can you say that operant behavior is influenced by events that follow it? If the behavior has already occurred, nothing can influence it. It's history."

Quite right. Once a behavior has occurred, nothing can change that particular instance of behavior. As you say, it's history; it's out of reach. But when I say that behavior is influenced by events that follow it, I don't mean that particular instance of behavior, but rather behavior of that type. If you pick up a hot kettle, for example, the fact that the kettle was hot does not alter the fact that you picked it up, but it might alter the likelihood of your picking it up again.

Carlotta? Do you have a question?

"Yes. If I get something in my eye, I blink. But I can blink any time I want to, whether there's something in my eye or not. So is blinking operant or respondent?"

Ah. It's not always easy to tell. Sometimes the same behavior, or at least what *seems* to be the same behavior, may be either operant or respondent, and the eye blink is a good example.

Behaviorists often talk about the operant-respondent distinction by saying that respondent behavior is *elicited,* whereas operant behavior is *emitted.* The difference has to do with the degree to which the behavior is evoked by an event. You get a speck of dirt in your eye and you blink. The blink is automatic, and it's hard to suppress; it's elicited by the speck of dirt contacting your eye, so it's . . . what, John?

"It's respondent behavior."

Right. But if someone quietly says, "Blink!" that word doesn't exert the same kind of control as the speck of dirt; you can blink or not blink. That kind of blinking is . . . Maya?

"Operant behavior?"

Yes. As this implies, you can't always identify a particular instance of behavior as operant or respondent based on the characteristics of the behavior. You have to look at the *relationship* between the behavior and things going on in the environment. Yes, John?

"I'm kinda confused. We've got, now, four different kinds of behavior? Behavior can be overt, covert, respondent, or operant. Is that right?"

Well, yes. Here, let me see if a simple fourfold table will help. Watch:

	Overt	Covert
Operant		
Respondent		

Now, if you look at the table, you can see that all overt behavior is either operant or respondent, and all covert behavior is either operant or respondent. Similarly, all operant behavior is either overt or covert, as is all respondent behavior. Let's try filling in the four cells of the table. What would be an example of an overt, operant behavior, Midori?

"Walking?"

Good. How about another example, Belinda?

"Picking up a book?"

And another, John?

"Reading a book."

Good. All of these examples involve emitted behavior—behavior that is not an automatic response to an event in the environment. Someone may ask you to read a book, and you may do so, but it's not an involuntary reaction, like the startle response. And all of these examples of behavior can be observed by people other than the person performing them, so they're overt. Now, how about an example of overt respondent behavior. Midori?

"Well, the knee-jerk reflex?"

Okay. How about another example, Maya?

"The pupillary reflex? When you shine a light in someone's eye, and the pupil gets smaller?"

A good example. It's involuntary and it's elicited, so it's respondent; but anyone looking at a person's eye can observe it, so it's overt.

Now can someone think of an example of *covert* operant behavior? Yes, John?

"I'm not sure about this, but wouldn't some thoughts be operant behavior? Like, maybe you're thinking about preparing a meal. If you were actually preparing the meal, that would be operant behavior, so why wouldn't thinking about preparing a meal be operant?"

A good point. There seem to be two differences between the two activities: One is that preparing a meal is overt—anyone can observe it—whereas thinking about preparing a meal is usually covert—only the person who's doing the thinking can observe it.

The other difference is that the overt behavior affects the person's surroundings, while the covert behavior does not. To put it another way, if you actually prepare a meal, you end up with something to eat, but if you just think about preparing a meal, you go hungry. (On the other hand, there's no washing up to do!) Can you give me another example of covert operant behavior, Jamal, one that doesn't involve food?

"Thinking about a problem. You might do an arithmetic problem in your head; that might involve the same steps as doing the problem on paper, but it wouldn't be observable to anyone but the problem solver."

Good. Now, let's have an example of covert respondent behavior. Brian?

"A person who isn't very afraid of snakes might still react to a snake in ways that couldn't be observed."

Such as?

"Well, his heart might beat a little faster, or his palms might sweat just a little; these reactions might not be noticeable to others without special equipment."

So you're saying that even if a person says he's unafraid, he might react in the same way as a person who is terrified, but not as intensely?

"Yes. The reactions would be private."

Okay. We've talked about four different kinds of behavior. Everything people can do, their entire behavioral repertoire, is composed of some combination of these four kinds of behavior.

"What was that term? Behavioral . . .?"

Behavioral repertoire, John. It refers to all of the kinds of behavior, overt and covert, operant and respondent, of which an individual is capable at any given time. That's another term you should know, so I'll write the definition on the board:

Behavioral repertoire: All the things an individual is capable of doing at any given moment.

If you can speak English, that's part of your behavioral repertoire. If you can also speak Greek, then speaking Greek is part of your repertoire. If you know three words of Latin, those three words are part of your repertoire. If you have a tendency to pull on your left ear, that's part of your repertoire. If you become frightened when you see a snake or you feel a rush of warmth and joy when you see a baby, that's part of your behavioral repertoire.

On the other hand, if you used to be a great baton twirler but now you can't twirl at all, then baton twirling is no longer part of your repertoire. And if you studied French in high school for four years but can't speak a word of it, then speaking French is not in your repertoire.

All the things that you do, or are capable of doing, are part of your behavioral repertoire. The concept is important because behavior analysis has a lot to do with changing behavioral repertoires.

Okay, so much for behavior. Our definition of behavior analysis does not say that it is the study of behavior. It says that it is the study of functional relations between behavior and . . . and what, Jamal?

"Environmental events?"

Right. So we need to talk about environmental events.

Environmental Events

The term *behavior* refers to things a person does; the term *environmental event* refers to things the environment does:

Environmental event:
Any event in a person's environment
that can be observed.[11]

Environmental events are the kinds of things we usually refer to as experience. But you need to keep in mind that we are talking about physical events—events that have some sort of measurable effect.[12] The ring of a telephone, for example, can be recorded on a tape recorder or monitored on an audiometer. When—

"Dr. Cee?"

Yes, John?

"Doesn't that leave out a lot? I mean, aren't there a lot of things that affect our behavior that aren't physical events?"

Such as?

"Such as the *meaning* of things! For instance, two people might say the same thing to you, but one person might be sincere and the other person might be sarcastic. They're both environmental events, but they have different meanings."

What tells you whether the person is sincere or sarcastic?

"Things like the way he looks and his tone of voice."

Those are physical events. Muscles of the face contract one way to produce a smile and another way to produce a sneer. The two faces are physically different. We can observe and measure those differences.

Tone of voice refers to differences in the physical properties of sound. For example, think about how you say, "Oh, really!" when you are sincere. Now think about how you say it when you are being sarcastic. There's a little different emphasis in the pronunciation. The difference in sound is physical, so we're still talking about physical events. Two people may be saying the same words, but they're not providing the same environmental event. Yes, Jamal?

"What about our own thoughts? They're not physical."

Remember, thinking and feeling are things we do, so they come under the heading of . . .

"Behavior."

Right. Thoughts and feelings are behavior, not environmental events.

"What about physiological events?"

Physical events that happen inside our skin certainly can affect our behavior. A brain tumor or an abscessed tooth may affect our behavior in important ways, for example. So do many commonly ingested drugs. The study of the effects of drugs, disease, or normal physiological processes on behavior is certainly a legitimate branch of behavior science. But, as far as most behavior analysts are concerned, they are not part of the subject matter of behavior analysis. Most behavior analysts are concerned with the effects of events in the external environment on behavior, and that will be our focus in this course.[13]

Environmental events can be described in terms of physical dimensions, including color, shape, size, brightness, texture, duration, and so on. We're all used to describing events in our environment in these terms, so I don't think we need dwell on that. However, one feature of experience deserves comment: the temporal relation of the event to behavior.

"Temporal relation?"

Yes, Maya. The word *temporal* means having to do with time, so we're talking about the relationship, in time, of environmental events to behavior. Most environmental events can be thought of as falling into one of two categories, depending on their temporal relation to behavior: those events that occur before the behavior, and those that occur after the behavior. The first events are called antecedents; the second are called consequences:

**Antecedents:
Environmental events that occur
<u>before</u> a behavior.**

**Consequences:
Environmental events that occur
<u>after</u> a behavior.**

Strictly speaking, we should speak of antecedents and *postcedents*. That's because the events that follow behavior are not necessarily consequences of the behavior. For example, you might shout an obscenity, and this might be followed by a flash of lightning and the boom of thunder. The lightning and thunder are postcedents of your behavior, but they are not consequences of it. In the same way, if someone annoys you, you might think to yourself, "I wish he'd drop dead." Obviously, there will be occasions when such thoughts are coincidentally followed by the wished-for event. That does not mean that the death was a *consequence* of the wish.

"You'd still feel guilty though, I'll bet."

That may be, Carlotta. Postcedent events can affect our behavior even if their occurrence is pure coincidence. The point I want to emphasize is that behaviorists apply the term *consequence* to any event that follows behavior, whether it was caused by the behavior or not. A question, John?

"Why don't behaviorists just call them postcedents then instead of consequences?"

For two reasons: first, because the postcedents that are important to behavior usually *are* consequences of the behavior. For example, if you're playing basketball and you score two points, those points are a direct consequence of throwing the ball. And if it's hot, you might open a window; the cool breeze that follows is a consequence of opening the window.

Second, calling postcedents consequences makes for a very nice acronym: We can speak of the ABC's of behavior analysis. What are the ABC's of behavior analysis, John?

"Oh, ah, let's see. That would be . . . antecedents, behavior, and consequences."

Exactly. If we used the term *postcedents,* then we'd have to talk about the ABP's of behavior, and that wouldn't have quite the same panache.

The subject matter of behavior analysis is contained in those three letters, *ABC.*[14] Behavior analysis is the search for functional relationships among behavior and its antecedents and consequences. Certain antecedents may make a behavior more likely to occur, others may make it less likely to occur. For instance, you're more likely to run for the door if I shout, "Fire!" than you are if I shout, "Chocolate!"[15] Similarly, certain consequences may make the behavior they follow likely to occur again, while others may make the behavior unlikely to be repeated. We will be talking about these relationships throughout this course. For now, the important thing to remember is that the subject matter of behavior analysis is entirely contained in those three letters, *ABC.* If you're not talking about antecedents, behavior, or consequences, then you're not talking about behavior analysis.

To be absolutely clear, let me add that behavior analysis is *not* concerned with drives, needs, expectations, unconscious conflicts, or the other intervening variables that most people (including many psychologists) point to when they attempt to explain or change behavior.[16] Behavior analysis is concerned with behavior and with the events in a person's surroundings that precede and follow behavior.

"Does that mean that Freud was wrong—that there is no unconscious mind, no id, ego, and superego?"

What it means, Carlotta, is that those concepts fall outside the purview of behavior analysis. Our subject matter is the effects of environmental events on behavior; Freud's concepts fall outside our scope. To someone who is interested in the mind, they might be useful. That's not for me to say. Our subject matter is the way events in a person's environment affect the person's behavior.

"Dr. Cee?"

Yes, Midori?

"Are behaviorists interested only in the effects of a person's present surroundings on behavior?"

That's a good question, Midori. The effects of antecedents and consequences are cumulative.

"So the answer is 'No'?"

The answer is "No." Two people, even identical twins from remarkably similar backgrounds, might behave very differently in a given situation. That's partly because each brings his or her unique learning history to that situation. *Learning history* may be a new term for you, so I'll put a definition on the board:

> **Learning history:**
> **All the environmental events (antecedents**
> **and consequences) that have affected**
> **a person's behavior up to the present.**[17]

Behavior is affected not only by what an individual experiences in a given situation but also by what the individual experienced prior to entering that situation. The effects of any given environmental event will depend, in fact, on that individual's unique learning history.

All right, that's enough of an introduction to behavior analysis; now let's consider applied behavior analysis.

Applied Behavior Analysis

We may as well start with a definition:

> **Applied behavior analysis:**
> **The attempt to solve behavior problems by**
> **providing antecedents and/or consequences**
> **that change behavior.**[18]

Behavior analysis is concerned with understanding how environmental events change behavior; applied behavior analysis is concerned with using environmental events to change behavior in desirable ways.[19] Our focus in this course is going to be on applied behavior analysis, on solving behavior problems by—

"Who decides what's desirable?"

Ah. A very good question, Brian. Of course, the question of who makes decisions concerning efforts to change behavior is not unique to applied behavior analysis. Anyone who attempts to change behavior must be asked this question: psychiatrists who prescribe psychoactive drugs; social workers who help people access community resources; educators who teach job skills; neurosurgeons who perform operations; and so on. Just because you *can* change someone's behavior doesn't necessarily mean you have the *right* to do so. Who decides whether you should change behavior, and who decides what behavior should be changed? These are difficult, important questions, but they are not unique to applied behavior analysis.

Among behaviorists and, I think, most other professionals involved in changing behavior, the rule of thumb is that the person whose behavior may be changed should participate in the discussion of the direction of that change in so far as he or she is capable of doing so. If you're working with a teenager who's having trouble getting along with his teachers, you might be able to work with that teen to establish a set of goals and a means of pursuing them. On the other hand, you don't ask a 6-month-old infant who habitually regurgitates her food whether she would like to stop engaging in that behavior, and you don't ask a 250-lb psychiatric patient who tends to behave violently if he would like to stop assaulting people. You have to balance the needs of the individual against the needs of society.

But we are getting into ethical questions here, and I think we should defer discussion of those issues until later in the course. I think you'll be better prepared to deal with them when you know more about the kinds of things behavior analysts do.

Now, where was I? . . . Oh, yes . . . Since applied behavior analysis is concerned with solving behavior problems, we need to talk a bit about the kinds of problems and what it means to solve them.

Behavior Problems

Who can give me an example of a behavior problem? Yes, Midori?

"A person might have a fear of something, like snakes or spiders."

Why would that be a problem? Isn't it a good idea to be afraid of snakes and spiders?

"Well, a little fear might be a good thing, because sometimes snakes and spiders can hurt you. But most of them are not really dangerous, and yet some people get really bonkers when they see one. So if somebody faints or becomes hysterical whenever he sees a spider, that could be more dangerous than the spider. If you're, like, driving down the highway, and a spider drops down from the ceiling of the car, if you overreact you could end up causing a major wreck. That could do a lot more harm than the spider, even a black widow. Also, it could be really embarrassing to be with a group of people and go bananas because you saw a spider."

So you're saying that a little fear is not a problem, but if the fear is out of proportion to the danger, that can be a problem. How about another example of a problem. Yes, Carlotta?

"Sometimes a person might be bothered by unpleasant thoughts, like when you think about some terrible experience you had when you were a child. Or maybe you were the victim of a crime, and you can't stop thinking about it."

And why would that be a problem?

"Well, it's unpleasant. I mean, you just keep thinking about this thing that happened and thinking about it and thinking about it. You feel like you wish you could just turn off your brain and not think about anything, but you can't stop. It's like when you hear a song and then you keep singing it in your head over and over even though you don't want to."

So it's unpleasant, and that makes it a problem. Is there any other reason why it's a problem? . . . Alfred?

"It might interfere with other things you're trying to do. Like, you might have trouble concentrating on a job if, in your head, you're singing, 'Ninety-nine bottles of beer on the wall, ninety-nine bottles of beer. If one of those—'"

Yes, yes, thank you, Alfred; we see your point. It might be difficult to deal with a task if you're engaged in some other behavior, such as reminiscing about some unpleasant experience. Most of us have been upset about something and found thoughts about it so intrusive that we found it hard to carry on a conversation with someone, or listen to a teacher, or read a book. If thoughts repeatedly interfere with our ability to perform daily tasks, the problem is called *obsessional thinking*. Obsessional thinking is a difficult problem to deal with, but it is one with which behavior analysts have had some success. Can someone suggest another behavior problem . . . Maya?

"A person might be extremely shy. She might feel very uncomfortable with other people, especially people she doesn't know. She might be unwilling to go places where she would be expected to interact with others, such as dances and parties—that could interfere quite a bit with a person's everyday life, since there are lots of situations in which you meet new people."

So extreme shyness might interfere with a job, just as a fear of spiders might, and of course it's unpleasant to be uncomfortable around others. John, can you give us one more example of a behavior problem?

"Uhm. Say a person can't read. In today's society that's a major problem, because if you can't read you can't drive a car safely or use a bus schedule, you can't follow the instructions on a medicine label, you can't use a computer. I knew a guy who graduated from high school and when his girl-friend—she was in the army—when she went to Kuwait during the Persian Gulf War, he had to ask one of his old teachers to read her letters to him because he couldn't read."

So the inability to read is another problem. Okay, let's put these problems on the board:

Problems

1. afraid of snakes
2. obsessed by bad thoughts
3. shy—seldom interact with others
4. can't read

Okay. Now let's take each one of these and talk about what solving the problem would mean. In other words, what would it require for us to say that the problem has been solved? Let's take the first one. Suppose you were terribly afraid of snakes. What would it require for you to say that your problem had been solved? Alfred?

"To live in a place where there aren't any snakes!"

Ah. Like Ireland. Well, that's a possibility, but there might be some problems with that solution. Maya?

"I think you'd still have a problem, because somebody might bring a snake into Ireland. And you'd be a prisoner; you'd never be able to go anywhere because there might be snakes."

So what do *you* think would be a good solution?

"It would mean overcoming the fear. It would mean feeling less afraid around snakes or spiders or whatever, and not fainting or running away."

Good. And what would it mean to say that we'd solved the problem of being obsessed by unpleasant thoughts? Midori?

"Not having those thoughts bothering you all the time."

All right, what about the third problem—extreme shyness? Jamal?

"Solving that problem would mean that they would be more outgoing, more comfortable meeting and being with people."

Excellent. And what about the last problem, illiteracy? Carlotta?

"Learning how to read."

Right. Okay, now let's put these solutions on the board:

Problem	Solution
1. afraid of snakes	less afraid of snakes
2. obsessed by bad thoughts	fewer bad thoughts
3. shy—seldom interact with others	interacts more often
4. can't read	reads

Does anyone see a pattern here?. . . Yes, Carlotta?

"In each case, solving the problem means changing how often a behavior occurs."

Excellent. That's exactly right. In two cases, solving the problem means . . .

"Decreasing the frequency of a behavior."

Exactly. And in the other two cases it means . . .

"Increasing its frequency."

Just so. Much of the time, a behavior problem means either that a behavior occurs too often or that it does not occur often enough. The task of the parent, teacher, manager, or therapist is to increase or decrease the frequency of the behavior. . . . You have a question, John?

"It seems to me there are problems that can't be solved just by changing how often the behavior occurs."

For instance?

"For instance, a student might mispronounce a word. The problem is not that he says the word too often or not often enough, but that he doesn't say the word correctly."

Solving behavior problems does often involve changing the form the behavior takes. But, tell me, how often does your hypothetical student say the word correctly?

"Never."

And how often would you like him to pronounce it correctly?

"All the time—whenever he uses the word."

Then the goal is to get him to pronounce the word correctly more often. That's a change in frequency.

"Well, what about when the behavior occurs in the wrong place or at the wrong time? Say somebody is invited to a formal dinner and shows up wearing a swimsuit. The problem is that the behavior isn't appropriate in that situation."

How often should people show up at a formal dinner wearing a swimsuit?

"Okay, never. So you're saying the problem still involves how often the behavior occurs."

Right. There are lots of cases in which the problem is that behavior occurs at inappropriate times and places, or *doesn't* occur at appropriate times and places. But in solving these problems, we're still going to be concerned with changing the frequency of the behavior in those situations. The point can be argued, but for our purposes we can think of solving behavior problems as *mainly* a matter of changing the frequency of some behavior.

"Are you saying that the main difference between a student who is a discipline problem and one who is not is just the frequency of certain kinds of behavior?"

That's exactly what I'm saying, Brian. The chief difference between the good student and the poor student has to do with how often each performs certain desirable and undesirable acts. Similarly, the main difference between a problem employee and one who is not is, again, a difference in the frequency of certain kinds of behavior.

> "But that wouldn't hold if you were talking about the difference between patients in mental hospitals and those on the outside."

Why not? It may be disconcerting, but the chief difference between the people who live inside mental hospitals and those who live outside of them is not that we never behave as they do, but that we behave as they do less often than they do.[20]

> "But if you view people's problems that way, and you just change their behavior, aren't you just treating the symptoms? I mean, even if the patient in a mental hospital stops ranting and raving, he's still crazy."

The Medical Model

Actually, John, very few people in mental hospitals spend much time ranting and raving. But never mind. Let's take a look at your criticism. It rests on something called the medical model, which assumes that behavior itself isn't very important, that the real problem is beneath the surface—in the mind. Here's a definition:

$$\text{Medical model:}$$
$$\text{The view that behavior problems}$$
$$\text{are merely symptoms of an underlying}$$
$$\text{psychological disorder.}$$

The medical model is accepted more or less implicitly, not only by many medical professionals but also by most psychologists, teachers, social workers, and others who deal with behavior problems.[21] According to the medical model, there is some sort of underlying psychological disorder that causes the behavior problem. The troublesome behavior, the theory goes, is just a symptom of this underlying problem. Behaviorists, on the other hand, maintain that the troublesome behavior *is* the problem, and that when you have changed the behavior, you have solved the problem.[22]

> It's true that a person who no longer rants and raves may continue to behave in other ways that are inappropriate, but he's no longer ranting and raving! That is a major improvement. In fact, he is less psychotic.

> "Less psychotic? I don't get that."

Psychiatric diagnoses are defined mainly by behavior, John.[23] For instance, the kinds of behaviors that define autism, a serious developmental disorder, are delayed or inappropriate speech, failure to interact with others, certain kinds of repetitive actions such as rocking back and forth, self-injurious acts, and so on.

Eliminate all the behaviors that *define* autism, and the person can no longer be diagnosed autistic. So, if you eliminate self-injurious behavior in a person with autism, he is literally less autistic.

"What about people with mental retardation?"

What about them?

"Well, people with mental retardation learn slowly. You might teach them to do all sorts of things, like do their laundry, buy groceries, and so on, but they still won't learn very fast."

Teaching them to do the laundry, to use a telephone, to earn a living, and so on may not produce much improvement in their ability to learn new things. But the diagnosis of mental retardation does not depend solely on learning ability; it also depends on what skills the person has. A retarded person who can dress himself, feed himself, do his laundry, buy groceries, and so on has less retardation than one who cannot do those things. Teach a person to do these things, and you have literally made that person less retarded.

One of the great things about applied behavior analysis is that it focuses on what people can do, rather than on a label or on some mysterious, unseen psychological disorder.[24] Yes, Jamal?

"Doesn't the medical model say that if you just treat the behavior, some new problem will take its place? So if you help someone overcome a fear of snakes, she'll just develop a fear of spiders or become a compulsive gambler or something."

Symptom Substitution

The medical model assumes that troublesome behavior is just a symptom of an underlying problem, and if you don't deal with the underlying problem some new symptom will take its place. That's called symptom substitution:

> Symptom substitution:
> The idea that if a behavior problem is solved
> without resolving the underlying psychological
> disorder, another behavior problem
> will take its place.

It has to be admitted that the idea of symptom substitution has a certain intuitive appeal. There's only one serious fault with it. Does anyone know what that is? Yes, Carlotta?

"There isn't any evidence—I mean, good research evidence—to support it, is there?"

There's very little. There's anecdotal evidence, but, as you know, you can find anecdotal evidence for almost anything. If someone proposed that sleep deprivation would cure the common cold, you could probably find anecdotal evidence to support it. But that's not the same thing as hard, scientific evidence.

I can't say that a person who is treated successfully for one problem will never develop another problem. You might overcome a fear of snakes and later develop a fear of spiders, just as anyone else might. The question is, does overcoming one problem make you succumb to another? Symptom substitution, if it occurs at all, is rare. The vast majority of people who get treatment that focuses on their behavior, rather than on attempting to analyze unconscious conflicts, do not develop new problems. In fact, a task force of the American Psychiatric Association looked into the literature on this issue and found no evidence for symptom substitution.[25]

We should also keep in mind that many behavior problems are not the sort that clinicians have in mind when they talk about symptom substitution. When a teacher teaches her pupils how to read, there is no reason to think that the student's former ignorance will be replaced with some new ignorance. A child who learns how to read does not, for example, forget how to count. And if a corporate manager is successful in reducing the frequency of accidents in a factory, there is no reason to believe that the workers will suffer more from nightmares.

There are, of course, plenty of people who will tell you emphatically that symptom substitution is a problem. But the fact that people say things emphatically does not mean that those things are true.[26] If you want to be scientific about behavior, you have to look at the best available evidence; and the best available evidence is that symptom substitution is seldom, if ever, a problem.

Caveat: Daniels' Dictum

Okay, enough of symptom substitution, a nonissue if there ever was one. There are, however, some limitations of behavior analysis, and I think you should know about one of them before we go any further, particularly since some of you may be thinking of going on to become behavior analysts. Solving behavior problems is harder than it looks. I like to tell students about what I call Daniels' Dictum:

> **Daniels' Dictum:**
> **If you think this stuff is easy,**
> **you're doing it wrong.**

Aubrey Daniels is a behaviorist who applies behavior analysis in the workplace. He helps corporations increase productivity, reduce the rate of accidental injuries, reduce losses due to damaged goods, and so on by helping them analyze and change the antecedents and consequences of employee behavior. He finds that businesspeople regularly underestimate the difficulty of achieving these ends. He tells people that if they think applying behavior analysis is easy, they're doing it wrong, so I call that idea Daniels' Dictum. You're not likely to find Daniels' Dictum in textbooks, but I think he's made a point that's worth crediting.[27]

Anyway, when you start learning about reinforcement and extinction and shaping and all the rest of it, the chances are you're going to think it's all just common sense, and easy as pie. It *will* sound easy, especially since I'm mostly going to be describing fairly simple problems that had fairly simple solutions. I'm going to do that because this is an introductory course, and I don't want to confuse or discourage you. But if you actually try to implement the principles and techniques we discuss, you will find out it is often difficult. And I'm not just talking about the treatment of people who are psychotic or mentally retarded; I'm talking about applications in homes, schools, and businesses.

This course will, I hope, give you some basic skills that will improve your ability to get along with others, to be better parents, to teach more effectively, to manage workers more productively. But please understand that it will *not* qualify you to use applied behavior analysis to solve serious behavioral problems; it will qualify you only for additional training in applied behavior analysis. Applied behavior analysis is not a set of prepackaged solutions to behavior problems; it is a set of tools for discovering and implementing solutions to behavior problems. Learning to use those tools properly requires years of study and practice. Remember Daniels' Dictum.

Before we call it quits for today, I think I'll erase all this stuff on the board, and then we can spend a few minutes reviewing today's key concepts.

Review

Let's start with behavior analysis. What is it? John, can you recall our definition?

"One was, the science of behavior change."

Yes. That's the one I prefer, because it's short and simple. But that's not the one you'll find in textbooks. What was the more formal definition I gave you?

"Uhmm . . . The study of the functional . . ."

Functional relations, yes, go on.

"The study of the functional relations between behavior and . . . "

And . . .

". . . environmental events."

Good. And what is a functional relation, Maya?

"That's like the tendency for one event to vary in a . . . regular way with . . . one or more other events."

Excellent! So we're looking for functional relations between behavior and events in the environment. Now, what is behavior, Midori?

"Anything a person does that can be observed?"

Exactly. And how many kinds of behavior are there?

"Four."

Yes. One kind of behavior can be observed by anyone who happens to be around when it is performed. Such public behavior is called . . . What, Alfred?

"Obvert?"

Not quite; try again.

"Overt?"

Right. So *covert* behavior is defined as . . . Jamal?

"Behavior that can be observed only by the person who performs it."

Excellent. Now, behavior is also identified as either respondent or operant. What is respondent behavior, Belinda?

"It's behavior that is a reflex reaction to something, like blinking your eye when you get a speck of dirt in it."

Okay, so respondent behavior is an automatic response to an event. What else helps define respondent behavior?

"It's not modified by its consequences very well. It's affected more by antecedents."

Good. And what about operant behavior, Alfred?

"That's behavior that isn't so automatic, but it can be modified by its consequences."

All right. It's sometimes said that if an event elicits a behavior, the behavior is respondent, and that if an event merely provides the occasion for a behavior, the behavior is operant. So, if you blink when you get dirt in your eye, blinking is respondent, but if Charlie Brown winks at the cute little redheaded girl in his class, his wink is operant.

You should be able to give original examples of operant and respondent behavior, and of overt and covert behavior. And if I give you examples of behavior, you should be able to tell me whether each one is overt or covert, operant or respondent.

You should also be able to tell me what a behavioral repertoire is. Can you, Brian?

"It's all the things a person can do at a particular point in time."

Good. Now, our definition of behavior analysis mentions environmental events. These are actions of the natural world that . . . What, Carlotta?

"That can be observed?"

Yes. Events that precede behavior are called . . .

"Antecedents."

Yes. Thank you, John. And what are those that follow behavior called?

"Consequences. Though they're really postcedents."

Right again. Yes, we're going to call them consequences, even though that's not entirely honest, because then we can talk about the ABC's of behavior analysis. The ABC's are.... Alfred?

"Antecedents, behavior, and consequences."

Right. Now, nobody comes to a situation as a blank slate. We all have been exposed to many environmental events—antecedents and consequences—that affect our behavior in a given situation. That history of exposure to antecedents and consequences is called the person's ... what? Yes, Brian?

"Learning history."

Right. We are all the products not only of our biological history, but of our learning history.

There are a number of aliases for behavior analysis and behavior analysts. A few of them are covered in today's endnotes. Be sure to learn them because they do appear in the literature.

Now, our emphasis in this course will be on applied behavior analysis. And the definition of applied behavior analysis is ... Carlotta?

"The field that attempts to solve behavior problems by providing antecedents and consequences that change behavior."

Excellent. You mentioned behavior problems. What are the two main kinds of behavior problems? How about it, Midori?

"One involves behavior that doesn't occur often enough; the other involves behavior that occurs too often."

Sehr gut.

"Zair what?"

Sehr gut. It means "very good," and it's just about the only German I know.

Behavior analysis says behavior problems are largely the result of experience; if we do something too often or not often enough, it's because of our learning history. But another view of behavior problems says that problem behavior is merely ... merely what, Jamal?

"A symptom of some underlying psychological disorder."

Right. And that view is called ... ?

"The medical model."

Right again. And according to the medical model, if you solve a behavior problem without dealing with the underlying disorder, the result will be ... What, Belinda?

"Symptom substitution."

Good. And how big a problem is symptom substitution?

"Not much. It doesn't seem to happen, really."

Right.

Well, that pretty much covers today's main points, although I have the feeling I've forgotten something. What could it be? Anybody know? . . . No? Well, it'll be in your notes—and on my exam—so be sure to find it. Not everything we cover in class will be in these reviews, you know.

I see we've run out of time. Please collect the handouts on your way out, and be sure to study them carefully.

◄ Exercises ►

 Feed the Skeleton

What follows is a skeletal outline of today's lesson. Your task is to put some "meat" on the skeleton by filling in the missing material. When you've done your best, check what you have written against your notes.

I. Behavior Analysis
   A. Behavior analysis is:
     1. the science of _____ .
     2. the study of the _____ relations between
     _____ and _____ events.
   B. A functional relation is the tendency of one event to _____ .
   C. Behavior
     1. Behavior is defined as anything a person does that can be
     _____ .

     2. There are four different types of behavior. These can be represented in a fourfold table. (Add appropriate labels and examples to the table.)

     3. Behavioral repertoire refers to _____ .

    D. Environmental Events
       1. An environmental event is any event in a person's surroundings that
         can be _____ .
       2. Behavior analysts distinguish between two kinds of environmental
         events, depending on when they occur in relation to behavior. These
         events are called _____ and _____ .
       3. Environmental events that have affected an individual's behavior are
         called the learning _____ .
       4. The ABC's of behavior analysis are _____ ,
         _____ , and _____ .

II. Applied Behavior Analysis
    A. Applied behavior analysis is defined as the attempt to solve
        _____ problems by providing _____
      and/or _____ that change _____ .
    B. Behavior problems usually take one of two forms.
       1. In one, the behavior occurs _____ .
       2. In the other, the behavior _____ .
    C. The medical model views problem behavior as a symptom of
      _____ .

    D. Symptom Substitution
       1. Symptom substitution says that _____ .
       2. The chief complaint against symptom substitution is that
        _____ .

III. Caveat: Daniels' Dictum is a warning that applying behavior analysis is
    _____ .

Daffy Advice:
Daphne Donchano Answers Your Questions

"Daffy Advice" is an imaginary newspaper advice column. Daphne ("Daffy") Donchano (pronounced "dont-ya-no") offers advice, usually bad advice.

Dear Daffy:

    My husband and I have three boys. The eldest is in college and the middle son joined the air force after completing high school. Both of these boys did very well in school and at home; neither ever got into trouble or caused any serious problems. The youngest boy, who just turned 13, is another matter. He seemed to be following in his brother's footsteps until about a year ago, when we moved and he entered a new school. Now he hangs out with a group of boys who wear nose rings and have green hair. Worse, he makes no effort to do well in school, cuts classes, and is rude to his teachers. Recently he was picked up by a truancy officer in the local mall, where he was trying to catch and eat goldfish from a pond. My husband and I have no idea what has gone wrong. We have always tried to treat all three boys alike. His brothers are as puzzled by his behavior as we are. What do you suggest?

Mother of a Monster

Dear Monster Mother:

You evidently have an unconscious desire to act out against society through your son. The clue to this is the fact that you signed yourself, "Mother of a Monster." Like Mary Shelley (author of *Frankenstein*), you unconsciously want to create a monster that would wreak havoc on the world. The fact that you have produced two well-behaved sons supports this theory: Since obviously you are capable of producing well-behaved sons, why is your third son becoming a monster? Perhaps because you wanted a monster. You will probably need many years of psychotherapy. In the meantime, you must be very patient with your son. If he fails his subjects, dyes his hair orange, and sticks pins through his skin, don't get upset or punish him. If you want to chastise the person responsible for his behavior, you have only to look in the mirror.

Daffy implicitly accepts a model we have discussed. What is that model, and what is wrong with Daffy's analysis?

Gertrude and Heathcliff Speak Out

People who know Gertrude and Heathcliff claim that they were named after the seagulls made famous by comedian Red Skelton. That's probably unfair, but it is true that they are locally infamous for the way in which they abuse the English language. Your task is to catch them mangling concepts and logic:

One day Heathcliff said to Gertrude, "I'm really bemuddled by this B. F. Skinner fellow. He says people think and feel, but he says thoughts and feelings don't explain behavior. That don't subtract, do it?"

"Course not. People do things because of what I'm thinking."

"They do?"

"Well, anyway, *I* do. I'll give you a sample so simple even you'll be able to stand it: I'm sitting in a chair, see, and I get up. Do I just get up? No! I *think* about getting up first. It goes like this: I'm sitting down . . . I think of getting up . . . then I get up. Notice, I don't get up and *then* think of getting up. Getting up follows thinking of getting up. So thinking of getting up must *cause* getting up. What more proof could anyone want that thoughts cause behavior?"

"You know, you're absolutely right. Nothing could be simpler. I don't know why that Skinner person couldn't grasp it. Sometimes smart people like Skinner can't see things as clear as people like us."

"What's that?"

"Not that *we're* stupid, Gertrude. I just meant that simpleminded people sometimes . . ."

"Quit while you're ahead, Heathcliff. In fact, quit while you've still got a head!"

Heathcliff is satisfied with Gertrude's argument that thoughts must cause overt behavior because they often precede it. Do you see any flaws in this argument? Hint: The rooster crows at dawn.

Practice Quiz

1. Behavior analysis is the science of _____ .
2. The ABC's of behavior analysis are _____ , _____ , and _____ .
3. Behavior is defined as anything a person does that can be _____ .
4. Behavior that can be observed only by the person performing it is called _____ .
5. An environmental event is an event in a person's surroundings that can be _____ .
6. Applied behavior analysis is the attempt to solve behavior problems by providing _____ and/or _____ that change behavior.
7. An example of a functional relation is _____ .
8. Daniels' Dictum reminds us that _____ .
9. The things that a person can do at a particular point in time constitute her behavioral _____ .
10. The tendency of one event to vary with another is called a(n) _____ relation.

Mini-Essay: Behaviorism and Behavior Analysis

This course is about behavior analysis, not behaviorism, but the two are closely related. *Behaviorism* (or behavior theory) is the set of assumptions that underlie the scientific analysis of behavior, including applied behavior analysis. These assumptions include the following:

1. *Behavior is lawful.* Behavior isn't a random phenomenon; it has an order and sense to it. This assumption is absolutely essential to a science of behavior and its application. If behavior is not lawful, it cannot be predicted, and there can be no technology for changing it and little hope of solving behavior problems.

2. *Explaining behavior consists of identifying functional relations between behavior and physical events.* The physical events referred to fall into two categories: biological events and environmental events. (Physiology and medicine are concerned with the role of biological events in behavior; behavior analysis is

concerned with the role of environmental events in behavior.) Note that behaviorism acknowledges that environmental events cannot, in themselves, entirely explain behavior; genetics and other biological variables are also assumed to be important. Thus, behaviorism does *not* assume that behavior is due entirely to experience.

3. *Thoughts and feelings do not explain behavior; they are part of the behavior to be explained.* A person may feel angry and slam a door, but he does not slam the door because he feels angry. Both feeling angry and slamming the door are part of being angry and must be accounted for in terms of the history of biological and environmental events. To say that a person slams a door because he is angry, amounts to saying that he is angry because he is angry. Similarly, to say that a person solves a problem because she has insight into it is to say that she solves the problem because she solves the problem. Such statements are absurd because a phenomenon can never explain itself.

These are the essential tenets of modern behaviorism, the behaviorism on which behavior analysis rests.

Reprint: A Behaviorist's Feelings
by B. F. Skinner

Skinner is frequently accused of thinking of human beings as empty organisms, devoid of thought or feeling. On occasion, it is even suggested that Skinner denied that people were conscious. In this excerpt, Skinner gives the lie to these reports, and also shows his treatment of this important subject.

A review of Gerald Zuriff's *Behaviorism: A Conceptual Reconstruction* (1985) in the *London Times Literary Supplement* (1985) begins with a story about two behaviorists. They make love, and then one of them says, "That was fine for you. How was it for me?" The reviewer, P. N. Johnson-Laird, insists that there is a "verisimilitude" with behaviorist theory. Behaviorists are not supposed to have feelings, or at least to admit that they have them. Of the many ways in which behaviorism has been misunderstood for so many years, that is perhaps the commonest.

A possibly excessive concern for "objectivity" may have caused the trouble. Methodological behaviorists, like logical positivists, argued that science must confine itself to events that can be observed by two or more people; truth must be truth by agreement. What one sees through introspection does not qualify. There is a private world of feelings and states of mind, but it is out of reach of a second person and hence of science. That was not a very satisfactory position, of course. How people feel is often as important as what they do.

Radical behaviorism has never taken that line. Feeling is a kind of sensory action, like seeing or hearing. We see a tweed jacket, for example, and we also feel it. That is not quite like feeling depressed, of course. We know something about the organs with which we feel the jacket but little, if anything, about those with which we feel depressed. We can also feel *of* the jacket by running our fingers over the cloth to increase the stimulation, but there does not seem to be any way to feel *of* depression. We have other ways of sensing the jacket, and we do various things with it. In other words, we have other ways of knowing what we are feeling. But what are we feeling when we feel depressed?

William James anticipated the behaviorist's answer: what we feel is a condition of our body. We do not cry because we are sad, said James, we are sad because we cry. That was fudging a little, of course, because we do much more than cry when we feel sad, and we can feel sad when we are not crying, but it was pointing in the right direction: what we feel is bodily conditions. Physiologists will eventually observe them in another way, as they observe any other part of the body. Walter B. Cannon's *Bodily Changes in Pain, Hunger, Fear, and Rage* (1929) was an early study of a few conditions often felt. Meanwhile, we ourselves can respond to them directly. We do so in two different ways. For example, we respond to stimuli from our joints and muscles in one way when we move about and in a different way when we say that we feel relaxed or lame. We respond to an empty stomach in one way when we eat and in a different way when we say that we are hungry. . . .

For centuries, of course, it has been said that we behave in given ways because of our feelings. We eat because we feel hungry, strike because we feel angry, and in general do what we feel like doing. If that were true, our faulty knowledge of feelings would be disastrous. No science of behavior would be possible. But what is felt is not an initial or initiating cause. William James was quite wrong about his "becauses." We do not cry *because* we are sad or feel sad *because* we cry; we cry *and* feel sad because something has happened. (Perhaps someone we loved has died.) It is easy to mistake what we feel as a cause because we feel it while we are behaving (or even before we behave), but the events which are actually responsible for what we do (and hence what we feel) lie in the possibly distant past. The experimental analysis of behavior advances our understanding of feelings by clarifying the roles of both past and present environments. . . .

Such an analysis has an important bearing on two practical questions: how much can we ever know about what another person is feeling, and how can what is felt be changed? It is not enough to ask other people how or what they feel, because the words they will use in telling us were acquired, as we have seen, from people who did not quite know what they were talking about. Something of the sort seems to have been true of the first use of words to describe private states. The first person who said, "I'm worried" borrowed a word meaning "choked" or "strangled." (*Anger, anguish,* and *anxiety* also come from another word that meant "choked.") But how much like the effect of choking was the bodily state the word was used to describe? All words for feelings seem to have begun as metaphors, and it is significant that the transfer has always been from public to private. No word seems to have originated as the name of a feeling.

We do not need to use the names of feelings if we can go directly to the public events. Instead of saying, "I was angry," we can say, "I could have struck him." What was felt was an inclination to strike rather than striking, but the private stimuli must have been much the same. Another way to report what we feel is to describe a setting that is likely to generate the condition felt. After reading Chapman's translation of Homer for the first time, Keats reported that he felt "like some watcher of the skies / When a new planet swims into his ken." It was easier for his readers to feel what an astronomer would feel upon discovering a new planet than what Keats felt upon reading the book. . . .

There are many good reasons why people talk about their feelings. What they say is often a useful indication of what has happened to them or of what they may do. On the point of offering a friend a glass of water, we do not ask, "How long has it been since you last drank any water?" or "If I offer you a glass of water, what are the chances you will accept it?" We ask, "Are you thirsty?" The answer tells us all we need to know. In an experimental analysis, however, we need a better account of the conditions that affect hydration and a better measure of the probability that a subject will drink. A report of how thirsty the subject feels will not suffice.

For at least 3,000 years, however, philosophers, joined recently by psychologists, have looked within themselves for the causes of their behavior. For reasons which are becoming clear, they have never agreed upon what they have found. Physiologists, and especially neurologists, look at the same body in a different and potentially successful way, but even when they have seen it more clearly, they will not have seen initiating causes of behavior. What they will see must in turn be explained either by ethologists, who look for explanations in the evolution of the species, or by behavior analysts, who look at the histories of individuals. The inspection or introspection of one's own body is a kind of behavior that needs to be analyzed, but as the source of data for a science it is largely of historical interest only.

Excerpted from "The Place of Feeling in the Analysis of Behavior," by B. F. Skinner. In *London Times* Literary Supplement. Copyright 1989 London Times. By permission of Julie S. Vargas, B. F. Skinner Foundation.

◄ Recommended Reading ►

1. Association for Behavior Analysis web site: http://www.wmich.edu/aba.
   This web site provides information about ABA and links to other pages related to behavior analysis.

2. Baer, D. M., Wolf, M. M., & Risley, T. R. (1968). Some current dimensions of applied behavior analysis. *Journal of Applied Behavior Analysis,* 1, 91–97. Discusses some of the defining characteristics of the field.

3. *Behavior Analysis Digest.* ($8/year). Write W. Joseph Wyatt, Editor, P. O. Box 844, Hurricane, WV 25526.
   BAD is a quarterly newsletter that publishes short, readable summaries of interesting research in behavior analysis. It is well worth the subscription price to any student of behavior.

4. Epstein, R. (1982). Introduction. In R. Epstein & B. F. Skinner (Eds.), *Skinner in the classroom: Selected readings.* Champaign, IL: Research Press.
   Epstein refutes a number of the more common misconceptions about Skinner, including the idea that he is a stimulus-response psychologist; that he sees people as "black boxes"; and that he is an extreme environmentalist.

5. Foxx, R. M. (1996). Twenty years of applied behavior analysis in treating the most severe problem behavior: Lessons learned. *The Behavior Analyst,* 19, 225–235.
   One of the most experienced applied behavior analysts discusses the difficulties of solving behavior problems.

6. Skinner, B. F. (1953/1965). *Science and human behavior.* New York: Free Press.
   B. F. Skinner is the founding father of behavior analysis, and this is the bible of behavior analytic theory. The book sets forth Skinner's revolutionary views of behavior. It assumes no background in behavior analysis and can be read profitably by any interested student.

7. Skinner, B. F. (1971). *Beyond freedom and dignity.* New York: Knopf.
   This is arguably Skinner's most controversial work. Contrary to popular opinion, he does not attack freedom and dignity per se, but their value as explanations for behavior.

◄ Endnotes ►

1. There is no true consensus concerning the definition of behavior analysis. Malott et al. (1993) define it as "the study of the operation of the principles of behavior with both human beings and other animals" (p. 10). Grant and Evans (1994) say behavior analysis is "the study of behavior and the variables that influence behavior" (p. 7)—a definition that includes the effects of physiology, genetics, maturation, and disease. Another definition is offered by the editor of *Behavior Analysis Digest* (a highly readable and interesting newsletter that summarizes recent research): "Behavior analysis is a natural science approach to the study of behavior, and the application and analysis of science-based interventions to problems of individual, social, and cultural

importance" (Wyatt, 1997, p. 13). The International Behaviorology Association defines behaviorology (a field closely related to, if not identical with,
behavior analysis) as "the science of contingent relations between behavior
and other events" (source: TIBA's web site, 11/13/96). For more on this, see
Carr (1993); Lee (1996); Pfaus et al. (1988); and Skinner (1987).

I should mention here that behavior analysis goes by other names,
including *behaviorology* and *the functional analysis of behavior.* There are subtle
distinctions among these terms, but there is clearly a great deal of overlap
among them, and for our purposes they will be taken as representing the
same field of study. The people who study behavior analysis are, of course,
called behavior analysts. But other, more or less equivalent terms include
behaviorist and *behaviorologists.* I will use only the terms *behaviorist* and *behavior analyst,* and I will use them as synonyms.

2. The term *behavior analysis* implies that it is the study of (the analysis of) behavior. But the term is somewhat misleading, since it isn't behavior that
behaviorists analyze but the relation between behavior and events in the
environment. Behavior analysis is divided into two fields: the experimental
analysis of behavior, which deals with basic research on functional relations
between behavior and environmental events, and applied behavior analysis,
which uses functional relations between behavior and environmental events
to change behavior.

3. Behavior is a more complicated concept than it first appears. Skinner (1953)
writes that behavior is "a process, rather than a thing. . . . It is changing, fluid,
and evanescent. . . ." (p. 14). Perhaps it is because behavior won't hold still
for examination that it is difficult to define. This may be why some textbook
authors (e.g., Baldwin & Baldwin, 1986) do not try to define it. Some who
have, follow tradition and define behavior as overt action. Malott et al. offer
two definitions of behavior; their "restricted" definition identifies behavior as
"a muscle or glandular activity" (p.10). Similarly, Grant and Evans (1993)
write that behavior "consists of specific categories of actions people perform,
what people do" (p. 2). They add that "behaviors have certain *physical . . .*
features" (p. 2; emphasis added). This very traditional (it can be traced back
to John B. Watson, 1924) view of behavior as overt action would seem to
exclude thoughts and feelings. Skinner (1938) continued this tradition by
defining behavior as any action by an organism that has a measurable effect
upon its environment. But Skinner (1953) later broke with tradition and
rejected this definition, along with Watsonian behaviorism. He made it clear
that, for him, behavior included thoughts and feelings. Most behaviorists
today stand with Skinner on this.

Some behaviorists (e.g., Graf, 1994; Malott et al., 1993) define behavior
as any activity that passes the dead-man test. The dead-man test is the cre-

ation of Ogden Lindsley (1968), a very prominent figure in applied behavior analysis. The dead-man test asks, "Can a dead person do it?" If the answer is yes, the activity doesn't qualify as behavior. Lindsley's idea was to get people to focus on what people did, rather than on what they failed to do. Parents, for example, would say, "Johnny doesn't put his toys away." Lindsley proposed the dead-man test to get people to focus on what their children, students, employees, or clients *do,* as opposed to what they fail to do. A dead man can, for example, leave toys out as well as anybody. Not everyone shares the enthusiasm of these authors for the dead-man test; see for example Allen & Miltenberger (1991). Nevertheless, the dead-man test is part of the behavioral literature, so it is helpful to be familiar with the term.

4. It is true that scientists sometimes study phenomena that are not directly observed but are inferred from other observable events. Physicists, for example, study black holes, even though, by definition, a black hole is something that cannot be seen. The black hole is a hypothetical event invented to account for phenomena that *are* observed. In reality, then, the physicist is not studying black holes but is studying these other events. For more on this, see Schlinger (no date).

5. Although behavior analysts acknowledge the existence of thoughts and feelings as covert behavior, they typically focus on overt behavior. This is mainly because it is most often overt behavior that presents problems. A person who has aggressive feelings, for example, does little harm compared to one who commits aggressive acts.

6. Even walking and thinking about walking are not entirely different: When people think about performing an action, such as walking, the muscles required for that action often contract in much the same way as they do when the act is performed. Thus, when you *think* about walking, in a sense you *are* walking.

7. Respondent behavior is also often defined as behavior that is mediated by the autonomic nervous system. The autonomic nervous system controls breathing, salivation, peristalsis (the rhythmic motion of the throat lining that carries food to the stomach), digestion, heart beat, and numerous other automatic actions that usually take place without our awareness.

   Behavior controlled by the autonomic nervous system is not readily modified by its consequences. In the 1960s, some research (e.g., Miller & DiCara, 1967) suggested that it might be possible to control autonomic behavior with biofeedback. This work raised the possibility that, for example, people with high blood pressure or heart arrhythmias might be able to control these health problems with feedback about when their pressure was falling or when their heart was beating properly. The idea was widely publicized (Jonas,

1973), and biofeedback training became very popular. Unfortunately, the promise of biofeedback training has not been fulfilled. Indeed, within a decade, Miller (1978) himself began to have doubts about his earlier findings. Dworkin and Miller (1986) finally concluded that "the existence of visceral learning remains unproven" (p. 299).

8. See, for example, Walster & Berscheid (1971).

9. Skinner chose the term *operant* because it "emphasizes the fact that the behavior *operates* upon the environment to generate consequences" (1953, p. 65). The term is quite appropriate when it applies to overt behavior; it is less apt when applied to covert behavior, since operant thoughts do not "operate upon" the environment.

10. Behavior analysis is often mistakenly referred to as an "S-R psychology." If behavior analysis dealt only with respondent behavior, the term would be acceptable: Respondent behavior is accurately represented by the letters *S* (for stimulus, an environmental event) and *R* (the response to that event). But behavior analysts are at least as interested in operant behavior as they are in respondent behavior, and operant behavior is *not* a reflex reaction to environmental events. In fact, it would probably be more accurate to describe behavior analysis as an "R-S psychology" than as an "S-R psychology."

11. Some behaviorists say that an environmental event is one that can be observed and that affects, or is capable of affecting, behavior. If, for example, you explode a balloon in the presence of a deaf person, you will probably not see a startle response. For that person, an exploding balloon is not an event unless the person sees it.

12. The phrase *physical event* is redundant. In behavior analysis, as in the natural sciences, there are no events *but* physical events.

13. Behavior analysts seem to differ over the extent to which their field embraces biological processes. B. F. Skinner, the founding father of behavior analysis, seemed to view behavior analysis as the study of the effects of environmental events on behavior. He writes (Skinner, 1989), for example, that "human behavior will eventually be explained (as it can only be explained) by the cooperative action of ethology, brain science, and behavior analysis" (p. 18). Notice that, contrary to the distortions of his critics (e.g., Sutherland, 1993), Skinner acknowledges the role of biology in determining behavior.

14. Antecedents, behavior, and consequences truly are the ABC's of behavior analysis. Skinner (1969) wrote, "An adequate formulation of the interaction between an organism and its environment must always specify three things: (1) the occasion upon which a response occurs, (2) the response itself, and (3) the . . . consequences" (p. 7). This is known as "the three-term contingency"; it is the fundamental unit of behavior analysis.

15. This is a little something I learned from the Smothers Brothers, two keen observers of human behavior. In one of their comic routines, Tommy Smothers sings about falling into a vat of chocolate and yelling, "Fire!" When his brother asks him why he yelled "Fire," he astutely observes that a person drowning in a vat of chocolate is unlikely to receive help by yelling, "Chocolate!"

16. I will make this point a number of times during the course. I have found that students have considerable difficulty accepting a natural science approach to behavior. Terms like *need, want, expect, intend,* and so on regularly creep into their sentences. For example, many students majoring in education know about the work of Robert Rosenthal and Lenore Jacobson (1968) on the effects of teacher expectations on student achievement. In this research, teachers were led to believe that certain students in their classes would advance more quickly. These students did, in fact, learn faster even though their names had been drawn at random. Unfortunately, this work has been widely misinterpreted to mean that teacher *expectations* affect student performance. But unless you believe in telepathy or psychokinesis, there's no way one person's expectation can affect another person's behavior. Subsequent research (Meichenbaum et al., 1969; Rosenthal et al., 1973) showed that changes in teacher *behavior* were responsible for the improved learning rates. When teachers were told that a particular student would advance quickly, they asked that student more questions, gave her more feedback about her performance, taught her more things, and so on. In other words, the exceptional progress of students identified as exceptional was due to the behavior of the teacher toward those students, not to teacher expectations.

17. An individual's biological (including genetic) history and learning history together produce a unique behavioral repertoire.

18. Applied behavior analysis is a distinct field of study and profession. However, certain other terms, including *behavior modification* and *behavior therapy,* refer to very similar, if not identical, fields and professions. While all three areas use the same basic intervention procedures, applied behavior analysis implies the application of rigorous research methods in the course of attempting to solve a behavior problem.

19. Some behaviorists have attempted to identify the defining characteristics of applied behavior analysis; see Baer et al. (1968, 1987). Behaviorists are often criticized for using techniques that actually play no part in behavior analysis. Psychoactive drugs (such as antidepressants and tranquilizers), psychosurgery, and electroconvulsive shock therapy (ECT), for example, are *not* part of applied behavior analysis, and people who use these techniques are *not,* when doing so, doing applied behavior analysis (Stolz and Associates, 1978).

20. Thousands of people around the world believe in reincarnation. There are many people who believe they were once Napoleon, when the concept of reincarnation requires that only one former Napoleon be alive at a time. How much difference is there between believing that one was *once* Napoleon and believing that one is *now* Napoleon? For more on this, see *The Three Christs of Ypsilanti* (Rokeach, 1964).

21. Some students may assume that the medical model of behavior problems has fallen into the wastebasket of history. If you are among them, please read *Let Me Hear Your Voice* by Catherine Maurice (1993). Maurice describes her encounters with the medical model in her efforts to get effective treatment for her autistic children. The book reveals that the medical model is alive and well, outmoded though it may be.

22. The famous British behaviorist Hans J. Eysenck wrote, "Get rid of the symptom and you have eliminated the problem" (Eysenck, H. J., 1959; quoted in Ullmann & Krasner, 1965, p. 2). This is not to say that behavior problems are never due in part to organic conditions.

23. Some psychiatric disorders (including epilepsy and some forms of mental retardation) are defined partly by the results of medical tests. Epilepsy, for example, is defined partly by the results of an electroencephalograph (EEG), whereas Down's syndrome (a form of mental retardation) is defined partly by certain facial characteristics. But these medical tests are rarely sufficient in and of themselves. A person who has an abnormal EEG but no seizures would probably not be called epileptic. Similarly, a person who has the facial features characteristic of Down's syndrome but who excels in regular academic classes cannot be called retarded.

24. Diagnostic labels have their uses, but they can also do great harm. One of their problems is that they give the impression that a solution is imminent. In fact, however, putting a label on someone may end a search for a solution, rather than suggest one. On a computer bulletin board, a teacher posted a question about a student with Tourette syndrome. Among other things, Tourette syndrome involves sudden and inappropriate outbursts, such as curses. Regrettably, some people replied that if the diagnosis were confirmed, the appropriate thing to do was give up! Though Tourette syndrome is a difficult challenge, it has been treated with some success with behavior analytic procedures (Peterson & Azrin, 1993; Woods & Miltenberger, 1995; Carr & Bailey, 1996). If the teacher had asked, "What am I to do about a student who periodically disrupts the class with very inappropriate remarks?" she might have gotten a more helpful answer.

    Because of this phenomenon, I like to tell students about what I call the truth *about* labeling law. To me, this law is more important than the truth *in* labeling law that regulates what is written on a cereal box. When we put a label on someone—he's retarded, she's a paranoid schizophrenic, he's a slow learner, she's hyperactive—we might feel that we have accomplished something, but all we have really done is given a name to the person's behavior. So, the truth about labeling law says: Labels don't solve problems, they just name them.

25. American Psychiatric Association (1973), reported in Myers & Thyer (1994). Two decades later, Myers and Thyer (1994) write, "There is little, if any, controlled research which points toward symptom substitution as a real phenomenon" (p. 101).

26. The fact that people say things repeatedly does not make them true either, yet we tend to be influenced by repeated messages, true or not. Charles Darwin, whose work was and is frequently misrepresented, wrote, "Great is the power of steady misrepresentation" (quoted in Todd & Morris, 1992, p. 1441). B. F. Skinner's work has also been steadily misrepresented. For an example of gross misrepresentation of Skinner's views, see Sutherland (1993). For further discussion of misrepresentation of behavior analysis and behaviorism, see DeBell and Harless (1992) and Myers and Thyer (1994).

27. People have asked me where they can read about Daniels' Dictum. This is a term I invented as a convenient way of reminding students that the apparent simplicity of behavior analysis is deceiving. Although I refer to Daniels' Dictum, other people have made a similar point.

Methods in Applied Behavior Analysis

Behavioral Assessment
    Defining the Target Behavior
    Identifying Functional Relations
    Identifying an Intervention

Recording Behavior Rates
    Continuous Recording
    Interval Recording

Measuring the Reliability of Rate Data
    Reliability of Continuous Data
    Reliability of Interval Data
    Improving Reliability

Graphing Behavior Rates
    Simple Frequency Graphs
    Cumulative Frequency Graphs

Evaluating the Effects of an Intervention
    Single Case Experimental Design
    ABAB Reversal Design
    Multiple Baseline Design
    Alternating Treatments Design

Review

Exercises

Mini-Essay: Measuring Behavior Change

Reprint: *The Queen's Scepter,* by Eric Haughton
    & Teodoro Ayllon

Recommended Reading

Endnotes

AT OUR LAST MEETING, you got a brief introduction to the ABC's of behavior analysis. What are the ABC's of behavior analysis, Midori?

"Antecedents, behavior, and consequences."

And why are the ABC's important to us?

"Because that's what behavior analysis is about, the way behavior is related to its antecedents and consequences."

Right. Behavior analysis is the study of the functional relations between behavior and environmental events. We also talked about applied behavior analysis, the focus of this course. What is applied behavior analysis? Maya?

"That's the attempt to solve behavior problems by changing the antecedents and consequences of behavior."

Very good. We change behavior by changing the functional relations between behavior and its antecedents and consequences. In applied behavior analysis, the treatment program, or intervention, consists of a change in the functional relations between behavior and its antecedents and consequences.

Before we actually begin talking about the kinds of interventions behavior analysts use to change behavior, I want to talk a little about the basic logic and methods they use to select and evaluate interventions. Problem solving begins with an assessment of the problem, so let's start with that process.

Behavioral Assessment

The traditional approach to behavior problems, especially in the area of clinical psychology, begins with a psychological assessment: an attempt to identify the underlying psychological problem that is presumed to produce the behavioral symptoms. Thus, psychological assessment rests on a model of behavior problems called . . . what, John?

"The medical model?"

Exactly. According to the medical model, the problem resides inside the person, possibly without his or her awareness. Given this assumption, it makes sense to talk to the client about dreams, fantasies, anxieties, and feelings about other people and to ask about childhood experiences that may have "planted" the seeds of psychological disturbance. It also makes sense, given the medical model, to

44

administer a battery of psychological tests such as the Minnesota Multiphasic Personality Inventory (better known as the MMPI), the Rorshach (the famous inkblot test), and the Thematic Apperception Test (the TAT). Although the tests I have mentioned are among the most popular, hundreds of others are available to the psychologist. In addition to the tests, there are numerous other assessment procedures, including surveys, questionnaires, and role-playing activities. Children, for example, are often given the opportunity to play with toys as the examiner observes or to play a game with the examiner. The purpose of these efforts, this psychological assessment, is to define what is wrong with the person's psyche.

Behaviorists take a very different view. They reject the medical model, holding that troublesome behavior is not the *symptom* of a problem, it *is* the problem. The source of the troublesome behavior is not in the person but in the functional relations between the behavior and its antecedents and consequences. So behaviorists don't do psychological assessment; they do *behavioral* assessment.

Behavioral assessment attempts to do three things:

> **Behavioral assessment:**
> **The attempt to (1) define the target behavior;**
> **(2) identify functional relations between**
> **the target behavior and its antecedents and**
> **consequences; and (3) identify an effective**
> **intervention for changing the target behavior.**

Let's talk about how each of these goals is achieved.

Defining the Target Behavior

Behavioral assessment begins by defining the target behavior, the behavior that needs to be changed:

> **Target behavior:**
> **The behavior to be changed**
> **by an intervention.**

Since applied behavior analysts are usually concerned about changing the rate of behavior, the target behavior is normally the behavior that needs to occur more or less frequently than it currently does.

The target behavior is typically defined in collaboration with the client or the client's legal guardian. This can be done by interviewing the client and sometimes other people who are close to the client, such as parents, siblings, teachers, co-workers, and spouses. Some of these people may be asked to complete questionnaires. So far, this looks superficially like the efforts of traditional psychological assessment; but whereas the traditional psychologist's interviews and questionnaires are intended to uncover information about things going on in the client's mind, those of the behaviorist are intended to identify things the client does and the relationship of that behavior to events in the client's environment.

The behaviorists may begin (much as the tradional psychologist does) by asking the client or others, "What seems to be the trouble?" Often the answers obtained are *not* initially very useful. Maybe I can illustrate this point by doing a little role playing. Jamal, let's say that you are a counselor and I am a high school student named Eddy. I have just been referred to you by one of my teachers, Mr. Jones. You begin by asking, "What seems to be the trouble?" I answer: Beats me. Mr. Jones just told me to come here.

"Oh. Ah, well, why did Mr. Jones send you here, Eddy?"

I don't know. I guess he's unhappy about something. He always is.

"You must have some idea why he sent you here. Did you do something to upset him?"

I didn't do nothin'. He's just always on my case.

Okay. Let's interrupt the role playing for a minute. You can see that Eddy is not very forthcoming. If Jamal keeps at it, and stays focused on behavior, he may eventually identify the behavior that needs to be changed.

Regardless of how things go with Eddy, you'll probably also want to talk to Mr. Jones. I'll be Mr. Jones and, let's see, Carlotta, you be the counselor. You've just asked me what the trouble with Eddy is:

I'll tell you what the trouble with Eddy is: He needs a trip to the woodshed.

"Why? What did he do?"

He's got an attitude.

"Yes, but what did he actually *do* that made you send him to me?"

It wasn't just one thing. Like I said, he's got an attitude.

"But I don't know what you mean when you say he has an attitude."

He's sarcastic, rude, belligerent, argumentative, hostile, and lazy. *Now* do you know what I mean when I say he has an attitude?

"Not really."

Okay. Let's stop again. Carlotta says she *still* doesn't know what the problem is. Can anyone define the target behavior for her? Yes, Alfred?

"I think Mr. Jones spelled out all sorts of target behaviors."

Such as?

"Such as sarcastic, rude, and lazy."

What sort of behavior is lazy?

"It probably means he doesn't do his schoolwork."

No, Eddy does his school assignments. In fact, he usually finishes his assignments ahead of the other students and then does his homework.

"So what does Mr. Jones mean by lazy?"

That's just it, Alfred, you can't know from what you've heard so far from Eddy or Mr. Jones. Words like *sarcastic, rude,* and *lazy* are vague—they don't specify a target behavior. At most, they give us hints about what the target behavior might be.

It's often the case that people who complain about a problem don't readily identify the kinds of behavior to be changed. Most people accept the medical model, even though they may never have heard of it by name; they assume that the problem is something inside the person—an attitude, an aggressive tendency, a lack of willpower or intelligence. But before you can do anything about a problem, you must be able to express that problem in terms of the behavior that is to be changed. So, Alfred, was Carlotta right to say she didn't understand Mr. Jones' complaint?

"Yes, because he hadn't spelled out a particular behavior he wanted changed."

Exactly. Let's take another example. Suppose you're a family therapist, and I tell you I need help with Sid, my 5-year-old son. You ask what the problem is, and I tell you it's anger. Sid, I tell you, is a kid with a lot of anger; I want you to reduce the amount of anger he has. What's the target behavior? How about it, Alfred?

"I guess I'd have to say I don't know."

Why?

"Because anger could mean a lot of things."

Like what?

"Like, it could mean Sid hits people. Or it could mean he yells at his dad. Or it could mean he walks around with his fists clenched and his jaw clamped shut. Or it could—"

I think you've got it, Alfred. Anger is not a specific behavior; it can mean the performance of any number of different acts.

Getting people to talk about a problem in terms of specific behaviors is not always easy. Fortunately, we may not need to rely exclusively on such secondhand information. Often we can observe the person interacting in those settings where the behavior problem typically occurs. These observations often help define the target behavior in concrete terms. Before we can help Sid, we have to define anger in terms of some specific behavior, or set of behaviors. That's what it means to define the target behavior, and it ain't always easy.

Identifying Functional Relations

Once you've defined the target behavior, the next goal is to identify functional relations between the target behavior and its antecedents and consequences. Interviewing the client or others is often helpful in this endeavor.

Let's say that Sid's anger is defined as a tendency to scream and throw things. We need to know when this behavior occurs. Again, the answers you get from Sid, his parents, his teachers, and others may not be very helpful at first. They may say, "It happens all the time." Or they may say, "It can happen anywhere, any time; there's no telling." In reality, the chances are it doesn't happen all the time, nor is it a random phenomenon. There are times and places in which Sid is likely to scream and throw things, and other times and places when he is unlikely to do these things. We need to identify those situations. More than that, we need to identify the specific kinds of antecedents and consequences that are usually associated with the target behavior. So if we don't get specific answers from Sid and his parents or teachers, we might ask them to describe specific instances in which they observed the target behavior.

Now suppose Sid's father describes a time when Sid started shouting and throwing things. They were in a grocery store picking up a few items. You ask, "What happened?" The father answers, "We were walking down an aisle, and, for no reason, Sid just picked up something from one of the shelves and threw it down the aisle. Then he started screaming." You spend some time talking about what was going on just before the tantrum started: Who was present? What time was it? Had anyone said anything to Sid? Had Sid said anything to anyone? What happened when Sid began to scream? Did his father shout at him? Did he threaten him? Did he take him out of the store? Did other patrons stare at Sid? Did the manager ask Sid's father to remove Sid from the store? You need a detailed description of Sid's environment before, during, and after the screaming episode.

When you have learned all you can about Sid's behavior during this episode and about its antecedents and consequences, you need to ask the same sort of questions about other episodes. After a while, you should have a pretty good idea of the antecedents and consequences that usually accompany the target behavior.

Your interview notes will probably suggest some hypotheses about the functional relations among these events—the target behavior and its antecedents and consequences. Based on your interviews with Sid and his parents, for example, you may have come to the tentative conclusion that Sid's tantrums tend to occur when food or other attractive items are present and Sid's request for them is denied. The tantrums usually are followed by his receiving the desired item. It's a reasonable hypothesis and fits all the facts, but is it correct? Are Sid's tantrums a function of receiving attractive items when such items are present?

The next step is to test your hypotheses about the functional relations by doing a functional analysis:

**Functional analysis:
The process of testing hypotheses about
the functional relations among antecedents,
target behavior, and consequences.**

A functional analysis begins with observations of the client. Whenever practical, these observations are made in the natural environment—in the home, the school, the workplace, the hospital ward—wherever the target behavior is a problem. (That is to say, in those situations where the rate of the target behavior is too high or too low.) In Sid's case, for example, you might actually go to a grocery store and watch Sid and his father as they shop. If Sid cries, you will try to note what happened before and after he started crying. Did the crying begin when someone entered the area? When someone said something? When the parent suggested leaving the store? What happened after he began crying? Was he shouted at? Spanked? Picked up and held? Given a toy?

Notice that when we talk about a functional analysis we are not talking about speculations about intentions, needs, or desires. We are talking about physical events that can be observed.

When you have identified a functional relation between the target behavior and certain antecedents and consequences—for example, you notice that Sid begins crying when he and his father reach the candy section, and that the crying continues until Dad gives Sid a bag of candy—then you may test these relationships by manipulating these antecedents and consequences. For example, you might have Sid's father go back to the candy area and see if the crying starts again. Or you might have Sid's father provide candy immediately after the crying starts to see if it then stops.

If it is not possible to observe Sid in the grocery store, you might create an analog of this situation. For example, you might have Sid and his father play on the floor of an office. If there are no tantrums, you might then introduce several attractive toys and see if Sid starts screaming when his father won't let him play with them and if he stops when his father turns over a toy. If he does, it suggests an explanation of the tantrums.

The example I've given is a very simple one. We've all seen children who cried when candy or other attractive items came into view and who stopped crying when they received the item. Unfortunately, not all functional relations are so easily identified. However, by carefully recording behavior and environmental events, it is possible to test hypotheses about the relationships among them. Later on, you will have a better understanding of the nature of these functional relations between behavior and environmental events. In fact, much of the rest of this course deals with different kinds of functional relations and their—

"Excuse me, Dr. Cee?"

Yes, Carlotta?

"It seems to me that this functional analysis you're talking about assumes that the behavior is the result of things going on at the time. But what if the behavior is the result of things that went on *before* the person got to that situation?"

Ah, well, that's an excellent question. Sid's crying might be the result of events that occur when his mother takes him shopping. Or they could be the result of things that happened months before when one of his grandparents took him shopping. Doing a functional analysis is not going to reveal the effects of such experiences. However, behavior problems normally persist because of functional relations between the target behavior and current environmental events, and a functional analysis can reveal those relationships.

Identifying an Intervention

You have a question, Belinda?

> "Yes. This is all very interesting, and I can see that functional analysis helps you understand why the target behavior occurs. But how does this solve Sid's problem?"

It doesn't, at least not immediately. But a functional analysis may help us come up with an effective intervention plan, which is the third and ultimate goal of behavioral assessment. The intervention plan will be tentative; we cannot know that an intervention will work until we implement it. And before we do that, it is usually necessary to discuss the plan with the person whose behavior we're trying to change, or with that person's guardian or representative. But doing a functional analysis can generate hypotheses about what sort of implementation might be effective.

You can see that behavioral assessment is very different from traditional psychological assessment. The behaviorist interviews the client and other people and may use surveys and questionnaires, but he or she does so for reasons that are very different from those of the person doing traditional psychological assessment. Behavioral assessment also relies a great deal more on careful observation of behavior. In fact, behavioral assessment and intervention both require carefully observing and recording events. For that reason, we need to turn now to some basic principles concerning the recording and analysis of behavior.

Recording Behavior Rates

Recording rate data means determining the number of times a particular behavior occurs in a given period.[1] But how is that number to be determined?

There are certain informal ways of estimating rate. One is to ask the person who engages in the behavior. I have noticed that young people today have a tendency to use phrases with the word *go,* as in "He goes" and "I go." This usually means *said,* as in "He goes, 'How ya doin, buddy?'" If I were interested in measuring the rate at which a person uses *go* in this way, I might simply ask the person. But this has an obvious limitation. And that is . . . Jamal?

"Well, it assumes that he knows, and he might not."

Exactly. People don't usually keep a running tally of such behavior, so the best the person can provide you with is an estimate. And there are problems with such estimates. . . . Yes, Carlotta?

"If a behavior is unflattering, aren't people likely to underestimate how often they engage in it? Or, if it's something they should do, they might overestimate its frequency. If you ask a person who's overweight how many bites of food he takes in a typical day, my guess is the answer will be too low."

Yes, you're right. People often give biased estimates. If you ask people who are married or cohabiting with someone how often they have intercourse, they may give you an answer they know is wrong in order to avoid the embarrassment of a figure that the interviewer might consider abnormally high or low.[2] So asking people how often they engage in a behavior is not always a good way of determining rate.

"What if you give them a survey? Something they can fill out and send in anonymously."

That might improve accuracy somewhat, John, but you're still basically asking a person to provide information the person probably doesn't have. The same thing is true of asking other people about a person's behavior. Instead of asking Sid how often he says, "He goes," you could ask his friends and members of his family. But again you are asking people for information they probably don't have.

"Does that mean there's no point in talking to a person with a behavior problem, or with his teachers and other people?"

No, Midori. You've already seen that talking with a person is an important part of behavioral assessment, and it may be useful in getting a rough idea of the rate of a target behavior. But when it comes time to pin down the rate with some precision, you can't rely on hearsay. Someone has to observe the behavior and tally the number of times it occurs in a given period. To be a behaviorist, you have to know how to count.

Continuous Recording

There are two ways of counting, or recording, behavior: continuous recording, and interval recording. In continuous recording, as the name implies, you record the behavior continuously:

> **Continuous recording:**
> **Recording each and every occurrence**
> **of a behavior during a prescribed period.**

To take the example of phrases such as "He goes," we might observe a person and count each and every time she uses such phrases. We would do this for a pre-arranged period of time, usually from half an hour to an hour. There would usually be one or two such observation periods per day for a number of days.

Now, the question arises, why not observe the person throughout the day? We could follow the person around, clipboard in hand, and make a tally every time she uses a *go* phrase. Why not do that? Jamal?

> "Well, this is just a wild guess, but it seems to me the person might not enjoy being followed into the bathroom, or having someone tagging along on dates."

Yes, people tend to be protective of their privacy. So let's suppose you decide to observe the person only when she is in public. Any problems?

> "It still might get pretty tiresome for them, always being under observation."

That's true, but it can be done. Anthropologists often move right in with a family or group they are interested in studying, and they can count the number of times a person in that group uses certain expressions. What about problems for the behavior analyst? Brian?

> "I think when anthropologists move in with a family or a village, they do it because they want to observe all aspects of the group's behavior. They're not trying to deal with a specific behavior problem, like poor student achievement or low worker productivity. If you're trying to solve a behavior problem, you probably don't need to observe the behavior in every situation."

Good point. In fact, a child may have tantrums at school but not at home, in the mall, or in the grocery store. There's usually not much point in observing the child in situations where the behavior hasn't been a problem. If tantrums have been a problem in school, then let's observe him in school. If we're interested in *go* expressions, they're going to occur in social contexts, so we could restrict our observations to certain situations, such as the dining hall and the classroom when the student is likely to talk to others.

Okay, so continuous recording does not mean 24-hour-a-day observation. It is usually sufficient to record the behavior in relevant situations for short periods. But during these observation periods, you record each and every occurrence of the behavior. This is often done with a tally sheet. The tally sheet, or recording form, typically shows the time and date of the observation period, the location where observations were made, the name of the person being observed, and the name of the observer. Each time the behavior being studied occurs, the observer makes a hash mark to indicate one occurrence. These hash marks can later be counted to determine the rate at which the behavior occurred.

I'm going to go "high-tech" now and use the overhead projector. . . . A typical tally sheet would look something like this:

Observer ___ *Phil I. Stein* ___

Person observed ___ *Mary Typhoid* ___

Date	Time	Location	Notes	"Go" expressions	Total
10-1	8 -8:30 a.m.	Dining hall	Alone except for 10 min w. Carole	~~////~~ ///	8
10-2	8:15- 8:45	Dining hall	Jon R., Diane, and Bob present	~~////~~ ~~////~~ ~~////~~ //	17
10-3	7:50- 8:20	Dining hall	Bob present	~~////~~ ////	9

Table 2-1. Tally sheet for continuous recording.

Another way of recording occurrences is with a mechanical counter, such as those used in museums and other public places to tally the number of visitors per day. Tallies are also kept with wrist counters similar to those that golfers use to keep score during a game. In either case, the recorder presses a plunger each time the behavior occurs.

Interval Recording

Continuous recording is fine if the behavior does not occur too frequently. If I were to set a metronome in motion at a slow pace—tick . . . tick . . . tick . . . tick—like that, you'd have no trouble keeping an accurate count of the number of ticks the metronome made during the course of a half-hour. But speed the metronome up dramatically, so that it goes tick-tick-tick-tick, and it becomes far more difficult to keep an accurate count. The same thing is true with behavior.

It might, for example, be hard to make an accurate count of the number of behavioral tics in some people. A tic is a sudden and abrupt movement of some part of the body. Examples include raising the eyebrows, opening and closing the mouth, twitching a facial muscle, and tapping a foot. In some individuals, tics occur at a fast and furious rate, too fast to be counted accurately. When the behavior being observed occurs at a very high rate, it is customary to turn to interval recording.

> **Interval recording:**
> **Recording whether a behavior occurs**
> **during each of a series of short intervals**
> **within an observation period.**

In interval recording, behavior is recorded during very short intervals—usually no longer than several seconds—during an observation period. No effort is made to count every occurrence of a behavior during these brief intervals. Rather, the recorder merely determines whether the behavior occurs. If it does, the recorder makes a hash mark for that interval; if it does not, the recorder leaves the tally sheet blank or makes a horizontal mark. The number of hash marks indicates the number of intervals during which the behavior occurred.

Suppose, for example, that I wish to record a facial tic—an eye twitch—that occurs at a very high rate. I might observe the behavior for an hour. Instead of trying to count every single twitch during that hour, however, I might divide the time into 10-second intervals. Then I would observe the person for 10 seconds and record whether or not the tic occurred during that interval. As soon as the 10 seconds were up, I would observe for another 10 seconds and record whether a tic occurred during that interval; and so on. The data record for the first 3 minutes might look something like this:

Observer ___ *Phil I. Stein* ___

Person observed ___ *Sally Salmonella* ___

Time and date ___ *8:45 a.m.* ___ *10-29-97* ___

10 second intervals

		1	2	3	4	5	6	Total
	1		/	/		/	/	4
Minutes	2	/				/		2
	3		/	/			/	3
	4							

Table 2-2. *Tally sheet for interval recording.*

What happened during these 3 minutes? Midori?

"There were tics during four of the six intervals in the first minute, during two of the intervals in the second minute, and during three of the intervals in the third minute."

Right. So the behavior occurred in 9 out of the 18 intervals, or 50% of the intervals. We can also express these data as a rate: The behavior occurred on average three times per minute.[3]

Now, recording data for each successive 10-second period can be difficult, since the behavior might occur while you're looking away to mark your record sheet. An alternative is to observe behavior for 10 seconds, then allow 10 seconds for marking the record sheet. This gives you three 10-second observation intervals per minute.

Even this method is rather demanding if the recorder also has other duties. For example, if you are a teacher, you may not have time to observe and record a particular behavior for one 10-second interval after another. In such cases, it's often possible to alter the recording procedure so as to accommodate observers who have other duties. For example, a teacher might observe a student for 10 seconds during each hour, beginning at half past the hour. During those 10 seconds, the teacher would either count each occurrence of the behavior (continuous recording) or note whether the behavior occurs at all during the interval (interval recording). There are problems when people attempt to combine data collection with other duties, but the realities of life are that sometimes there is no other option.

You can see that continuous recording would work very well for relatively infrequent behavior of short duration, such as cursing, getting up from a seat, and calling out in class. But continuous recording might not work so well if it is hard to tell when a behavior begins and ends, if it occurs at very high rates, or if it is of long duration. If we're going to study a child's tantrums, we're probably better off using interval recording because . . . why is that, John?

> "Because it's sometimes hard to tell when one tantrum ends and another begins, and because tantrums can go on for a long time."

Exactly. What if the behavior is something like head banging? Every now and then, an autistic child bangs his head against a piece of furniture. How would you record rate in that case, Brian?

> "Continuous recording."

Why?

> "Well, each instance of head banging should be pretty easy to count; his head either comes in contact with a piece of furniture or it doesn't. And you said he does it 'every now and then,' so it doesn't occur at a high rate."

Good point. You've got to think about these kinds of things before you start collecting data or you may end up collecting data that aren't very useful. You also need to be able to estimate how reliable the data are.

Measuring the Reliability of Rate Data

Suppose you ask someone to record the number of times a student gets out of her seat without permission. The recorder uses, let's say, interval recording. Every 30 minutes, he observes the student for a 10-second interval and records whether she leaves her seat during that time. These data show that the student is out of her seat on 50% of the intervals. Now, how can you determine if that 50% figure is accurate? Yes, Maya?

"You could have two people record the behavior."

How does that help?

"Well, if they observe at the same time, they should both come up with the same figure. If one recorder says the behavior occurred 50% of the time, and the other says it occurred 75% of the time, something is wrong. They can't both be right."

Yes. It's like asking two people to add the same column of figures. If they both come up with the same answer, we feel fairly confident that the answer is correct. On the other hand, if they come up with two different figures, then we know that at least one of them is wrong. In trying to determine the accuracy of data tallies, researchers usually look at the degree of agreement between two observers, something called inter-observer reliability:[4]

> **Inter-observer reliability:**
> **A measure of the degree of agreement**
> **in data tallies made by two or more observers.**

There are several ways of calculating inter-observer reliability.

Reliability of Continuous Data

With data obtained by continuous recording, it is customary to calculate inter-observer reliability by dividing the smaller tally by the larger tally and multiplying the resulting ratio by 100. Multiplying by 100 converts the ratio to a whole number.[5]

Let's take an example. A 10-year-old boy has been diagnosed as having ADHD—attention deficit hyperactive disorder. This means, among other things, that his eyes wander: He changes the focus of his gaze far more often than most 10-year-olds do. This is one of the things that lead people to say that such children have short attention spans. His teacher calls on the friendly, neighborhood behavior analyst, who decides to get some data on eye movements. She has two observers sit in on the teacher's class during a silent reading period and count the number of times the boy looks away from his book during a 30-minute period. The observers take positions in different parts of the room. Each can see the boy clearly, but neither is likely to be influenced by the other's tally. The record sheets show that observer 1 counts 100 instances of eye wandering, while observer 2 counts 150 instances. How useful are these data? The behaviorist calculates inter-observer reliability: She divides 100 by 150, which yields a ratio of .666. She rounds this to .67 and multiplies by 100. The inter-observer reliability is 67.

Reliability of Interval Data

The procedure is somewhat different when computing inter-observer reliability with interval data. You get interval tallies from two observers and compare their records for each interval. You count the number of intervals on which the two observers agree. Then you divide that number by the total number of intervals both observed. You multiply this number by 100 to convert the ratio to a whole number.[6]

Let's suppose the friendly, neighborhood behavior analyst tells the teacher, "I'm sorry, but we're all out of observers. However, you and your teacher's aide can collect the data we need." The teacher gets a little huffy. "And how are we supposed to do that?" she asks. "We've got our hands full as it is. We can't spend 30 minutes watching one student." The behavior analyst says, "I understand, but there's another way. During silent reading, look over at the student in question once every minute. Watch him for 5 seconds, and record whether he looks away from his book at any time during those 5 seconds. You can just count for 5 seconds—1001, 1002, and so on. That'll give you close to a 5 second interval. Do your observations during the first 5 seconds of each minute. That way you'll both be observing the boy at the same time. Do this for 30 minutes. That will give us 30 observations."

The teacher and his aide agree to collect the data. To calculate reliability, the behaviorist compares the records of the two observers, noting the number of intervals in which they agreed. Let us say that our hypothetical observers saw the same thing on 20 of the 30 intervals, and on the other 10 intervals their observations differed. The behaviorist divides the number of agreements, 20, by the total number of intervals, 30, and that gives a ratio of agreements to total observations of .666. Round off to .67 and multiply by 100 and you get a reliability score of 67.

There are other ways of computing reliability, but these two are the ones you're most likely to encounter in reading behavioral studies. If the observers come up with very different tallies, you can't be very confident that the results obtained are valid. You have a question, John?

> "Yes. I'm not sure what we're measuring with these ratios. I mean, two people can add a column of figures and come up with the same wrong number. Agreement doesn't necessarily mean accuracy."

That's a good point. The reliability score expresses the degree of agreement in tallies between the two observers. It does not directly measure the accuracy of either observer's tally. Suppose that you have a cold, and you cough and sneeze a good deal. During a 30-minute period two observers record the number of times you cough. One observer's tally is 9; the other's is 11. The inter-observer reliability is 9 divided by 11, which is . . . who has a calculator?

> "It's .818."

Thank you, Maya. So, round off to .82, multiply by 100, and you have 82. But in fact, the number of coughs was 10. Both observers were wrong. What reliability tells you is how far apart two tallies are, not how accurate they are.

"So, in the example of the hyperactive boy, the correct tally could be 25, or 50, or 200. The inter-observer reliability won't tell you what the correct tally is, or even which observer is closer to being right."

Well . . . yes, Midori, that's true. It's an imperfect world.

"Then what good is inter-observer reliability? They could both be a mile off."

Ah, now that's not quite true. One of them has to be closer to the truth than the other. Our example said that one observer tallies 100, and the other comes up with 150. If the correct number is 50, then the first observer is closer to being right. If the correct number is 200, then the second observer is closer to being right. If we split the difference between the two tallies, then the first observer will be closer to right if the true number is below 125, and the second observer will be closer if the true number is higher than 125. The best guess, then, of the true number is . . . is what? Yes, Brian?

"One hundred twenty-five."

Explain why.

"Because, on average, that number is going to be closer to the correct answer than to any other guess."

Exactly. The implicit assumption with reliability measures is that the true number *probably* lies somewhere between what the two observers come up with. This means that the smaller the gap between the two tallies, the smaller their combined error is likely to be. So you want a high degree of agreement between observers. With an inter-observer reliability of 66, I'd be pretty squeamish about accepting the conclusions of a study.

"What *would* be a good reliability figure?"

I'm not sure there's a consensus on that, Carlotta, but anything below 80 is usually looked on with suspicion. I think most behaviorists would probably be pretty happy with a reliability score of 90.

"What if the reliability is low?"

A good question, Midori. Let's talk a bit about how you might improve the reliability of your data.

Improving Reliability

First, let's try a little experiment. Imagine that a teacher has a fourth-grader, Betty, who tends to be overly aggressive with the other students. To study this problem, you have to count aggressive acts. I'll give you a running account of her behavior, and you count aggressive acts. (Remember, readers, you're expected to do this, too!) Ready? Here we go:

Betty bops a student on the top of his head with her fist. Then she turns to another youngster and gives him a little shove so that he falls to the floor. She sits on top of him and bounces up and down three times. Next she gets up and throws a cup of water in a student's face. Then she grabs a toy another student is playing with, and they get into a tug of war over it; Betty yanks at the toy three times but the other child won't let go. Then she stomps on the child's toe, and he lets go of the toy. Betty promptly tosses the toy over her shoulder, and it happens to land on the head of another student. At this point, the teacher comes over to Betty, grabs her by the arm, and reproaches her. Betty tries to pull away. She grabs the teacher's wrist, then she bites the teacher's hand.

Okay, how many aggressive acts did Battling Betty perform? John?

"I counted 16."

How about you, Maya?

"I got 12."

Jamal?

"13."

It would appear there's quite a bit of disagreement in the counts. In other words, the inter-observer reliability is rather low. Some of you may have counted grabbing the teacher's wrist and biting her hand as two aggressive acts. Some of you may have counted that as one action. Others of you may not have counted interactions with the teacher, because I implied that the teacher was concerned about aggression toward other students. Some of you may have counted throwing the toy as an aggressive act, because the toy hit another child. Some of you may not have counted that because she apparently did not throw the toy *at* the child. We could go through each of Betty's actions and discuss whether it qualifies as aggression, and we would see a lot of disagreement. That's because we don't have a consensus about exactly what qualifies as an aggressive act.

It follows that one thing we can do to improve reliability is to define the behavior so that the observers are recording the same kind of behavior. For example, in Betty's case, aggression might be defined as any contact with another person that appears to cause pain to that person. By this definition, a pat on the back would not be recorded as an aggressive act, nor would shoving a child or taking away a toy. On the other hand, biting the teacher and hitting a student on the head would qualify if the victims showed evidence of pain.

This definition would probably improve inter-observer agreements, but it's a long way from perfect. It doesn't, for example, tell us whether tossing a toy over the shoulder constitutes aggression when it hits another child. Another possibility would be to define aggression as any action that causes another person to say

"Ouch!" or "Ow!" or to cry. By identifying the specific effects the behavior must have on the environment to qualify as aggression, we should increase the reliability of observations. . . . You have a question, John?

> "Doesn't that leave out a lot? If Betty jabs someone with a pencil and he doesn't say anything or cry, according to the definition there's been no aggression. That's obviously wrong."

You're right, but you've missed the point. The point is to have a consistent measure of the behavior we're studying. It's okay if we underestimate or overestimate the frequency as long as we do so consistently. It's like when the Audubon Society does their Christmas bird count every year. I don't think anybody imagines that the observers get a truly accurate count of the number of rufous-sided towhees in Maryland. Undoubtedly, many birds are counted three and four times by different observers, while many other birds aren't counted by anyone. But if the procedure for counting birds is the same each year, we can get some idea of whether the numbers are going up or down. The same is true of behavior. It's not usually important whether a behavior occurred 47 or 45 times; what matters is whether the rate changed. As long as we are recording behavior in a consistent manner, we can get some idea of whether the rate is going up or down.

Another thing we can do to improve reliability is to have the observers practice recording the data together and compare notes. When one records an act and the other does not, they can discuss the matter and reach a consensus so that, when such instances occur in the future, the observers will agree. This sort of training is often essential to obtain reliable data.

Once reliable data have been collected, the question arises, What does it mean? Interpreting data is greatly facilitated by presenting it in graphic form.

Graphing Behavior Rates

Students often hate graphs. The reason seems to have to do with the association of graphs with mathematics, which they hate even more than graphs. I once knew a librarian—a college graduate—who said that before he read a magazine article, he would flip through the pages and see if there were any graphs. If there were, he wouldn't read the article. This fear of graphs is very unfortunate, since graphs are generally not complicated. In fact, their chief purpose is to make difficult material easier to understand. In any case, the kinds of graphs used in applied behavior analysis are nearly always very simple, even when they appear formidable. So, take heart. You will survive this short discussion of graphs.

Simple Frequency Graphs

I'm going to tell you about the two kinds of graphs you are most likely to encounter in your reading in behavior analysis: simple frequency graphs, and cumulative frequency graphs. A simple frequency graph is:

Simple frequency graph:
A graph in which each data point indicates
the number of times a behavior occurred
at a particular time.

For example, suppose your company offers a course in basic arithmetic for employees who haven't completed high school. The class meets each weekday for an hour. The course is designed to be self-paced, so each student works through a succession of modules. When a student is able to demonstrate mastery of the skill in one module, she goes on to the next. When she masters that one, she goes on to the next, and so on. The modules are designed to take about 20 minutes each, assuming the student has already mastered the prerequisite modules. Let's suppose you keep track of the number of modules each student does each day. The data can be plotted as a simple frequency graph, with the horizontal axis designating the class days and the vertical axis designating the number of modules completed. Each point on the graph indicates the number of modules completed on a particular day. I've put this graph on a transparency so you can see what it looks like:

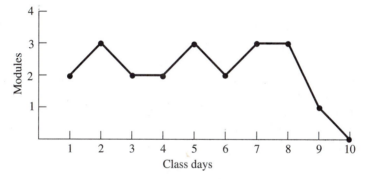

Figure 2-1. Simple frequency graph. Modules completed per day. (hypothetical data)

The data points are connected to help us see any trends or anomalies. Do you see any trends or anomalies here? Yes, Belinda?

"It looks like the student usually does two or three modules a day."

Yes. Anything else?

"The student didn't do very well on days 9 and 10."

Yes, there does appear to be a drop in performance. What do you suppose is going on?

"I guess maybe those modules are harder than the others."

You think so? Well, let's look at the data from another hypothetical student:

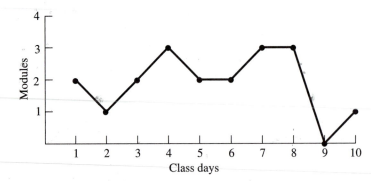

Figure 2-2. *Simple frequency graph: Modules completed per day. (hypothetical data)*

We see the same sort of dip on days 9 and 10. What do you make of this? Does this confirm Belinda's hypothesis about the difficulty of the modules? Midori?

"No, it doesn't."

Why do you say that?

"Because they're not working on the same modules those days. It's something to do with the day, not the module."

Congratulations, Sherlock. You've reached a logical deduction. Perhaps those were the days when regular work in the factory stopped and everyone took inventory, so the students were unusually tired. The point is, plotting the data on a graph makes anomalies of this sort easier to spot and may help in deducing the reason for the anomaly.

Frequency graphs can also make it easier to see trends. If the number of daily modules increases or decreases, that will be more apparent when the data are presented in graphic form. This is especially so if the change is gradual. Here's an example:

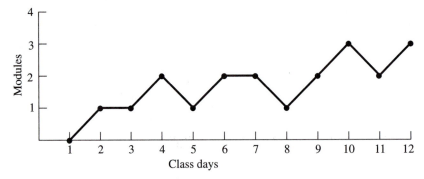

Figure 2-3. *Simple frequency graph: Modules completed per day. (hypothetical data)*

Do you see a trend in these data, John?

"It looks like there's a gradual increase in the number of modules the student does each day. It takes him two days to do the first module. Then he's doing at least one module a day. Toward the end, he's getting to where he can sometimes do three modules a day."

Yes. There's a gradual upward slope to the data points. There's a good deal of variability in these data, as is often the case in human behavior, but there is a gradual increase in the number of modules done each day.[7]

Incidentally, there's a simple tool you can use to help see data trends of this sort: a straightedge. Just take a ruler or any other straightedge and rest it over the data points of a figure. The idea is to cut through the middle of the data points. Then mark a line with a pencil. The resulting trendline is a way of highlighting the change in the data—the tendency of the data points to go up or down. Of course, trendlines can be drawn more precisely with computers, but in applied work it's usually not necessary.

You can see that plotting data on a simple frequency graph is a piece of cake. Reading such a graph is also no great challenge. Interpreting changes in the data, such as the dip in performance on days 9 and 10, is more difficult. But that's not a difficulty that the graph causes; the graph merely helps us see what the data are trying to tell us. Sometimes the data speak very clearly; sometimes they are more circumspect.

Cumulative Frequency Graphs

Okay, so much for simple frequency graphs. Now on to cumulative frequency graphs:

> Cumulative frequency graph:
> A graph in which each data point indicates
> the total number of times the behavior
> has occurred up to that point.

While a simple frequency graph shows the number of times a behavior occurred during a particular period, a cumulative graph shows the total number of times the behavior has occurred during that and all previous periods. Let's take a look at the data from the first figure and see how they would be plotted on a cumulative graph. On the first day, the student completed two modules, so day 1 would show a point indicating two modules completed. On day 2, he completed three modules. Two modules for day 1 plus three for day 2 gives you a total of five modules completed by the end of day 2. On the third day, he does two modules, so the total as of that point is . . . is what, Alfred?

"Seven; 5 plus 2. I'm not too dumb."

So I see. Okay, I've already plotted these numbers on a transparency. They look like this:

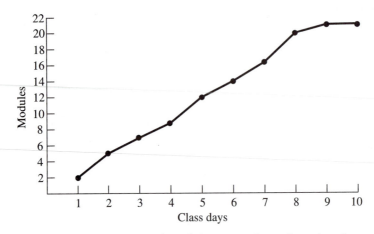

Figure 2-4. *Cumulative graph. Each data point indicates the total number of modules completed as of that date. (hypothetical data)*

You'll notice a difference between simple and cumulative graphs right away. With the simple frequency graph, if you look at the data point for any given day and look across to the numbers on the vertical axis, you can determine how many modules were completed on that particular day. With the cumulative frequency graph, you look at the data point for any given day and look across to the numbers on the vertical axis and determine the total number of modules completed as of that day. The two graphs present the same data in very different ways.

For example, the change in student performance on days 9 and 10 is represented as a dip in the line in the simple frequency graph. But there is no dip in the cumulative frequency graph. In fact, the line progresses upward slightly and then levels off. If the student had done no modules at all on those days, the line on the cumulative graph would be flat; a horizontal line means the behavior is not occurring at all. A *straight* line that moves upward means the behavior is occurring at a steady rate—in this case, the same number of modules each day. A line that curves indicates that the rate is increasing (if it curves away from the horizontal) or decreasing (if it curves toward the horizontal).

"What does it mean if it goes below the horizontal?"

It means someone has made a mistake, Jamal. With a cumulative graph, the line can never go below the horizontal because the lowest number you can add to the previous data point is zero. A student can't complete "minus 2 modules," for example.[8]

Frequency graphs are very neat things because they make the data so, so . . . graphic. But the real benefit of a frequency graph is that it allows us to see the effects of variables on behavior. If you're trying to solve a behavior problem, for example, and you try intervening in some way, you need to be able to evaluate whether the intervention worked. It takes more than a good graph, however, to evaluate an intervention.

Evaluating the Effects of an Intervention

The job of applied behavior analysts is to solve behavior problems. Usually they do this by increasing or decreasing the rate of some behavior. But how can they be sure that the changes in behavior that they get are due to their efforts?

A lot of people believe that if a black cat crosses your trail, misfortune will soon follow. Often they'll support their belief by pointing to experiences they've had or heard about, such as when a person saw a black cat and then fell into an open manhole. But such evidence is selective: Black cats cross the paths of a lot of people without anything bad happening to them, but the true believer remembers only those who fell into open manholes.[9]

Do black cats bring bad luck? To get accurate answers to such questions, we must ask them properly. That's what experimental research is all about: asking questions in such a way as to get accurate answers.

You are all familiar with group design experimental research. That's where you get data on two or more different groups of people. Those in each group perform under different conditions. You compare the performances of the various groups and run statistical tests to tell whether the differences are greater than would be expected.

Single Case Experimental Design

Group designs are not particularly suitable for answering questions about the effects of experience on *individual* behavior. For such questions, single case experimental designs are more appropriate:

> Single case experimental design:
> A research design in which the behavior
> of an individual is compared under
> experimental and control conditions.

In a single case design, we compare the performance of an individual under one condition with that same individual's performance under other conditions.[10] Instead of running statistical tests, we plot the data on a graph and examine it. It is possible to do statistical analysis with individual data, but the assumption is that if we can't see an effect without a lot of mathematical gymnastics, then the effect isn't very important. We want effects that are of *practical* significance, not statistically significant trivial differences.

Now, to test the effects of a particular variable on behavior, you must manipulate that variable while holding all other variables constant—so far as is possible. In a traditional group design experiment, you do that by . . . by doing what, John?

"By exposing one group to the variable but not the other group."

Right. But single case research is done differently. You're not comparing one group with another or one person with another. You're comparing one person's performance under one circumstance with that same person's behavior under a different circumstance. There are various ways of doing this, but they all start with a baseline period:

Baseline:
A period during which the behavior under study is recorded, but no attempt is made to modify it.

A baseline period in single case designs serves the same purpose as the control group serves in traditional group designs: It provides a basis for comparison. During the baseline period, you record the behavior but you don't introduce the variable in which you're interested. This gives you a standard—a baseline—against which you can measure the effects of the independent variable.[11]

After you have established a relatively stable baseline, you can introduce the independent variable. Since you are now not merely recording behavior but attempting to change the rate of the behavior, this stage of the experiment is called the *intervention period*. To determine the effects of the intervention, you compare performance during the baseline with performance during the intervention. The way you make this comparison is by looking at graphic representations of the data.

Let's take a hypothetical example. We'll take a student who is completing modules on arithmetic. You plot the number of modules done by the student each day. After five days, the graph looks something like this:

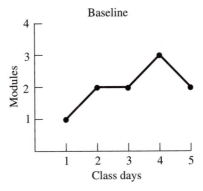

Figure 2-5. *Baseline. Data collected before an intervention are plotted on a frequency graph. (hypothetical data)*

This is the baseline period. The student is working under standard conditions, and his rate of module completion is about two modules per day.

Now you introduce the independent variable. Let's say you want to see whether presenting the modules on computer will make a difference. During the baseline, the modules were in booklet form; during the intervention period, the modules are on computer. You plot the data for seven more days, and the resulting graph looks like this:

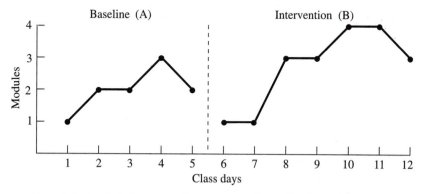

Figure 2-6. *Simple frequency graph: Intervention effects. The effects of an intervention may be seen by comparing modules completed during a baseline period (A) with modules completed during an intervention period (B). (hypothetical data)*

You can see that during the intervention, the rate of module completion first fell sharply and then increased steadily and finally stabilized at about three modules per day. It appears that the student can do the modules faster when they're on computer.

"Are the baseline and intervention periods always for five and seven days?"

No, Midori. There is no set length for either period. Ideally, you continue the baseline and intervention periods until the rate of behavior is very stable. In our hypothetical experiment, for example, it would have been a good idea to have continued the baseline for another five or ten days to be sure that the rate of module completion would remain steady at about two modules a day. For the same reason, it would have been a good idea to continue the intervention for several more days. But practical considerations, such as the severity of the problem and the availability of staff and funds, also play a role in these decisions. For example, if you're helping parents deal with a kid who screams like a siren whenever he doesn't get his way, it may be difficult to convince the parents that you need to get three weeks of baseline data before you begin the intervention.

Now, let's have a little practice at interpreting single case research data. Suppose you have an idea about how you might increase the rate at which students complete arithmetic modules. You implement your idea, and you plot the data. Suppose your graph looks like this:

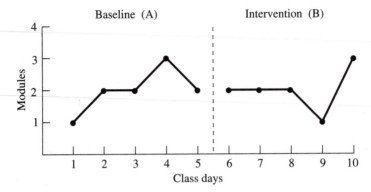

Figure 2-7. *Simple frequency graph: Intervention effects. The broken line indicates that an intervention began on day 6. (hypothetical data)*

The broken vertical line indicates that the intervention went into effect on day 6. Now, what does this figure tell you about the effectiveness of your intervention? What do you say, Jamal?

"Well, I can't see much effect. It looks like the student is doing about two modules a day before and during the intervention."

I agree. Now suppose you get data like this:

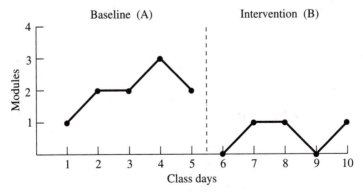

Figure 2-8. *Simple frequency graph: Intervention effects. (hypothetical data)*

"Whoa! With that kind of help, the students will get nowhere fast."

Right. The graph makes it very clear that the intervention is having a negative effect—it's reducing the rate at which modules are completed. With frequency graphs, you don't usually need to collect data for long periods to see what's happening; you can see it almost immediately. The same thing is true with cumulative graphs. Look at this cumulative graph. It shows math modules done before and after an intervention:

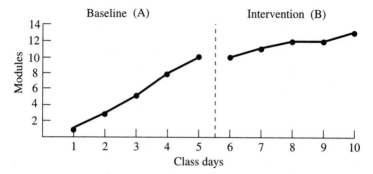

Figure 2-9. *Cumulative graph: Intervention effects. The broken line indicates that an intervention began on day 6. The effects of the intervention are reflected in the change in the slope of the data line. (hypothetical data)*

Is the intervention having an impact? John?

"I think it's hurting."

How can you tell?

"The graph was climbing at a steady rate, but during the intervention the line is just about flat. The rate of module completion slowed down."

Right. In fact, this is the same data we just saw as a simple frequency graph. If the intervention were helping, the slope of the line would be steeper during the intervention.

"But, Dr. Cee, that's just one student. Maybe other students would be helped by the intervention."

That's true. Sometimes an intervention will work with one person but not another. So if you're interested in a group of people, such as the students in a class, the workers in a factory, or the residents in a dormitory, you have to plot data for more people. Ideally, you'd plot data for everybody involved. But if the group is large, that's not practical. One alternative is to plot the data for a few people who are picked at random. Another possibility is to select a few people who are likely to be representative of the group. Plotting their data should provide a pretty good picture of the class as a whole. You—

"Why don't you just average the data?"

Sometimes that's useful, Carlotta, but averaging data can hide as much as it reveals. Here are the cumulative graphs of two students:

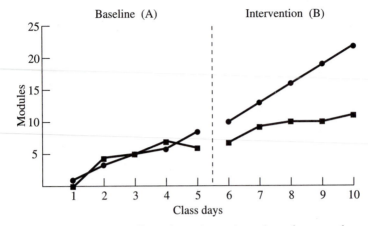

Figure 2-10. *Intervention effects. The two lines indicate the performance of two students before and during an intervention. (hypothetical data)*

Now, Carlotta, what would happen if you averaged these data?

"It looks to me like it would show that, on average, the intervention had no effect."

Exactly! One student's performance cancels out the other. An intervention that is beneficial with one student and harmful with another appears, when the data are averaged, to be having no effect at all. The same thing can happen if you average the data from a large group. Some people may be helped by an intervention, and some may be hurt by it; but when you average the data, it looks as though the intervention had no effect. Or, an intervention might have a powerful effect on a few people and little or no effect on others. When you average the data, it looks as though the intervention had only a mild effect.

Behaving is something *individuals* do, so you have to look at *individual* data. Because of this, and because averaging data necessarily hides individual performance, you won't see many graphs depicting averages in the behavior analysis literature. Behavior analysis recognizes that people are different, and that an intervention that helps one person may not help another.

"But how do you do statistical analysis with this kind of data?"

A good question, Brian. There is usually no need to do statistical analysis if you're looking at individual behavior, and so you don't often find t tests, analysis of variance, and the like in behavior analysis journals.

"Then how do you decide what the data show?"

You look at the graphed data. If you're trying to solve a behavior problem and you can't see a definite improvement in behavior without doing a sophisticated statistical analysis, then you haven't been very successful. Even if a statistical test showed that the differences obtained were significant at the .0001 level, it's of no practical importance if the change in behavior isn't obvious from a graph. You may have learned something of theoretical value, but you haven't solved the person's problem. Statistical tests are good for teasing out the subtle effects of an intervention, but when your tooth hurts you don't want subtle effects; you want relief. You have a question, Carlotta?

"You're saying, you plot the data from a single person on a frequency graph and you eyeball it. You look at the data line to see if there's been a change since the baseline. Right?"

Not only right, but succinctly said. The process is usually referred to as "visual inspection," but *eyeballing* is a good enough term. What you're looking for in applied behavior analysis is a very definite effect on behavior, something that will pop out at you from a graph.

"But how do you know that what 'pops out at you' is the result of the intervention? I mean, there could be a lot of things that changed the behavior."

ABAB Reversal Design

You're absolutely right, Carlotta. Something other than the intervention may have been responsible for the change in performance.

Consider the experiment in which we put arithmetic modules on computer. At first the student did fewer modules with the computer, but then he did more. It looks like the computer helps. Now, suppose that, unknown to us, the worker's supervisor called him aside on the first day of intervention and said something like, "If you don't start doing better in this math course, there's no way I'm going to recommend you for that promotion you want." The subsequent improvement in performance might have been due to the modules being on the computer, or it might have been due to the supervisor's comment. One way to rule out that possibility is by repeating the experiment. This can be done in what is called an ABAB reversal design:

ABAB reversal design:
A single case design in which baseline
and intervention conditions are repeated
with the same person.

In an ABAB design, you essentially perform the experiment twice. In our modules experiment, you might get data that look like this:

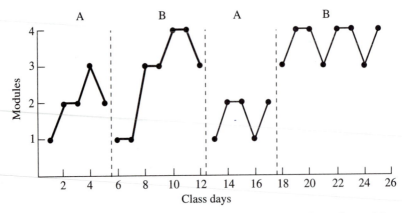

Figure 2-11. *ABAB reversal. Repetition of A and B periods helps rule out the possibility that changes are due to variables other than the intervention. (hypothetical data)*

After the initial baseline period (the first A) and intervention period (the first B), you return to the baseline condition (the second A) and then follow that with another intervention period (the second B). This figure shows that when you switched back to the paper-and-pencil modules, the student once again completed about two modules per day. When you returned to the computer modules again, the rate returned to about three per day.

The first time you switched from baseline to intervention conditions, the change might have been due to some uncontrolled variable that coincidentally changed at the same time. But it is unlikely that this sort of coincidence would occur a second time.

The ABAB design makes it possible to study the effects of an intervention on behavior in much the same way as you would test a light switch. If you want to know whether a particular switch affects a particular light, you throw the switch and see what happens to the light. To make sure the result wasn't due to coincidence (a momentary power failure, for example), you return the switch to its first position and throw it again. You can even repeat the experiment over and over again—ABABABAB . . . —But this is rarely necessary. A single replication is usually sufficient. In traditional group designs, replication is done by conducting the experiment again with different subjects. With the ABAB design, each time you repeat the baseline and intervention sequence, you are replicating your initial experiment.

You can see that the ABAB design is extremely powerful. There are times, however, when you can't use an ABAB design. Can anyone think of an example of a time when an ABAB design would be inappropriate? Yes, Carlotta?

"If you were treating a patient for cancer and the tumor was getting smaller, you wouldn't want to stop treatment for a while to see if the tumor got bigger again and then treat it again."

Well, that's true enough—although, actually, I think there are some experiments in medical history in which something of this sort was done. But your example involves a medical problem, and our subject matter is behavior problems. Can you think of an example of a behavior problem that you might not be able to treat with an ABAB design?

> "Hmmm. Suppose you're teaching someone to read. He's making good progress. You wouldn't want to stop teaching him just to prove that the lessons were helping."

No, you wouldn't. Of course, you *could* use an ABAB design in that case. You could test the person every day during a baseline and record the number of words the person reads per minute. Then you could provide instruction and continue to record the reading rate. Then you could discontinue instruction for a time, and then begin instructing again. If you did this, what do you think you'd find? Midori?

> "I think you'd see faster progress during the intervention periods, when you were teaching him to read, than you would during the baseline periods, when you didn't teach him."

I think you're right. If you start with someone who can't read at all, then the reversal is not going to make the person illiterate again. But you probably will see a difference between baseline and intervention periods in the rate of reading improvement. Of course, you probably wouldn't want to interrupt the intervention. Who can give me another example of a case in which you wouldn't want to use an ABAB design? Yes, John?

> "If the problem involved violent behavior, and your intervention reduced the rate of violence, you might not want to return to the baseline condition."

Multiple Baseline Design

Yes. If you've solved a serious behavior problem, you probably wouldn't want to reinstate it just to make sure your intervention worked. In situations like this, you need to replicate without returning to the baseline condition. Behaviorists do this with what is called a multiple baseline design:

> ### Multiple baseline design:
> ### A single case design in which the effects
> ### of an intervention are recorded across
> ### situations, behaviors, or individuals.

In multiple baseline experiments, as the name implies, there are two or more baseline periods with which the intervention period is compared. For example, consider the case of 4-year-old Teddy Tyrant. Little Teddy has been tormenting his betters for most of his short life, issuing commands and then producing ear-piercing screams until the commands are obeyed. He does this at home, in preschool, at church, on outings with adults—pretty much everywhere. People always give him what he wants to shut him up. It might be interesting to see if steadfastly ignoring his screams would put an end to this obnoxious behavior. But if this procedure were to work, there would not be much support for the idea of discontinuing the treatment to reestablish Master Tyrant's unpleasant ways.

Another option is to gather baseline data in various situations and then begin applying the intervention in each of those situations at different times. You might record the amount of time spent screaming at home, in school, and in public places. When the baseline is stable in the home, you begin the intervention. Then, perhaps a few days later, you begin the intervention in the school. Then, after a few more days, you apply the new procedure in public places. The data obtained might look something like this:

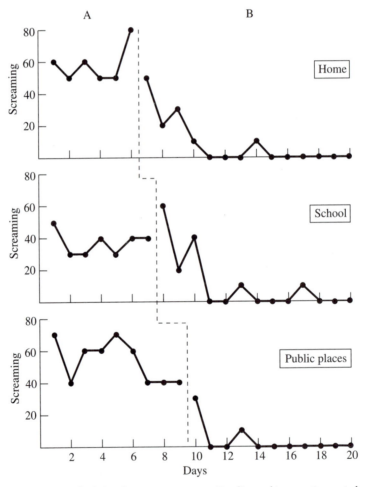

Figure 2-12. *Multiple baseline across situations. Baseline and intervention periods are different for different situations. (hypothetical data)*

You've got three different baseline periods (indicated by A), and three different intervention periods (indicated by B). In essence, you've got three different experiments, and you've gotten similar results in all three of them. This is a multiple baseline experiment across situations. You compare the behavior that occurs during intervention and baseline in each situation. In other words, you look to see how well the intervention worked in the home, in the school, and in public places. If you get similar results in all three situations, there's not much doubt that the change is due to the intervention.

Now, just to be sure you understand how to read multiple baseline graphs, let's see if someone can tell me when the intervention began in the home. How about it, John?

"Day 7."

Right. You can look at the broken line, indicating the start of the intervention, and follow it down to the horizontal axis where the days are indicated. Or, since there was one data point for each day, you can count the number of data points to the left of the broken line.

Now, look at the figure again. How long was the intervention period in the home setting? Alfred?

"Ah, let's see. Fourteen?"

Aren't you sure?

"One, 2, 3, 4, . . . 14. Yes, I'm sure."

And you're also right.

How long was the baseline in public places, Maya?

"Nine days?"

Right. Okay, so much for multiple baseline research across situations. We can also look at the effects of an intervention on different kinds of behavior. How could you set up such a study with Teddy Tyrant? Brian?

"Hmm. Well, Teddy probably does more than just scream. He probably does things like shout and stamp his feet, and maybe he knocks things about or hits people. I guess you could get baselines on two or three of those behaviors, and then intervene with one after the other."

Good. Let's say we assume that in addition to screaming, Teddy stamps his feet and hits the adults who are not fulfilling his commands. What might the data look like?

"I think it would look like the last figure you showed us, except that the three different graphs would be for different behaviors rather than different locations."

Excellent, Brian. You're exactly right. And here it is:

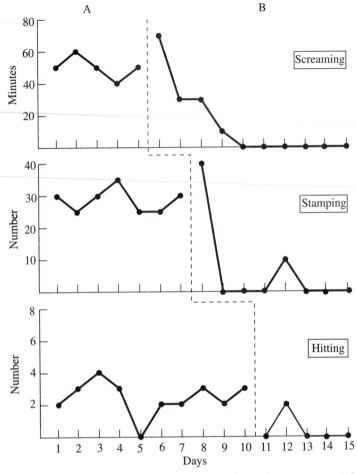

Figure 2-13. Multiple baseline across behaviors. Baseline and intervention periods are different for different behaviors. (hypothetical data)

Again, you have three different baselines and three different intervention periods. You've conducted the same basic experiment three times. You've tested the effects of the intervention on screaming, on foot stamping, and on hitting. The assumption is that if you get similar changes in two or three different behaviors, it's probably the result of the intervention.

Now, each of these examples of multiple baseline experiments has involved only one person. You're getting data in different situations or on different behaviors, but you're getting them from the same person. It is also desirable to know whether an intervention is likely to work for different people. To answer this question, behaviorists perform multiple baseline experiments across individuals.

In this case, data on time spent screaming might be collected as before, but the data come from different people. The result looks like this:

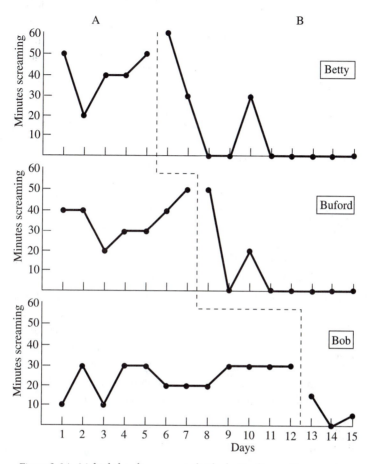

Figure 2-14. *Multiple baseline across individuals. Baseline and intervention periods are different for different people. (hypothetical data)*

You're looking for trends. If a behavior changes for the better after an intervention, then you can tentatively conclude that change was brought about by the intervention. If you replicate those effects with different people, then you can also have some confidence that it will work with many people.

"But you're using only one intervention in all of these experiments. What if you wanted to compare two different interventions?"

Alternating Treatments Design
An excellent question, Carlotta. If you want to study the effects of different treatments, one way to do it would be to use a traditional group design experiment.

However, you can also investigate problems of this sort with an alternating treatments design:

> **Alternating treatments design:**
> **A single case experimental design**
> **in which two or more interventions**
> **alternate systematically.**

As an example, suppose a therapist is interested in the effectiveness of two different treatments for obsessional thinking. The traditional way of determining which treatment is better is to randomly assign people troubled by obsessional thoughts to one of two treatment groups or to a no-treatment control group. Then you would look at the average improvement of subjects in the three groups and analyze the results with statistical tests to determine if the differences were mathematically reliable. You have to assume that there are no important differences among the groups before treatment. The smaller the groups are, the less likely that assumption is to be valid. So you need large groups. But a therapist may have only three or four clients troubled by obsessional thoughts.

The alternating treatments design will let you compare the effectiveness of different interventions with one client. Suppose you have a client who is troubled by obsessional thinking. You collect data on the frequency of obsessional thinking, perhaps by having the person keep a record of the number of times he is troubled by unwanted thoughts each day. When you have a stable baseline, you begin testing your interventions. You do this by alternating them. You could use one treatment on one day and a second treatment on the next day. In this case, data on obsessional thinking might look something like this:

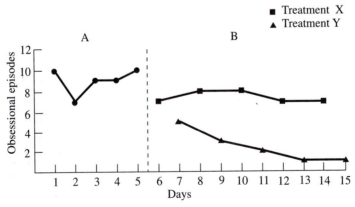

Figure 2-15. *Alternating treatments design. In this case, two interventions, X and Y, are used on different days. (hypothetical data)*

Another approach is to have more than one treatment session each day and use one treatment in the first session and another treatment in the second session. Then the data would look something like this:

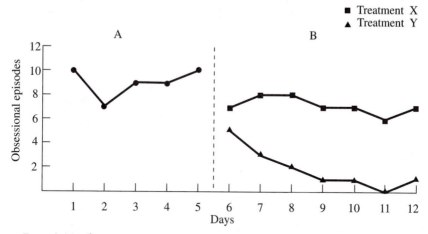

Figure 2-16. Alternating treatments design. In this case, two interventions, X and Y, are used at different times on the same days. (hypothetical data)

"Doesn't this method leave open the possibility that the results are due to *when* the treatment was given?"

How do you mean, Brian?

"Well, let's say you use one treatment on even-numbered days, and the other on odd-numbered days. Or maybe you use one treatment in the morning, and the other treatment in the afternoon. You get better results with one treatment than with the other. How do you know the difference is due to the treatment, and not to something associated with when the treatment was done?"

Like what?

"I don't know. Maybe the client is getting chemotherapy on even-numbered days and he feels too rotten to obsess about things. Or maybe he sees his mother in the afternoons, and those sessions stir up all sorts of things to obsess about, so he's more obsessional."

What do you think about Brian's comment, Carlotta? Has he got a point, or is he obsessing unnecessarily?

"Well, I do think he is a little obsessional, but what he says makes sense."

I agree. Now, what can you suggest to control this problem—so that Brian won't lose sleep obsessing about it?

"Why couldn't you vary the treatment times?"

How would you do that?

"Well, if you're doing morning and afternoon sessions, you could use one treatment in the morning for the first week, and then use it in the afternoon for the next week. The other treatment would be used in the afternoon during the first week, and then in the morning in the second week."

Good idea. You could even flip back and forth like that for several weeks if necessary. What if you're giving treatments on different days?

"Well, maybe during the first week you could provide one treatment on even-numbered days, and the other treatment on odd-numbered days. Then the next week you could switch treatment days."

Okay, I think that works. Of course, another thing you can do to rule out the possible influence of extraneous variables is to repeat the procedure with different clients. It's not likely that three people will be receiving chemotherapy on odd-numbered days, for example.

Before we move on, I want to be sure you understand that I'm *not* saying that group designs are terrible things that should never be used. They definitely have their place; in fact, there may be questions that can be answered only with a group design. Behaviorists are partial to single case designs because they are very powerful designs when it comes to identifying effective procedures for changing an individual's behavior.

Now, I hope you realize that this introduction to research methods in behavior analysis covers just the main points. There are other ways of measuring behavior change, other ways of recording changes in behavior, other ways of calculating inter-observer reliability, other ways of graphing data, other kinds of research designs. My goal in discussing some of the research methods of behavior analysis wasn't so much to prepare you to do behavioral research; it was to give you the background you will need to understand the research we will be considering in this course.

If you understand the material we've covered here today, you have completed the most difficult part of the course. Let's review a bit and see what you've learned.

Review

Our first topic today was behavioral assessment. How does behavioral assessment differ from psychological assessment? Jamal?

"Psychological assessment is based on the medical model that says that behavior problems are the product of some sort of psychological problem. Behavioral assessment says that the problem is the behavior itself."

Well said. Psychological assessment and behavioral assessment both attempt to find the cause of the troublesome behavior. The difference is in where they look. When people do psychological assessments, they are looking for the cause of behavior . . . where, Belinda?

"Inside the person's mind?"

Yes, somewhere inside the person. And when people do behavioral assessment, they are looking for the cause of behavior . . .

"In the person's environment."

Yes. The cause of the behavior is assumed to be in the person's learning history. There may be biological factors involved as well, but the behaviorist is interested in the role of the environment.

Now, behavioral assessment attempts to do three things. What are they, Carlotta?

"Define the target behavior; identify . . ."

Yes?

". . . identify the functional relations between the target behavior and its antecedents and consequences; and identify an intervention."

Excellent. What is a target behavior, Maya?

"That's the behavior that needs to be changed, like it might need to occur more often or less often."

Good. How do you define a target behavior?

"You talk to people about the behavior problem. You try to get them to describe the problem in terms of actual behavior. And you observe the person, so you can see what he does that is troublesome to him or others."

Okay. And what's a functional analysis, John?

"That's where you look for functional relations between the target behavior and other events."

What sort of other events?

"Things that happen before or after the behavior—antecedents and consequences—like things people say or do."

Right! Okay. What's our definition of a behavior problem? Jamal?

"Behavior that occurs too frequently or not frequently enough."

Yes. So frequency or rate is a basic datum in applied behavior analysis. That means that recording rate is very important. We identified two formal ways of recording rate data. One of those was . . . Midori?

"Continuous recording."

Which consists of . . . ?

"Which consists of tallying every single occurrence of the behavior during an observation period."

What's an observation period?

"That's the time that has been designated for recording data. It might be a whole day, or an hour, or 15 minutes."

Good. So that's continuous recording. What was the alternative to continuous recording that we discussed, Jamal?

"Interval recording?"

Yes. And how is that different from continuous recording?

"In interval recording, you don't tally every occurrence of the behavior. Instead, you record whether the behavior occurred at all during a short period. These observation periods are separated by much longer intervals."

And when would you use interval recording rather than continuous recording?

"When the behavior occurs so frequently that it's hard to count it accurately."

Yes. Are there any other times you would use interval recording?

"When it's hard to tell when instances of the behavior start and end, and when the behavior lasts a long time."

Good. How do you determine if your data are reliable? John?

"You use two recorders, and use a formula for computing inter- . . . inter-something."

Well, who's doing the recording?

"Oh, yeah. Inter-observer reliability."

Right. For continuous data, the formula for determining inter-observer reliability is . . . what, Carlotta?

"You divide the smaller number by the larger and multiply by 100."

Good. As you obtain rate data, it's customary to plot it on a graph. What are the two kinds of graphs we talked about? Maya?

"Simple frequency graphs and cumulative frequency graphs."

That's correct. And what's the difference?

"A simple frequency graph plots the number of times the behavior occurred in each observation period. A cumulative frequency graph plots the total number of times the behavior has occurred as of a particular observation period."

Well done, Maya. The last topic we took up today was the kinds of single case research designs. What does that term *single case research design* mean? How about it, Brian?

"That's a design in which the person whose behavior is being studied acts as his own control. In other words, you record the behavior under different conditions and compare them."

What are these different conditions?

"Well . . . one is a baseline period."

Which is . . . ?

"That's when you make no effort to change the behavior; you just record how often it occurs. Then there's an intervention period. That's when you do something to change the rate of the behavior."

What does that tell you?

"If you intervene and the rate changes, that suggests the change is the result of your intervention."

Can you illustrate that for me?

"Hmmm. Okay. Suppose you sneeze and sneeze over and over again, and . . ."

You want me to begin sneezing now?

"No, I'm saying, *suppose* you were having some sort of allergic reaction to something in the room. You'd want to remove whatever it is that's making you sneeze. You could get a baseline of your sneezing rate by counting how many times you sneeze in a 15-minute period. Then you could remove something in the room that might be making you sneeze, like flowers. That's your intervention. Then you count the number of times you sneeze in a 15- or 30-minute period. If the rate of sneezing is lower after the intervention than it was before it, that implies that the flowers made you sneeze."

You say, *implies*. That term doesn't inspire a lot of confidence.

"That's why you need an ABAB design."

Go on.

"Well, if all you do is collect baseline data and then collect data after intervening, you can't be absolutely certain the change you get is due to the intervention."

And with an ABAB design . . . ?

"With an ABAB design, you return to the baseline condition and record data for a while, and then you reintroduce the intervention condition. For example, you could bring the flowers back into the room for a half-hour, and then remove them again. If the sneezing increases when the flowers are back, and then falls off when the flowers are taken out again, that makes a strong case for concluding that removing the flowers solved your problem. It's like flipping a light switch on and off and then on and off."

A light switch. A very clever analogy; I wish I'd thought of that. Okay, Brian has given us a good review of the ABAB design. Who can tell me briefly about multiple baseline designs? Yes, Jamal?

"A multiple baseline design is an alternative to the ABAB reversal design. You collect more than one baseline and test the intervention after each baseline. You might collect baseline data in different situations, on different behaviors, or from different people. If you get similar results following interventions in the different baselines, that confirms that the intervention produced the changes."

All right. And what if you want to test the effects of more than one intervention?

"You use an alternating treatments design. That's where you get a baseline and then provide two or more interventions alternately. You'd alternate between the interventions and record behavior to see which intervention works better. Another thing—"

That was an excellent summary, Jamal, and I'd like to hear more, but I'm afraid we're out of time. Be sure to collect the handouts before you leave. See you next time.

◄ Exercises ►

Feed the Skeleton

I. Behavioral Assessment
   A. Behavioral assessment differs from psychological assessment in that

   _____ .

   B. One goal of behavioral assessment is to define the _____
      behavior.
   C. Another goal of behavioral assessment is to identify _____
      _____ relations between behavior and environmental events.
   D. A third goal of behavioral assessment is to identify an _____
      _____ that might change the problem behavior.

II. Recording Behavior Rates
   A. Obtaining accurate estimates of behavior rates requires direct observation
      of _____ .
   B. One method of estimating behavior rates is called _____
      recording.
   C. Another method of estimating behavior rates is called _____
      recording.

III. Measuring the Reliability of Rate Data
   A. Rate reliability measures are needed because human behavior tends to be
      highly _____ .
   B. The reliability of continuous data is estimated by _____ .
   C. The reliability of interval data is estimated by _____ .

    D. Rate reliability can be improved by

       1. _____ .

       2. _____ .

IV. Graphing Behavior Rates

    A. In a simple frequency graph, a data point shows _____ .

    B. In a cumulative frequency graph, a data point shows _____ .

V. Evaluating Interventions

    A. The problem with anecdotal evidence as a way of evaluating an interven-
       tion is _____ .

    B. A research design in which the same individual serves as her own "con-
       trol group" is called _____ .

    C. A research design that is analogous to turning a light switch on and off is
       the _____ design.

    D. In multiple baseline designs, the dependent variable may be

       _____ , _____ , or _____ .

    E. A design for testing the relative effectiveness of two or more interventions
       is called the _____ design.

Plotting Data

A teacher gave fourth-grade students smiley face stickers at the end of a 50-minute silent reading period for 10 days. At the end of each lesson, the teacher would ask the students to write down the number of pages they had read and would then give each child a smiley sticker. Later, the teacher would calculate the average number of pages read and record it on a graph. She was interested in seeing if the smiley faces increased the number of words read. Plot the data as a simple frequency graph and then as a cumulative frequency graph.

Date	Pages Read	Date	Pages Read
9/30	42	10/7	49
10/1	38	10/8	52
10/2	45	10/9	50
10/3	47	10/10	49
10/4	49	10/11	53

Harassing Explanations

A survey (Anonymous, June 2, 1993) found that sexual harassment is commonplace in our nation's schools. Four out of five teens said that they had experienced some form of sexual harassment (unwanted and unwelcome sexual behavior) while at school. About two-thirds of the girls and 42% of the boys reported being touched in a sexual way. The most frequently selected explanation for the behavior was, "It's just part of school life." From the standpoint of behavior analysis, what is wrong with this "explanation" of harassment?

Targeting Labels

Think of someone you know who is often described by each of the adjectives below. Then, in one sentence, translate that adjective into specific behaviors the person performs that earn him or her that adjective. Restrict yourself to very specific overt acts. For example, the adjective *stupid* might be translated as "learns slowly," but that phrase does not specify a specific behavior the person performs. A better translation might be, "repeatedly destroys data files he needs on his computer."

1. Stupid: _____ .

2. Cruel: _____ .

3. Macho: _____ .

4. Immature: _____ .

5. Lazy: _____ .

Practice Quiz

1. _____ assessment assumes that behavior problems arise from problems within the person.

2. Usually, the goal of an intervention is to increase or decrease the frequency of a(n) _____ behavior.

3. A(n) _____ analysis tests hypotheses about the functional relations among antecedents, behavior, and consequences.

4. When behavior occurs at a high rate, it is best to use _____ recording.

5. One way to study the effects of an intervention in different situations is to use a(n) _____ baseline research design.

6. In a cumulative frequency graph, a flat line indicates that the target behavior _____ .

7. One problem with averaging data from several people is _____
_____ .

8. A period in which a target behavior is observed, but no attempt is made to change it, is called a(n) _____ .

9. In a(n) _____ design, the intervention effort is discontinued for a time and then renewed.

10. IOR stands for _____ .

Mini-Essay: MEASURING BEHAVIOR CHANGE

Behavior problems can be defined in terms of their frequency or rate: Sometimes the problem is that a behavior occurs too frequently; sometimes the problem is that a behavior does not occur often enough. Rate or frequency is therefore a fundamental datum in applied behavior analysis.

Rate measures behavior as a ratio of the number of occurrences of a behavior to a unit of time—usually a minute, hour, or day. For example, a child who has 30 separate epileptic seizures during a 15-day period has seizures at the rate of 2 per day. Similarly, a student who offers comments 2 times during class discussions totaling 4 hours comments at the rate of .5 times per hour. And a psychiatric patient who shouts unprovoked obscenities 12 times in a 15-minute period curses at the rate of .8 times a minute. Rate is very important in applied behavior analysis because it provides a simple and precise way of measuring the severity of a behavior problem and the effects of an intervention. However, there are other dimensions of behavior that can be used to define problems and to measure efforts to solve them. They include topography, intensity, duration, and latency.

Most people associate the word *topography* with maps. A topographical map shows the physical features of the earth's crust. When behaviorists talk about the topography of behavior, they're talking about the physical features of a person's actions. Topography answers the question, What form does the behavior take? If the behavior in question is a person's movement around a room, we might describe it by referring to how the person moves and where. Does he walk, run, crawl, skip, or somersault? Does he walk around in circles? Does he pace back and forth? These questions all get at topography.

If the behavior under study is speech, topography may refer to what the person says and how she says it. Is she talking about school? About her parents? About the philosophy of Schopenhauer? Does she reminisce about real experiences or speak about events that never occurred? Does what she says make sense, or is it absolute gibberish? Is it grammatical? Does she speak with a lisp? Does she roll her *r*'s?

One way of measuring the effects of experience on behavior, then, is to measure changes in topography. If a child is capable of walking but gets around on all fours instead, then we might be interested in providing experiences that would change the topography of his behavior from crawling to walking. If a student spells Mississippi "M-i-s-i-s-i-p-i," his teacher might provide experiences that change the topography of his behavior to M-i-s-s-i-s-s-i-p-p-i. If a worker in a factory does not operate a piece of machinery in a safe manner, the worker's supervisor might provide experiences that will get him to operate the machine safely. And if a psychiatric patient talks about having been abducted by people from another planet, then her therapist might provide experiences that produce changes in her topics of conversation.

Another way to measure changes in behavior is to focus on the *intensity* of the behavior. Intensity refers to the energy expended by a person in producing a behavior. Tapping on a window pane with your fingers is different from pounding on a window pane with your fists. Similarly, a boy who gives another child a gentle shove behaves differently from one who knocks another child to the ground.

Topography and intensity are closely related. Tapping on a window pane with your fingers involves different physical features than pounding on the pane with your fists. A change in the intensity of behavior probably does involve a change in topography. But topography and intensity are both useful measures of behavior. In fact, there are times when the topography of the behavior is not particularly important, while the intensity is. The child who is having a tantrum provides an example. The child might be making a lot of noise, but it might not make much difference to a parent or a teacher whether the child is screaming, crying, or pounding on a table. The noise level—a measure of the intensity of the behavior—is more important than the topography of the behavior. Or a teacher might have a student who speaks much too softly. Getting him to speak more loudly will involve subtle changes in topography, but it is the change in volume—the intensity of the behavior—that is critical.

A third way of measuring behavior change is in terms of its *duration*: the time during which the behavior persists. Behavior takes time. A child having a tantrum may scream and shout and stamp his feet for 30 seconds, 1 minute, 5 minutes, or 2 hours. How long the tantrum persists is its duration. Other examples are how long a person reads a book, watches TV, or does calisthenics. Duration is how long behavior endures once it starts.

Another way of measuring changes in behavior is to measure the lapse of time before a behavior begins following some signal. That is called *latency*. Suppose that a student is asked the question, "How much is 8 times 7?" After a pause of 20 seconds, he finally says, "56." Then, after additional practice, the student is again asked, "How much is 8 times 7?" This time he gives the correct answer after a pause of only 1 second. The better a student has learned a lesson, the shorter the delay in answering questions about the subject covered.

These measures of behavior are not the only ones available to us, but they are among the most important. Each has its strengths and weaknesses. Topography is commonly used to measure behavior when new skills are being learned or old skills are being improved. A student learning to read learns to make certain sounds when presented with certain letters and letter combinations. A dancer learns to step this way and that. A lathe operator learns to hold the chisel against the wood at just the right angle to produce a given effect. Learning usually, perhaps always, involves changes in topography.

Intuitively, topography might seem to be the only measure of behavior we might need, but describing the topography of a particular act is difficult and time-consuming, and changes in topography are often hard to quantify. We can see that the accomplished gymnast and the novice perform differently on the parallel bars, but how is that difference in topography to be expressed? Gymnastic judges assign a number to the overall performances, but that number doesn't describe the topography of the performance. And thoughts and feelings are difficult, if not impossible, to describe topographically. What, for example, is the shape of anger?

Intensity is often much easier to quantify. We can record, for example, the loudness of a child's screams during a tantrum, and we can note with precision increases and decreases in decibel level. But intensity is not as simple a measure as it first appears. A child having a tantrum does not scream constantly at 90 decibels. The decibel level may vary from a barely audible sniffling to a 110-decibel blast. What level do we use to describe the tantrum? The highest level? The lowest? Should we compute an average?

Intensity may be even more problematic. How are we, for instance, to measure the force exerted by a child when he pinches other children? And how are we to gauge changes in the intensity of these actions? We may infer, from the reactions of the child's victims, that the offending child is using more or less force than in the past, but this is mere guesswork. Guesswork is not very useful when we're trying to solve behavior problems.

Duration is a very useful measure of behavior in certain situations. How long a tantrum lasts may be more important than how loudly the child screams and stamps his feet. And duration is often easy to measure: We simply note the time when the behavior starts and note it again when the behavior stops. Unfortunately, these two points are not always as easy to pinpoint as it may seem. A child screams and throws things for 20 minutes in classic tantrum fashion. One of the toys she throws knocks over a large stuffed animal, and she straightens the animal, picks up the missile, and throws it again at the stuffed animal. Is she still having a tantrum, or has she begun to play a game? If she sits down and begins to wail again, is she having a new tantrum, or is this a continuation of the first tantrum?

Latency is useful when reaction time is important. A student is not accomplished at addition if he takes 5 seconds to answer the question, "How much are 5 and 4?" Similarly, the physician on duty in an emergency room should be able to deal properly with injured patients without delay. On the other hand, there are many instances in which latency is of no particular importance. Whether a disappointed child begins tantrumming 3 seconds after a refused request or 30 seconds later probably does not matter much to those who must endure his screams. And latency in the reaction time of a physician is less important during routine physical exams than it is in treating accident victims in an emergency room.

Sometimes different measures of behavior are used in combination. Rate in particular is often combined with other measures. For instance, instead of counting the number of tantrums a child has in a day, we might count the number of times the child's vocalizations reach 90 decibels. We are then combining rate and intensity. We can combine rate with duration by, for example, counting the number of times a child screams for 10 minutes or longer without interruption. Rate may be combined with topography as when we measure body rocking by counting the number of times a person's upper body moves through an arc of more than 15 degrees.

Combining rate with accuracy (topography that meets certain criteria) yields *fluency.* Fluency is an increasingly popular measure of behavior change, especially among behaviorists interested in education and job training. Fluency is often defined as the number of correct performances per minute. For instance, a student who solves 12 division problems in a minute, 10 of them correctly, has a fluency level of 10 per minute. He is twice as fluent at division as a student who solves 5 problems correctly per minute. Fluency level is thought to be related to, among other things, how well skills are retained over time.

Although each of the various measures of behavior has its uses, the king of all measures is *rate.* Rate is not the only way of measuring behavior change, and it is not the ideal measure in all situations. But for scientific rigor, for ease of measurement, and for all-around practical value, rate takes first prize.

Reprint: THE QUEEN'S SCEPTER
by Eric Haughton & Teodoro Ayllon

> *The excerpt below describes research that demonstrated that bizarre behavior could be produced merely by altering the antecedents and consequences of behavior. The study raises serious doubts about the validity of psychodynamic explanations of unusual behavior:*

. . . Repetitive responses that resist modification and tend to be "purposeless" often come to the attention of the psychiatric or psychological clinician. A variety of interpretations are often made regarding the etiology and current factors maintaining the responses at a high level. . . .

Subject. P [patient] S was a fifty-four-year-old schizophrenic patient who had been hospitalized for twenty-three years. According to ward reports the patient stayed in bed or lay on a couch most of the time. She was an "idle" patient who simply refused to do anything on the ward except smoke. These reports also indicated that she had consistently refused to work and participate in recreational or occupational activity for the preceding thirteen years.

Procedure. A daytime baseline of the behavior exhibited by P S was obtained by observing her every thirty minutes. During this period she was given only one cigarette at each meal to induce a level of deprivation with respect to cigarettes. The baseline data indicated that the patient spent sixty percent of her waking time lying in bed. She spent approximately twenty percent of her time sitting and walking. The rest of the time was accounted for in behaviors associated with meals, grooming, and elimination.

To develop a novel class of behavior in the repertoire of the patient, an arbitrary response was selected and cigarettes were used as reinforcement. The objective response defined for the staff was "holding the broom while in an upright position." . . .

. . . a staff person gave the patient a broom and while she held it, another staff member approached the patient and gave her a cigarette. . . . In a matter of a few days, the patient developed a stereotyped behavior of pacing while holding the broom.

Discussion. Several behaviors associated with the patient carrying a broom were observed in this experiment. For example, when other patients tried to use the broom and attempted to take it away from the patient, she resisted firmly and sometimes rather aggressively. The behavior of carrying the broom quickly became so stereotyped that there was no difficulty in recording the behavior. Her response seemed to bear many of the characteristics associated with behavior clinically described as "compulsive" behavior. In this respect it seemed useful to have other people evaluate the patient's behavior. Two psychiatrists were asked to observe and evaluate the patient from behind a one-way mirror. These two evaluations which were independently arrived at, help to put the experimentally established behavior into better clinical perspective.

Dr. A's evaluation of the patient's behavior was:

The broom represents to this patient some essential perceptual element in her field of consciousness. How it should have become so is uncertain; on Freudian grounds it could be interpreted symbolically, on behavioral grounds it could perhaps be interpreted as a habit which has become essential to her peace of mind. Whatever may be the case, it is certainly a stereotyped form of behavior such as is commonly seen in rather regressed schizophrenics and is rather analogous to the way small children or infants refuse to be parted from some favorite toy, piece of rag, etc.

Dr. B's evaluation of the patient's behavior follows:

Her constant and compulsive pacing holding a broom in the manner she does could be seen as a ritualistic procedure, a magical action. When regression conquers the associative process, primitive and archaic forms of thinking control the behavior. Symbolism is a predominant mode of expression of deep-seated unfulfilled desires and instinctual impulses. By magic, she controls others, cosmic powers are at her disposal and inanimate objects become living creatures.

Her broom could be then:

1. a child that gives her love and she gives him in return her devotion;

2. a phallic symbol;

3. the sceptre of an omnipotent queen.

Her rhythmic and prearranged pacing in a certain space are not similar to the compulsions of a neurotic, but because this is a far more irrational, far more controlled behavior from a primitive thinking, this is a magical procedure in which the patient carries out her wishes, expressed in a way that is far beyond our solid, rational and conventional way of thinking and acting.

The apparent uselessness and irrelevance of the patient's behavior is indeed the hallmark of behavior often clinically described as "compulsive" or "psychotic." Yet, examination of some of the environmental conditions under which the response was developed, may make it easier to understand how similar classes of behavior are developed and maintained by environmental contingencies.

"Production and Elimination of Symptomatic Behavior" by Eric Haughton and Teodoro Ayllon, in *Case Studies in Behavior Modification* by Leonard P. Ullmann and Leonard Krasner, copyright 1965 by Holt, Rinehart and Winston and renewed 1993 by Leonard Krasner, reprinted by permission of the publisher.

‹ Recommended Reading ›

1. Bachrach, A. (1962). *Psychological research: An introduction*. New York: Random House.
   A highly readable little book; an excellent place to begin study of behavior science methods.

2. Eysenck, H. J. (1965). "Little Hans or Little Albert." In *Fact and fiction in psychology*. Baltimore: Penguin.
   This chapter compares clinical case studies and experimental method.

3. Johnston, J. M., & Pennypacker, H. S. (1981). Strategies and tactics of human behavioral research. Hillsdale, NJ: Erlbaum.
   A popular text in the methods of behavior analysis.

4. Sidman, M. (1960). *Tactics of scientific research*. New York: Basic Books.
   A classic, but not for the faint-of-heart beginner.

5. Skinner, B. F. (1956). A case history in scientific method. *American Psychologist, 11*, 221–233. Reprinted in B. F. Skinner (1961), *Cumulative record* (pp. 76–100). (Enlarged ed.) New York: Appleton-Century-Crofts.
   Another classic; Skinner's methods are not what you might expect.

‹ Endnotes ›

1. Skinner (1938) once defined *rate* as the length of the intervals between instances of behavior. However, in practice, he used the number of instances of

behavior per minute as his measure of rate. The two measures are mathematically equivalent but not synonymous: A pigeon that pecks a disk at the *rate* of 10 times a minute has an average *interval* between pecks of 6 seconds.

    Another dimension of behavior, speed, is closely related to rate. *Speed* is defined as the time it takes to perform the behavior. For example, a student first struggling to recite the alphabet may take a minute to get through it, but after considerable practice he may go from A to Z in under 10 seconds. That's a change in speed, not rate, yet the two measures are obviously related: The faster a student can recite the alphabet, the more frequently he can recite it in a given period of time.

2. Social psychologists and sociologists are well acquainted with this bias. They refer to the tendency to provide the "socially desirable response" to questions.

3. Although it's customary to report interval data as percentages, it's important to remember that we are still dealing with rate data: If observations are made in 10-second intervals and the behavior occurs on half of those intervals, it follows that the behavior occurred at a rate of 3 or more times a minute.

4. In laboratory research, it is often possible to record behavior by machine; then reliability isn't a problem. In *The Behavior of Organisms,* Skinner says he was able to record something like 2 *million* separate acts in a 6-year period. But Skinner was working with rats and pigeons; recording human behavior mechanically is often much more difficult, even in the laboratory. Outside of the laboratory, it is often a practical impossibility.

5. The formula for determining the reliability of continuous data may be expressed as IOR = (S/L) 100, where inter-observer reliability (IOR) is equal to the smaller number of observations (S), divided by the larger number of observations (L), multiplied by 100.

    An IOR of 100 does not mean perfect agreement among the observers on all of the observations; it merely means that the frequency counts of the observers are the same. For example, two observers might count the number of times a student calls out in class. Both observers may record seven instances of calling out during one 50-minute class period. Close examination of the data might reveal, however, that one observer counted two instances of calling out in the first 5 minutes of observation and none in the last 5 minutes, whereas the other observer counted no instances during the first 5 minutes and two in the last 5 minutes. Clearly, the two observers are not in perfect agreement, yet their IOR is 100. Nevertheless, the IOR is useful because it is the *rate* at which the behavior occurs that is usually of most interest.

6. The formula for determining the reliability of interval data may be expressed as IOR = (A/T) 100, where IOR equals the number of intervals in which the observers agree (A), divided by the total number of observation intervals (T), multiplied by 100.

7. Variability is a fact of life in all research. Indeed, the aim of experimental research may be said to be to identify the factors responsible for variability in the phenomenon under study. You're never going to see a person behaving in precisely the same way in two different situations or, for that matter, in the same situation. Richard Herrnstein (1966) pointed out that people don't even sign their name exactly the same way twice. One of the great advantages of single case designs is that, by comparing the same individual's behavior under experimental and control conditions, you eliminate the variability contributed by comparing different individuals with one another. Another important advantage of single case designs is that the variability in behavior isn't hidden by group averages.

8. It is possible, however, for a cumulative record to go down under special circumstances: If students earn points for doing work and *lose* points for misbehavior, their point totals may both rise and fall.

9. Anecdotes are not of much scientific value, but they can be very useful pedagogically, and I plan to use them whenever I can to make a point.

10. The more common terms for this kind of research design are *single subject* or *within subject* experimental design. However, this use of the word *subject* is sometimes taken to imply that people are no different from rats, which have traditionally been referred to as subjects. The term *single case design* avoids that impression but runs the risk of being confused with the case study method. It is important to remember that single case experimental design is by no means a synonym for case study, which is not an experimental design at all.

11. Students sometimes confuse the terms *independent variable* and *dependent variable*. It may help to consider that in experimental research, one *changes* an *independent* variable and looks for *changes in* a dependent variable. Goldiamond (1974) suggests that the terms *independent variable* and *dependent variable* are roughly equivalent to the terms *cause* and *effect,* respectively. Most behaviorists are reluctant to speak of causes (they prefer to speak of functional relations among events), but his idea may help you remember which is which.

Reinforcement

Law of Effect
  Reinforcement Defined
  Reinforcer Defined

Kinds of Reinforcers
  Positive and Negative
  Primary and Secondary
  Contrived and Natural

Illustrative Studies
  Ann Doesn't Socialize
  Mary Refuses to Eat

Rules for Using Reinforcement
  Define the Target Behavior
  Select Appropriate Reinforcers
  Make the Reinforcer Immediate and Certain
  Monitor Results

Problems with Reinforcement
  Inappropriate Use
  Moral Objections
  Negative Side Effects

Review

Exercises

Mini-Essay: Finding Reinforcers

Reprint: *The Rewards of Coaching,* by Hilary Buzas
      & Teodoro Ayllon

Recommended Reading

Endnotes

Let's BEGIN WITH A BIT OF REVIEW. Jamal, what is the subject matter of this course?

"Uhm, applied behavior analysis?"

Okay. And what is applied behavior analysis?

"The attempt to solve behavior problems by . . ."

Yes?

". . . by providing antecedents and consequences that change behavior."

Good. Now, we looked at behavior problems earlier and we said that all, or at least most of them, take one of two forms. And they are . . . Midori?

"One type is when the behavior doesn't occur often enough, and the other is when it occurs too often."

Sehr gut. Today we're going to focus on the first kind of problem: that in which the behavior does not occur often enough. Can someone suggest an example of such a problem? Yes, John?

"Shyness. The shy person is someone who doesn't interact with others very often."

Yes, that's one we discussed before. How about a fresh example? Maya?

"A student might not study enough."

Right. Alfred, do you have an example?

"Yeah. My mother says I don't call home often enough. She says I just call home when I need money."

Okay, these are typical examples of problems involving behavior that occurs but does not occur as often as it should. Sometimes the problem is identified by the person whose behavior is involved. Shy people, for example, often wish that they were more outgoing. Sometimes the problem is identified by someone else. A teacher may recognize that a student needs to study more, while the student may not. When the problem is that a behavior does not occur often enough, the question arises, How can we increase the frequency of this behavior? The answer relies heavily on a basic principle of behavior called the law of effect.

Law of Effect

The law of effect has to do with the idea that the strength of behavior depends on the effects it has on the environment. It is stated formally like this:

> **Law of effect:**
> **In any given situation, the probability of a behavior occurring is a function of the consequences that behavior has had in that situation in the past.**

Notice that this law refers to the three terms of interest to the behaviorist: antecedents, behavior, and consequences. In fact, I can amend this statement to emphasize this fact: In any given situation, A, the probability of a behavior, B, occurring is a function of the consequences, C, the behavior has had in that situation in the past.

The law of effect was first formulated (in somewhat different form) by E. L. Thorndike, one of the first behaviorists, around the turn of the century.[1] Some of you have read about his experiments with cats in puzzle boxes. You may not know that Thorndike was primarily interested in human learning; in fact, he practically invented the field of educational psychology. Anyway, Thorndike's law of effect recognized that whether a behavior is repeated depends on the *effects* the behavior has had in the past. Thorndike's law can be expressed more simply this way:

> **Law of effect:**
> **Behavior is a function of its consequences.**

In considering this abbreviated version of the law, keep in mind that the roles of antecedents and consequences over time are implied. The law of effect recognizes that behavior becomes more or less likely depending on the consequences the behavior has had.

Now, the law of effect may seem rather obvious. You might find yourself saying, "Well, doesn't everybody know that?" The same thing might be said of Newton's first law of motion. Everybody knows that an object at rest tends to remain at rest, and an object in motion tends to remain in motion, until acted on by an outside force.

But *does* everyone know this? If you are a *Star Trek* fan, you may have noticed that there are lots of times when the *Star Trek* writers don't seem to know Newton's first law. I don't know how many times I've seen the Starship *Enterprise* come to a rapid stop after the ship has run out of fuel or had a malfunction. But what stops it? There is no gravity in outer space; there is no atmosphere, so there is no friction. So why does the ship stop? In fact, a ship traveling at warp whatever speed would continue traveling at that speed until it ran into something, such as a planet or a planet's atmosphere.[2] But how many viewers notice this violation of Newton's first law? If "everybody knows" Newton's first law—if it's really just common sense—then everyone should notice its violation in the *Star Trek* stories. Scientific principles often seem like formalized common sense, but they often help us see things that would otherwise go unrecognized.[3] In the same way, Thorndike's law of effect helps us recognize the importance of consequences in changing behavior.

In Thorndike's day, nobody paid much attention to the effects that consequences had on behavior. Even today, many people give little thought to the role of consequences when they consider behavior problems: Is your 6-year-old still wetting the bed? He must be immature. Did an unmarried 13-year-old get pregnant? Perhaps she lacks moral restraint. Are you having trouble staying on a reasonable diet? You lack willpower. Is a student unable to solve an arithmetic problem? Perhaps he lacks mathematical aptitude. Has an employee neglected to do his work? He must lack ambition. Has a psychiatric patient assaulted an aide? Probably his id forces have overwhelmed his superego. Has another patient slashed her wrists? Evidently she has a death wish.

Such commonly heard explanations look for the causes of behavior inside the person. But such explanations are not very helpful, since they seldom suggest an effective course of action. Can you give a child a dose of maturity or an adolescent some moral restraint? Is there a store where you can buy an ounce of willpower, a quart of mathematical aptitude, or a foot of ambition? The law of effect draws our attention to the important role that environmental *consequences* play in behavior. It also provides the basis for what is probably the most important tool we have for changing behavior, reinforcement.

Reinforcement Defined

Consequences can have either of two kinds of effects: They can strengthen behavior (make it more likely to occur), or they can weaken it (make it less likely to occur). For now, we are concerned with consequences that strengthen behavior. Providing such consequences is called reinforcement:

> ### Reinforcement:
> #### The procedure of providing consequences
> #### for a behavior that increase or maintain
> #### the frequency of that behavior.[4]

Please note that reinforcement strengthens *behavior,* not *people*. Everyone slips up now and then and speaks of reinforcing a person, as in, "John was studying very hard so I reinforced him." You don't increase the strength of people with reinforcement; you increase the strength of their *behavior*. Please try to remember that.

The definition I've given you implies that reinforcement is something people do—it's a procedure. Actually, reinforcement is also a natural phenomenon that is a normal and inevitable part of human experience. When you hit a nail with a hammer and the nail drives home, that consequence probably reinforces your use of the hammer. When you ask someone a question and receive a satisfactory answer, that consequence very likely reinforces the act of asking questions. When you hail a cab and the cabby pulls over to the curb and stops, that consequence probably reinforces waving at cabs.

Reinforcer Defined

Reinforcement is a natural phenomenon, but it is also a tool we can use in solving behavior problems, and it is mainly in that sense that we will be using the term. If a behavior does not occur often enough, we can increase its frequency by providing reinforcing consequences. Such consequences are called reinforcers:

> **Reinforcer:**
> **An event that, when made contingent**
> **on a behavior, increases or maintains**
> **the frequency of that behavior.[5]**

The word *contingent* means "dependent on." So, if the occurrence of an event depends on the performance of a behavior, and if it then results in that behavior occurring more often, the event is a reinforcer. Carlotta, do you have a question?

"Yes. Isn't *reinforcer* just another name for *reward*?"

Not quite, but I'm glad you brought that up. Some people think that people with Ph.D.'s go around thinking up new terms for everyday words just so what they say will sound more sophisticated. There may be some truth to that, but the word *reinforcer* is not just a synonym for reward. Here's the essential difference: Rewards are defined by consensus; reinforcers are defined by results. Can anyone tell me what that means? Jamal?

"I suppose you mean that something is a reward if people generally agree that it's a reward, but something is a reinforcer only if, uh, . . ."

Keep going, you're doing fine.

". . . only if it strengthens or maintains behavior. You have to look at what happens, so reinforcers are defined by their results."

Very good. That's exactly right. Reinforcers are defined by their effects on behavior. If an event strengthens the behavior it follows, it is a reinforcer. It doesn't matter whether the event was intended to strengthen the behavior. A reward, on the other hand, is something that is given in recognition for some act; it may strengthen the act or it may not.

Now, is *mm-hmm* a reward? If I said "mm-hmm" periodically, would people say that I was rewarding you? Midori?

"I don't think so."

Nor do I. Most people probably would not consider *mm-hmm* a reward. Now, could *mm-hmm* be a reinforcer?

Suppose I conducted an experiment in which I asked people to say words— any words at all. They're not to speak in sentences or count; they're just to say individual words until I tell them to stop. And suppose that whenever a person comes out with a plural noun such as horses, bananas, or books, I say "mm-hmm." Would that increase the frequency of plural nouns? Jamal, what do you think?

> "I guess if you tell a person that *mm-hmm* means he's done something right, then he might figure out that you want him to say plural nouns."

What if I say nothing to him about *mm-hmm*. What if, as I'm listening to him, I just casually say *mm-hmm* whenever I hear a plural noun, but I don't tell him what I'm doing. Would it have any effect?

> "It doesn't seem likely, but I have a feeling you're going to say it would."

You're right. A fellow named Joel Greenspoon performed the experiment I've just described, and people who heard *mm-hmm* whenever they used plural nouns produced more plural nouns than did people who heard nothing.[6] So in this instance, *mm-hmm* was a reinforcer, even though it is not a reward.

So, reinforcers are not always rewards. It is also the case that rewards are not always reinforcing. You might give someone money each time she said a plural noun, for example, yet plural nouns might not increase. Money is widely recognized as a reward, but if it doesn't strengthen the behavior it follows, then it's *not* a reinforcer.

Now, how about this example: You enter a dark room, and as you feel your way around the room, you happen to hit a small panel on the wall and suddenly the lights go on. The consequence of touching the wall panel is that the room changes from dark to brightly lit. Now, has touching the panel been reinforced by that consequence? What do you think, Midori?

> "Sure. It's no fun stumbling about in the dark. The light would be a reinforcer."

Brian, do you have a different opinion?

> "Well, it seems like it would probably be a reinforcer, but according to the definition, you can't tell."

Why not?

> "Well, a reinforcer would strengthen or maintain the tendency to touch the wall panel in the dark, but we don't know yet whether the light will have that effect."

Midori, would you care to reply?

> "I guess, strictly speaking, he's right. But it's just common sense that the light would be a reinforcer. I mean, some things we know are reinforcing from our

personal experience with them. When it's dark, and you do something that makes a light come on, that's going to be reinforcing."

Rebuttal, Brian?

"I still think you have to wait and see what the effects are. It might not be reinforcing."

Let me give you a bit more information and see if that helps. The room is in the Fun House at an amusement park. Now, in a fun house, all sorts of spooky and scary things happen to you in the dark. What do you think now about the light going on, Midori?

"Well, in that case I don't think it would be reinforcing. If the lights came on, it would spoil everybody's fun."

Ah. So now you say it would *not* be reinforcing. Well, let me give you some additional information: Your companion in the Fun House was startled by a sudden blast of air. She inhaled a great wad of bubble gum. You can hear her gasping for breath, but you can't see her. That's when you happen to touch the wall panel and the light comes on. Is the light a reinforcer, Midori?

"I have a feeling that if I say yes, you're going to tell us something else about the situation that will make me think the light *wouldn't* be a reinforcer. So I'm going to say you can't tell until you see how it affects her behavior."

Good for you. The point I'm trying to make is that a reinforcer is defined by its effects on behavior. If an event strengthens or maintains the behavior it follows, it's a reinforcer; if it doesn't, it isn't a reinforcer. There is no other defining characteristic of a reinforcer.

This is a really important point; one students often miss. People often get the impression that a behaviorist is someone who carries a bag of reinforcers about and whenever behavior needs strengthening, he reaches into the bag and hands out reinforcers. The essence of behavior analysis is not handing out reinforcers but analyzing the effects of antecedents and consequences on behavior. That includes identifying consequences that are reinforcing. And you do that by noting what effect consequences have on behavior. Now let's talk a bit about the kinds of reinforcers.

Kinds of Reinforcers

Positive and Negative

Literally thousands of different events can be reinforcing, but most of these events fit reasonably well into a few categories. One pair of categories distinguishes between positive reinforcers and negative reinforcers:

Positive reinforcer:
A reinforcing event in which something
is added following a behavior.

Negative reinforcer:
A reinforcing event in which something
is removed following a behavior.

When the words *positive* and *negative* are applied to reinforcers, they denote whether something is added or removed, so think of the words as arithmetic signs: *Positive* means add; *negative* means subtract.[7]

Who can give me an example of something that is likely to be a positive reinforcer? All right, John?

"Receiving candy or some other kind of food—if a person is hungry."

Okay, good. How about another, Midori?

"Well, *mm-hmm* was a positive reinforcer in the study by Greenfork, wasn't it?"

Yes, it was, but the researcher's name is Green*spoon*. You had the wrong piece of flatware. How about an example we haven't used in class. Carlotta?

"Well, what if the phone rings and you pick up the receiver and the person on the line is a good friend you haven't talked to in a long time?"

Yes, that's likely to be a positive reinforcer. Or if you pick up the phone and someone says, "Congratulations! You've just won a million dollars." Or even if you just pick up the receiver and someone says, "Hello," that probably would reinforce the behavior of picking up a ringing phone. Now, how about an example of a negative reinforcer? Alfred?

"Well, I guess if you were on a date and you said something crass and your date smacked you, that would be a negative reinforcer."

Look at the board, Alfred. What does it say a negative reinforcer is?

"It's something that strengthens behavior when it is removed."

Right. In your example, is something removed or presented?

"Presented, because you get hit. So something is, like, added. And it wouldn't strengthen the behavior—saying crass things—it would probably weaken it."

Right. Lots of people make the same mistake Alfred made. They confuse negative reinforcement with punishment—a procedure that weakens behavior.[8] Just remember that if we're talking about reinforcement, we're talking about consequences that strengthen behavior.

Now, Alfred, how about an example in which behavior is strengthened when something is removed?

"Uhm, well, if you have a poison ivy infection, and you spray on some medicine and the itchiness starts to go away, that might reinforce using that medicine."

Yes, it might negatively reinforce taking that particular medicine, and it might also reinforce the act of taking medicines when ill. How about another example, Alfred, just to be sure you have the concept.

"Well, suppose you're confronted with a vampire, and you take a bite of garlic and then breathe in the vampire's face. He'll go away, right? Because vampires hate garlic. And the next time you're confronted with a vampire, you'll eat garlic and breathe on him. So a fleeing vampire is a negative reinforcer because anything that makes him go away is reinforced."

Now there's an example I can really sink my teeth into. And it is similar to examples from everyday life. For instance, probably every woman here has learned that there are certain things she can do to discourage the unwanted attention of a man. She might make sarcastic remarks, or give him a dirty look, or look away when he talks to her. If the man leaves, her behavior has been negatively reinforced. How about another example of negative reinforcement? Maya?

"Would nagging be an example?"

Tell me what you mean.

"Well, when I lived at home my mother was always nagging me about my room. I'd pick up the room to escape the constant nagging. If she hadn't nagged, I'd probably never have cleaned my room."

Good example. People do a lot of nagging. Parents nag their kids; teachers nag their students; students nag their roommates; employers nag their employees; husbands nag their wives; and wives nag their husbands. It's very common. We keep bugging the person until the person escapes by doing what we want. It's unfortunate, because the same thing can usually be accomplished with positive reinforcers.

Okay. One way of classifying reinforcers is as positive or negative. All reinforcers fall into one of these two types, but they can "move about," as it were. Something that is a positive reinforcer for one person or in one situation may be a negative reinforcer for another person or in another situation.

Negative reinforcement requires the use of aversives—events the person will avoid or escape, given the opportunity. Because of this, negative reinforcement is often said to involve *escape-avoidance learning*. The behavior involved results in the person escaping from or avoiding exposure to the negative reinforcer.

Let's consider a garden variety case of negative reinforcement and you'll see why it's called escape-avoidance learning. Suppose you have a boyfriend or a girlfriend. (It could happen!) Your significant other is perfect in every way *except* when he or she drinks. Since men are more likely to drink to stupidity, let's assume you're a woman and your boyfriend has the drinking problem. At first when he drinks, he just gets a little silly. As he continues to drink, he gets rude, and then he gets downright obnoxious. The first time this happens you stay with him until the obnoxious stage, when he shouts at you and calls you various names; then you leave. What's happening here? Midori?

"Escape. My boyfriend creates an unpleasant situation and I leave it."

Right. Your boyfriend provides aversives in the form of silliness, shouting, and so on. You terminate the aversives by leaving the area where they are present. Now, the next day, Bozo Boyfriend apologizes profusely. (They almost always apologize profusely.) The two of you patch it up, but it turns out that every time your Mr. Right drinks, he becomes Mr. Wrong. During the course of your relationship, something interesting happens: Each time your boyfriend drinks, you leave earlier. The second time he drinks, you leave when he begins to get obnoxious. The next two or three times it happens, you leave at the rude stage. Then you start leaving when he gets to the silly stage, and next you disappear as soon as he begins drinking. Finally you break off the relationship. What has happened here? There has been a progression from escape to what? Maya?

"From escape to avoidance."

Exactly. At first you escape the aversives by leaving, and finally you avoid them altogether by not going out with the jerk. Escape-avoidance.

Now, the examples we've discussed seem clear enough, but there are many instances in which the distinction between positive and negative reinforcers is questionable. For example, suppose you are in an elevator and somebody is smoking a big, fat cigar. The elevator fills up with smoke, and you start coughing. You get off at the next floor, and as you do you gasp for air. No doubt the change in your environment is reinforcing, but is the reinforcer escape from smoke or the addition of fresh air? Has leaving the elevator been reinforced negatively or positively? It seems to me that the answer is completely arbitrary.

It is clear that certain kinds of changes in the environment are reinforcing, but it is not always clear whether these changes should be categorized as positive or negative reinforcers. Because of this, the distinction between positive and negative reinforcers is of dubious value.[9] Nevertheless, the distinction is part of the language of behavior analysis, so you need to be familiar with it.

Primary and Secondary

There are other ways of classifying reinforcers that we need to discuss. All reinforcers can be classified as primary or secondary:

> **Primary reinforcers:**
> **Reinforcers that are <u>not</u> dependent**
> **on their association with other reinforcers.**

Secondary reinforcers:
Reinforcers that <u>are</u> dependent
on their association with other reinforcers.

Primary reinforcers are reinforcing as a result of our evolution as a species. They include food, water, oxygen, sexual stimulation, warmth (when body temperature is low), and coolness (when body temperature is high).

As these examples suggest, primary reinforcers often have to do with biological processes. But there are other examples in which that is less clear. For instance, if you are restrained or immobilized in some way, the opportunity to move about can be reinforcing. In fact, the opportunity to engage in physical exercise is often reinforcing, especially for young, healthy people. The opportunity to modify the environment also seems to be a primary reinforcer. If you dangle an object above a baby's bed, just within his reach, he will hit the object with his hand. And if there is no object within reach, he will play with his own feet. It is not clear whether all of these reinforcers have to do with biological processes, yet they seem to be primary reinforcers.

Secondary reinforcers depend on learning—they acquire their reinforcing powers through their association with other reinforcers. So, for example, if a parent smiles while providing food to a baby and the food is reinforcing, then smiles will become reinforcing. If the parent then says, "Good" and smiles, then the word *good* will become reinforcing. Secondary reinforcers get their name from the fact that they are ultimately derived from, and are therefore secondary to, primary reinforcers. This business of pairing neutral events with reinforcers may sound familiar to you. What does it remind you of, Brian?

"Pavlovian conditioning?"

Right. The process of pairing events with reinforcers resembles Pavlov's experiments in conditioning, as for example when Pavlov paired a sound with food. Some reinforcers that might seem to be innately reinforcing actually become reinforcers only because of their association with reinforcers. For instance, praise probably becomes a reinforcer by being paired with food, pats on the back, and other reinforcers. Because the process by which neutral events become reinforcing is Pavlov's conditioning procedure, secondary reinforcers are also called *conditioned reinforcers*.

Common secondary reinforcers include praise, positive feedback, money, awards, smiles, and hundreds of other things. Make a list of the things you like to do—read, watch TV, visit with friends, draw or paint, talk on the phone, play cards, go bowling, and so on—and most of the items on your list will be secondary reinforcers.

Primary and secondary reinforcers each have their strengths and weaknesses. Primary reinforcers are much more susceptible to *satiation,* the loss of reinforcer effectiveness resulting from excessive exposure to the reinforcer. If you haven't had anything to eat all day, a tasty treat can be a powerful reinforcer. But food tends to lose its reinforcing power rapidly with each bite. Secondary reinforcers are less susceptible to satiation. Even if we've been complimented many times, a compliment is still likely to be reinforcing.

Secondary reinforcers, on the other hand, are more dependent on the context. A compliment that is powerfully reinforcing in one situation may not be reinforcing at all in another situation. The same is true of money. So much—

"Wait. I have to ask about that. I can't imagine a situation in which money wouldn't be reinforcing."

No, Alfred? Well, the next time you go on a date, and you're about to take your leave, hand your date $20 and say, "Thanks, I had a great time."

"Whoa. I get it."

Contrived and Natural

So much for primary and secondary reinforcers. Now let us consider contrived and natural reinforcers:

Contrived reinforcers:
Reinforcers that have been arranged by
someone for the purpose of modifying behavior.

Natural reinforcers:
Reinforcers that have <u>not</u> been arranged by
someone for the purpose of modifying behavior;
spontaneous or unplanned reinforcers.

Contrived reinforcers are part of an instructional or therapeutic program. So, if a 12-year-old boy answers a teacher's question correctly and the teacher smiles and winks at him, the smile and wink are contrived reinforcers: They are provided by the teacher in order to strengthen the student's behavior. On the other hand, if the cute little redheaded girl two rows over smiles and winks at him, she has provided natural reinforcers. Yes, Carlotta?

"If they're both smiling and winking, I don't see how you can say one is a natural reinforcer and the other is contrived."

Contrived reinforcers are arranged by someone for the purpose of changing behavior, while natural reinforcers are those that occur as a result of the interactions between a person and his or her environment. If a reinforcer is presented by a teacher or a trainer or a therapist or someone else as part of a program to change behavior, then it's a contrived reinforcer. If the reinforcer is just the natural consequence of the behavior, then it's a natural reinforcer.

"Dr. Cee? Some of my education professors say that teachers shouldn't provide contrived reinforcers. They say students should learn from the natural consequences of behavior."

Maybe they *should,* Midori; the question is, *do* they?

"I don't understand."

Natural reinforcers are often weak or rare. Particularly in the early stages of learning, some sort of contrived reinforcers are usually necessary. To take one classroom example, what's the natural reinforcer for getting the right answer to a multiplication problem?

"Isn't getting the right answer itself reinforcing?"

But what tells the student she has gotten the right answer?

"Maybe she can look up the answer in the back of the book."

Yes, but that's a contrived reinforcer. It was contrived by the author of the textbook.

"Someone could tell her she got the right answer."

The person who's in the best position to do that is the teacher, and then it's a contrived reinforcer.

There's another problem with relying on natural reinforcers: It can be dangerous. If you were to learn to drive without benefit of contrived reinforcers, for example, you might have to crash a few times before the natural reinforcer of avoiding injury took effect. The natural reinforcer for stopping at a red light is that you don't get broadsided by someone going the other way. But if avoiding a collision is to be reinforcing in and of itself, you might have to be in a few traffic accidents. Similarly, if someone were training a surgeon without contrived reinforcers, a few extra patients might have to die before the natural consequences would take effect.

It is sometimes possible to make use of natural reinforcers in the classroom— and elsewhere—but if we try to rely exclusively on them, progress is apt to be very slow. In many situations, contrived reinforcers are essential.

The distinctions we've been making among reinforcers—positive and negative, primary and secondary, natural and contrived—are somewhat arbitrary. For example, we've said food is a primary reinforcer, but we know that food preferences are determined partly by experience. We learn to like some foods and to dislike others. Similarly, the distinction between contrived and natural reinforcers tends to get fuzzy if it's looked at closely. For example, eating is naturally reinforcing, but food can be used as a contrived reinforcer. Nevertheless, these categories have some value when we talk about reinforcers, so it's good to know them.

Now let's take a look at some studies that illustrate the use of reinforcement.

Illustrative Studies

Ann Doesn't Socialize

One problem teachers see from time to time is a child's tendency to avoid interacting with other children. The study I'm going to describe was reported by Eileen Allen and others.[10] The child was a 4-year-old enrolled in the university's laboratory preschool. Ann was not especially withdrawn or fearful; she interacted with adults readily and enjoyed their attention. But she showed very little interest in interacting with other children. She seldom approached them or responded to their efforts to engage her in play. Since adult attention seemed to be reinforcing, the researchers decided that the teachers should provide attention only when Ann interacted with another child.

Two observers collected data on Ann's behavior during the course of the study. They did this by using a form that looked something like a bowling score sheet. Here, I've got a transparency I can put on the overhead projector:

From "*The Effects of Social Reinforcement on Isolate Behavior of a Nursery School Child,*" by *K. E. Allen, B. M. Hart, J. S. Buell, F. R. Harris, and M. M. Wolf. In* Child Development, *Vol. 35, copyright 1965 The Society for Research in Child Development, Inc. Reprinted by permission.*

Each of the cells indicates a 10-second interval. The top row of cells is for recording Ann's interactions with adults; the bottom row is for recording her interactions with children. If Ann interacted with an adult during a 10-second interval, the observer would put an X in that box. If the interaction continued into the next 10-second period, the observer would make another X. A hash mark indicates that Ann drew close to someone but didn't interact with the person.

Okay, so the observers took their trusty record sheets and counted interactions every morning for five days to get a baseline. A baseline is . . . what, Carlotta?

"A record of the target behavior when there's no attempt to change the behavior."

Right. You need a baseline to . . . well, why *do* you need a baseline, Jamal?

"As a control?"

What do you mean?

"Well, if you want to change the frequency of some behavior, you have to know how often it occurs before you try to change it. That way you have a basis for comparison."

Good. In this case, our intervention is reinforcement. To see if the consequences we provide are reinforcing behavior, we have to compare the results we get with the results obtained before reinforcement.

At the end of the baseline period, the teachers started providing special attention to Ann whenever she interacted with other children. If Ann played with another child, a teacher would make a comment such as, "Ann, you are making dinner for the whole family." If she played alone, the teachers paid no particular attention to her.

The researchers expected to see an increase in the number of interactions over the baseline rate. Unfortunately, that didn't happen. The data showed that the attention the teachers provided did *not* reinforce interacting with other children. Apparently, the teacher's comments drew Ann's attention away from the other children and toward the adult. Be that as it may, what seemed like a likely reinforcer—adult attention—wasn't reinforcing. Daniels' Dictum strikes again!

If one consequence proves ineffective, you try another. And that's what Allen's group did. Instead of commenting specifically on Ann's behavior, the teachers commented on her role in the group. For instance, if Ann were playing house with some other children, the teacher might say, "You three girls have a cozy house!" When possible, the teacher would also give Ann a toy or utensil to use in the ongoing activity. She might, for example, give Ann more cups to use in a tea party.

This new effort at reinforcement produced a dramatic change in Ann's behavior: During the baseline period, Ann spent only 10% of her time interacting with other children. On the day that the teachers began providing attention for interacting with other children, Ann spent nearly 60% of her time with other children. As long as the new consequences were in force, Ann continued to spend the great bulk of her time with other children.

"Dr. Cee?"

Yes, Brian?

"Why didn't Ann interact with other kids in the first place? Why did she need this special reinforcement program?"

That's an interesting question. It's usually impossible to reconstruct the learning history that produced a behavior problem. It's possible Ann received very little attention at home, so when she came to school and adults noticed her, it was very reinforcing. Or it may be that she was an only child and did not have opportunities to learn to play with other children. Or it could be that she kept to herself one day because she wasn't feeling well, and the teachers paid special attention to her, thus reinforcing avoiding other children. There are any number of learning histories that can lead to a particular behavior, including problem behavior.

Whatever the reason a child plays alone, it is easy to see how this behavior could be reinforced. If you saw a preschool child off by herself much of the time, it's likely that you would approach her, speak pleasantly to her, and attempt to involve her in play with other children. If she went off by herself again, you might very well go to her again. In doing this, you would not intend to reinforce social isolation, but reinforcement doesn't depend on what you intend. Anyway, this is a likely scenario of how Ann's isolation might have been strengthened. Fortunately, dealing effectively with a behavior problem seldom requires a detailed understanding of the learning history that produced the problem in the first place. Yes, Jamal?

"I wonder if it's a good idea to try to get Ann to interact more. Is it such a terrible thing if some kids spend time by themselves?"

That's one of those questions that behaviorists are always trying to answer—not just in the abstract but in specific situations. It's an ethical dilemma. If the behavior isn't a problem for the child, you might have to question whether anybody has a right to change it. In this case, we have a little girl who spends very little time interacting with others her age. She seems to have been normal in every way except for not playing with other children. But what would have happened if she had remained a loner at such an early age? Would the other kids have started making fun of her? Would she have missed out on important social experiences? It's a judgment call. It seems to me the teachers and researchers were right to intervene, but the point is arguable.[11]

All right, I have one more thing to tell you about the Ann study. After reinforcing social interactions for six days, the researchers had the teachers stop reinforcing group play and start providing attention for playing alone. Social play immediately dropped off to the baseline level. When the teachers began attending to social play again, that behavior shot up. These last two steps turn the study into a research design known as . . . John?

"An ABAB reversal design?"

Right. During the A periods, the "natural" conditions are in force. In this case, teachers reinforced playing alone. During the B periods, the intervention is in force. In this case, teachers reinforced playing with other children. In an ABAB experiment, the researchers get a baseline (A) and then intervene (B), then return to the baseline condition (A), and then intervene again (B). Now, why would researchers want to return to the baseline condition once they had an intervention that was working? Yes, Maya?

"To see if the intervention was really what changed the behavior."

Tell me what you mean.

"Well, you try reinforcing the behavior, and the frequency goes up, compared to baseline. But how do you know the increase was due to the reinforcer?"

Well, why wouldn't it be?

"It could be just a coincidence. Maybe something else happened that affected her behavior."

Such as?

"I don't know. Maybe her parents started treating her better at home, or maybe she started seeing a counselor, or maybe she was put on some kind of medication, or taken off of medication."

Good point. Any number of things could have occurred coincidental to the reinforcement effort; these things, rather than teacher attention, might have produced the change. So behaviorists sometimes reverse a reinforcement procedure to see if the improvement in behavior deteriorates. If it doesn't, then we can't be sure the reinforcement helped. If it does, then we can reinstate the reinforcement; if the behavior bounces back, there's little doubt that reinforcement produced the change.

Of course, a teacher probably wouldn't use a reversal design. Once a teacher sees an increase in desired behavior, he's probably content to assume that the intervention produced it. The same thing is true of a parent dealing with the problem behavior of a child or a manager dealing with a problem involving the behavior of employees. But for the researcher, or the person trying to ensure that an intervention was effective, a reversal is often essential.

A child who doesn't interact much with other children represents a fairly common problem, and one that is not especially difficult to treat with reinforcement. Let's consider a more difficult problem.

Mary Refuses to Eat

This next example involves a woman admitted to the hospital because she claimed that her food was being poisoned and refused to eat.[12] Probably because of her low weight, the nurses took to spoon-feeding her. At the beginning of this study, Mary had been in the hospital for seven months and was usually spoon-fed by one of the nurses.

The goal was to get Mary to feed herself. Mary seemed to care a good deal about her personal appearance; she always kept her clothes neat and clean. This gave the researchers, Teodoro Ayllon and Jack Michael, an idea. They asked the nurses to continue spoon-feeding the patient but to be careless about it, so that a few drops of food would fall on Mary's dress. Whenever Mary ate on her own, the nurses were to stay with her for a while as she ate. The idea was that by eating on her own, Mary could avoid getting her dress messy.

During an 8-day baseline period before the intervention, Mary ate 5 meals on her own, was spoon-fed 12 meals, and refused to eat 7 meals. So she was being spoon-fed about twice as often as she was feeding herself. Once the nurses became a little sloppy at spoon-feeding, this began to change. At first Mary typically began with spoon-feeding, but reached for the spoon once an "accident" occurred. After a while, she began feeding herself right from the start.

The goal was to get Mary to feed herself, and that was achieved. However, there were also some interesting positive side effects. Once she started feeding herself, Mary skipped fewer meals. This in turn meant a healthy weight gain, from 99 to 120 pounds. She also talked less about her food being poisoned. There had been no effort to change this behavior; it was merely a side effect of reinforcing self-feeding. Since the reason for Mary's admission to the hospital was her refusal to eat and claiming that her food was poisoned, there was no longer any reason to keep her in the hospital and she was discharged.

Now, Mary's case was very different from Ann's. In the case of Ann the reinforcer was . . . what, Midori?

"Adult attention."

Right. And what was the reinforcer in Mary's case, John?

"Was it avoiding the drops of food?"

Exactly. One consequence of being spoon fed was that her clothes became soiled. She could avoid this by feeding herself, which means this used what kind of reinforcer? Jamal?

"A negative reinforcer."

Yes, but why is it negative?

"Because getting your clothes messed up is negative?"

Nope. Try again. Remember that the terms *positive* and *negative* can be thought of as mathematical signs.

"Oh, right. It's negative because something is being taken away: She's able to avoid the spills by feeding herself."

Right. Avoiding food spills was, for her, reinforcing.[13]

These studies provide illustrations of how reinforcement can be used to solve behavior problems. This course is not a practicum, but all of you have the opportunity to use reinforcement every day in your interactions with others. And some of you will be in occupations (such as teaching, counseling, human resources, employee supervision, and health care) in which reinforcement can be a tremendously useful tool. And most of you will be parents; no procedure is more important in child rearing than reinforcement. So I want to describe some basic rules for using reinforcement effectively. I'll put each rule on the board, and then we can discuss it.

Rules for Using Reinforcement

We can't very well implement an intervention effectively if we don't have a very clear idea of what behavior we are trying to change. In the case of reinforcement, we need to know precisely what behavior we are trying to reinforce. So, the first rule for using reinforcement is:

1. Define the target behavior.

Now, when I say, "Define the target behavior," I mean that quite literally: *Write* a brief description of the behavior, or set of behaviors, that will qualify for reinforcement.[14] Let's consider an example. Suppose you're working with a 9-year-old girl who is diagnosed ADHD—attention deficit hyperactive disorder. She is highly impulsive and has a very short attention span. What might be an appropriate target behavior for her? Belinda?

"Not running around so much; not being so active . . ."

Just a minute. We're talking about rules for the use of reinforcement, right? And reinforcement increases the frequency of behavior. So, are you identifying behavior you want to occur more often?[15]

"Oh. No, I'm listing things the person should do less often. Let's see . . . the target behavior might be sitting in a chair continuously for, say, 2 minutes, or working on a task without interruption for 2 minutes."

Okay, that's better. So the first step in using reinforcement effectively is to decide what behavior is to be reinforced. The second step is to decide what consequences you will provide to strengthen the target behavior.

2. Select appropriate reinforcers.

Before you can reinforce a target behavior, you have to select one or more reinforcers. There are a few rules of thumb that will help you make a good choice:

First, Think Positive. We talked before about positive and negative reinforcers. Negative reinforcers often work quite well—that's why they're so popular. But they involve aversives, and aversives often have negative side effects. We will talk more about the negative side effects of aversives when we discuss punishment. For now, I'll just say that if you use aversives, you run the risk of running into some serious problems.

The most important thing to remember when selecting reinforcers is to never use negative reinforcers if positive reinforcers are available. The second most important thing to remember is that positive reinforcers are always available. When selecting a reinforcer, think positive.

Second, Secondaries First. Other things being equal, it is better to use secondary reinforcers than primary reinforcers. Of course, if you have a choice between a very powerful primary reinforcer and a very weak secondary reinforcer, you probably have to go with the primary reinforcer. But primary reinforcers tend to satiate quickly, while secondary reinforcers do not. And the use of secondary reinforcers is more likely to help sensitize the person to the natural reinforcers available for the behavior. (More often than not, the naturally occurring reinforcers are secondary reinforcers.) It is sometimes necessary to begin a program with primary reinforcers, but it is usually possible to shift to secondary reinforcers once the behavior begins to change. You might, for instance, offer praise (a secondary reinforcer) when you present food (a primary reinforcer). After a while, you'll be able to rely more and more on praise and less on food. The trend over the course of training should be toward secondary reinforcers.

Third, Go Natural. I've said that contrived reinforcers are usually a necessary part of a reinforcement program. If naturally occurring reinforcers were up to the job, behavior problems would not occur and there would be no need for applied behavior analysts. By deliberately arranging reinforcers, we can rapidly boost the frequency of behavior, but—

> "A person can't spend his life in an environment that has been specially designed to have lots of reinforcers."

Exactly, Carlotta. A person can't spend his life in a contrived environment. Contrived reinforcers have their place, because with them we can produce rapid changes in behavior. But, as you say, we can't always provide an environment that is loaded with contrived reinforcers. So, it's important to make use of whatever natural reinforcers are available. And while we may rely heavily on contrived reinforcers to begin with, we need to shift from those contrived reinforcers to naturally occurring reinforcers as the frequency of the target behavior increases.

3. Make reinforcement immediate and certain.

There are lots of variables that can affect the power of reinforcement.[16] However, by far the most important are how quickly the reinforcer follows the behavior, and how likely the reinforcer is to follow the behavior.

The more closely the target behavior is followed by a reinforcer, the more likely the reinforcer will be effective.[17] Usually, the ideal procedure is to provide reinforcement while the behavior is still occurring. Why do you suppose it's so important to reinforce immediately after the target behavior? Midori, what do you think?

"Well, if you delay, then when the reinforcer arrives the person may be doing something else and that behavior might be reinforced instead of the target behavior."

That's exactly right. Any delay allows time for other behavior to occur, and that behavior may be accidentally reinforced. Suppose you would like to increase your 10-year-old daughter's tendency to read. You know from past experience that giving her the opportunity to read aloud to you is reinforcing. After dinner, while you are washing the dishes, you notice that instead of watching TV, your daughter has picked up a book and begun reading. You decide that to reinforce this behavior, you will ask her to read to you as soon as you finish the dishes. Unfortunately, 5 minutes later when you are ready, she is no longer reading; she is now watching TV. Odd as it may seem, if you ask her to stop watching television and read to you, you might actually reinforce TV viewing.

The other factor I mentioned was certainty. The more likely the target behavior is to result in reinforcement, the more rapidly the behavior will increase in strength. It is not enough, however, merely to hand out lots of reinforcers to the person whose behavior we want to change; the reinforcers must be contingent on the occurrence of the target behavior.[18] Best results are usually obtained when reinforcement is almost certain to occur when the target behavior occurs, but is unlikely to occur otherwise.

Unfortunately, reinforcers are often no more certain to occur following desirable behaviors than at other times. In fact, sometimes it's the other way around. Parents and teachers often ignore children when they behave well, for example—but let those children whine or cry or be destructive, and suddenly they have the adult's undivided attention. If attention is reinforcing, these parents and teachers are making reinforcement likely when *undesirable* behavior occurs and unlikely when *desirable* behavior occurs. Strange as it may seem, some psychodynamically oriented therapists actually advocate making reinforcers more likely when children misbehave or act crazy than at other times.[19]

The importance of making reinforcement immediate and certain (or at least, highly likely) is such that, if you do not follow this rule scrupulously, you may see little benefit from your efforts.

Okay, there's one more rule for using reinforcement:

4. Monitor results.

In applied behavior analysis, every intervention includes monitoring the results of the intervention—usually on a daily basis—and modifying the intervention in accordance with the data obtained.

Often when people attempt to change behavior, they fail to monitor the results they get or do so only in an informal way. A psychotherapist may, for example, look for changes in behavior during a therapeutic interview, or he may talk to relatives about a client's progress. A teacher may be on the lookout for lisping in a student whose speech she is trying to improve. But such subjective and informal observations of behavior are of limited value. Behavior varies from moment to moment and day to day, even without any effort at intervention. Is the change we see due to the intervention, or is it just the normal variation in behavior? Subjective observations are also subject to bias. Anyone who attempts to solve a behavior problem is likely to be eager to see improvements in behavior. This raises the possibility that setbacks will go unnoticed, while any sign of progress may be exaggerated.

Because of these problems, behavior analysis calls for systematic approaches to monitoring results. In fact, it sometimes seems to me that the biggest difference between behaviorists and others who try to solve behavior problems is that behaviorists *count*. When a behaviorist is working on a problem, someone actually counts the number of times the target behavior occurs during a particular period of time. To many people, this seems excessive, but if you don't actually count the number of times the target behavior occurs, it is easy to be misled about the effects of an intervention.

Carefully monitoring the effects of an intervention can, for example, reveal changes in the effectiveness of a reinforcer. A consequence that was powerfully reinforcing at one time may be far less effective at another time.

Moreover, as the target behavior changes, other behavior may change, and that may create new challenges. For example, suppose you are a counselor in a corporation and you're working with a supervisor whose workers find him offensive. As his behavior improves, he becomes more popular with the workers he supervises, but the productivity of his group goes down. That is going to make him unpopular with his supervisors. You need to see what is going on—what he is doing differently—that is reducing the productivity of his workers or your helpfulness may get him fired.

The point is that you must monitor the performance of the person whose behavior you're trying to change, because it's only by monitoring performance that you can be sure that your intervention is continuing to have beneficial effects. If the results of your observations indicate that the intervention is not working, is not working as well as it might, or is producing undesirable side effects, you can then modify the intervention accordingly. For example, if your efforts at reinforcing a target behavior are unsatisfactory, you might try using a different reinforcer, improving the contingency or contiguity of the reinforcer, or redefining the behavior that qualifies for reinforcement.

Now, we have discussed four simple rules for using reinforcement effectively, and . . .

"Dr. Cee?"

Yes, John?

"Should you tell the person what you're doing? I mean, if you're trying to reinforce some behavior, should you tell the person what you're going to do?"

That's an excellent question. It's often a good idea to involve the person in discussions about the goals and nature of an intervention. A reinforcer is often more effective when the person knows what behavior you want and what consequences you will provide. However, it is sometimes possible to change a person's behavior without the person's active participation—as Greenspoon demonstrated when he reinforced plural nouns.

Your question, by the way, illustrates that the rules we've covered are just very basic guidelines; there are lots of other rules that could be discussed.

One problem with presenting only the most basic rules of thumb about using reinforcement is that you're likely to conclude that using reinforcement is a piece of cake. But even if I had a list of all the rules concerning effective use of reinforcement (assuming there were such a list), and even if you learned the list by heart, this would not necessarily make you an expert at applying reinforcement. You can learn all the rules for riding a bicycle, but that would not mean that you could ride a bike. Riding a bike and talking about riding a bike are two different things. Using reinforcement and talking about using reinforcement are two different things. If you want to become proficient at using reinforcement to solve serious behavior problems, such as those a behavior therapist or special education teacher faces, you will need to practice using it under the supervision of an expert.

Still, we all use reinforcement in our everyday lives, whether we've been trained to do so or not. Knowing a little something about reinforcement should help you use it more effectively. Reinforcement is a powerful tool, and it can help you do a lot of good. Despite this fact, there are people who oppose the use of reinforcement to change behavior.

Problems with Reinforcement

Those who oppose the use of reinforcement to change behavior do so mainly for one of three reasons, which I will call inappropriate use, moral objections, and negative side effects.

Inappropriate Use

The argument is made that reinforcement can make matters worse, rather than better. There is some merit to this argument.

You have to remember that the effects of a reinforcer have little if anything to do with the intentions of the person providing it. For instance, suppose you have a son who whines for things he wants. It's a safe bet that he whines for things because he gets them. In other words, whining is reinforced. Now, you can tell the boy, "I'm going to give you this toy, but it has nothing to do with the fact that you've been whining for the last half-hour." You can *tell* him that, but the fact is that whining produced the toy, so you're likely to hear whining the next time there's an attractive toy around.

The misuse of reinforcement can have disastrous consequences. Truck drivers are typically paid by the mile, which encourages them to drive fast and for long hours. It is therefore hardly surprising that there are thousands of fatal accidents involving heavy trucks each year.[20] It's the contingency between behavior and a reinforcer that matters, not the intentions of the person providing the reinforcer.

Delays in the delivery of a reinforcer can also result in the reinforcement of unwanted behavior. To be maximally effective, a reinforcer usually has to appear within a few seconds of the target behavior. So, if you have a daughter who seldom says "thank you," you shouldn't expect much change in her behavior if you wait ten minutes before complimenting her for doing so.

Another way that unwanted behavior gets reinforced is by what is known as bootleg reinforcement:

Bootleg reinforcement: Reinforcement that is not part of, and tends to undermine, an intervention.

Some of you may have heard the term *bootleg gin*. This is liquor manufactured illegally, usually in homemade stills. Teodoro Ayllon and Jack Michael coined the term *bootleg reinforcement* to refer to natural reinforcement of inappropriate behavior.[21]

Often bootleg reinforcement is provided by a parent, teacher, or other well-intentioned person. Sometimes it is provided by people whose intentions are suspect. Suppose, for example, that you are a teacher and you want your students to raise their hands and wait to be called on, rather than interrupting you or someone else by calling out comments and questions. To reinforce the desired behavior, you call on those who raise their hands, and you often compliment them for their patience. All well and good. But little Fred has just thought of a witty remark to make and offers it, without being called on, in a loud, clear voice; the class shows its appreciation with loud laughter. Even if *you* are able to resist laughing (and that is not always easy), the chances are that Fred's impulsiveness has been strengthened by bootleg reinforcement—the laughter of his peers.

Bootleg reinforcement of inappropriate behavior is a serious problem, not only in schools but in most settings. For instance, an institution for delinquent girls should be a place in which appropriate behavior—behavior that comes under the heading of good citizenship—is reinforced, and inappropriate behavior is not. But in one experiment involving delinquent girls in an institution, researchers found that antisocial remarks were approved *70% of the time* by other inmates.[22] More socially acceptable remarks were approved by inmates far less often. Staff members were more likely to praise appropriate behavior, but the net result was that inappropriate behavior was more likely to be reinforced than appropriate behavior.

You have to remember that although you may be the only person in a situation who is attempting to reinforce behavior in a systematic way, you may not be the only source of reinforcement in that situation. To the extent that reinforcement is available for inappropriate behavior, your efforts to reinforce appropriate behavior will be diminished.

Okay, so one complaint against reinforcement is that it can be misused, with the result that unwanted behavior is reinforced. A second problem that you may have with reinforcement is opposition on moral grounds.

Moral Objections

The person whose behavior is being reinforced is unlikely to object to the procedure, but parents, teachers, and traditionally trained health providers may. Sometimes they do so quite vehemently.

One kind of objection says that reinforcement is manipulative and controlling. *Brave New World,* a novel about a utopian world gone wrong, may be mentioned, though the book doesn't describe anything remotely resembling an effective reinforcement program.

Of course, reinforcement is controlling in the sense that it changes behavior. But by that measure, *any* effective technique for influencing behavior is controlling. Lecturing, pleading, encouraging, suggesting, reinforcing—all are efforts to modify behavior. To the extent that they work, they are controlling. The real difference among these approaches is in their effectiveness. Lecturing people about how they *should* behave usually has very little effect on their behavior; the same may be said of most other commonly used forms of influence. Altering the consequences of the desired behavior, on the other hand, often has very pronounced effects on behavior. Reinforcement is called controlling because reinforcement *works.*

It's hard to know how to respond to opposition to a procedure when the opposition is based on the fact that the procedure is effective. Basically, the criticism is a way of saying, "We don't want you to use procedures that work." But what is the point of using procedures that *don't* work?

Some people argue that reinforcement violates the Puritanical principle that there is virtue in suffering. Reinforcement makes changing too easy and too pleasant. The idea is that good medicine has to taste bad.

Often this objection comes from parents concerning reinforcement programs in school. Once, when I was at a PTA meeting, the parents and teachers were discussing the problem of what to do about student misbehavior, which was getting worse and worse each year. The discussion focused on the kinds of punishment to provide for various offenses. They had compiled a list of student offenses and the consequences each offense should have. I made an innocent observation. "No one," I offered, "has said anything about what happens when a student behaves well. What about providing some *positive* consequences for *good* conduct?"

Some parents strongly opposed the idea. "Nobody gave *me* anything for behaving myself when I was in school," said one.[23] But the fact that schools haven't been very good about reinforcing desirable behavior does not mean that they should not do so now. The schools never used to use computers, but that hasn't kept us from putting them in the schools.

Negative Side Effects

Another objection to reinforcement is that reinforcement has unacceptable side effects. One argument is that if people become accustomed to earning attention, privileges, or even praise by working hard, they will become spoiled. They will expect some "pay off" for everything they do. For example, it is said that if students receive recognition for behaving well and for learning, they will no longer work hard and learn when such benefits are no longer available.[24] This would be a very powerful argument against reinforcement if it did have this effect, but it doesn't.

In one study, Donald Dickinson looked at the academic and social behavior of 50 eighth-graders who had gone through a reward program in the fifth and sixth grades.[25] He compared the performance of these students with similar students who had not been involved in a reward program. What Dickinson found was that those students who had once earned rewards by behaving well and working hard had made *greater* progress in the two years following the program (that is, when rewards were no longer available) than had students who had never received rewards. Dickinson also found that behavior problems were less common among the once-rewarded students. It appears, then, that there is no reason to believe that reinforcers will corrupt the youth—or anybody else. Nevertheless, the idea that reinforcement undermines interest is still widespread, especially among educators.

A similar argument against reinforcement is that it undermines a person's natural interest in the reinforced activity. If this were a side effect of reinforcement, it would condemn its use—particularly in schools. In fact, however, the evidence suggests that the proper use of reinforcement *increases* a person's interest in the reinforced activity and that the increased interest persists even when reinforcers are no longer available. This finding has been confirmed repeatedly by reviews of the research literature.[26]

Not all of the negative side effects of reinforcement are imaginary, however. One particular problem that can arise is something called behavioral contrast:

Behavioral contrast:
The tendency for a reinforced behavior
to occur <u>less</u> often in situations
in which it has not been reinforced.[27]

For example, suppose you are a therapist working in a psychiatric hospital. One of the patients, a schizophrenic, is rather quiet, and you decide to attempt to reinforce talking. You get together with the nurses and aides on the ward, and they decide that any time the patient says anything within their hearing, they will smile at him, respond appropriately to his remark, and spend a bit of time with him. Your data graphs show that the number of words the patient speaks on the ward is increasing dramatically. Then one day you run into the occupational therapist, and she mentions she has seen a change in the patient. "Yes," she says, "he never was very talkative, but lately he's been like a monk under a vow of silence."

What has happened is that while the reinforcement procedure has produced an increase in the target behavior on the ward, it has produced a corresponding *decrease* in the behavior in other settings. This is behavioral contrast. The question now is, what do we do about it? Yes, Brian?

"I suppose you have to reinforce the behavior in the other settings."

Exactly right. You don't always get behavioral contrast, because sometimes the natural reinforcers available are sufficient to maintain the behavior at the new rate. But you have to be alert for the possibility of behavioral contrast, and if it occurs, you need to reinforce the behavior in those settings.

And once again, we're just about out of time. Before we go, let's have a brief review of today's topic.

Review

We've been talking about reinforcement, which is based on a law called . . . Midori?

"The law of effect?"

Right. And the law of effect says?

"It says, uhm, that whether a behavior is repeated depends on its effect."

True, but can you recall the language I put on the board earlier?

"Let's see . . . behavior depends on its consequences."

Good enough. What I actually wrote was "Behavior is a function of its consequences." But that's the same idea. Whether a behavior is repeated depends on its consequences, its effects. I also provided a more formal statement. Can anyone recall it? Yes, Carlotta?

"In any given situation, the likelihood of a behavior occurring is a function of the consequences that behavior has had in that situation in the past."

Excellent. Now, the law of effect is important because it provides the basis for reinforcement. What is reinforcement? Belinda?

"That's the procedure of providing consequences for a behavior that . . ."

Yes, keep going.

". . . that increase or maintain the frequency of that behavior."

Good. What do you call the consequences that Belinda just referred to? Alfred?

"Reinforcers?"

Right. And what is a reinforcer, Alfred?

"That's like food, or water, or sex, or praise, or money."

Well, those things are often reinforcing, but what is the definition of a reinforcer?

"That's like an event that makes a behavior more likely to occur in the future."

Close, but no cigar. Can you help Alfred, Jamal?

"A reinforcer is an event that, when it is made contingent on a behavior, increases or . . ."

Or?

". . . or maintains the frequency of that behavior."

Excellent. Now, Alfred, about those examples you gave us—food, water, praise, sex, money. Are these things *necessarily* reinforcers?

"Not really. They usually are, but they might not always be. Like if you have just eaten all you can eat, then food might not be a reinforcer for a while, and if you're really old, like maybe 50, sex might not be a reinforcer."

Well, I might argue with you about the age, but you're on the right track. So while some events may always be considered rewards, at least by some people, they might not always be reinforcers. We talked about some of the different ways of classifying reinforcers. For example, there are positive and negative reinforcers. This distinction gives students a lot of trouble. What's the difference between them, Brian?

"A positive reinforcer is something that's added following a behavior; a negative reinforcer is something that's taken away."

Good. And what do they have in common?

"Well . . . they're both reinforcers. They both strengthen the behavior they follow."

Exactly right. Just remember that a reinforcer increases the frequency of a behavior. And both positive and negative reinforcers are things people generally are glad to have happen. For example, if your headache goes away, that's usually a good thing. If that reinforces some behavior, the reduction in pain is a *negative* reinforcer.

We discussed some studies. One involved Ann, a girl who didn't interact with other children; the other involved Mary, a woman who refused to feed herself. We don't have time to review those studies; make sure you know what their problems were and how they were solved.

We also talked about some rules for using reinforcement properly. What was the first one, Jamal?

"That would be define the target behavior, the behavior you want to reinforce."

Yes. Before you begin using reinforcement, you need to be very clear about what kind of behavior will qualify for reinforcement. Once you have defined the target behavior you need to select something. What do you have to select, Belinda?

"The reinforcers you're going to use?"

Right. Then, as you provide reinforcers you need to remember to . . . what, John?

"To make reinforcement immediate and certain."

Right. What does that mean, Carlotta?

"Reinforce immediately means that you should provide the reinforcer, whatever it is, as soon as the behavior occurs, or at least immediately after it."

Good. What about certainty?

"That means performing the behavior makes reinforcement very likely. You can't just hand out reinforcers. If the behavior occurs, then the reinforcer occurs; if the behavior doesn't occur, then there's no reinforcer."

Okay, we have one more rule. Can anyone recall it? Yes, Brian?

"Monitor results."

Right. But why do you have to monitor results?

"To see how you're doing. Things might not be going the way you expected."

Yes. And that's one reason why we talked about graphing data, so you can monitor the results you're getting. And if you find things are not going as you would like, then what? Belinda?

"Well, you modify your intervention. If you monitor the results you're getting, and things aren't going right, then you need to change what you're doing."

Right. Now, reinforcement is a very powerful and useful procedure, but I did identify some problems with it. One was . . . Midori?

> "It can be misused. Like, you can reinforce behavior unintentionally and create a problem or make a problem worse, like when a parent reinforces whining by giving in."

Exactly so. Troublesome behaviors don't pop up out of nowhere for no reason. Most of the time troublesome behavior occurs because it has gotten good results—in other words, it has been reinforced. We reinforce undesirable behavior in others all the time. People say, "The squeaky oil gets the grease." What that really means is that obnoxious behavior is sometimes more likely to get reinforced than polite behavior is. So we have to be careful to avoid oiling squeaky wheels. What was the second problem with reinforcement? John?

> "There's some opposition to it on moral grounds. There are people who say it undermines intrinsic interest, that it spoils people, that it's bribery."

Yes. The opposition generally comes from people who don't understand what reinforcement is or how it is to be used. For example, the opponents of reinforcement often don't know the difference between reinforcers and rewards. Still, the reality is that there's sometimes a lot of opposition from parents, teachers, shop foremen, managers, and other people when they are asked to reinforce behavior systematically. It's something you have to be prepared to deal with if you're ever involved with setting up a reinforcement program.

> We also talked about negative side effects. Actually, reinforcement is a very safe procedure, provided that the intended behavior gets reinforced. Negative side effects of reinforcement—properly used reinforcement—are rare.

> Oh, but I see we're out of time. I have another set of entertaining exercises to keep you out of trouble. Devote all of your attention to these handouts between now and our next class, and I guarantee you won't flunk the course before then.

◄ Exercises ►

Feed the Skeleton

As usual, your task is to fill in the missing material.

I. The Law of Effect

    A. The more formal statement of the law of effect is that in any given situation _____ .

    B. The less formal statement of the law of effect is that behavior

_____ .

II. Reinforcement
    A. Reinforcement is the procedure of _____ .
    B. A reinforcer is an event that, when _____ .

III. Kinds of Reinforcers
    A. The chief difference between positive and negative reinforcers is

    _____ .

    B. The chief difference between primary and secondary reinforcers is

    _____ .

    C. The chief difference between contrived and natural reinforcers is

    _____ .

IV. Illustrative Applications
    A. The study of Ann showed that _____ .
    B. The study of Mary showed that _____ .

V. Reinforcement Rules
    A. Define the _____ .
    B. Select _____ .
    C. Make reinforcement _____ and _____ .
    D. Monitor _____ .

VI. Problems with Reinforcement
    A. One objection to reinforcement is that it can make a problem worse if

    _____ .

    B. Some people object to reinforcement on _____ grounds.
    C. Another complaint against reinforcement, especially in schools, is that it
       has _____ .

Ophelia's Complaint

Your poor old aunt, Ophelia, is known as "poor old" Aunt Ophelia because, although she seems to be fairly healthy for her age, she always seems to be suffering from something or other. In fact, Aunt Ophelia has so many aches and pains that medical students could use her for simulation training. If there's something that can go wrong with the human body, chances are Aunt Ophelia suffers from it—or will, as soon as she hears of it. Conversations with Aunt Ophelia tend to involve exchanges about her endless ailments. They go something like this:

Ophelia: "I'm so terribly weak; I just don't have any energy these days."

You: "I see. Maybe you should try eating something. You didn't eat much of your breakfast."

Ophelia: "Oh, I couldn't eat it. I just don't have any appetite any more."

You: "Poor dear. What's wrong with your appetite?"

Ophelia: "I just don't have any interest in food. And my arthritis bothers me so much it's difficult to open cans and such."

You: "Really! It's as bad as that?"

Ophelia: "Oh, my, yes. And I can't stand at the stove long or my feet swell up. And . . ."

And on and on. Visiting with Aunt Ophelia is a kind of water torture. Moreover, with all her talk about aches and pains, by the time you leave, you feel almost as decrepit as she does.

Aunt Ophelia's behavior is interesting, and deserves examination. Given what you now know about behavior analysis, what is your best guess about why Ophelia behaves as she does? Design a study to determine whether your theory is sound.

Problem at Holdemdown Elementary

Mr. Flibberty-Gibbet teaches fourth grade at Holdemdown Elementary. One of his students, Buster, is particularly aggressive. Buster rarely strikes anyone, but he makes liberal use of verbal threats, nasty facial expressions, and body language to intimidate the other children. They are terrified of him and do whatever he says. Buster is not openly aggressive toward the teacher, whose authority he seems to accept grudgingly because of his superior strength. The teacher looks into Buster's future and sees a bully at best and a mass murderer at worst. He calls in the school psychologist, Dr. Pickemup, who happens to have been trained in behavior analysis.

After observing Buster casually during recess for several minutes, Dr. Pickemup can see that there is a problem. She decides that the first step is to get a baseline of Buster's aggressive behavior. She has two parent volunteers who are willing to collect data, and she decides to have them count three kinds of aggressive behavior: (1) verbal threats of harm directed at other children; (2) threatening gestures involving the hands, such as a raised fist; (3) any unfriendly physical contact, such as shoving, hitting, or throwing an object at another child.

You are Dr. Pickemup's assistant, and she asks you to help out in two ways: First, design a simple form the parent observers can use to tabulate the three kinds of behavior mentioned. Second, prepare a set of written instructions to accompany the form.

Superstitious Follow-Through

Are you superstitious? You may not think so, but superstitious behavior can be more subtle than carrying a good luck charm or a rabbit's foot. And some superstitious beliefs are so widely accepted that calling them superstitious will provoke an argument. Consider the widely held belief among athletes and coaches in the importance of follow-through.

Follow-through refers to the movements an athlete makes after performing a sport-related move. For instance, in baseball, the batter's object is to hit a ball thrown over a plate. Many baseball coaches and players believe that the form of the swing after hitting the ball is important to successful batting. To continue swinging the bat in a particular way after the bat has hit the ball is to follow through. Belief in the importance of follow through is common among coaches and players in most, and possibly all, sports.

But once a bat hits a ball, the ball immediately is set on a course away from the bat; nothing the batter does after this point can have any effect on the ball.

If follow-through does not (indeed, cannot) affect a batter's performance, then the belief in the importance of good follow-through is superstitious (Hernnstein, 1993). This raises an interesting question, which I would like you to answer: What reinforces the batter's belief in follow-through?

Field Work

Go to a place where you are sure to have the opportunity to observe adults interacting with children for at least several minutes: a grocery store, restaurant, shopping mall, doctor's office, bus station, airport, etc. Find an adult and a child you can observe easily. Look for some behavior that occurs with notable frequency. The behavior you observe may be that of the parent or the child. Then:

1. Write a brief description of the behavior you have selected.

2. Record each occurrence of the behavior and its consequences for at least five minutes. For instance, if you count the number of times the child asks a question, then you should record what the parent does immediately *after* each question (e.g., answers the question; turns to the child and says, "No!"; continues talking to another adult, etc.).

3. List the generalizations, if any, you can draw about the kinds of consequences the behavior has.

Practice Quiz

1. The law of effect states that in any given situation, the _____ of a behavior occurring is a _____ of the _____ that behavior has had in that situation in the past.

2. A reinforcer is an event that, when made _____ on a behavior, increases or _____ the frequency of that behavior.

3. One thing that positive and negative reinforcers have in common is that both _____ the frequency or rate of behavior.

4. In using reinforcement, it is important to make the reinforcer _____
_____ and _____ .

5. _____ reinforcers are those that have *not* been arranged by someone as part of an intervention program.

6. Unplanned and inappropriate reinforcement is called _____ reinforcement.

7. Escape training involves _____ reinforcers.

8. Unlike rewards, reinforcers are defined by their _____ on behavior.

9. _____ reinforcers are not dependent on their association with other reinforcers.

10. The tendency of behavior to occur less often in situations in which it has not been reinforced is called behavioral _____ .

Mini-Essay: FINDING REINFORCERS

Reinforcers are defined by their effects on behavior, and there is no way of predicting with certainty what those effects will be. You have to experiment and monitor the results. However, there are some things you can do to identify consequences that are *likely* to be reinforcing:

1. Ask. One way of finding out what a person might find reinforcing is to ask. You can do that by having the person review a list of reinforcers and select the top three or rate each one on a scale from 1 to 10. Or you can give the person a list of the consequences you are prepared to make available and have her check off those that interest her.

Sometimes this straightforward approach is inappropriate. (The person you're working with may be retarded or uncooperative, for example.) In these instances, you might contact people who know the person well: a parent or other relative, a teacher, a friend, or a social worker. You might ask these people for suggestions or have them complete a reinforcer survey based on how they believe the client would complete it if she were able to do so.

2. Observe behavior freely engaged in. A second approach to finding reinforcers is to observe the behavior of the person in question. You can get valuable information about reinforcers just by noting how a person spends his or her time. If, for example, a child has the opportunity to do a number of things but spends most of the time watching TV, then we know that watching TV will probably be reinforcing. Watch ordinary kids in a classroom and you will see them doodling in their notebooks, whispering to one another, and sending notes back and forth. It follows that these activities might be used as reinforcers.

This approach makes use of an important idea known as the *Premack principle*. David Premack demonstrated in laboratory experiments that the opportunity to engage in a favorite activity can be used to reinforce the performance of some other, less favored activity. In other words, the Premack principle states that high-probability behavior reinforces low-probability behavior.

For instance, if a child is given the opportunity to do all sorts of things—playing various games, singing songs, using a computer, talking with an adult, playing with other children, and so on—but spends more time using the computer than doing anything else, we can use that high-probability behavior to reinforce behavior that doesn't occur as often as we'd like.

Parents can use the Premack principle at home. Most American children spend considerably more of their free time watching television than they do reading. It is probably safe to say that reading contributes to intellectual and academic development far more than TV viewing does. So how do we get children to read more? One way is to require them to earn TV time by reading. The high-probability behavior, watching TV, will reinforce the low-probability behavior, reading.

3. Try common reinforcers. Although you can't *know* something will reinforce behavior until you try it, certain kinds of experiences are usually reinforcing. Praise, positive feedback, eye contact, a congratulatory hug, applause, special privileges, food, music, and games are often reinforcing. You can begin a reinforcement program by trying one of these or other familiar reinforcers. If you monitor the results, chances are you will find that the behavior is being strengthened.

4. Create them. You have learned that an event that is regularly paired with a reinforcer is likely to become a reinforcer itself. This is how secondary reinforcers are born. One implication of this is that you can literally create reinforcers by pairing events with existing reinforcers. In clinics and hospitals, behaviorists who work with seriously disturbed clients do this all the time. They pair praise, smiles, and hugs with events that are already reinforcing, such as food. The typical result is that praise, smiles, and hugs soon become reinforcing in their own right.

Reinforcers are defined by their effects on behavior, but you can often find reinforcers without a lot of trial and error—if you know where to look.

Reprint: THE REWARDS OF COACHING
by Hilary Buzas & Teodoro Ayllon

The principal goal of coaching is to improve a skill. That means getting the person to perform correctly more often. How do coaches do that? A lot of coaches concentrate on pointing out errors: "No, not like that!"; "You were too slow on that pivot!"; "Don't bend your wrist!" The philosophy behind this approach is widely accepted: Nearly everyone, it seems, believes that

> *"we learn from our mistakes." But positive reinforcement suggests another approach: pointing out what people are doing right. Which approach gets better results, pointing out mistakes or pointing out what the person does right? In this study, Buzas and Ayllon attempt to find out.*

. . . The present study compared the effects of the coach correcting errors in a typical tennis class to selectively ignoring errors and attending to correct performance. . . .

Method

Subjects
Three female students, ages 13–14, were chosen from a physical education tennis class at a junior high school. The students were beginning tennis players who were selected by the tennis coach because their proficiency level was below 20% on the execution of three tennis strokes: forehand, backhand, and serve.

Setting and Personnel
The tennis class was held on an outdoor tennis court at a junior high school. A female tennis coach held class daily from 12:00 to 12:30 p.m. For purposes of the study, an experimenter-observer-recorder and a reliability observer were present at the tennis sessions, but they did not interact with the players.

Response Definition
Three tennis skills—forehand, backhand, and serve—were examined. These three skills were assessed to be correct based upon appropriate form and also upon appropriate placement of the tennis ball in the court. To be judged correct, each of the following components of the skills analyzed must have been observed:

(1) Forehand

(a) the player must use either the Eastern forehand, the Continental, or the Western grip;

(b) when stroking the ball, the player must pivot and step toward the net with his left foot forward if he is right-handed or with his right foot if he is left-handed;

(c) while stepping toward the net the weight of the player would transfer from the back foot to the front foot (foot closest to the net);

(d) the player's front knee should be bent;

(e) as the player pivots, placing his foot forward, his racket should be brought back passing the right shoulder (if he is right-handed) or the left shoulder (if he is left-handed);

(f) the backswing should continue until the racket is perpendicular to the net;

(g) the racket should be waist level as the forward swing begins and the player should swing through into the ball ending with the racket head on the other side of the body at head height with the arm fully extended;

(h) the ball must land over the net without touching the net, and land on the other side of the court inside or on the single's court lines.

(2) Backhand

(a) the player must . . .

Tennis Coaching

During baseline the coach was asked to instruct the player in her usual manner. The coach typically held a class instruction period lasting approximately 5 to 10 minutes. During this time, the coach discussed and demonstrated the specific components necessary to execute each of the three tennis skills correctly. Following those instructions, practice sessions were held in which each player was given the opportunity to execute the skills while the coach generally pointed out the errors in execution. Most often, the coach's comments were of a negative nature. The coach focused on what the player was doing incorrectly, thereby frequently ignoring correct or near correct components of a specific skill.

Behavioral Intervention

As during baseline, the coach held her class instruction period prior to the practice sessions. However, during the practice sessions the coach was asked to discontinue her comments on errors, poor form, and other negative behavior. Instead, the coach was to give praise/attention for near correct performance, such as "Good! You started to bend your knees!" as well as for correct target behavior, such as "Great serve!" The players usually performed at least one component of the skill correctly which enabled the coach to praise that component behavior. However, only when the target behavior was displayed (all components executed correctly) was it recorded as correct.

Results

The behavioral procedure, praising correct performance and ignoring incorrect performance, increased correct execution of three tennis skills for all three players.

During the baseline, reliability ranged from 80.5% to 91% for each of the three skills examined and from 79% to 87.7% for the verbalizations for the instructor. Reliability during intervention ranged from 83% to 94% for each of

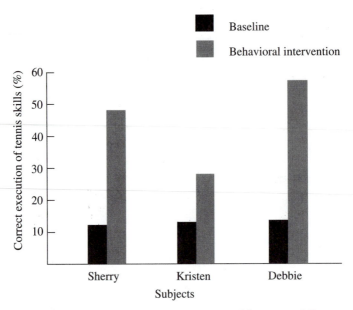

Figure 1. *Average percentage correct execution of three tennis skills during baseline and behavioral intervention.*

the skills examined, and reliability of the tennis coach's verbal behavior ranged from 82% to 88%. . . .

Figure 1 shows the average percentage correct execution of the three skills together during baseline and intervention for Sherry, Kristen, and Debbie. It can be seen that during baseline correct performance of skills ranged from 11.6% to 12.9%. When the behavioral procedure was applied, correct execution of skills ranged from 28.3% to 56.8%, which was an increase of two to four times over baseline measures. . . .

Excerpted from "Differential Reinforcement in Coaching Tennis Skills," by H. P. Buzas and T. Ayllon. In *Behavior Modification, Vol. 5,* copyright 1981 by Sage Publications, Inc. Reprinted by permission.

◄ Recommended Reading ►

1. Hopkins, B. L., & Conard, R. J. (1975). Putting it all together: Superschool. In N. G. Haring & R. L. Schiefelbusch (Eds.), *Teaching special children.* (342–385). New York: McGraw-Hill.

   This study demonstrated that it is possible for students to learn far more in a school year than they normally do. Positive reinforcement played a major role.

2. Eisenberger, R., & Cameron, J. (1996). Detrimental effects of reward: Reality or myth? *American Psychologist, 51,* 1153–1166.
   The most recent analysis of research studies finds that the much-reported negative effects of rewards are more myth than reality.

3. Kaplan, J. S., with Kamperman, M. G. (1996). *Kid Mod: Empowering children and youth through instruction in the use of reinforcement principles.* Austin, TX: Pro-Ed Books.
   A program for teaching kids ages 9 to 12 how to use reinforcement in their everyday lives.

4. Maurice, C. (Ed). (1996). *Behavioral intervention for young children with autism.* Austin, TX: Pro-Ed Books.
   A collection of articles on the application of reinforcement and other behavioral procedures in the treatment of autism.

5. Skinner, B. F. (1968). *The technology of teaching.* Englewood Cliffs, NJ: Prentice-Hall.
   Don't let the title fool you; the book is not primarily about teaching machines.

◄ Endnotes ►

1. Thorndike's (1898) formulation of the law of effect was possibly the single most important contribution to the science of behavior. His early experiments are often represented as studies of trial-and-error learning, but Thorndike (1911) believed that learning was a matter of trial and success. Skinner (1938, 1953) moved us well beyond this early view of behavior, yet his work—and modern behavior analysis in general—rest firmly on Thorndike's Law.

2. *Star Trek* aficionados, take note: One trekky has informed me that the reason the Starship *Enterprise* comes to a halt when its drive system fails has to do with traveling at warp speed. He explains that within the realm of science fiction, warp speed does not obey Newton's laws. However, I have noticed that the *Enterprise* also stops following engine failure when the ship is under "impulse power"—when, apparently, Newton's laws still hold. Go figure.

3. Research findings on human behavior often have a familiar ring to them. We hear about a research finding and say, "I already knew that," or "It's just common sense." But research shows that behavioral findings are not as obvious or commonsensical as people think; see, for example, Wong (1995).

4. Two points are worth noting about this definition: First, many textbook definitions of reinforcement do not include the phrase "or maintain." I have included this phrase because at some point providing a reinforcer will no longer increase the frequency of the behavior it follows, yet continued reinforcement may be necessary if the behavior is to continue occurring at the

same rate. Second, this definition equates the strength of behavior with its rate, but there are other ways of measuring the strength of behavior (Nevin, 1974). For example, one measure of strength is the tendency for behavior to persist even when reinforcement is available for other behaviors; another is the tendency for behavior to persist when it is no longer reinforced. Catania (1998) has identified what many consider to be the defining characteristics of reinforcement: First, a behavior must have a consequence. Second, the behavior must increase in strength. Third, the increase in strength must be the result of the consequence. Also see Higgins & Morris (1985) on this point.

5. Note that a reinforcer is an event, not an object. Thus, the *arrival* of food may be reinforcing to a hungry person, while the *removal* of food may be reinforcing to a nauseated person. It is not the food, per se, that is reinforcing in either case, but the arrival or removal of food—an event.

6. See Greenspoon (1955). The first study of this type seems to have been the doctoral dissertation of R. S. Ball (1952). A number of other people have conducted similar experiments; for a discussion of this topic, see Michael (1984).

7. If you have trouble keeping positive and negative reinforcers straight, it might help to think of positive reinforcers as events that a person will work to produce, and negative reinforcers as events that a person will work to escape or avoid. Note that this still means that reinforcers are defined by their effects on behavior.

8. One reason for the confusion is that both punishment and negative reinforcement use events the person will escape or avoid, if possible.

9. See Michael (1975).

10. Allen et al. (1964).

11. It is very easy to sit on the sidelines and say, "Let nature take its course." If an unplanned exposure to a virus threatens a person's health, we do not hesitate to make every effort to interfere with nature's course. Why then do we hesitate to act when an unplanned exposure to reinforcement contingencies threatens a person's ability to function effectively?

12. Ayllon & Michael (1959).

13. Again we see the variability of reinforcers. For many people in Mary's situation, avoiding food spills would not be sufficiently reinforcing to be effective.

14. Ideally, the target behavior should be overt, discrete (i.e., countable), and important (i.e., something that, if increased in frequency, is likely to make a practical difference in the life of the client or student).

15. A common mistake in the analysis of behavior problems is to focus on what the person should *not* do (Goldiamond, 1974). This approach often leads to the use of threats and other aversives: "Johnny, if you get out of that chair one

more time, I'll brain you!" Focusing on what we want the person to do *more* often, rather than on what we want him to do *less* often, inclines us toward the use of reinforcement. As you will see later in the course, reinforcement is preferable to aversives for a number of reasons.

16. One such variable is the level of deprivation: If you've just eaten a big meal, food is less likely to be reinforcing than it would be if you'd had nothing to eat all day. Thus, if you are going to use bits of food as a reinforcer—as you well might if you were working with a retarded or autistic person, you will probably get better results if the training sessions are held just *before* a meal than if held just after a meal. Deprivation is a particularly important factor when primary reinforcers are involved. The opportunity to socialize with others is more reinforcing when you've been without company all day than it is when you've spent the day visiting with friends. So, depriving a person of contact with a reinforcer will often increase the effectiveness of that reinforcer. Other variables that affect the reinforcement procedure are the amount of reinforcer provided, the quality of the reinforcer, the number of times the target behavior is reinforced and the availability of reinforcers for other behaviors.

17. See Renner (1964); Schneider (1990). Timing is so important to a reinforcer's effectiveness that some authors incorporate it into the definition of reinforcement. According to Malott et al. (1993), for example, if a reinforcer does not follow a behavior "immediately," any increase in the strength of the behavior is not due to reinforcement. One problem with this definition is that it demands a definition of *immediately*. Malott et al. suggest that immediately means under an hour, and probably under a minute. I have a lot of trouble with this: Bill puts a coin into a vending machine. A minute later food drops into a tray, and the tendency to put money into that machine is stronger, so we say the behavior has been reinforced. Jack puts a coin into a vending machine. Sixty-one seconds later food drops into a tray, and the tendency to put money into that machine is stronger, but now we say the behavior has *not* been reinforced because the food fell into the tray one second later. Increasing the time limit to one hour does not help any. Malott and his colleagues believe that when the interval between behavior and a reinforcer is long, the increase is due to other factors, such as instructions or rules about behavior and its consequences. Instructions and rules certainly influence the effectiveness of reinforcers; so does deprivation; so does the presence of reinforcers for other activities. To me, this does not seem sufficient reason for arguing that some process other than reinforcement is involved.

18. Strictly speaking, if reinforcers are provided noncontingently, the procedure is not reinforcement. What is usually meant by the phrase *noncontingent reinforcement* is that reinforcers are not made contingent on the target behavior.

The procedure does not usually increase the frequency of the target behavior, yet it is widely used. Workers are, for example, commonly paid "by the hour," meaning that pay is contingent on showing up for work, rather than for working (see, for example, Aldis, 1961; O'Brien & Dickinson, 1982).

19. These therapists also tend to blame the mothers for their child's disorder. (The mothers are called "schizophrenogenic.") For more on this, see *Let Me Hear Your Voice,* by Catherine Maurice (1993). Maurice describes her attempts to find effective treatment for her autistic children. Initially hostile toward behavior analysis, she eventually turned to it because of the compelling evidence in its favor, and her children made remarkable progress.

20. Burrell (1995).

21. Ayllon & Michael (1959).

22. Bueler et al. (1966).

23. It is interesting that people who object strenuously to providing positive consequences for good behavior often have no objection whatever to providing negative consequences for bad behavior.

24. See Deci & Ryan (1985) and Lepper & Greene (1975); but also see the critiques of this work (e.g., Dickinson, 1989; Eisenberger & Cameron, 1996). A brief, but readable discussion of this issue can be found in Chance (1992). Even those researchers who believe rewards have negative effects do not oppose the use of all rewards (see Deci & Ryan, 1985; Greene & Lepper, 1974). Yet this fact is often ignored. One hears some parents and educators attacking not only prizes, certificates, gold stars, and other forms of recognition but even praise and simple positive feedback. I know a school principal who tells teachers not to praise their students because it will undermine their natural interest in learning! *I know of no researcher who would endorse such a statement.*

25. See Dickinson (1974).

26. As of this writing, the most recent meta-analysis of the research in this area seems to be that of Eisenberger and Cameron (1996). They write that "our analysis of a quarter century of accumulated research provides little evidence that reward reduces intrinsic task interest" (p. 1162). Earlier reviews resulted in similar conclusions; see, for example, Cameron & Pierce, 1994; Dickinson, 1989; Skaggs, Dickinson, & O'Connor, 1992.

27. Williams (1983).

Prompting and Fading

W_{ELL}, NOW. Last time we discussed reinforcement, which is the procedure of . . . of what, Jamal?

"It's the procedure of providing consequences for a behavior that increase or maintain the frequency of that behavior."

Very good. And what are the consequences Jamal refers to called, Midori?

"Reinforcers?"

Yes. So what's the definition of a reinforcer?

"That's a . . . I forget. I mean, I know, but I can't remember how it's defined."

Let's see if I can help you. The definition starts, "An event that . . ."

"Oh, yeah, an event that, when made . . ."

Contingent . . .

"when made contingent on a behavior . . ."

Increases or . . .

"Increases or maintains the rate of that behavior."

Right. Let's try it again: A reinforcer is an . . .

"A reinforcer is an event that, when made . . ."

Contingent on . . .

"when made contingent on a behavior, increases or maintains the rate of that behavior."

Good. See if you can do it on your own.

"A reinforcer is an event that, when made contingent on a behavior, increases or maintains the rate of that behavior."

Excellent. Now, Midori and I have just demonstrated today's topic, prompting and fading. Reinforcement is a powerful procedure, but you cannot reinforce a behavior that does not occur. One way to get a behavior to occur is to use prompts.

Prompts

Informally, a prompt can be defined as a cue or hint meant to induce a person to perform a desired behavior. Our definition is slightly more formal:

Prompt:
An antecedent that induces a person to perform a behavior that otherwise does not occur.

Lots of antecedents affect the likelihood of a behavior occurring. If you're at home around noon and someone says, "Lunch time!" you are much more likely to move to the dinner table than you were before the announcement. Such natural antecedents are not normally considered prompts. A prompt is an antecedent that is provided when the ordinary antecedent is ineffective.[1] If, for example, you are watching a game on TV and do not respond to the call, "Lunch time!", the cook may appear before you and say, "I spent an hour preparing this meal. Now get in the kitchen and eat!" *That's* a prompt—at least it is if you then go to lunch.

Behaviorists generally recognize five different kinds of prompts: verbal, gestural, physical, modeling, and environmental. I need to talk briefly about each of these.

Verbal Prompts

Verbal prompts involve spoken or written words or parts of words. The person who whispers Hamlet's next line is providing a verbal cue for the actor to help him produce the rest of the soliloquy. When Midori couldn't answer my question, I provided the first part of the definition; this helped her produce the next part. Similarly, when you meet a shy 2-year-old, you might say, "What's your name?" His mother may say to him, "Say, *Billy*." She is attempting to prompt the appropriate reply to your question.

Parents do the same thing—or used to, anyway—in teaching their kids good manners. If someone gave a child some candy or a toy, the father or mother would say, "Say, 'Thank you,' Mary."

Teachers use verbal prompts a good deal in the classroom. A teacher who has taught the word *transportation* may ask a student to recall it. If the student is unable to do so, the teacher may say, "A *train* is a means of . . ." Her hope is that the similarity of *train* to *trans* will trigger the response "transportation." Of course, if that doesn't work, she might say, "trans . . ." She gives the first part of the word as a prompt for *transportation*.

Instructions are another kind of verbal prompt. If the student in my example still doesn't come up with the answer, the teacher may just say, "Say, *transportation*." Similarly, a tennis coach may say, "To put topspin on the ball, turn your racket forward slightly as you hit the ball at an angle." If this has the desired effect, then the coach has successfully prompted the behavior.

A textbook writer can pose a question in the hope that it will prompt a reader to answer it. He might insert a question such as, "What's the definition of *reinforcer?*" with the idea of prompting the reader to say, aloud or to herself, the definition of *reinforcer*. But raising the question in a textbook is no guarantee that the reader will attempt to answer it. The reader may simply move on without attempting an answer, in which case the question did not serve as a prompt. In that case, the answer the text supplies does not serve as a reinforcer.

The same thing is true of questions that teachers ask in class. Teachers may think they are "stimulating thought" by asking questions; but if the questions don't produce a response, there's no reason to think they stimulate thinking or anything else. And, of course, if the student doesn't attempt to answer the question, there's no behavior to reinforce.

Gestural Prompts

Gestural prompts involve facial expressions and posture. An orchestra conductor moves her hands about to indicate that the tempo should be speeded up or slowed down or to indicate that the brass section should play more softly. An experienced teacher may restore order to a class by standing with her hands on her hips, or even by simply raising an eyebrow.

I once saw a program for kids on PBS called *Kidsong*. There was a lot of singing, as you might have guessed. Anyway, they sang a song about a dog named Bingo. I don't remember it very well, but the chorus involved spelling the dog's name. The first time through the kids sang out the letters, B-I-N-G-O three times. In the second chorus, instead of saying B, they clapped their hands once, and then sang, I-N-G-O. The third time through they clapped once for each of the first two letters: CLAP-CLAP-N-G-O. And so on, until in the last chorus they clapped five times in unison with the music. The viewers were supposed to sing along, but when the kids on TV clapped, the kids at home were supposed to say the letter. Clapping is a form of gesture, and in this case it acted as a prompt for saying the appropriate letter.

"How do you know that?"

How do I know what, Carlotta?

"How do you know clapping acted as a prompt for saying the appropriate letter?"

Oh. Good point. I don't, since I didn't get to see what kids watching the program actually did. That's one of the problems with what is called educational television. The "Bingo" song was supposed to prompt the kids at home to sing, "B-I-N-G-O," but they may have merely imitated the chorus and clapped. The assumption is that the viewers are doing what the program creator intended, but how often does anyone check to see if the program actually produces those effects? Probably not very often.

Well, on to physical prompts.

Physical Prompts

The use of physical prompts is often called *physical guidance*. It means guiding the person's body through the required movements. The mother of a boy who is now able to stand for a moment on his own may stand behind the child, grasp his hands in her own, and "walk" him a few steps. When it is time to dress the child for an outdoor excursion, Mom may grasp her son's hand and put it into a coat sleeve. When the boy is a few years older, his golf instructor may take his hands and mold them about a club to get him to form the proper grip. In all of these cases, the teacher is physically prompting the appropriate behavior.

Modeling Prompts

Another way of prompting a behavior is to demonstrate or model it. Most children learn to imitate modeled behavior sometime during infancy. Once a child will imitate modeled behavior, models are an extremely efficient way of prompting desired behavior.[2]

Parents often make very effective use of modeling to teach all sorts of skills, from the proper use of eating utensils to baking a cake. Similarly, teachers show students how to do all sorts of things, from printing the letters of the alphabet to performing long division. It's interesting to note that the word *teach* comes from a word that means *to show*.

You want to teach little kids how to use the 911 system in an emergency? You pick up a disconnected phone, you dial 9-1-1, and you say, "We need an ambulance (or the police, or the fire department) at 409 Rover Street." You have someone else playing the part of the 911 dispatcher. She says things like, "What's the problem?" or "Is the person breathing?" or, in the case of a fire, "Is there anyone in the house now?" and so on. And you respond appropriately to these questions. Then you let the child have a turn pretending to call for help and answer the dispatcher's questions.

The tennis coach may not need to tell you how to put topspin on the ball or move your hand through the proper steps. He may be able to get the appropriate behavior merely by demonstrating it. Likewise, the golf pro can show you the proper way to grip the club. Often such demonstrations are enough to prompt the behavior.

Now, that covers the four basic kinds of prompts. Some people recognize a fifth kind of prompt, the environmental prompt.

Environmental Prompts

An environmental prompt is an arrangement of the physical environment that induces the desired behavior. For example, I once had an old dog named Sunny that was having a lot of trouble negotiating the steps from the deck to the yard. She just couldn't handle them well, and sometimes she'd fall. I built her a ramp, just like the ones that are built for older people and people in wheelchairs. But Sunny wouldn't use the ramp; she'd walk right past the ramp and use the stairs, even though she'd sometimes fall. Since the use of the ramp did not occur naturally, I had to find some way to prompt it.

First I tried modeling the desired behavior. With the dog on the deck, I walked down the ramp. She watched me, sniffed about the ramp a bit, and then went down the stairs. Then I tried physical guidance. I took her by the collar and led her up and down the ramp a few times. She went willingly enough, but when left to her own devices, she went for the stairs. I'm pretty sure physical guidance would have worked eventually, but I decided to try modifying the environment to increase the likelihood of her using the ramp. Do you know what I did? Yes, Maya, what do you think?[3]

"I think maybe you blocked off the stairs."

That's exactly what I did. If Sunny couldn't use the stairs, she *had* to use the ramp. I had modified the physical environment in such a way that the desired behavior was much more likely to occur. That's what is meant by an environmental prompt.

"I see what you mean with the example about the dog, but I don't see how I could use that with people. I mean, I can't block off the stairs to get people to use a ramp."

You might, if you worked at a nursing home with Alzheimer's patients. Blocking off the stairs might be an effective way of inducing patients to use a ramp. You might put a gate in front of the stairs. The gate might have a latch controlled by a keypad. The staff could use the stairs if they wished by punching in a four-digit code, but the patients would have to use the ramp.

Another problem nursing homes run into is that some of the patients wander off. One minute they're sitting in the sun room staring into space; the next minute they're wandering across Main Street or getting themselves lost in a nearby woods. Well, how can you restructure their environment to deal with this problem? Yes, John?

"Maybe you could have a fenced area outside the sun room. When they went for a walk, they'd eventually come to the fence and they'd have to walk in the safe area."

That's a possibility. Any other ideas?

"You might build a special sidewalk, with railings on either side, that would keep them on the path."

That's an interesting idea. You could carry it a step further and make it a covered walkway. Then it could be used in inclement weather.

"I have a question."

You look a little annoyed, Belinda. What's the problem?

"Well, we spent all that time on reinforcement and now you tell us that all we need to do is prompt the desired behavior—"

Whoa! Who said all you need to do is prompt the behavior? Prompting is a way of getting the person to perform behavior that doesn't normally occur, or occurs only rarely. But you still have to reinforce it. Tell me why you have to reinforce it, Belinda.

"I guess because the point is to strengthen the behavior."

Exactly. The reason you prompt behavior is *so that you can reinforce it.* If you repeatedly prompt a behavior and don't reinforce it, pretty soon you may not be able to prompt it. That, by the way, is an error commonly made by parents: They prompt a desired behavior, and then ignore it. You often hear parents complain that their children pay no attention to them. Well, that's exactly what they've taught the kids to do by ignoring the kids when they did what they were told.

So reinforcement is still very important. Prompting is just a way of getting the behavior to occur so that it can be reinforced. You have a question, Belinda?

"Is it ever appropriate to use more than one kind of prompt at the same time?"

Different kinds of prompts are often used together or in sequence. If you're teaching someone how to do the Fox Trot—

"The *what?*"

Yes, I guess the Fox Trot is not exactly a popular dance these days. Well, then, if you're trying to teach someone how to Shimmy and Shake, or whatever today's dancing is called, you might model the behavior, but you might also provide instructions as you're demonstrating the steps. If you're a golf pro, and you're teaching someone how to tee off, you might demonstrate the correct procedure and explain what you're doing as you do it. If you do, you're combining modeling and verbal prompts. Then you might use physical guidance to help your student through the motions.

So, you aren't restricted to using one kind of prompt. However, you may find that combining prompts hurts more than it helps. It can be confusing to people to have more than one thing (such as instructions and a demonstration, for example) going on at the same time. This is especially the case if you work with retarded or autistic people, or with certain kinds of special education students. You always have to monitor the results you're getting and modify your methods accordingly.

Now, prompting is only the first step of the prompting and fading procedure. If your 2-year-old doesn't answer the question, "What's your name?" appropriately, you won't mind prompting him with, "Say, 'Bill-ee.'" But if you have to do this when Billy is 22, it could be a bit annoying. That's why fading is important.

Prompting and Fading

Prompting

If you've ever acted in a play, you know that there is a person, usually called the prompter, whose job is to help actors with their lines when they get stuck. If you're out there on the stage trying to do Hamlet's soliloquy, and you say, "To be, or not to be, that is the question," and suddenly you realize you haven't the foggiest idea what comes after the question, you look over at the prompter and he'll whisper, "Whether tis nobler" and more than likely those words will get you started again.

In the theater, *prompting* means assisting an actor by providing a few words of dialogue. This is helpful because it makes it easier for the actor to produce his or her lines. Most people would say that prompting "jogs the memory" of the actor, but no one ever sees a memory being jogged. What we see is one person (the prompter) doing something that induces another person (the actor) to speak his lines. And that is basically how we will define prompting:

Prompting:
The procedure of providing antecedents that evoke a target behavior.

Prompting means inducing the person to perform a desired behavior by presenting a prompt. Prompts are like crutches; they're a kind of artificial support. When you say "Hello" to someone, you expect that salutation to get a response such as, "Hi. How are you?" You don't expect to have to follow your greeting with some hint about what the other person should say, such as "Now say, 'Hi. How ya doin?'" So, while prompts are very helpful, it's important to wean people off of them if possible.

Fading

It usually is possible to wean people off prompts through a procedure called fading.

Fading:
Gradually reducing the strength of a prompt.[4]

Let's take, as an example, shy little Billy. If you say, "What's your name?" you get no response. But if you add the prompt, "Say, *Billy,*" he says, "Billy." So how do you get him from that point to the point at which he will give his name when asked for it, without any prompting by you? The answer is by gradually fading the prompt. How do you fade "Say, 'Billy'"? Yes, John?

"Could you say it softer?"

You mean whisper it?

"Not at first. Just say it more quietly. And gradually say it softer and softer. Then you'd be whispering it."

Excellent. Then what?

"Huh?"

Well, what do you do after you get to the softest whisper you can do?

"Oh. You could just mouth the words, like the lip-synchers do."

The Lip Singers? Is that a new rock group?

"No, that's when people pretend to sing while a recording of their voice is played. The point is, they mouth the words, but they don't make any sound. You could do that, and gradually reduce even the lip movements."

That's a very good way of fading a verbal prompt. How else could you fade a verbal prompt? Any ideas, Carlotta?

"Maybe you could say less of the prompt. When someone asks, 'What's your name?' instead of saying, 'Say, "Billy,"' you'd say, 'Say, "Billll . . ."' and *Billll* might work just as well as *Billy* as a prompt."

Good. Then what?

"Then you'd say, 'Say, *Bill* . . .' And if that worked pretty well, you could go to 'Say *Bi* . . .' Then when that worked well, you'd just say the word, *Say*."

So you'd get to a point where you wouldn't actually *say* the word he's to produce, you'd just remind him that he's to say something. Okay. Then what?

"I guess then you could just sort of say, 'Ssss,' as though you were going to say, *Say* but got stuck on the first letter."

Good. Let's take another example. When kids first learn to print, they're given sheets of paper with the alphabet printed on it and they're asked to trace the letters. The printed letters prompt the appropriate pencil movements. But the kids need to be able to write without the letters guiding them. How could you fade the letters? Brian?

"You could begin with letters in bold type, and gradually give them letters that were made with finer and finer lines, until the lines were so small you couldn't see them."

That sounds good. How else could you fade these prompts? Belinda?

"I'm not sure. Maybe you'd start with bold type, like before, and then you'd provide letters that had less ink in them. The lines that make up the letters would be just as wide, but they wouldn't be as dark. And they'd gradually get grayer and grayer until finally you couldn't see them at all."

Excellent.

Okay, how about an example of fading a gestural prompt? Any ideas? . . . No? Remember the example of the kids singing Bingo? They clapped to prompt the audience to say the letters B-I-N-G-O. How could you fade the prompts? John?

> "Could you clap for each letter, but clap more softly? And then each time you went through that part of the song, you'd clap more softly until finally you weren't clapping at all."

Yes, that should work nicely. Okay, now let's look at physical guidance. Somebody give me an example of a physical prompt. Yes, Jamal?

> "How about if you're teaching a person with mental retardation to cut up his own food? You might start by putting a knife and fork in his hands, and then hold his hands and cut the food."

Okay, so how are you going to fade that prompt?

> "Well, at first, he's not really cutting the food, I am. I'm the one who's controlling what the knife and fork do. But then I would ease up on my grip, so that he would have to do more of the work. And if he did, I'd reinforce that with praise and, of course, he'd get to eat the food he's just cut up. I'd just keep reducing the amount of force I was applying to the knife and fork, and reinforce his efforts as he did more of the cutting himself. Eventually I'd just barely be touching his hands, and he'd be doing all the work. And then I'd just sit beside him as he cut his food."

A very nice example, Jamal. Now, let's take modeling. Somebody give me an example of fading a modeling prompt. How about you, Carlotta?

> "Well, if you were teaching a baby to feed herself, and she could pretty much use a spoon, you might model eating by taking a spoon and using it to eat some of the baby's food. Then when she imitates your actions pretty reliably, you could maybe perform most of the behavior. You could take some food with the spoon, and move the spoon toward your mouth, but not actually eat the food. If she fed herself with that prompt, you could reduce it further. You might just pick up the spoon and get a bit of food. You'd reinforce the baby's performance of the whole step, but you would model less and less of the behavior until finally when you give her the food and a spoon, she feeds herself."

That seems pretty solid. Okay, we're down to the last kind of prompt. When we discussed environmental prompts, one of the things we talked about was the idea of prompting nursing home residents to walk in a safe area by putting up a fence. Now, how would you fade these prompts? Alfred?

"You could make the fence shorter and shorter, until they would finally stay on the path when there was no fence at all."

Yes, that sounds like the fading procedure all right. Now, tell me, is that what you would do?

"Sure. Why not?"

A fair question. Why not? Does anyone have any thoughts on the matter? Yes, Brian?

"There's going to be new patients coming into the nursing home from time to time. Are you going to put the fence back up and begin fading all over again every time a new patient is admitted? It doesn't seem very practical."

Excellent. Those are exactly the points I hoped you'd make. Just because you have a tool, such as fading, doesn't mean you have to use it. You have to decide if it's appropriate. In this case fading the environmental prompt is probably not a good idea.

Okay, we've talked about the prompting and fading procedures, and we've discussed a number of hypothetical examples. Now let's look at some actual studies in which prompting and fading proved useful.

Illustrative Studies

Prompting and fading are widely used, after a fashion, by teachers, parents, and others who try to build new skills. However, most of the published research on prompting and fading involves severely disturbed or handicapped people. Perhaps the reason for this is that most people can acquire new skills with a little prompting and very rapid fading. If you wanted to teach someone how to use a new VCR, for example, you would probably say something like, "This button is to play a tape; this one is for fast forward; this one is for rewind; . . ." and so on. While you were saying these things, you'd point to the relevant buttons, and you might demonstrate their use by pushing the buttons and pointing out what is happening on the TV screen. You would repeat these prompts as necessary, and fade them pretty quickly.

This informal approach to prompting and fading is far from ideal, but it is usually sufficient. It's a different story with people who are dyslexic, who have difficulty attending, who have physical handicaps, or who are retarded or psychotic. With such people, prompting and fading needs to be done with considerable care. One example is provided by a study by Montrose Wolf and his colleagues.[5]

Dicky Has an Echo

Dicky was a 3½-year-old autistic boy. This young fellow had lots of problems—tantrums, eating problems, and so on. On top of everything else, he did not speak. He was not altogether mute, however; he knew the words of various songs and would sing them. One of his favorites was *Chicago*. He would sing, "Chicago, Chicago, it's a wonderful town . . ." and so on, yet he wouldn't say ordinary kinds of things. He did do a certain amount of mimicking. If you said, "Hello, Dicky," he might parrot back, "Hello, Dicky."

One of the therapist's goals, then, was to get Dicky talking in a more normal way. The training began by presenting Dicky with five pictures, one at a time, and prompting him to name the item shown. For example, the teacher would show him a picture and say, "This is a cat; now say, *cat*." The teacher would repeat this procedure several times until Dicky mimicked the answer. When he said "Cat," the teacher would praise him and give him a bit of food.

At first the researchers tried candy and fruit as reinforcers. These are usually effective as reinforcers, but they didn't work well with Dicky. The researchers ended up using Dicky's breakfast and lunch meals as reinforcers. When he answered correctly, the teacher would give him a bit of his breakfast cereal, for example. After several days of training, the researchers were ready to begin fading the prompts. In three weeks, Dicky responded correctly to ten pictures.

After Dicky was able to name ten pictures, the training shifted to naming household objects. The teacher would hold up a spoon and say, "This is a spoon. Say, *spoon*." Each time Dicky said, "spoon," he received a bit of his breakfast or lunch. When he had learned to say *spoon,* the teacher would move on to another item.

When Dicky had learned a number of common household items, the researchers moved on to more abstract tasks, such as replying to queries such as, "Where are you going tonight?"

Dicky's progress continued, so that by the time he was 5 years old, he was much more verbal, used pronouns correctly, made requests and comments—all without adult prompting.

"Was he normal then?"

He was not normal for a 5-year-old, but he was much closer to normal than he had been when he started treatment at age 3. And, given the fact that this study was done in the 1960s, I suspect he was much closer to normal than any of the medical staff expected him to be. Prior to the development of techniques such as prompting and fading, autistic kids like Dicky were not expected to make much progress at all. It was quite common for parents of these children to be told by pediatricians and psychiatrists, "The best thing you can do is put your child in an institution and forget about him." That is what people were told before applied behavior analysis began proving its usefulness.

This study illustrates the way that prompting and fading is normally done, but there is another way of prompting and fading. Let's take a look at it now.

Teresa Won't Say "Hi"

Stephen Wong and James Woolsey used prompting in a little different way to reestablish elementary conversational skills in chronic schizophrenics.[6] They used a system of graduated prompts. The way this works is, you provide the natural cue for the behavior. If the behavior does not occur, you provide a weak prompt. If the behavior still does not occur, you use a stronger prompt. If the behavior still does not occur, you use a still stronger prompt, and so on. When the behavior finally occurs, you reinforce it. On the next trial, you repeat this procedure. Normally, what happens is that the behavior begins to appear in response to the weaker prompts, until finally it occurs in response to the normal cue, with no prompting at all. Although this procedure looks very different from the fading procedure we discussed earlier, you're still gradually reducing the strength of the prompt used.

One of the patients was named Teresa, a 44-year-old woman with a diagnosis of undifferentiated schizophrenia. She was a high school graduate and had been a secretary and homemaker; at the beginning of this study, she had spent the previous 14 years in psychiatric hospitals. Teresa literally spent part of her day talking to the walls. A good deal of her speech was incoherent and delusional. She would say things such as, "Here's a check for a million dollars." At the time of the study she was on medication.

Wong and Woolsey hoped to reestablish five basic conversational skills, including returning a greeting, addressing a person by name, and saying something like "Fine" when asked, "How are you." To get a baseline on these skills, the trainer would approach Teresa on the ward and say, "Hello, Teresa." Then the trainer would say, "How are you?" and then offer some bit of small talk, such as "It's cold outside today." Finally the trainer would say some sort of farewell and leave. Teresa's behavior during these encounters was recorded; these assessments were done once or twice a day, five days a week.

Training consisted mainly of prompting and reinforcing the appropriate behavior. The trainer would provide the natural cue (such as, "Hello, Teresa") and wait 10 seconds for a reply. If Teresa failed to reply or replied inappropriately, the trainer would provide instructions about what was wanted and model the appropriate behavior. He might say, for example, "When someone says 'Hello,' to you, the right thing to do is say 'Hello' to him." Then the trainer would give the normal cue: "Hello, Teresa" and wait 10 seconds for her reply. If Teresa still didn't respond appropriately, the trainer would try a stronger prompt: He would hold one of her favorite treats (such as a bit of candy) before her and tell her that if she replies with "Hello," she will get the treat. Then the trainer would provide the ordinary cue, "Hello, Teresa," and wait 10 seconds for a reply. When Teresa replied appropriately to the trainer's greeting, the trainer would praise her performance and provide her with the treat. Each training session lasted 1 or 2 minutes.

Baseline data showed that Teresa's conversational skills were close to non-existent. With prompting and reinforcement, they improved dramatically. Here's what her performance was like on returning a salutation and addressing the trainer by name:

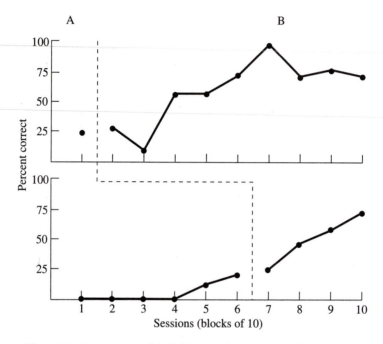

Figure 4-1. *Prompting social skills. Teresa learns to return a salutation (top) and address the trainer by name (bottom). Adapted from Wong and Woolsey (1989).*

Each data point represents the percent of correct replies on 10 training sessions. You can see that her performance improved during the training on both returning a greeting and using the trainer's name. By the end of the training, all five of the target behaviors had stabilized at nearly 100% accuracy.

Now, I don't want to mislead you. I've told you before that behavioral procedures don't always work as well as you'd like. Wong and Woolsey write that "Systematic prompting, reinforcement, and fading of prompts eventually over-rode psychotic behavior," but they add that "many training trials were required for this process to occur."[7]

Progress was slow for all of the patients—slower than what might be expected of moderately retarded people. And one of the patients, a 53-year-old woman named Helen, benefited little from the program. Keep in mind, however, that these patients represent quite a challenge for any kind of intervention. Helen, for example, had been hospitalized continuously for 34 years. During their training the patients would often say bizarre things, become aggressive, or walk away from the trainer. To produce any progress toward normal social behavior in such patients is no small accomplishment.

Okay, so proper use of prompting and fading can be a very important part of an effort to increase the frequency of a target behavior. Now let's consider some rules for making effective use of this procedure.

Rules for Prompting and Fading

Please tell us the first rule, John.

"Define the target behavior."

Right:

1. Define the target behavior.

As always, we begin by defining exactly what behavior we want to change. In this case, that means identifying the behavior we want to prompt.

Next, we need to identify some event, or events, that are likely to bring out the target behavior.

2. Identify suitable prompts.

You need to identify a prompt that will reliably produce the behavior, and use that. There are usually any number of events that will serve as prompts. In selecting one, it's generally best to begin with the weakest one. Next—

"Excuse me, Dr. Cee."

Yes, Jamal?

"I don't know what you mean by *the weakest one*."

Ah. Well . . . I guess the best I can do to explain is to give an example. Suppose you become a parent, and your child is diagnosed as ADHD. He's got the attention span of a mosquito. One aspect of this attention span problem is that he doesn't look at people when they talk to him; he glances at them and then his eyes wander about the room. You want to get him to make eye contact for longer periods, so you need to prompt the behavior of looking at you when you're talking to him. So how do you prompt this behavior? Let's say one thing that works is saying loudly, "Johnny! Look at me!" But another thing that works is saying softly, "Johnny!" Which prompt do you use?

"The second one?"

Right. Eventually you want to fade the prompt completely, so you begin with the prompt that is closest to no prompt at all. You see?

"Yeah. You don't want to start at the bottom of the ladder if you can start on the third step."

That's a good way to put it. Okay, so you begin by selecting an appropriate prompt and prompting the behavior. Then you . . .

3. Prompt, reinforce, and fade.

The reason for prompting behavior is so that you can reinforce it. As I said before, if you repeatedly prompt a behavior and *don't* reinforce it, the prompt will no longer work, and getting the behavior to occur will be even more difficult. So reinforcement of the prompted behavior is fundamental.

This business of prompting and not reinforcing behavior is a fairly common mistake. Teachers and parents often say to a child, for example, "Look at me when I'm talking to you," but how often do they reinforce that behavior when it occurs? If you want to strengthen a behavior that rarely occurs, then you should prompt it and reinforce it.

Since the object of prompting is to get the behavior to appear so that you can reinforce it, it's important to give the person time to respond. So, after presenting the prompt, you wait several seconds, maybe as long as 10 seconds, before prompting again. If you prompt again and still don't get a response, you try a stronger prompt and wait again. You continue escalating, as necessary, until the target behavior occurs. Then you reinforce it.

Okay, so you prompt and reinforce the target behavior. You do this several times, of course, until the behavior occurs without hesitation at the prompt.[8] Now what? Carlotta?

"You begin to fade the prompt."

Right. You don't just drop the prompt. You present a prompt that is slightly weaker than the original but strong enough to produce the behavior. When the behavior occurs, you reinforce it. You prompt and reinforce, several times if necessary, to be sure that the behavior will occur immediately at the prompt. Then you reduce the strength of the prompt again. You keep at this, prompting, reinforcing, and fading until the behavior occurs without any prompt at all.

That's all there is to it, except for one last rule, which I hope you can guess. What is it, Maya?

"It must be, monitor the results."

It must indeed:

4. Monitor results.

You must always monitor the intervention so that you'll know whether you're progressing satisfactorily. Are you fading the prompt too quickly? Are you providing an effective reinforcer? If you don't monitor the results of your intervention closely, you won't know.

Prompting and fading are basically simple procedures, but they're not so simple that nothing can go wrong. Let's take a quick look at some of the problems that can arise.

Problems with Prompting and Fading

The goal of prompting and fading is to have the target behavior occur reliably in appropriate situations. You prompt the behavior in those situations so that you can reinforce it, and you fade the prompts so that you can get to the point at which the behavior occurs without special hints. To achieve that goal, you have to fade gradually, but what's gradually? When you reduce the prompt too much, the target behavior won't occur. If you use a prompt two or three times without effect, then you have to return to the previously effective prompt. You have to prompt and reinforce again, possibly several times, before trying to fade again. And this time when you fade, you have to reduce the prompt by less than you did before.

On the other hand, fading may take a very long time if you reduce the prompt strength by very small steps. You have to experiment a bit during the fading process to determine how rapidly you can fade the prompt.

Another problem arises if you reinforce the behavior too few times before you reduce the prompt. That can result in the behavior not occurring in response to the prompt.

> "So how many times should you reinforce the behavior at one prompt level before you modify the prompt again?"

A very good question, Midori. I wish I had a very good answer. Unfortunately, all I can say is that you continue reinforcing the behavior until it occurs reliably and without hesitation when you present the prompt. When it does, you're ready to reduce the prompt strength again. But I can't give you a simple definition of the terms *reliably* and *without hesitation*. Applied behavior analysis is a very young field, so a lot of these things have not been pinned down precisely. At this time, prompting and fading are a combination of science and art. Perhaps they always will be.

Now, how about a short review of today's lesson?

Review

What is a prompt, Midori?

> "A prompt is . . ."

Yes?

> "A prompt is an antecedent that . . ."

Yes, an antecedent that induces . . .

> "that induces a person to perform a behavior that otherwise does not occur."

Excellent. And once again Midori has helped me demonstrate the use of a prompt.

Okay. There are five kinds of prompts. Let's see if you can tell one from another. A boy enters a store, allowing the door to slam in the face of an old lady who's bent in the middle by osteoporosis. A young Republican sees the boy's rudeness and says, "Hey! Pus-face! Pick up that old lady and hold the door open for her." What sort of prompt is the young Republican using? Alfred?

"A threat? Just kidding. How about a verbal prompt?"

Right. And you're right, the young Republican probably is threatening the boy with bodily harm. You don't call someone "Pus-face" to put him at ease. So in this example, the prompt was a threat.

Now, when I was a boy, back in the days of black-and-white films, when you went to the movies they often included a sing-along segment. The words to the song would be displayed on the screen, and everybody in the theater would sing along. One of the songs was often "God Bless America." Anyway, to keep everybody together, the announcer would say, "Follow the bouncing ball." Then a little ball would appear over the first word or syllable you were supposed to sing, and it would bounce from word to word with the music. This prompted the appropriate behavior so that everyone sang together. The question is, what sort of prompt was the bouncing ball? Yes, Belinda?

"A gestural prompt?"

A gesture is something the teacher or trainer does. Who's making this gesture?

"Nobody; it's a bouncing ball. So . . . is it an environmental prompt?"

What do you think?

"Yeah, I think it is."

You may be right. Now, what if, instead of a bouncing ball, the theater manager came out onto the stage and used a long stick to point to the words. What sort of prompt would that be?

"Gestural?"

Yes, since the stick is really just a way of pointing.

Okay, new situation: Your Spanish teacher is teaching you various forms of greetings. She tells you that *hola* is Spanish for *hello,* then says, "What's the Spanish word for *hello*?" but you're unable to remember. She says, "Hoaaaa . . ." And you say, "*Hola*!" What sort of prompt is *Hoaaaa . . .*? Midori?

"A verbal prompt."

Right. Now, suppose the Spanish teacher says "Hoaaa . . ." and you still can't remember the word. So she says, "*Ho-la*." What sort of prompt is that?

"Well, it's still a verbal prompt."

Is it? Does anyone see any other possibilities? Yes, Brian?

"It could be considered modeling. She's demonstrating the behavior she wants performed."

Good point. So a prompt that uses words, or parts of words, is a verbal prompt; but if the words used are the behavior we want performed, then you could argue that the person is modeling the behavior. Now, how about this one—

"Wait. Which is it—a verbal prompt or modeling?"

You know, Brian, I think a teacher should leave some questions unanswered. It might force the student to do some thinking, so I'm just going to let you wonder about that one.

"In other words, he doesn't know."

Thank you, Alfred, for that vote of confidence. Now, prompting behavior is fine as far as it goes, but it doesn't go far enough. A prompt is like a crutch, and you don't want a person to be dependent on crutches if she can walk on her own. So, how do we avoid dependence on prompts? Carlotta?

"By fading them. You gradually reduce the strength of the prompt."

Right. So we speak of prompting and fading behavior. What are the three steps of prompting and fading? Yes, John?

"First, prompt the behavior. Second, reinforce the behavior when it occurs. Third, fade the prompt."

Good. You keep prompting and reinforcing the behavior, but you gradually reduce the strength of the prompt until finally the behavior occurs without a prompt.

Well, I think that's enough for today. Don't forget—

"The handouts! We don't need *that* prompt any more."

I'll try to remember that, Alfred.

◄ Exercises ►

Feed the Skeleton

I. Prompting and Fading
  A. Prompting means _____ .
    1. A prompt is a _____ .
    2. There are several kinds of prompts:
      a. V _____ prompts involve _____ .
      b. G _____ prompts involve _____ .
      c. P _____ prompts involve _____ .
      d. M _____ prompts involve _____ .
      e. E _____ prompts involve _____ .

B. Fading means _____ .

II. The rules for prompting and fading properly are:
   A. _____ .
   B. Identify _____ .
   C. Prompt _____ .
   D. _____ .

III. Problems
   A. One source of difficulty with prompting and fading is fading too

   _____ .

   B. Problems can also arise if _____ .

$$$ Contest $$$

THE MANUAL TYPEWRITER COMPANY invites you to offer your suggestions on how instruction in touch typing can be improved through the power of prompting and fading. In particular, we ask you to suggest how the keys on a typewriter might be modified so as to prompt the correct actions during the learning process. Also suggest how these prompts could be faded. Use your imagination! Don't worry about expense or practicality! Any suggestion, so long as it might work if implemented, qualifies. All suggestions will be carefully considered, and the person making the best suggestion will win **$10,000.** (Or a congratulatory letter, whichever seems in the best interests of MANUAL TYPE-WRITER COMPANY.)

Balancing Act

Harry's 7-year-old, Jill, is learning to ride a bicycle, and she's using a bike that has training wheels—two little wheels attached to the bike's rear wheel that keep the bike from tipping over. Now, Jill is zipping around pretty well, and it looks as if she doesn't need those wheels all the time. Harry considers the training wheels prompts, and he decides to fade them.

He raises the training wheels ¼ inch off the ground and then lets Jill ride the bike until she's having no problems. Then he raises the wheels another ¼ inch. Jill rides the bike some more, and when she is riding well, Harry raises the wheels another ¼ inch. After some additional practice, Harry removes the wheels entirely.

Do the training wheels act as prompts, and do the steps Harry took constitute fading? Why or why not?

Going Metric

There are good reasons the United States should switch to the metric system of weights and measurements, but the American people have been slow to adopt it. As an employee of your state's department of transportation, you have been asked to design signs that will get drivers to use kilometers rather than miles on the highways. What do you propose?

Practice Quiz

1. Prompting is the procedure of providing _____ that _____ a _____ behavior.

2. Instructions such as "put your left foot on the clutch" are examples of _____ prompts.

3. A fence is a kind of _____ prompt.

4. One mistake people often make in using prompting and fading is that they prompt the target behavior and then fail to _____ it.

5. Prompts should be provided only when the target behavior _____ _____ .

6. Fading means _____ of a prompt.

7. The golf instructor who pushes on a student's elbow to straighten the arm is using a kind of _____ prompt.

8. The text describes an autistic boy named Dicky. In an effort to teach him to speak normally, the teacher might show him a picture of a cat and say, _____ .

9. The text gives four rules for using prompting and fading. The second rule is to identify _____ .

10. _____ is a way of prompting behavior that may not work if the client or student has not learned to imitate others.

Reprint: RULES TO LIVE BY
by B. F. Skinner

Rules and instructions are a kind of prompt: "Always look both ways before crossing a street"; "Use i before e, except after c, and in sounding like a, as in neighbor and weigh"; "Go to the intersection and turn right; then go about three blocks. Look for the restaurant on your left." Such statements prompt behavior that is likely to be reinforced. Indeed, we learn to follow rules and instructions precisely because doing so usually has reinforcing consequences. Once we have learned to follow rules, we can often perform new forms of behavior, even though they have never been reinforced. We do not learn to use an automatic teller machine through "trial and error." We follow instructions that lead to success. Thus, Skinner argues, behavior may be strengthened by its consequences, or it may be prompted by verbal behavior. He calls these two kinds of behavior, "contingency-shaped" and "rule-governed." Here he discusses some of the differences between them.

A scientist may play billiards intuitively as a result of long experience, or he may determine masses, angles, distances, frictions, and so on, and calculate each shot.

He is likely to do the former, of course, but there are analogous circumstances in which he cannot submit to the contingencies in a comparable way and must adopt the latter. Both kinds of behavior are plausible, natural, and effective; they both show "knowledge of contingencies," and . . . they may have similar topographies. But they are . . . different operants. The difference appears when the scientist examines his behavior. In the first case he *feels* the rightness of the force and direction with which the ball is struck; in the second he feels the rightness of his calculations but not the shot itself. . . .

The behavior evoked by a rule is often simpler than the behavior shaped by the contingencies from which the rule is derived. The rule covers only the essentials; it may omit features which give contingency-shaped behavior its character. The sanctions which make a rule effective also often make the behavior "cold." Some rule-governed behavior, however, may be more complete and effective than contingency-shaped behavior. This is particularly the case when the contingencies are defective. . . . Few people drive a car at a moderate speed and keep their seat belts fastened because they have actually avoided or escaped from serious accidents by doing so. Rules derived from contingencies affecting large numbers of people bring these consequences to bear upon the individual. Ethical and legal consequences work synergically with the natural consequences which by themselves are ineffective. . . .

Many classical distinctions can be reduced to the distinction between rule-governed and contingency-shaped behavior.

(1) *Deliberation vs. impulse.* Deliberate or reasoned behavior is marked either by an examination of possibly relevant rules and the selection of one or more to be obeyed or by an examination of current contingencies and the derivation of a rule on the spot. Acting on impulse is not preceded by behavior of this sort.

(2) *Ultimate vs. proximate gains.* Rules tend to bring remote consequences into play; without rules only immediate consequences affect behavior.

(3) *Culture-bound vs. "natural" behavior.* Rules evolve with the culture and differ among cultures; behavior shaped by nonsocial contingencies is as universal as the contingencies. . . .

(7) *Logical argument vs. intuition.* The behavior shaped by the contingencies which arise as one solves a problem may yield a solution "intuitively." The solution appears, the problem is disposed of, and no one knows why. The intuitive mathematician will, however, probably be asked for a proof. He will be asked to supply rules which will lead others from a statement of the problem to the solution. . . .

(9) *Monotony vs. variety.* Rule-governed behavior is usually designed to satisfy contingencies, not to duplicate other features of the behavior shaped by

them. Contingency-shaped behavior is therefore likely to have a greater variety or richness.

(10) *Conscious vs. unconscious.* Since it is often the function of a rule to identify stimuli, responses, and their consequences, reasoned behavior is marked by reflection and awareness. . . .

(11) *Knowing vs. knowing how.* The knowledge which appears to be objectified in rules is owned or held by those who know the rules. Contingency-shaped behavior, simply as knowing how to do things, is less likely to suggest a prior form of possession. . . .

(16) *Reason vs. passion* (or vs. *instinct* or vs. *nature*). . . .

"The heart has its reasons which reason cannot know." Pascal may have been talking about reason and passion, but passion was not just emotion. . . . Pascal seems to be saying simply that rule-governed and contingency-shaped behavior are different and that the former cannot simulate all the latter. Contingencies contain reasons which rules can never specify.

Excerpted from "Differences Between Rule-governed and Contingency-shaped Behavior," by B. F. Skinner. In *Contingencies of Reinforcement: A Theoretical Analysis*, Appleton-Century-Croft, 1969. By permission of Julie S. Vargas, B. F. Skinner Foundation.

◂ Recommended Reading ▸

1. Bandura, A. (1971). Psychotherapy based on modeling principles. In A. E. Bergin & S. L. Garfield (Eds.), *Handbook of psychotherapy and behavior change* (pp. 653–708). New York: Wiley.
   Bandura is famous for his work on modeling.

2. Lovaas, O. I. (1966). A program for the establishment of speech in psychotic children. In J. K. Wing (Ed.), *Early childhood autism* (pp. 115–144). Oxford: Pergamon Press.
   Illustrates the use of physical guidance.

3. Pace, G. M. et al. (1994). Stimulus fading as treatment for obscenity in a brain-injured adult. *Journal of Applied Behavior Analysis, 27* (2), 301–305.
   Sometimes one consequence of head injury is the inappropriate use of language. This study used fading to deal with the problem.

4. Ziegler, S. G. (1987). Effects of stimulus cuing on the acquisition of ground strokes by beginning tennis players. *JABA, 20*, 405–411.
   Stimulus cuing is a form of prompting.

◂ **Endnotes** ▸

1. Donnellan et al. (1988) define a prompt as "assistance provided . . . to assure a correct response" (p. 160).

2. The tendency to imitate modeled behavior is so important that if it is not present, one of the first goals of an intervention will be to establish it. (See, for example, Baer et al., 1967.) When a person has learned not merely to imitate a particular behavior, but modeled behavior in general, behaviorists speak of *generalized imitation.*

3. By the way, this was one of those questions that was meant to prompt my reader to respond.

4. Fading can also be thought of as the gradual replacement of one antecedent event with another. For example, the antecedent "Say, Billy" is gradually replaced by the antecedent "What's your name?"

5. Wolf et al., 1964.

6. Wong & Woolsey (1989).

7. Wong & Woolsey (1989, p. 427).

8. At some point you may suspect that prompting is no longer necessary. If so, you may periodically omit the prompt or present it in very weak form. This is called a *probe.* If the person continues to perform the target behavior, you may conclude that prompting is no longer necessary.

5

Shaping and Chaining

Lᴇᴛ's ʙᴇɢɪɴ ᴛᴏᴅᴀʏ ᴡɪᴛʜ ᴀ ʜʏᴘᴏᴛʜᴇᴛɪᴄᴀʟ ᴘʀᴏʙʟᴇᴍ: Suppose you work in a retirement community named Sleepy Hollow. One of the residents is an octogenarian named Gilroy. Mr. Gilroy, a confirmed couch potato, has been told repeatedly by the facility's doctor that he needs to exercise more. Sleepy Hollow is equipped with an Olympic-size swimming pool, and Mr. Gilroy's doctor would love to see him swimming five days a week. You are the athletic director for Sleepy Hollow, and the doctor has asked you to encourage Mr. Gilroy to swim. You approach Mr. Gilroy and invite him to join a swimming class.

"Why would I want to do that?" shouts Mr. Gilroy, who is a little hard of hearing.

"It's fun!" you shout in return.

"No need to shout; I ain't deaf!" he shouts. Then he says, "I'm not interested," and he mumbles something about smart-mouthed kids. Since Mr. Gilroy refers to anyone under the age of 60 as a kid, you surmise he is referring to you.

You explain that his doctor would like him to get more exercise, that exercising would help him stay healthy. He replies that he is a lot older than you or the doctor and suggests that neither of you have any business giving people advice on being old until you've had some experience at it. You consider mentioning that the advice to exercise is based on research with old people, but decide against it; Mr. Gilroy, like most people, is not usually persuaded by scientific evidence.

Now, what do you do about Mr. Gilroy? Yes, Jamal?

"Reinforce swimming: Find something Mr. Gilroy likes, and provide it whenever he goes swimming."

He doesn't go swimming. *Ever.* He never goes near the pool. He rarely gets any sort of exercise beyond walking from his room to the dining hall and back.

"Maybe you could prompt the behavior. You know, you might say, 'Let's go swimming, Mr. Gilroy!'"

You tried prompting the behavior six ways to Sunday; it didn't work.

"But you can't reinforce behavior if it never occurs."[1]

An astute observation, Midori. Behavior has to occur in order for it to be reinforced. So, if it doesn't occur, it can't be reinforced.

"So you're saying the problem can't be solved with reinforcement?"

No, Midori, I'm saying we can only reinforce behavior that occurs. Often, that is enough. Did you ever play the game, "Hot and Cold"?

"Sure. That's where you hide something and then other people have to try to find it. Whenever they go near it, you say, 'You're getting warmer' and when they move away from it, you say, 'You're getting colder.' When they get real close, you yell, 'You're hot!'"

Almost everybody who grew up in this country has played "Hot and Cold" at least once. It's a fun game that uses reinforcement.[2] What is the reinforcer, Belinda?

"Words like *warmer* and *hot*?"

Of course. Those words tell you you're getting close to the goal. What about *cold* and *colder*? Are they reinforcers?

"No."

Right. They make the behavior less likely to occur. Let's forget about *cold* and *colder.* We can help someone find something without pointing out the mistakes; all we have to do is reinforce steps in the right direction.

"I don't see what this has to do with Mr. Gilroy. Are you suggesting that we yell 'Hot' every time he walks toward the pool?"

In a manner of speaking, Alfred, that's just what I'm suggesting. We've talked about increasing or decreasing the frequency of behavior by modifying the consequences of the behavior. But there are lots of times when the behavior we want to reinforce never occurs, or occurs only very rarely. Mr. Gilroy never goes swimming, so we can't reinforce swimming. But when you play "Hot and Cold," you don't wait for the person to go to where the prize is and then yell "Hot." If you did, the searcher might never find it. You reinforce behavior that takes the person *in the right direction.* In other words, you start with what the person does and build on that toward the behavior you want. This process is called *shaping.*

Shaping Defined

Shaping is used when the target behavior does not yet exist. In shaping, what is reinforced is some approximation of the target behavior:

Shaping:
The reinforcement of successive
approximations of a target behavior.[3]

By *approximation* I mean any behavior that resembles the desired behavior or takes the person closer to the desired behavior. Successive approximations are steps toward the target behavior, the behavior you want to shape.

In playing "Hot and Cold," you reinforce any movement that takes the player closer to the prize. Each of those successive movements is a closer approximation of the desired behavior. Suppose the player is in the middle of a room, facing south, and the prize is under the seat cushion on a chair that is against the north wall. What is it that you want the person to do? Maya?

"Move to the north?"

Exactly. Any movement toward the north is an approximation of the desired behavior and should be reinforced. Let's say the person turns his head to the left. As soon as he does, you yell "Hot." Next he turns so that he is facing east; you yell, "Hot." He steps forward, toward the east wall. Do you say "Hot?" John?

"No."

Why not?

"Because that takes him east; moving in that direction doesn't get him closer to the chair, which is on the north wall."

Right. Next he turns to the right. Do you say "Hot?"

"No. That takes him south."

Very good. Now he turns to his left, and you yell "Hot" because once again he's turning toward the north. When he's facing north, you reinforce any movement forward until you have him standing in front of the chair. Now what do you reinforce? Yes, Brian?

"Any movement toward the cushion."

Such as?

"Such as bending over or moving a hand toward the cushion."

Okay, but what if he doesn't bend over or move a hand toward the cushion?

"Well, he might look down at the chair. I could reinforce that."

Good. Each step that gets the person closer to the desired behavior is a successive approximation of that behavior. You can think of the shaping process as a matter of reinforcing a series of sequential steps toward the target behavior. We reinforce steps along the way, not because we want to establish those steps, but because by reinforcing those steps the person then becomes more likely to perform the *next* step, the next approximation of the target behavior. What you—

"How big should these steps be?"

That's a very good question, Belinda, for which I don't have a very good answer. Shaping is as much an art as it is a science. The behavior you are most likely to get after providing reinforcement is the behavior you just reinforced. If you don't reinforce that behavior again, the person may return to the *previously* reinforced behavior. In other words, he may go backward. So, the general rule of thumb is that you should reinforce any behavior that is a closer approximation of the target behavior than the behavior you reinforced last. However, if a new approximation does not occur, you reinforce the last approximation again. If an approximation is repeated and reinforced three times, withhold reinforcement the next time that behavior appears; often this will induce the person to try some new things, and one of the new things is apt to be a closer approximation of the target behavior.

If no new approximation appears, you have to drop back to a previously reinforced behavior. Sometimes you will get good progress for a while, only to have the person emit a behavior that was reinforced several steps before. You may then have to reinforce that old behavior and shape through the sequence again.

The shaping procedure is rather like helping someone up a staircase. Sometimes progress is fast and effortless, but other times progress is slow and difficult. Sometimes the person may leap over the next step; then he may turn and go down the stairs a few steps and you have to help him up those same steps again. So, while the procedure is simple, it is not always easy to implement. Yet a skilled shaper can accomplish some remarkable feats. Let's look at some examples of shaping at work.

Illustrative Studies

Steve, the Stutterer

A study by Henry Rickard and Martha Mundy used shaping to treat stuttering.[4] They worked with a bright, 9-year-old boy I'll call Steve.

Steve had been stuttering for about 5 years. He had received speech therapy off and on for 2 years, but his stuttering was very pronounced. The researchers defined the problem as repetition errors. For instance, if the boy said "g-g-g-going," he had made three repetition errors. The goal, then, was to reduce the frequency of these errors. This was to be accomplished by reinforcing stutter-free speech.

At first, the boy had only to read short phrases printed on cards. The researchers provided positive feedback and praise whenever he read without errors, but they later supplemented these reinforcers with ice cream. The reinforcers were contingent on meeting certain standards of performance, with the standards increasing slowly as the youngster progressed.

In the next stage of treatment, the boy practiced reading sentences. He earned one point for each sentence read perfectly; the points could later be exchanged for a prize. The sentences averaged six words in length and were composed of fourth-grade level words.

Next, Steve moved on to reading paragraphs. Each paragraph consisted of a poem, joke, short story, or fable. Again, he earned one point each time he read a card without a repetition error.

Reading is not the same thing as talking, so once Steve was reading substantially without repetition errors, it was time to try conversational speech. This stage of treatment proved more difficult than you might think. Rickard and Mundy started by showing Steve ambiguous pictures and asking him to make up a story about them. They also asked him to tell stories he had heard. Then the therapist simply engaged the boy in conversation; if he talked for 5 minutes without a repetition error, he earned points. This worked for a while, but the boy soon ran out of things to say. Someone then suggested that the researchers provide bonus points periodically. The researchers arranged to have a buzzer sound at random intervals, and if the boy happened to be talking when the buzzer sounded, he received bonus points. This additional reinforcement helped, and when Steve was speaking well for short periods, the researchers began providing additional points for longer periods of errorless speech.

Steve showed marked improvement in the various reading exercises, and further testing left no doubt that he was much improved. Conversational stuttering also diminished, though not as much.

This treatment made good use of shaping. It began with phrases and progressed to . . . to what, Jamal?

"Sentences."

And from sentences to . . .

"Short passages—poems, jokes, little stories. And from that they went to conversational speech."

Right. There was a series of successive approximations of the target behavior, which was reading and speaking without repetition errors. You can see from this study that shaping is a useful tool, but you can't really appreciate the power of shaping until you see what it can accomplish with the most difficult behavior problems.

Chuck, the Hopeless One

Chuck was a profoundly psychotic 6-year-old: He did not play; he spent a good deal of his time engaged in self-stimulatory behavior, such as rocking back and forth; he did not interact with others; he sometimes engaged in head banging or other self-injurious behavior. Although Chuck occasionally made vocal sounds, he did not speak at all, and did not imitate the speech or other actions of others.

Ivar Lovaas and his colleagues decided to see if they could teach Chuck to imitate adult speech. Imitation is extremely important in learning language and other skills, so if they could teach Chuck to imitate words, this would raise the possibility that he would make additional progress toward normality.

The shaping effort took Chuck through a sequence of steps, or successive approximations, of imitative speech. The first step involved reinforcing any sort of vocalization Chuck might make. Social rewards, such as eye contact and praise, were not effective reinforcers for Chuck, so the trainer provided a single spoonful of food as a reinforcer. The trainer sat opposite Chuck and provided a spoonful of food each time he made the slightest vocal sound. Since imitating speech is easier if the child looks at the trainer's mouth, Chuck also received food whenever he looked at the trainer's mouth. When Chuck was making some sort of vocal sound about once every 5 seconds and was looking at the trainer's mouth more than 50% of the time, training progressed to step two.

The goal of step two was to get Chuck to respond vocally in response to the trainer's vocalization. The trainer would make some sort of vocal sound about once every 10 seconds. Chuck continued to receive a spoonful of food for vocalizing, but only if he made the sound within 6 seconds after the adult had vocalized. Chuck wasn't required to make the same sound the trainer made; he simply had to make some sort of vocal sound within the time limit. When Chuck was meeting this criterion fairly regularly, it was time to move on to step three.

Step three was similar to step two except that Chuck now had to make the *same* sound the trainer made. The trainer helped him do this by providing prompts, such as exaggerating the movements of the lips made in making a sound, such as *emmmm*. The trainer also used sounds that Chuck himself had been heard to make often. The trainer might say *emmmm*, and if Chuck then said *emmm*, he received a bit of food. When Chuck had mastered this step, the trainer added new sounds, then words, then phrases.

The training was intense: 7 hours a day, 6 days a week. But after 26 days of training, Chuck was imitating new words and phrases with ease and had the foundation skills necessary to begin using language in a communicative way.

That may not seem like much of an accomplishment to you, because you could teach similar skills to ordinary 6-year-olds without shaping. But you have to remember that Chuck was no ordinary 6-year-old; he was utterly psychotic. At the time of this study, children like Chuck were often confined to a psychiatric hospital where they got nothing more than custodial care their entire lives. Lovaas and his colleagues demonstrated that with shaping and other procedures, such children can be helped.

All right, let's consider one more study of shaping. This one you'll see is a little different than the others.

Matilda, the Clotheshorse

Teodoro Ayllon used a kind of shaping in the treatment of a 47-year-old schizophrenic woman in a hospital setting.[5] I'll call her Matilda.

Matilda exhibited various forms of bizarre behavior, among them a tendency to put on extra items of clothing. We are not talking here about a person who wore an extra sweater; we're talking about a person who wore 18 pairs of stockings, multiple layers of undergarments, 6 or 7 dresses, several sweaters, and a shawl or two. She then wrapped herself up in sheets, and topped off this display of sartorial splendor with a kind of headdress made of towels. Matilda also carried two or three cups in one hand and a bundle of clothing and a large purse in the other.

To determine how much extra clothing Matilda was wearing, Ayllon had the nurses weigh her before each meal and then subtracted this figure from her actual body weight. This was done over a period of 2 weeks to obtain a baseline, and revealed that she typically wore about 25 pounds of clothing—about 22 or 23 pounds of excess clothes. The goal, of course, was to have her wearing just a few pounds of clothing, as most people do. That was the target behavior.

Ayllon decided that food might reinforce the shedding of excess clothing, so he made access to the dining hall contingent on meeting certain requirements concerning clothing. Before she could enter the dining hall, she had to step onto a scale. At first she was given a "clothing allowance" of 23 pounds: She could weigh in at up to 23 pounds more than her body weight. If she was over that limit, the nurse told her, "Sorry, you weigh too much; you'll have to weigh less." At that point, she could remove a few articles of clothing to meet the limit and enter the dining hall; otherwise she would be turned away and would miss a meal.

It might seem a little cruel to deny a person food, even as a treatment for such bizarre behavior. But in fact Matilda was dangerously overweight, so the prospect of her missing some meals was not viewed with alarm by the medical staff. As it happens, she missed only a few meals at the start of the program.

What happened? Just what you would expect: Matilda started shedding clothes. At first she left behind the cups and bundles of clothes she had carried in her arms. Next she abandoned the towel turban and the various sheets and shawls.

Sometimes in attempting to meet the weight requirement, Matilda would show up wearing fewer pounds of clothing than she was permitted. When this happened, the new figure became the weight limit from then on. Thus, the standard she had to meet changed as closer approximations of the target behavior appeared.

And so it went. Eventually, she weighed in wearing a dress, undergarments, one pair of stockings, and shoes. Her clothing weight had fallen from 25 pounds to 3 pounds.

At the beginning of the program Matilda engaged in some emotional outbursts: crying, shouting, and throwing chairs around. This behavior was ignored, however, and soon disappeared. A positive side effect of the program was that as she began dressing normally, she also began to participate in small social events in the hospital. Previously she had been something of a recluse, remaining in her room most of the day. In addition, her parents visited and insisted on taking her home for a visit. That was the first time in 9 years Matilda's parents had asked to take her home.

Now, the studies I've just described should give you some idea of the range of uses to which shaping can be put. It's a very powerful procedure if used properly. Let's consider some guidelines for its proper use.

Rules for Shaping

I assume you know what the first rule is . . . John?

"I'll take a wild guess and say it's define the target behavior."

What a clever lad! Yes, you're right. When shaping is involved, some people refer to the target behavior as the *terminal* or *goal behavior.* The reason, I suppose, is that the behavior you want doesn't actually occur yet; it's the goal that appears only at the end of the process, hence the terms *goal* or *terminal behavior.* But I see no reason to use a new term so I'll stick with *target behavior.* So, our first rule is:

1. Define the target behavior.

The first step in shaping is to decide what behavior is to be "shaped up." What is it you want the person to be doing at the end of the shaping procedure? For example, you might want Mr. Gilroy to go to the pool on his own at least three times a week and spend a half-hour or more propelling himself through the water. To get to the target behavior, we have to have a very clear idea of what it is. Once you've identified the target behavior, you're ready to . . .

2. Reinforce successive approximations of the target behavior.

Something the person currently does can be said to resemble the target behavior to some degree. You shape up a target behavior by reinforcing the nearest approximations of that behavior.

There is a classic demonstration of shaping in which behaviorists got a schizophrenic man to speak.[6] This fellow was a catatonic schizophrenic, and he had been mute for 19 years. He not only didn't talk, he didn't communicate with people in any way. He was fond of chewing gum, however, and he would follow a stick of gum with his eyes. That was the nearest approximation he made to speaking, and the behaviorists began by reinforcing that behavior. Yes, Belinda?

"I don't see how looking at a stick of gum is an approximation of talking."

Where do you usually look when you talk to someone?

"At their face?"

Right. If you're going to talk to someone, you usually look at them. And in order to look at them, you have to turn toward them. By turning his head, this fellow was emitting part of the behavior involved in talking with someone. The similarity between following a stick of gum with one's eyes and talking to someone is pretty weak, but it was the nearest approximation of the target behavior in this person's repertoire, so it became the therapist's starting point.

When you have reinforced the nearest approximation of the target behavior, other approximations of the behavior will usually appear. Some of these approximations will be even closer to the target behavior. You reinforce the nearest approximations of the target behavior as they appear. Shaping is rather like helping someone up a ladder or a staircase. Each step up the ladder is reinforced—

> "But if you're reinforcing what they're doing at a particular step, why would they move on? Why wouldn't they just keep performing that same behavior over and over?"

That's a good question, Midori. An important characteristic of behavior is its variability; we never do anything exactly the same way twice.[7] It is this fact that makes shaping possible. You look for variations that are closer approximations to the target behavior, and you reinforce those variations.

For instance, if you say to a 2-year-old, "Say cookie," and you do this three times, you will get three slightly different answers. His three answers might be *cuck, ook,* and *cook.* In this case, the last attempt is a closer approximation of "cookie" than the others. You might reinforce all three of these efforts, but once he says *cook,* you hold out for that. You don't reinforce *cuck* and *ook* once he has said *cook.* If he says *cook* again he gets a bit of cookie, otherwise he gets nothing. Before long *cuck* and *ook* will drop out, but his behavior will still vary. Eventually he will say something that sounds a bit more like *cookie* than *cook* does. He might say something like, *cookay.* As soon as this next approximation occurs, you reinforce that. From now on, saying *cook* is no longer acceptable; he has to say *cookay.* But he won't always say *cookay* the same way. Before long he will say something that sounds a bit more like *cookie.* Once he does, you reinforce that, but no longer reinforce *cookay.* And so on. You use the natural tendency for variability in behavior. You look for variations that more closely resemble the target behavior. When they occur, you reinforce them, and you no longer reinforce behavior that used to be acceptable.[8] If a person—

> "This sounds something like evolution."

That's a very astute observation, Carlotta. Shaping is a lot like evolution.[9] Evolution depends on variation and natural selection. Some variations have favorable consequences for the species and are selected; they live on. Similarly, the shaping of behavior depends on variation and selection. Some variations in behavior have favorable (reinforcing) consequences and are selected; they live on. I suppose the major difference between evolution and shaping is that the latter often involves an agent, the behavior shaper, while evolution is an unplanned phenomenon. Of course, shaping may also occur naturally without any person's deliberate intervention, as when you learn to keep your balance on a bicycle, and a sort of artificial evolution is involved when, for example, an orchid enthusiast crosses specific varieties to produce new hybrids.

If a person gets "stuck" at a particular step, repeating the same level of performance over and over again, you can usually induce variability in behavior by withholding reinforcement. Some of the new behavior will be in the direction you want the behavior to go, and can be reinforced. So, if you're teaching Little Johnny to say "cookie," and he gets to where he can say "kuck" easily but never provides anything better, then you stop reinforcing *kuck* until he makes another step forward. He might eventually say, "kuck-ee" or "cook." Either is a step in the right direction, and should be reinforced. You have a question, Brian?

> "So when Little Johnny comes up with something better, you reinforce that. How many times do you reinforce that behavior before you withhold reinforcement to induce variability?"

A good question, Brian. Unfortunately, I don't think anybody knows the answer. If I reinforce a new approximation once and then hold out for something better, Johnny might revert to some inferior version of *cookie* that was reinforced yesterday. That means he's going in the wrong direction. On the other hand, if I reinforce an approximation too many times, then I may not see better approximations of the target behavior. Perhaps the best rule of thumb to follow is: Reinforce an approximation several times or until a closer approximation appears, whichever comes first; if no new approximation has appeared after several reinforcements, withhold reinforcement until a new approximation occurs.

Now, if all goes well, the person will progress rapidly up the ladder. But shaping is as much an art as it is a science, and there are no clear cut guidelines to follow concerning *when* to raise the requirements for reinforcement, or how *much* to raise them. In general, shaping progresses more rapidly when the increases in the requirements for reinforcement are small. When you hold out for something better, the something better should be only a very slight improvement. If an approximation appears that is a big advance, reinforce it; but don't hold out for big advances. Remember that a lot of small improvements add up to a big improvement.

You have to make judgments about when to raise the ante and by how much, and sometimes you will be wrong. If you err on the side of caution, reinforcing behavior at a given step more often than is necessary and making very small increases in the requirements for reinforcement, the worse that is likely to happen is that progress will be slow. If you make the mistake of moving too quickly, then progress will stop and you may see some strong emotional reactions. If you expect too much of the child who is learning to say "cookie," for example, you may have a very upset child on your hands.

"So what do you do then?"

Well, if progress breaks down, you can move back to a previous level. This is sometimes called a *backstep*. Obviously, you want to be moving forward, toward the target behavior. But if you get stalled, you may have to take a backstep in order to go forward again. If you find yourself having to take numerous back-steps, it's a pretty good bet that your requirements for reinforcement are too high; in other words, your *forward steps* are too large.[10] You should—

"I *still* don't see how this gets a mute catatonic to talk."

Why not, Belinda?

"Well, I can see how you can begin by reinforcing eye movements, and then eye contact. But once he's looking at the therapist, it seems like progress would end. If he talked nonsense, I can see how you might shape talking sensibly. But if he doesn't vocalize at all, I don't see how the therapist has anything to work with. How did they do it?"

You really want to know?

"Yes."

Then read the original article. The lead author is Isaacs; the reference is in the recommended reading list you'll get later. It's a good article.

"Why don't you just tell us how they did it?"

Because of Sherlock Holmes. Sherlock Holmes observed that once he had revealed how he had solved a problem, people were apt to think the solution was obvious. Just common sense. People are the same way about behavior science: Once the solution to a behavior problem is explained, it seems obvious. Because of this, I like to leave students hanging now and then, in hopes that they may appreciate the difficulties involved in solving these "simple" problems. So, if you really want to know how the therapists got from eye movements to speech, read the article—or figure it out for yourself. Now for rule number 3:

3. Monitor results.

The only way you can gauge how successful you are being at shaping behavior is by noting what changes in behavior are occurring. Are you seeing progress toward the target behavior? Is the behavior that occurs *now* closer to the target behavior than the behavior you got earlier? Is it time to hold out for a closer approximation of the target behavior? Has the behavior begun to break down?

Should you take a backstep? These are questions you must ask while shaping behavior, and you can answer them only if you are paying close attention to changes in behavior.

As a practical matter, it is difficult to shape behavior and, at the same time, keep track of the number of new approximations that have been reinforced and the number of times you've had to back up. And it is usually not necessary to record changes in behavior during shaping. However, it *is* necessary to monitor your progress. If progress is slow, or if you find yourself repeatedly having to reinforce older steps again, then it is likely that your steps are too large. That is, you are probably not reinforcing small enough steps. That is probably the most common error made in shaping: failing to reinforce a new approximation that is only slightly better than the last reinforced approximation. Remember that so long as you are reinforcing closer approximations to the target behavior, you are making progress. Even very small steps will reach the target behavior in surprisingly little time. So, when it comes to approximations, think small.

Today's topics are shaping and chaining. We've talked about shaping; now let's look at chaining.

Chaining Defined

Sometimes—quite often, in fact—the new behavior you want to build is a series, or chain, of behaviors. A behavior chain is a series of related behaviors that produce reinforcement. Here, I'll put a definition on the board:

> **Behavior chain:**
> **A sequence of related behaviors, each of which provides the cue for the next, and the last of which produces a reinforcer.**

Actually, almost everything we do can be considered part of a behavior chain. Tying your shoes, for example, can be thought of as a series of separate acts, beginning with holding the laces in your hands, then pulling them, crossing them, turning one lace under the other, pulling them tight, and so on. We think of tying our shoes as one act, but it's really a series of acts, a chain. Tying your shoes is part of a larger chain, called putting your shoes on. Putting your shoes on is part of a larger chain called getting dressed. Getting dressed is often part of a larger chain called getting ready to go out. And so on.

Each step in a behavior chain serves as a cue for the next step. In fact, you can think of a behavior chain as a series of signals and behaviors. The completion of one behavior in a chain produces the signal for the next action. When you pull the laces on your shoes, for example, the tight laces provides the signal for the next step, crossing the laces. When you see the laces crossed, that provides the signal for the next step, and so on. Each behavioral link in a chain provides the signal for the next link.

Practically everything we do in the way of operant behavior is part of a chain, or a multitude of chains: eating, getting dressed, using a telephone, reciting the alphabet, writing a letter, ordering food in a restaurant, driving a car, going on vacation, swimming. Practically any complex behavior you can think of can be thought of as a behavior chain. So behavior chains are pretty important. The procedure for building chains, called chaining, is also important:

Chaining:
The reinforcement of successive elements of a behavior chain.

If you are attempting to teach a youngster how to tie his shoes, you are attempting to build a chain. If you are teaching a student how to write a business letter or solve an algebra word problem, you are attempting to build a behavior chain. If you are training a worker to operate a piece of machinery, you are attempting to build a behavior chain. If you are working with a retarded man who can't dress himself, you are attempting to build a chain. And you will probably be more successful in all of these and similar efforts if you use chaining.

Forward Chaining
There are two chaining procedures, forward chaining and backward chaining. *Forward chaining,* as the name implies, starts at the beginning and moves forward:

Forward chaining:
A chaining procedure that begins with the first element in the chain and progresses to the last element.

In forward chaining, you start with the first task in the chain. Once the person is able to perform that element satisfactorily, you have him perform the *first and second* elements and reinforce this effort. Notice that you don't just go from the first to the second element. The second element isn't performed unless the first element has been performed.

When the first two elements can be done competently, you have the person perform the first three elements, and so on. You don't teach the elements in isolation from one another; you teach them as part of a series, a chain.

Backward Chaining
Forward chaining is often a very effective way of developing complex sequences of behavior, but another approach also works very well. This approach is called *backward chaining.* Forward chaining starts with the first component and works forward; backward chaining starts with the last component and works backward:

Backward chaining: A chaining procedure that begins with the last element in the chain and progresses to the first element.

Backward chaining is counterintuitive. It's not something you'd ordinarily think of, and it probably sounds like something that wouldn't work. In fact, however, it's often more effective than forward chaining.

"I'm confused, Dr. Cee."

What are you confused about, John?

"If the person learns the tasks in reverse order, then he's going to do the chain backward. It doesn't make sense."

You're right, John, it doesn't make sense. But that's not what you do in backward chaining. It's true that you teach the elements in reverse order, but your student always performs them in the proper order. So, if you're teaching a brain-injured person to wash his hands, you hand him a towel and have him return it to the rack. When he has mastered that task, you have him wipe his hands with the towel (even though they aren't wet) and then *return it to the rack*. When he does these last two components of the task without hesitation, you back up one more task, and so on. You teach the tasks in reverse order, but your student is always performing them in the correct sequence.

Another example might help. One of the longest words in the English language is *antidisestablishmentarianism*. If I asked you to teach an average 9-year-old how to spell this word, you'd probably protest that it's too hard. That's because most people would attempt to teach the word as one behavior, instead of a behavior chain—a series of tasks. If you analyze the chain, you might identify 28 discrete components, since there are 28 letters to be written in sequence. If the child has learned some phonics, you might identify 11 components, one for each syllable. Knowing phonics makes spelling easier because it reduces the number of tasks in spelling chains. Let's assume that our pupil has learned some phonics, so we need to teach him to perform the 11 components of the behavior chain known as an-ti-dis-es-tab-lish-ment-ar-i-an-ism. Where do we begin?

We could begin by teaching him to write the first component. We could write "___-ti-dis-es-tab-lish-ment-ar-i-an-ism" on a blackboard, say the word, and ask him to write the first syllable. When he writes *an* we praise him, or tell him he's right. If he has any difficulty, we might repeat this stage until he writes *an* without hesitation. When he has the first component mastered, we go on to the second component: We erase *an* and the next syllable so that he is presented with "__ __ -dis-es-tab-lish-ment-ar-i-an-ism." Now he has to write *anti*. When he is able to do that without difficulty, we erase the third syllable, so he is presented with "__ __ ___-es-tab-lish-ment-ar-i-an-ism." And so on. Notice that each time he learns a new syllable, he writes it after the preceding syllables. If you teach spelling this way, you're using what procedure—Midori?

"Forward chaining?"

Right. Now, to teach the same task with backward chaining, you would do the same thing except you would start at the other end of the word and go backward. So you would write *an-ti-dis-es-tab-lish-ment-ar-i-an-ism* on the board, and then you would erase the last syllable, *ism*. You'd ask your student to fill in the missing letters, and you'd reinforce a correct effort. You'd repeat the process until she is able to write *ism* without hesitation. Then you'd present her with an-ti-dis-es-tab-lish-ment-ar-i-___ ___, and she'd have to provide the missing letters, *anism*. Notice that even though you've started at the end of the word, your student is spelling the word in the correct order. You would keep backing up in this way until you had only to say, "Spell *antidisestablishmentarianism*," and she would write the word without hesitation—to the amazement of herself and her parents.

Of course, there's no reason you couldn't teach a task like this to an entire class of students at the same time. You might want to have them spell the word aloud together, since it might be easier to monitor their oral behavior than their written behavior in this situation, but the basic procedure is the same.

Notice that you provide reinforcement at the end of the performance. So, if one syllable is missing, the student is praised when she correctly fills it in; when three syllables are missing, you praise her when she has filled in the missing three syllables. When she has mastered the entire chain, the reinforcer she receives (perhaps a word of praise or just the feedback, "That's right") is delivered when she finishes writing the word.

Now let's look at a study that used chaining to solve a behavior problem.

Illustrative Study

Howard Walks to School

Barbara Gruber and her colleagues used chaining, in conjunction with other procedures, to train four institutionalized adult men to walk from their living quarters to a school about 1000 feet away on the institution's grounds.[11] All four young men were profoundly retarded, with IQ scores ranging from 8 to 14. They also engaged in various forms of bizarre behavior, such as facial contortions, spinning in circles, slapping or hitting themselves, and hitting or scratching others. They had mastered basic self-help skills, such as dressing themselves, but occasionally had toileting accidents. The brightest of the men could utter a few words or phrases; the slowest made only meaningless sounds. None of the men could walk from the living quarters to the institutional school unattended. When instructed to "go to school," they typically wandered off the route. For the sake of simplicity, I'll focus my attention on Howard, one of the slower members of the group.

The intervention was more complicated than it will seem from my description, because I want to focus on the role of chaining. Training began by escorting Howard to the front door of the living quarters and saying to him, "Howard, go to school." The trainer then escorted Howard to the school, frequently praising his efforts by saying things such as, "Good walking, that's the way!" If Howard stopped walking or wandered off course he was prompted to continue on the correct path by, for example, giving him a gentle push on the arm to move him in the right direction. When Howard reached school, the trainer praised him and gave him a food treat and then escorted him back to the living quarters.

The next stage of training consisted of testing Howard's ability to reach the school without help from various points along the way. The idea behind these tests was to avoid spending time on unnecessary training: If Howard had been able to get to the school from, say, 250 feet away, then training could have begun at that point.[12] Unfortunately, Howard (like the other three men) failed these tests and had to begin training at the school entrance.

The next stage of training involved chaining. Beginning near the school, the trainer told Howard to go to school. As Howard walked off, the trainer, who did not accompany him, watched his progress. If Howard wandered off the course, the trainer would catch up to him, instruct him to go to school, and nudge him in the right direction if necessary. When Howard reached the school he was met in the lobby by another trainer who praised him enthusiastically for walking to school and gave him a food treat. The trainers repeated this procedure until Howard performed successfully on three consecutive trials. Once Howard met this criterion he was escorted to a point 50 feet farther from the school and training resumed from that point. In this way, Howard gradually made his way to school from farther and farther away until he was finally able to walk from the living quarters to the school without assistance. This is, of course, a chaining procedure. Which kind of chaining is it, Jamal?

"It must be backward chaining."

Why must it be backward chaining?

"Because Howard is starting at the end point and the training progresses backward toward the beginning."

Good. That's correct. Now, the researchers don't tell us Howard's IQ, but we know it's very low. We also know about the lack of language skills and the bizarre behavior. So, given this information, how long do you think it took Howard to learn to walk from the living quarters to the school by himself? What do you think, Carlotta?

"I don't have any idea. Three months?"

What do you think, Brian?

"Howard had to begin training right at the school, so I'd say it must have taken a long time. Six months, maybe longer."

I have a graph based on information provided in the article. I'll put that on the overhead projector:

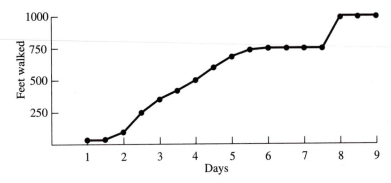

Figure 5-1. *Independent walking. The greatest distance Howard walked to school each day. Adapted from Gruber et al. (1979).*

What does this graph tell you, Alfred?

"It tells me that the two class brains are not always right."

Can you be a little more specific, and a little less personal?

"The graph shows that Howard was walking the entire distance on his own in a little over a week."

That's right. The graph shows the greatest distance from which Howard walked to the school on each day. By the 9th day, he was able to walk to school all the way from the living quarters. In those 9 days, Howard had a total of 17 training sessions. Two of the residents learned faster than Howard, one learned more slowly. The men mastered the task in 4 to 15 days. Even 4 days is a long time to train someone to find their way between two buildings 1000 feet apart. But keep in mind that this training gave these men a certain degree of autonomy; they no longer had to be escorted to school. This is something that might never have been accomplished without the use of chaining.

Ordinarily, teaching students to find their way to school and back does not require the systematic use of chaining. However, there are times when even very bright children need some help in learning a chain. The rules for using chaining successfully are similar to those for using shaping.

Rules for Chaining

1. Define the target behavior.

To teach someone to perform the links of a chain, you need to know exactly what those links are. Sometimes the components of a chain are fairly obvious, and you have only to write them down. The chain known as hand washing, for example, consists of:

1. Turning on the faucet

2. Wetting the hands

3. Turning off the faucet

4. Picking up the soap

5. Lathering the hands

6. Putting the soap back

7. Turning on the faucet

8. Rinsing the hands

9. Turning off the faucet

10. Picking up a towel

11. Drying the hands

12. Returning the towel

Other times the links of a chain may not be so obvious, and you may have to call on the help of experts in the area. For example, if your assignment is to develop a program for training new workers on an assembly line, you may need to interview current line workers as well as observe them as they work. Or, if you need to teach a diabetic person how to administer insulin to himself with a syringe, you may need to speak to a diabetic person who uses insulin and to nurses and doctors who treat such patients. You will probably also need to observe diabetics self-injecting insulin.

This sort of *task analysis,* as it is called, may seem unnecessarily tedious, and it is not necessary in every situation.[13] Normal kids, for example, will typically pick up the hand washing chain simply by watching adults perform it—especially if their efforts are reinforced by adult attention and praise. But what if the child is blind? What if she is retarded? What if the person you're teaching is a former college student whose head collided with a windshield on the ride home from a drinking party? People who have had head injuries often have difficulty performing simple, everyday behavior chains. You might take a brain-injured person to the bathroom, have him stand in front of the sink, and say to him, "John, wash your hands." And he may have no idea how to begin. In situations like these, you need to have a very clear idea exactly what the components of the chain are. In fact, the hand washing chain I have described may not be detailed enough for some people. You may, for example, have to treat turning on a faucet as a chain in itself, and you may have to build that chain before you can work on the longer chain.

Once you have a very clear idea about the elements of the chain you want to build, you are ready to . . .

2. Reinforce successive elements of the chain.

The elements in a behavior chain must be reinforced in sequence. Of course, first you have to get an element to appear, and that may require shaping. In some cases, each link in the chain will have to be shaped up. When you have shaped up one element and reinforced it, you go on to the next. You continue shaping and reinforcing elements until all components of the chain have been mastered.

So, we've got a sequence of behaviors, links in the chain, that we want to reinforce:

$$B1 \ldots B2 \ldots B3 \ldots B4 \ldots B5 \ldots B6$$

What you learn in a chain is not just a number of discrete tasks; you learn to perform those tasks *in the right order.*

You can start at the beginning of the chain and work your way to the end. Or you can accomplish the same thing with backward chaining, in which case you would start . . . where?

"With the last link—putting the towel away."

Right. Okay. So, whether you go forward or backward, you're reinforcing successive links in the chain. The third rule is . . . Jamal?

"Monitor results."

Exactly:

3. Monitor results.

As with any intervention, you must keep track of the effects of your efforts. Has a particular element been mastered? Should it be performed and reinforced a few more times? Is it time to move on to the next element? These are judgments that must be made during the chaining process, and they can be made accurately only if you carefully monitor the results you are getting.

Okay, so much for how chaining is done. Shaping and chaining are certainly similar, which is one reason I'm taking them up together. And some textbooks on behavior analysis don't talk about chaining, perhaps because the authors consider it merely a form of shaping. But I think it is worth distinguishing between the two. Let's compare them.

Shaping versus Chaining

The crucial similarity between shaping and chaining is . . . is what, Carlotta?

> "Hmm. Well, the goal in each case is to establish a target behavior that doesn't yet occur."

Exactly right. The behavior you want doesn't occur, or it occurs only rarely. If you want to teach someone how to read, you can't simply wait for reading to occur and then reinforce it. You have to do something to get the behavior to occur. A person may perform several elements of a chain, but if the elements aren't performed in the correct sequence, then you need to use chaining. So shaping and chaining are both used when the target behavior doesn't occur and needs to be developed.

There are, however, several differences between the two procedures. For one thing, shaping always moves forward. If progress breaks down, you may have to take a step back before moving forward again, but there is no such thing as backward shaping. It is, however, quite possible to do backward chaining, as you have seen.

Another difference between shaping and chaining concerns when reinforcers are delivered. In shaping, the reinforcers are provided "along the way" so to speak; each new approximation is reinforced. In chaining, reinforcers are provided mainly at the conclusion of the chain, or at the conclusion of as much of the chain as the person can currently do.[14] For instance, suppose you are using backward chaining to teach a brain-injured person to dress himself. He has already learned to tie his shoes, and now you are teaching him to put on his shoes. He gets one shoe on, and you praise his efforts; he gets the other shoe on, and you provide more praise. Next he ties his shoes. When he completes this last item in the chain, you heap on the praise and provide a hug and maybe a special treat, such as a piece of candy. The performance of a new link is reinforced, but the heavy-duty reinforcers come after the completion of the *last* link in the chain.

The distinction between shaping and chaining is subtle. It is possible to think of practically any behavior as comprising a chain of smaller tasks. And shaping can be viewed as reinforcing successive approximations of a chain. The situation is further complicated by the fact that in chaining it is sometimes necessary to shape a component that is not in the person's repertoire. Still, I think there is enough difference between shaping and chaining to warrant the distinction.

Shaping and chaining are important concepts. Let's see if you understand them.

Review

Let's start with shaping. Who can give me a definition? Yes, Midori?

"It's the procedure of reinforcing successive approximations of a desired behavior."

Yes. Shaping is, in principle, a simple procedure consisting of only three steps. The first of these is . . . Alfred?

"The first is *Alfred*!? Oh, you mean, you want *me* to tell you what the first step is. I gotcha."

What would we do without your witticisms, Alfred?

"I don't like to think about it. Your readers would probably fall asleep."

Could we get back to the question? The first step in shaping is . . . ?

"Define the target behavior."

Right. And the second step in shaping, Belinda?

"Reinforce successive approximations."

What are successive approximations?

"That's behavior that resembles the target behavior in some way more than anything else the person does."

Can you give me an example?

"Well, if you wanted someone to walk in counterclockwise circles, you might start by reinforcing any movement to the left, such as twisting the torso to the left, or turning the head to the left, or maybe even looking to the left. Then you'd reinforce stepping to the left. Then you'd require taking two steps to the left, then three, then four, until you had the person walking in counterclockwise circles."

Where do these successive approximations come from?

"Pardon?"

You said you're going to reinforce successive approximations—turning to the left, stepping to the left, and so on. Where do these approximations come from? How do you know that if you reinforce turning to the left, you're going to get stepping to the left? How do you know if you reinforce taking one step to the left, the person will then take two steps to the left?

"Ah . . . hmm. I don't know; it just happens."

Can you help Belinda, Carlotta?

"I think what you're getting at is that there is always some variability in behavior. Like you said, nobody ever really does the same thing twice. So if you reinforce turning to the left, sometimes you'll see some foot movements" to the left. And if you reinforce that, you'll get more foot movements. In shaping, you look for and reinforce the variations in behavior that more closely resemble the target behavior."

Oh, what a head, that has such wisdom in it!

"Does that mean she's right?"

It does indeed, Belinda. All right, so much for shaping. What's chaining? Maya?

"Chaining is the procedure of reinforcing successive elements of a behavior chain."

And what, pray tell, is a behavior chain?

"That's a series of related actions, the last of which produces reinforcement."

Okay. So, Jamal, how do you do chaining?

"There's three steps. First, you define the target behavior. That may involve doing a task analysis to identify the elements of the chain."

All right, and then?

"Then you reinforce the performance of the links, or elements, in order."

What order?

"Well, that depends. You can start with the first element in the chain and work forward."

So if there are five elements in a chain, you start by reinforcing element number 1, then reinforce 1 and 2, then 1, 2, and 3, and so on. Right?

"Right. That's called forward chaining. But you can go the other way around. You can start with the last element, and work backward, like start with number 5, then do 4 and 5, then 3, 4, and 5, then 2, 3, 4, and 5, and finally 1, 2, 3, 4, and 5."

What's that called, John?

"It's called backward chaining."

Good. So what's the third rule for chaining?

"Monitor results."

Right. Well, it sounds like shaping and chaining are very similar. Are there any differences, Brian?

"Uhm, yes. Let's see . . . shaping always moves forward, toward the target behavior, but chaining can work forward or backward. There's no such thing as backward shaping."

Anything else?

"In shaping, you're providing heavy-duty reinforcement from the very beginning. In chaining, the main reinforcer comes at the end of the chain. That final reinforcer reinforces the entire chain. Like when you make a cake, you get to eat the cake."

So, a student is learning to make a cake. He mixes the batter and the teacher says, "Very good," or something. Then the student pours the batter into a pan and the teacher says, "Good job," and so on. Is that it?

"You could do that. But those contrived reinforcers are not the only reinforcers for performing the links."

What others are there?

"I think the opportunity to go on to the next element in the chain would reinforce the previous element. Mixing the batter is reinforced by pouring the batter into the pan; pouring the batter would be reinforced by putting the pan into the oven; and so on. Each element of the chain is reinforced by the fact that it brings the person closer to the reinforcer for the final element."

So the whole chain is maintained by the fact that we get to eat the cake?

"Or maybe the fact that we get approving smiles from our family when *they* eat the cake. My mother was diabetic, so she rarely ate cake, but she still liked to make them because we all enjoyed eating them and she got a kick out of that."

Nicely done, Brian.

We've talked now about how to increase the frequency of behavior. Next time we will talk about how to get behavior to occur less often. See you then.

◄ Exercises ►

Feed the Skeleton

I. Shaping is the _____ of successive _____ _____ of a _____ behavior.

II. The rules for shaping include:
A. defining the _____ .
B. reinforcing _____ .
C. monitoring _____ .

III. Chaining is the _____ of successive _____ _____ of a _____ behavior.
A. When chaining proceeds from the first element of the chain to the last, it is called _____ .
B. When chaining proceeds from the last element of the chain to the first, it is called _____ .

IV. The rules for chaining include:
    A. def _____ .
    B. re _____ .
    C. _____ results.

V. One difference between shaping and chaining is _____

_____ .

Daffy Advice:
Daphne Donchano Answers Your Questions

Dear Daffy:

    My problem is my husband, Elroy. When he comes home from work, he gets undressed and spends the rest of the evening in his boxer shorts and his sleeveless undershirt. In the summer, he doesn't even wear the undershirt. Daffy, he even comes to the dinner table dressed like this.

    When we were first married, he changed into casual clothes when he got home, but over the months, his evening attire began to fall away bit by bit. I tried to use "psychology" on him: I made extra nice meals, sympathized with him about his problems at work, and sometimes I even had flower arrangements and candelabra on the table. I figured if I fancied things up a bit, he'd feel out of place in his shorts. But there he sits, eating by candlelight in his BVDs.

    What has happened to this man? Is there anything I can do to change his ways?

Desperate in Dallas

Dear Desperate:

    Who knows why these things happen? Personally, I think men are programmed to deteriorate after marriage. As for changing his behavior, I suggest a bit of shock therapy: Invite a couple of neighbors for dinner, but don't tell Elroy about it. When the guests arrive, let Elroy scramble for his clothes.

Can you provide a better theory about how Elroy might have come by this behavior? How could Desperate in Dallas use shaping to improve Elroy's evening attire?

911 Lifesaver Kit

A 6-year-old child died when he mistook some pills on the kitchen table for candy. His parents were at work, and when he became sick he simply waited for them to return; he didn't know what else to do. As the governor's advisor on public safety, it has fallen to you to prepare the "911 Lifesaver Kit." This is to be a complete program to help parents, teachers, and others teach children how to use the 911 emergency system. The kit must cost the state no more than $10 each, and it must be simple to understand and use. (Many of the kids most at risk have parents with less than a high school education.) Describe your kit.

Chained Poetry

You are required to recite a poem of at least ten lines in your speech class. Since you will not be permitted to read the poem or use notes, you must learn it by heart. You have selected Robert Frost's poem, "On Stopping by Woods on a Snowy Evening."

How could you use chaining to learn this poem?

Overcoming Mental Conflicts

In an article published in 1963, Teodoro Ayllon complained that "the current emphasis in psychotherapy is on 'mental-conflict resolution' and little or no attention is given to dealing directly with the behavioral problems which prevent the patient from returning to the community." How do you account for the fact that many therapists still focus more on "mental conflicts" than they do on changing behavior?

Practice Quiz

1. Shaping is used when the target behavior _____ occurs.

2. Rickard and Mundy helped Steve by having him read aloud—first short phrases, then sentences, then paragraphs. This was all part of a program to deal with the problem of _____ .

3. If, during shaping, progress breaks down, it is sometimes helpful to reinforce a previous approximation. This is called a _____ _____ .

4. Chaining is the reinforcement of successive _____ of a behavior chain.

5. Shaping is the reinforcement of successive _____ of a target behavior.

6. In _____ chaining, the last element of a chain is performed and reinforced, then the last two elements are performed and reinforced, and so on.

7. Barbara Gruber and her colleagues used _____ chaining to get retarded students to walk to school.

8. In chaining, the most important reinforcement comes after the _____ _____ element in the chain.

9. When shaping is used, the target behavior is sometimes called the terminal or _____ behavior.

10. To identify the parts of a behavior chain, it is often useful to do a _____ _____ analysis.

Mini-Essay: THE THIRD REVOLUTION

There have been three major revolutions in the way we think about human nature.

The first revolution was started by the Polish astronomer Nicolaus Copernicus. Before Copernicus, people believed that the earth was the center of the universe. The sun (as anyone could plainly see) revolved around the earth. That put people at the center of the universe—the center, it seemed, of God's attention. Then Copernicus said that the earth revolved around the sun. Suddenly the earth and its people were not the center of anything. We were off to one side, as it were. This was a mighty blow to the vanity of human beings, and it was a long time before it was widely accepted.

The second revolution came with the English naturalist, Charles Darwin. Before Darwin, people were thought to be separate from the animal world, above the beasts and below the angels. In suggesting that human beings were the products of millions of years of evolution, Darwin said that we are *of* the animals, not above them. Like Copernicus, Darwin not only offended conventional theology, he struck a blow at human vanity. It was a blow from which many people are still reeling.

The third revolution in human nature came in this century with American psychologist B. F. Skinner. Before Skinner, most people believed that behavior originated in the mind, a noncorporeal essence in recent times thought to have resided in the brain. The mind was a kind of little man, or homunculus, within us that decided our every action. Skinner showed that by modifying the environment, he could modify behavior in systematic and predictable ways. This meant that behavior was lawful and that (with biological variables held constant) changes in behavior could be accounted for by the antecedents and consequences of behavior. There was no longer any need for a homunculus to explain behavior. Skinner's discoveries, like those of Copernicus and Darwin, forced a new assessment of human nature.

It took hundreds of years for the Copernican view to become widely accepted. And people still struggle to keep Darwin's ideas about human nature out of our schools. We must, therefore, assume that it will be many years before the third revolution will win acceptance. But science is patient.

Reprint: SHAPING SIGHT

by Judith R. Mathews, Gary D. Hodson,
William B. Crist, & G. Robert LaRoche

There are times when children do not act in their own best interests: Given half a chance, they may avoid eating vegetables, taking medicine, and washing their hands after using the bathroom. What's a parent to do? Sometimes the parent may be helped by turning to shaping, as the excerpt below illustrates.

Visual impairment in infants and young children can have serious developmental implications, including limitations in motor and cognitive development (Lewis, 1987). For children with surgically removed lenses (aphakia) and extreme near-sightedness, thick glasses can result in image distortion, altered peripheral vision, compromised visual acuity, and even eventual loss of vision if only one eye is aphakic (Michaels, 1980). Aphakia occurs in approximately 30 children per year in the three provinces of Nova Scotia, New Brunswich, and Prince Edward Island, which have a total population of 1.7 million. Children with aphakia and extreme nearsightedness have benefited from the early introduction of contact lenses (Levin, Edmonds, Nelson, Calhoun, & Harley, 1988).

In infants and very young children, lenses are inserted by simply restraining the child during the procedure. This is less appropriate for toddlers and preschoolers, who are less easily restrained and may exhibit noncompliance in other aspects of their lives. Physical resistance to lens insertion can result in injury to the eye or discontinuation of lens use. For this reason, it is important to teach children to comply with lens insertion and removal.

Shaping, the differential reinforcement of successive approximations to an end goal (Catania, 1984), has been used successfully to teach a variety of skills, including conversation skills (Bourgeois, 1990), glasses use (Wolf, Risley, & Mees, 1964), inhalation therapy responses (Renne & Creer, 1976), and compliance with radiation therapy (Mathews & Grantmyre, 1985). The purpose of this study was to document and evaluate systematically the effectiveness of a shaping procedure to teach contact lens use in young children.

Method

Subjects and Setting

Four children, aged 5 years 1 month (Pierre), 1 year 11.5 months (Charles), 3 years 11.6 months (Adam), and 4 years (Joel), were enrolled in the study over an 18-month period as referrals were made. Three were being fitted with lenses for the first time and showed some noncompliance during eye exams. Charles had been using lenses since 6 weeks of age, but was noncompliant to their insertion. Joel had Down syndrome. All were admitted to a care-by-parent unit in the hospital and seen intensively for contact lens instruction over a 4- to 5-day period. . . .

Measures

Daily lens use and visual acuity were the ultimate dependent variables in this study. However, immediate measures of compliance and noncompliance in response to adult commands were recorded during training sessions and follow-up observations. Compliance was defined as the initiation of a response within 5 seconds of an adult command. Noncompliance was defined as no initiation of a response within 5 s, as well as the following physical responses: moves head away, blocks eye, squeezes eye shut, pushes adult away, or physically resists. The presence or absence of any crying or behavior necessitating physical restraint was recorded at the end of each 1-min interval. The number of minutes needed to insert and remove the lens and the frequency and length of time-out were also recorded. All sessions were videotaped.

After discharge, parents were phoned weekly for 2 months. They were asked to rate seven behaviors during that morning's insertion (five compliance scores, one crying score, and one restraint score) on a 5-point Likert-type scale. At discharge, parents rated the success of and their satisfaction with the procedure on the same type of scale. . . .

Interobserver Reliability

Interobserver agreement, assessed for 25% of the observations over all phases of treatment, was 84.9% (range, 76.9% to 92%) for minute-by-minute occurrence and 98.1% (range, 93.5% to 100%) for minute-by-minute nonoccurrence of the observed behaviors. . . .

Design

Because children were seen over an 18-month period as referrals were received, the study used a noncurrent multiple baseline design across subjects, with changing criteria (Kazdin, 1982).

Procedure

Baseline. Due to time constraints, after referrals were received and consent was obtained, each child was randomly assigned to a baseline of one, two, or three points. Because of potential aversive conditioning during baseline, actual insertion of the lens was not attempted. Instead, six steps in the shaping hierarchy were randomly ordered and introduced twice during each session. They included touching the child's face, pulling open the eyelid, having the child pull open an eyelid, placing drops in eyes, approaching the child's eye with a finger, and touching the child's eye with a finger.

Initial lens shaping. The initial shaping procedure consisted of systematic introduction of variations of eight steps, including the steps described in baseline as well as touching a soft lens and then a hard lens to the corner of the eye. Child compliance to requests was rewarded with praise, stars, bubbles, food, or access to toys. Noncompliance was followed within approximately 30 s by warning, followed almost immediately by brief time-out for Pierre, Charles, and Adam, and physical restraint for Joel (whose parents reported this to be effective). . . . Because of noncompliance in baseline, Charles was taught general compliance first. This consisted of rewarding compliance with commands unrelated to contact lenses and using time-out for noncompliance.

Lens insertion. At the start of the week, parents were taught lens care and practiced lens insertion and removal using the therapist's eye. Generally, the therapist first inserted the child's lenses on Wednesday, and parents inserted the child's lenses on Thursday and Friday. . . .

Follow-up. Parents were contacted weekly by phone for 2 months. The primary therapist conducted the standardized interview and recorded the parents' responses. At approximately 3-, 6-, and 10-month follow-ups, parents and children returned to the hospital, where the parents were videotaped removing and inserting the lenses.

Results

. . . Mean percentage of compliance for Pierre, Charles, and Adam was 65.8% (range, 36.7% to 94.4%), with a much lower compliance percentage for Joel, who was restrained (M = 20.5%, range 0% to 55.5%).

At home following hospital discharge, the parents of Pierre, Charles, and Adam reported a steady improvement in compliance. . . .

Joel, who was restrained and introduced to the lenses early in the week, showed low compliance throughout treatment. Although the parents reported excellent compliance for the first 3 weeks after discharge, poor fit and an eyelid infection resulted in a drop in compliance. At 16 weeks, because insertion was taking up to 2 hr and poor fit resulted in frequent loss of lens, the parents chose to discontinue the use of contact lenses.

There was a mean of 18.8 sessions over the week (range, 16 to 24), lasting a mean of 18 min (range, 2 to 66 min). Sessions were followed by frequent breaks of 30 to 60 min. Mean therapy time was 5 hr 59 min (range, 3 hr 18 min to 7 hr 42 min).

At discharge, all 4 parents rated their satisfaction with and the success of the intervention very high. . . .

Excerpted from "Teaching Young Children to Use Contact Lenses," by J. R. Mathews, G. D Hodson, W. B. Crist, and G. R. LaRoche. In *Journal of Applied Behavior Analysis,* Vol. 25, © 1992 by the Society for the Experimental Analysis of Behavior, Inc. Reprinted with permission.

Reprint: CHAINED ROUTINE
by Melvyn Hollander & Vivian Horner

This study by Hollander and Horner illustrates the utility of chaining in establishing (or reestablishing) daily routines in institutionalized patients. Learning to perform basic hygiene skills (such as brushing one's teeth), ordinary household chores (such as making a bed), and doing some sort of useful work (such as sweeping the ward floor) not only add to the fullness of the patient's life, but are generally prerequisites for returning to the community. Some people oppose such training, arguing that it amounts to forced labor. Ironically, denying people the opportunity to get such training may, in effect, deny them the opportunity to leave the institution.

On the selected open ward it was observed that most patients were apathetic and withdrawn. Many of them sat motionless for hours in the day in their bedroom. Others escaped from the lack of stimulation on the ward by wandering around the hospital grounds all day. Furthermore, the majority of patients did not attend group activities and refused to participate in the ward clean-up program. Similar observations have been made for other hospitalized patients (Ayllon and Azrin, 1968; Schaefer and Martin, 1969). Therefore, target behaviors were selected which would engender a higher activity level, more responsibility and greater independence in patients. . . .

Target Behaviors

Three behavioral configurations were chosen for modification. They were working (ward-maintenance assignments), grooming, and care of personal property (bed-making). These target behaviors appeared to satisfy the selection criteria. All target behaviors could potentially be maintained by the contingencies of the outside community. Development of work skills is a prerequisite for gainful employment in the community, and gainful employment is reinforced with money. Similarly, appropriate grooming and self-care habits set the occasion for community approval and enhance the probability of access to gainful employment. . . .

Regarding an integrated series of activities, the target behaviors represent what might be called a "work day routine." Basically the behavioral chain was, in sequence, grooming, bed-making, and working, followed by eating lunch. Each link in the chain involved many behavioral routines. For example, patient work activities were posted weekly on a large public chart and patients were expected to consult the chart for their particular assignment. Also, patients performed their ward maintenance tasks as part of small groups. It was necessary for them to learn cooperative skills or the assignment could not be completed satisfactorily.

The desired "work day routine" began with patients rising at 7:00 A.M. to take care of their personal hygiene. They then ate breakfast. Then they cleaned their rooms and attended to putting away their personal effects. Afterwards, they reported for work, picking up their supplies and joining their work group. At a specific time, later in the day, patients went to the play area to be reimbursed (with a meal ticket) for their work. Finally, they had the opportunity to spend their earnings at noon for the hospital meal. As may be seen, this patterned sequence to activities is, in many respects, comparable to the schedule that a typical worker in the community follows. . . .

There were some preliminary factors which had to be examined. It was important to ascertain whether the target behaviors were already part of most patient's repertoires. As they were not, all of the pieces of the behavior chain were modeled by the ward staff before the conditioning procedure was undertaken. In order to deal with the delay between target behaviors which were scheduled to be performed early in the morning and at lunch, a meal ticket was delivered to patients immediately after the target behaviors were completed. The patient's name and the date were inscribed on each ticket to provide safeguards for theft and bartering. . . .

During the A_1 condition, baseline measures of target behaviors were recorded and patients were randomly assigned to defined jobs and work groups. All patients were informed that it was their responsibility to complete the posted assignments in addition to caring for their personal hygiene and making their beds. Reinforcement was not now provided, but the lunch ticket was established during this phase as a secondary reinforcer by directing patients to pick up the lunch ticket at a designated time and place if they wanted lunch. Access to the dining room was made contingent on the presentation of a lunch ticket.

The B condition was the behavioral intervention phase. As the conclusion of the baseline phase, the contingency management and response chaining procedures were instituted. Basically, the delivery of the lunch ticket was now contingent on the performance of the target behaviors. The previously established contingency between eating the lunch and the lunch ticket was still in effect.

The response chaining procedure was conducted in the following manner. The last behavior in the chain (work behavior) was conditioned first. Receipt of the lunch ticket became contingent on the completion of ward maintenance tasks according to prescribed standards. The next target behavior, bed-making, was introduced only after a patient's work behavior met a criterion performance level of 75 percent for 2 weeks. In other words, the contingency was expanded to include two behaviors only after an average of 75% of patients were emitting work behavior daily for 2 weeks. . . .

The last major target behavior to be sequentially conditioned was grooming. This time it was required that the combined performances of work and bed-making reach a criterion level of 75% for 2 weeks before the grooming contingency was added. When the conditioning of the response chain was completed, patients were grooming, making beds, and working in that sequence to earn a lunch ticket.

In the final or A_2 condition the response chain-lunch contingencies were suspended. The target behaviors were no longer reinforced and access to the dining room was permitted without restrictions.

Results

Figure 1 presents the data collected on a total of 17 patients who resided on the experimental ward throughout the three phases of the program. All patients were officially diagnosed as schizophrenic and had been continuously hospitalized for over 2 yr. Each target behavior was analyzed separately and is represented graphically as the percent of patients emitting that target daily for each week.

The findings show that a significantly greater number of patients were emitting the target behaviors during the B-phase-lunch contingency than during either the A_1—baseline or the A_2—non-contingent phases. . . .

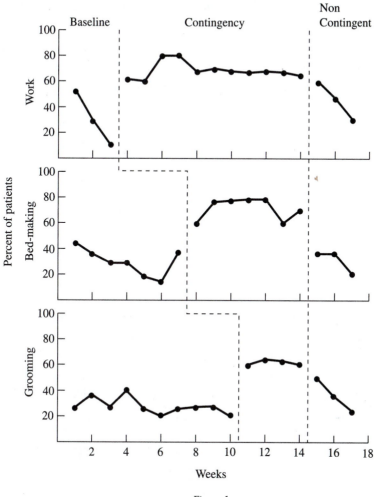

Figure 1

Discussion

The success of the patient operant conditioning program is attributed, in part, to the identification and evaluation of those factors in the institutional environment which facilitated or impeded program implementation. In this context, particular attention was paid to such factors as the availability of reinforcements, the motivation and morale of the ward staff, the degree of environmental control afforded project directors, and the prevalent institutional practices which either supported or interfered with program objectives. The behavioral assessment also included the community environment into which patients were likely to be placed on discharge. The value of the latter assessment becomes apparent when one attempts to develop those skills which will allow patients to maintain themselves in the community (Atthowe, 1973). . . .

Reprinted with permission from *Journal of Behaviour Therapy and Experimental Psychiatry, Vol. 6.* M. Hollander and V. Horner, "Using Environmental Assessment and Operant Procedures to Build Integrated Behaviors in Schizophrenics," 1975, Elsevier Science Ltd., Oxford, England.

◄ Recommended Reading ►

1. Isaacs, W., Thomas, J., & Goldiamond, I. (1960). Application of operant conditioning to reinstate verbal behavior in psychotics. *Journal of Speech and Hearing Disabilities, 25,* 8–12.
   This study describes the use of shaping, with chewing gum as a reinforcer, to develop conversational skills in a mute psychotic. It is a classic.

2. Paniaqua, F. A., & Baer, D. M. (1982). The analysis of correspondence training as a chain reinforceable at any point. *Child Development, 53,* 786–798.
   It is important that people tell the truth and keep their promises. Paniaqua and Baer suggest that chaining can be used to increase such "say-do correspondence."

3. Skinner, B. F. (1951). How to teach animals. *Scientific American, 185,* 26–29.
   Skinner's "how to" includes the use of shaping and chaining.

4. Skinner, B. F. (1975). The shaping of phylogenic behavior. *Acta Neurobiologiae Experimentalis, 35,* 409–415.
   Skinner draws attention to the similarity of the process of shaping to that of evolution. In both cases, what "works" survives.

◄ Endnotes ►

1. If a behavior never occurs, we say that it is not in the person's repertoire. Shaping is a way of adding behaviors to a person's repertoire.

2. "Hot and Cold," as it is usually played, includes both reinforcement ("You're getting hot!") and punishment ("You're getting cold!). Shaping, by definition, relies exclusively on reinforcement.

3. Skinner (1938) was the first to demonstrate the power of shaping and chaining (though he originally called shaping *response differentiation*). Skinner's heart was in basic research, and these first experiments involved rats, but

Skinner clearly saw the value of shaping and chaining in dealing with human problems, and other behaviorists soon put the procedures to good use in helping people.

4. Rickard & Mundy (1965).

5. Ayllon (1963).

6. Isaacs et al. (1960).

7. Herrnstein (1966).

8. J. S. Bruner (1983) describes how parents shape the language skills of their children, though he never mentions shaping or reinforcement by name. Much of Bruner's work is very behavioral. That is to say, it identifies functional relations between observed behavior and physical events. Unfortunately, Bruner insists on using mentalistic concepts to interpret his findings.

9. Skinner (e.g., 1975, 1984) often noted the similarity of operant learning to evolution. On one occasion (Skinner, 1981), he wrote that the selection of behavior by reinforcement "resembles a hundred million years of natural selection . . . compressed into a very short period of time" (p. 502). Incidentally, naturalists have described animals training their young in a manner that suggests shaping. Teale (1946), for example, has observed a mother fox take captured prey into the den after the kits have been weaned. Later the vixen drops the prey at the den entrance. Still later she drops the prey several yards from the entrance. Next the pups must search an area of several hundred square yards around the den. Finally, the mother buries the prey under leaves in the search area. "In this practical, progressive manner," Teale writes, "the school for foxes educates the young animals for the vital work of hunting" (p. 189). Apparently, this use of shaping is innate, the result of evolutionary "shaping."

10. Todd (1995).

11. Gruber et al. (1979).

12. Such "tests" are probes. The idea is to "probe for" the target behavior so as to avoid unnecessary training. If, for example, you are asked to teach students a list of spelling words, you might begin by asking them to spell each word. This way you can avoid spending time teaching them what they already can do.

13. As an illustration of the application of task analysis to mathematics instruction, see Engelmann and Carnine (1982).

14. The last element of a chain normally provides extrinsic reinforcement; other elements of a chain become conditioned reinforcers by their association with the ultimate reinforcer. Each time you complete an element in the chain

known as shoveling snow from a sidewalk, you are closer to the reinforcer—seeing a clear sidewalk. Hence, people often report feeling a sense of satisfaction as they complete successive elements in the chain. Smart parents offer their youngster hot chocolate or other treats when the job is complete. This adds to the reinforcer value of completing elements in the chain. Some chains do provide extrinsic reinforcers prior to the last element. Cooks not only get to eat their cake, they get to taste the batter.

6

Extinction and Differential Reinforcement

W'E'VE TALKED ABOUT BEHAVIOR PROBLEMS, and we've seen that most behavior problems fall within one of two categories. What are those categories, John?

"One is when a behavior doesn't occur often enough; the other is when a behavior occurs too often."

Right. So far we've been talking about the first kind of problem. What procedure does a behaviorist use when behavior doesn't occur often enough? Midori?

"Reinforcement."

Right. Reinforcement means providing consequences that increase the frequency of behavior. Shaping, chaining, and prompting and fading are procedures that are used in conjunction with reinforcement to increase behavior rate. Now I want to turn your attention to problems in which the behavior occurs too often. Let's have some everyday examples of behavior problems in which a behavior occurs too frequently. Carlotta?

"When I was living at home, my parents said I talked on the phone too much."

A good example. Parents complain that their kids talk too much on the phone, eat too much, go out too much, complain too much, and cost too much. (I threw that last one in as a joke.) What about school? What kinds of student behavior do teachers find troublesome? Jamal?

"Staring out the window, walking around the room, throwing spitballs, fighting, crying, calling out answers, daydreaming, passing notes . . ."

Yes, very good. Most teachers probably would like it if those kinds of behavior occurred less frequently. What about the clinic or mental hospital? Do psychiatric problems ever involve behavior that occurs too often? Maya?

"I think so. Some patients hallucinate. They have delusions. They say things that make no sense, like 'Today the Germanic telephone on the treetops of the mysteries.'"

Good. Those are all things that therapists would like to see occur less often. Anything else? Yes, John?

"Aren't they violent? If I worked in a mental hospital, I wouldn't want patients attacking people."

Interestingly enough, only a small percentage of psychiatric patients are aggressive. Those few, however, can be a serious problem for other patients and staff, and anyone working around them would be interested in reducing the frequency of violent behavior.[1]

Okay, so there are lots of problems involving behavior that occurs too often. With these problems, the task is not to strengthen the target behavior but to weaken it, to get it to occur less frequently. Today we will discuss two procedures for reducing the frequency of problem behavior. The first is called extinction.

Extinction Defined

Operant behavior is maintained by its consequences. Preventing the consequences that maintain a behavior should weaken it. Put another way: If a behavior occurs with annoying frequency, we can be reasonably sure that it pays off in some way. And if we can arrange the environment so that the behavior no longer pays off, then it will occur less often. That's extinction:

Extinction:
Withholding the reinforcers that maintain a target behavior.

Behaviorists often speak of a behavior as having been extinguished. This means the frequency of the behavior has been reduced by the extinction procedure. It is not the same as saying, however, that the behavior no longer occurs; extinction does not, in other words, render behavior "extinct." Rather, the effect of extinction is to reduce the frequency of the target behavior.

Suppose, for example, that during the course of a day, Nervous Nellie drums her fingers on the table; she usually does this five or six times a day. But suppose that, on one occasion, a co-worker notices the finger tapping and inquires about Nellie's well-being. "Is something bothering you, Nellie?" she asks. This inquiry leads to a conversation about Nellie's current troubles, during which her inquiring co-worker is very supportive and attentive. Periodically, when Nellie drums her fingers, her co-worker inquires about her problems and listens attentively as Nellie complains. The behavior of the co-worker turns out to be reinforcing, and the rate of finger tapping climbs to 30 or 50 times a day. Nellie's co-worker eventually takes a job with another company. The reinforcer that had strengthened Nellie's finger tapping is no longer available; the behavior is on extinction, and the rate falls. After a few weeks, however, the rate of finger tapping levels off at about five or six times a day—the frequency at which it occurred before the co-worker intervened. In other words, the behavior returns to its baseline (or preintervention) level. The tapping does not disappear entirely. Presumably, the behavior produces reinforcers other than the inquiries of the coworker, and those reinforcers continue to maintain the behavior at some level.[2] You have a question, John?

"Is extinction the same thing as forgetting?"

A good question. People sometimes confuse extinction with forgetting, but they are quite different. *Forgetting* is usually defined as a deterioration in performance due to the lack of opportunity to perform the behavior. Chopin said that if he skipped practice one day, only he could tell the difference in his playing. If he skipped two days, only he and his tutor could tell. But if he skipped three days, everyone could tell. He was talking about forgetting, the deterioration in performance that comes with not performing a skill.

In extinction, the person may remain quite capable of performing the behavior but does not do so. Suppose, for example, that you smile or laugh when your 6-year-old uses a swear word. The frequency of swearing increases, and you make a determined effort not to giggle when he says "Mrs. Warner is a blankey-blank good teacher!" The swearing drops off. That does not mean, however, that Junior has forgotten how to swear, only that the rate of swearing has declined.

We've mentioned some examples of behavior problems that might be solved with extinction, but let's examine some actual cases in which extinction was put to use.

Illustrative Studies

Let's start with a problem many of you are going to face as parents, and possibly as teachers: the crybaby. Babies and young children often cry when they fall and hurt themselves, when they are sick, or when they are very hungry. That's to be expected. But sometimes children cry when there's no apparent reason for crying. These are the crybabies. Their crying is an annoyance to others and interferes with their own healthy development. One such was a boy named Bill.[3]

Bill, the Crier

Bill was just over 4 years old. He was a normal, healthy boy attending the University of Washington's Laboratory Preschool. Based on the description of his behavior, Bill was probably above average in intelligence and social skills. But Bill had one failing: He was a crybaby. He cried more than any other child in the school— five to ten times each morning. If he bumped into furniture, he cried; if he fell down, he cried; if he had difficulty doing something, he cried; if he was threatened by one of the other children, he cried. And when Bill cried, he didn't just sit down and weep quietly; he cried so that everybody in the neighborhood knew about it. And he would keep crying until a teacher had given him several minutes of comforting. Bill cried so easily and so often, his teachers began to wonder if he wasn't crying because of the attention he got when he cried.

A group of behaviorists, headed by Betty Hart, thought the teachers might be right and decided to see if extinction might help.[4] To begin with, the researchers asked a teacher to keep tabs of the crying using a pocket counter. (These are like the ones used to record attendance at museums and other public places. Each time a person depresses a plunger, the counter adds one to the running total.) The researchers defined the target behavior, crying, as vocal sound loud enough to be heard 50 feet away that lasted for at least 5 seconds. At the end of each day, someone recorded the total number of crying episodes on a cumulative graph. A cumulative graph is one that shows . . . what *does* a cumulative graph show, Midori?

> "Oh, ah, it shows the total number of times the target behavior has occurred at a given point in the program, I think."

You think right. The teachers recorded crying episodes for 10 days without making any effort to modify the behavior. This provided a baseline against which the effects of treatment could be compared.

Treatment consisted of putting crying on extinction: When Bill cried, his teachers were to glance his way to ensure that he was not actually hurt, and then they were to pay no attention to him: They were not to look at him, go to him, or speak to him when he was crying. If he began crying when a teacher was nearby, the teacher was to walk away. However, if Bill fell down or had some other unpleasant experience and did *not* cry, then the teacher was to give him praise and attention.

What happened was that the frequency of crying fell off sharply. Within 5 days after the extinction procedure had been started, Bill was crying no more than twice a day. . . . Alfred, you have a question?

> "I can see that the crying probably fell off because the teachers stopped paying attention—"

They didn't stop paying attention. They just stopped paying attention following crying. Attention was no longer contingent on crying.

> "That's what I meant. Anyway, how do you know it wasn't just a coincidence that he stopped crying after they started extinction? I mean, maybe he cried a lot at home and his parents got fed up and started walloping him whenever he cried. Or maybe he's just growing up, and the intervention has nothing to do with it."

That's a reasonable question. Does anybody have any ideas about how you could rule out the possibility that another variable is the important one? Yes, Jamal?

> "You could ask the parents if they have been doing anything different lately."

Yes, you could, and it might be worth doing that. But suppose you found out they had begun spanking Bill whenever he cried; you still wouldn't know for sure what was reducing crying at school. Any other ideas?

> "Wait. I don't get that. If his parents said they'd started spanking him for crying, why wouldn't you know that that was the reason his behavior changed?"

Can someone answer Alfred's question? Yes, Carlotta?

"You've got two possibilities, the spankings and extinction. Either could be responsible."

Satisfied, Alfred?

"Yeah, I get it."

Good. Now, any other ideas about how we can determine if withholding attention is responsible for the change in behavior? Yes, Brian?

"You could do a reversal. You could have the teachers give him attention again whenever he cried and see if he cries more, and then you could use extinction again, and see if the crying drops off again."

Excellent, Brian. If crying is reinforced by attention, then making attention contingent on crying will increase its frequency. And if that happens, we should be able to reduce the frequency of crying again with extinction. Interestingly enough, that is exactly what the researchers did in this case. After several days with crying on extinction, the researchers asked the teachers to go back to providing attention whenever Bill cried. The rate of crying shot up almost immediately and continued to occur at a high rate for several days. Then they put the behavior on extinction again, and within a few days crying had been practically eliminated. So, the cumulative record looked something like this:

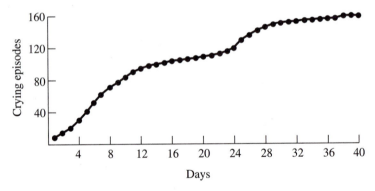

Figure 6-1. *Crying and extinction. Adapted from Hart et. al. (1964).*

This is only a rough approximation of the cumulative record, but it shows the basic idea. Looking at this graph, who can tell me when the first extinction procedure started and ended? Jamal?

"The first extinction period must have started just before that fairly level section, because that means crying became less frequent."

Right. Very good so far. And when did the first extinction period end?

"About where the line starts to shoot up again. That steep line means the behavior is occurring at a high rate again."

Right again. And where does the second extinction period begin, Midori?

"It has to be right before the point where the line goes flat again, because you said crying dropped off fast when they reinstated extinction."

Excellent. I can draw some vertical lines to indicate the changes in procedures, and I can label the periods when extinction was in effect. What I end up with looks like this:

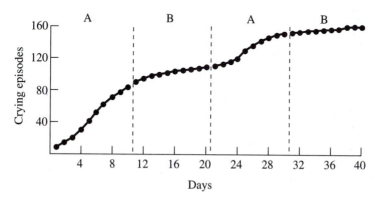

Figure 6-2. Crying and extinction. Adapted from Hart et. al. (1964).

This is, of course, the kind of research design known as . . . as what, John?

"ABAB reversal design?"

Right. The A-B-A-B labels are sort of a giveaway. Now, the idea of getting rid of a troublesome behavior and then reestablishing it again just to verify that the treatment worked is controversial. You certainly would not want to do this sort of reversal if the target behavior were potentially harmful to the client or someone else. But it is a very powerful research tool, since it demonstrates beyond reasonable doubt that the treatment was effective. As I've said before, it's rather like throwing a switch on and off and observing the effects on a lamp.

Okay, so much for crybaby Bill. Let's see if extinction can help with a more serious problem.

Laura, the Vomiter

The case I want to tell you about was treated by Montrose Wolf and his colleagues.[5] The target behavior this time is rather unpleasant, so I apologize if I spoil your lunch.

The case involves a 9-year-old girl named Laura. Laura was mentally retarded, could not speak, and was easily upset. She also suffered from cerebral palsy and brain damage. Laura was a patient in an institution for people with mental retardation, where she attended class 3 hours a day. About a month after she started attending class, she began vomiting. The frequency of vomiting increased, and within 3 months she was vomiting practically every day during class. Laura received medication for the vomiting, but it didn't help. After 3 months, she was dropped from school.

The researchers had a hunch that the vomiting might be operant behavior—

"I thought vomiting was a reflex. Wouldn't that make it respondent behavior?"

Ordinarily, Carlotta, vomiting is a reflex elicited by toxins in the stomach or by other conditions created by certain kinds of illness, such as flu. But in this instance, the researchers suspected the vomiting was operant behavior. In other words, they suspected that it was being influenced by its consequences.[6] One reason they thought this was that the vomiting was accompanied by certain other operant behavior; Laura didn't just vomit, she screamed, tore her clothes, and damaged property. Another reason for their hunch was the fact that Laura didn't just spill her beans on the floor; she vomited on her clothes, on the table where she and other kids were working, and on the teacher's desk. If somebody throws up on your desk, you have to wonder if it's just a reflex.

"Do you mean she was up-chucking *deliberately*!?"

No, Alfred. I simply mean that it was operant behavior: It was influenced by its consequences. Words like *deliberately* usually refer to the thoughts and feelings a person is presumed to have before or while performing some overt act. But remember, those thoughts and feelings don't explain the overt behavior, and they're usually not particularly helpful in changing it. Laura might have thought, "I think I'll go throw up on the teacher's lap" before doing so, but knowing that wouldn't have helped in changing her behavior.

A teacher was willing to work with Laura, so the researchers devised a plan based on the assumption that the vomiting was operant. Mont Wolf (as he is usually called) and his colleagues found that what often happened when Laura vomited was that the teacher then took her to her dormitory. Wolf and his colleagues reasoned that this might be reinforcing the behavior, so they asked the teacher *not* to take Laura to the dorm, no matter how many times she vomited. If returning to the dorm was a reinforcer, then vomiting would be on extinction.

Apparently the researcher's hunch was right because the frequency of vomiting gradually declined to zero over a 6-week period. The extinction procedure worked.

Extinction is basically a very simple procedure: Prevent the target behavior from being reinforced and it declines. But, as with reinforcement, extinction is more difficult to implement than it appears. In fact, it is rather easy to make a mess of things with extinction if you aren't careful. It is, however, a fairly safe procedure provided that you follow a few simple rules. Let's discuss those rules now.

Rules for Using Extinction

You know that when the goal is to increase the frequency of a behavior, the first rule is to define the target behavior, the behavior you want to increase. When the goal is to *decrease* the frequency of a behavior, the first rule is to:

1. Define the target behavior.

The same rule! Defining the behavior you want to change is just as important when it comes to *decreasing* the rate of behavior as it is when attempting to *increase* the rate of behavior. Any time you are attempting to change the frequency of a behavior, you must have a very clear idea of what that behavior is. It's common sense, but that doesn't mean it's commonly done. People often set out to change behavior without really knowing what it is they want to change. So, before using extinction, always decide in advance what behavior will qualify for extinction.

2. Identify the reinforcers that maintain the target behavior.

If an operant behavior occurs on a regular basis, you can safely assume that it is being reinforced. To put the behavior on extinction, you have to identify the reinforcer. That is easier said than done.[7]

Of course, you might try asking the person who has temper tantrums why he screams, cries, and throws things. You can ask, but that isn't to say you will get a helpful answer. In many instances, they don't seem to know. And when they do know, they may not be willing to tell you. A man who pouts whenever his wife displeases him in some way may understand that if he pouts long enough, his wife will do various things "in order to make up." But that husband is not likely to say, "I pout because it pays to pout." Similarly, the child who has screaming tantrums does not announce, "I'm screaming because, in the past, screaming has produced adult attention."

So how do you determine what reinforcer is maintaining the target behavior? Observe the behavior and its consequences for a time. If the behavior tends to have a particular consequence, there is a good chance that that consequence is reinforcing the behavior. For instance, whenever Bill cried, a teacher went to him and comforted him, so it was reasonable to suppose that crying was being reinforced by adult attention. Similarly, when Laura vomited, someone took her to the dormitory. It was a good bet that escaping from class was the reinforcer that maintained her Mt. Vesuvius imitations.

Behavior can have all sorts of consequences, and identifying those that are reinforcing a particular behavior is sometimes difficult. Temper tantrums are often maintained by adult attention, and so in dealing with this problem, you may withhold adult attention during tantrums. If doing so has little or no effect, it's likely that adult attention was not the reinforcer. Extinction means withholding the reinforcer that maintains the target behavior; if you withhold some *other* consequence, you have not put the behavior on extinction.

3. Withhold all reinforcement of the target behavior.

Extinction is a very simple procedure: All it requires is that the target behavior not be reinforced.[8] But even assuming that you have identified the relevant reinforcers, withholding them is not always easy. Consider the case of Crybaby Bill. Bill's crying was reinforced by adult attention, so withholding reinforcement required only the cooperation of his teachers. But if Bill falls and cries, a teacher must investigate to ensure that he has not been hurt. In doing so the teacher must take great care to avoid accidentally reinforcing crying.

The difficulty of using extinction in Bill's case would have been even greater had the source of reinforcement been the other students in the class. Consider the case of a third-grader whose silly remarks disrupt the class activity. Very often such behavior is not maintained so much by the behavior of the teacher as by the behavior of other students. A teacher may ignore a silly remark, but the class may erupt in laughter. In such circumstances, laughter can be powerfully reinforcing. Getting a group of students to withhold reinforcement (in this case, to avoid laughing) is not so easy. You might get the kids to cooperate most of the time, but that is not good enough when using extinction. Extinction requires that *all* reinforcement for the target behavior be withheld, and that is often easier said than done. . . . Yes, Alfred; you have a question?

"I can't see what harm it does if the behavior is reinforced once in a while, like when once in a while the kids laugh at a student's silliness. What's the big deal?"

Ah. The big deal is that occasional reinforcement can maintain behavior at very high rates and may even make the behavior more difficult to eliminate. This phenomenon is called the partial reinforcement effect:

Partial reinforcement effect: Increased resistance to extinction following intermittent reinforcement.

The partial reinforcement effect, or PRE, as it is called, is a topic of some controversy today. Recent research by John Nevin and others has shown that under certain circumstances, resistance to extinction varies directly with the frequency of reinforcement.[9] In other words, the more often a behavior is reinforced, the more resistant it is to extinction. This runs counter to the PRE. The issue is unresolved, but it is clear that behavior can be maintained by occasional reinforcement, and that means that it is not a good idea to initiate an extinction procedure unless you can be reasonably certain of withholding virtually all reinforcement of the target behavior. If it is likely that the behavior will be reinforced from time to time, then it is better not to attempt extinction because you might only make matters worse.

4. Monitor results.

As with reinforcement, it is essential that you monitor behavior during extinction. The only way you can be certain that the extinction procedure is working is to note changes in behavior during extinction. If you do not see typical extinction effects, the chances are the consequence you are withholding is not the relevant reinforcer.

Now, before we extinguish the extinction light, let's talk about some of the problems you might encounter when using extinction.

Problems with Extinction

Uncontrolled Reinforcement

What makes extinction simple is that all you have to do is prevent the target behavior from being reinforced. What makes it difficult is—you have to prevent the target behavior from being reinforced!

The problem is that the target behavior may produce reinforcement from a number of sources, and those sources are often difficult to control. Parents, teachers, spouses, classmates, friends, neighbors, grandmothers, and lots of other people sometimes gum things up by reinforcing behavior you are trying to extinguish. You recall that inappropriate reinforcement that undermines an intervention is called . . . what, Belinda?

"Hmmm . . . is it bootleg reinforcement?"

Yes. And it can be a major problem when extinction is used. Even if the reinforcement happens only occasionally, that may prevent the intervention from being effective. Even very infrequent reinforcement is sometimes enough to maintain a target behavior indefinitely.

There's another source of reinforcement that is difficult to control; I wonder if anyone can think of it? How about it, Carlotta?

"It seems to me some things we do are reinforcing. They aren't reinforced by anything else; the behavior itself is reinforcing."

How about an example?

"Well, nobody has to pat me on the back to keep me eating chocolate; I eat it because I enjoy it. And I have a puppy named Ginger, and she chews the furniture. I don't think she does that because somebody does something reinforcing; I think that, for puppies, chewing on stuff is just reinforcing in itself."

Good point. Children provide another example. They have a lot of energy to burn. It may be that running around the house occurs, not because someone is providing a reinforcing consequence for that behavior, but because it feels good to run around. And it may be that some bizarre behaviors seen in certain psychiatric patients are reinforcing in and of themselves. We know that some autistic and retarded people injure themselves—by, for example, banging their heads against a wall—at least partly because the behavior produces attention or other reinforcers. But it's also possible that head banging has physiological effects that are reinforcing.

The point is that if a target behavior is going to be reinforced, either because someone is not cooperating with the intervention effort or because the behavior itself is reinforcing, then extinction is probably not going to work. With extinction, it is not enough to prevent the behavior from being reinforced *most* of the time; you have to be able to prevent the behavior from being reinforced virtually *all* the time. This is sometimes impossible.

So, uncontrolled reinforcement is a major problem when using extinction. What's another problem? Yes, John?

"Considering the cases you described, it looks to me like extinction might be kind of slow. That could be a problem."

Slowness
You're right, sometimes it is rather slow.[10] But why is that a problem?

"Well, I think the longer it takes to get rid of a behavior, the more likely parents and other people would be to give up."

Good point. So you're saying that if there are people involved who might not persevere, who might start reinforcing the behavior again, then extinction could be risky. What else might make extinction inappropriate? Yes, Brian?

"What if the target behavior is head banging, or some other self-injurious behavior? By the time the behavior had been extinguished, the kid might be blind."

An excellent point. It's hard to justify using extinction with behavior that is harmful, either to the person we're working with or to others. Suppose you're a teacher, and you've got a student who hits other kids? Or maybe he throws things across the room. The behavior might be reinforced by teacher attention, so you could get rid of the problem just by ignoring it. But you might have some students sent to the hospital before that happened. That's too high a price to pay for the solution.

A similar problem arises when the target behavior involves destruction of property. You can't merely walk away when a youngster tears pages out of a book. This is not to say that if a person is destructive or violent, you should allow that behavior to be reinforced. But in these situations, extinction alone is no longer an acceptable choice.

Side Effects

Extinction produces some rather dramatic side effects, and these can be problematic. The long-term effect of extinction is a steady and pronounced reduction in the frequency of the target behavior. But the immediate effect of putting a behavior on extinction is often a sudden and abrupt *increase* in the target behavior. This is called an extinction burst:

Extinction burst:
A sharp <u>increase</u> in the frequency of the behavior on extinction.

Laura the vomiter provides an example. Before the intervention, Laura usually vomited once or twice a day. But when the researchers put the behavior on extinction, the rate of vomiting increased dramatically. One day she vomited 21 times! Such extinction bursts are fairly common during the early stages of extinction. Now, why would an extinction burst be a problem? Carlotta?

"If you didn't know there was such a thing, you might think that extinction wasn't working and give up on it."

Exactly right. And unfortunately, this happens all the time. Suppose you become a parent and your child develops some sort of obnoxious behavior—let's say she uses swear words. You decide that the reinforcer for this behavior is probably the reaction it produces in adults, especially your spouse. He (or she) smiles at your daughter's verbal antics, and says things such as, "Don't talk like that, Sweetie," while smiling and patting her on the head. You discuss your theory with your spouse, deftly avoiding an argument by suggesting that you are both reinforcing the behavior, and you suggest that from now on you must both ignore the behavior totally. Your spouse doesn't believe a word of it, of course, but agrees to go along.

So you begin the extinction procedure—cursing no longer produces smiles, comments, or any other discernible reaction from you or your spouse. And what happens? The behavior gets worse! Your sweet little daughter starts adding indelicate modifiers to every noun and verb she has: "Pass the blankety-blank salt," she says. "Where's that blankety-blank dog of mine?" she asks. "Wow! This is a blankety-blank TV show!" she complains.

Your spouse notices the abrupt change for the worse and says sarcastically, "Well, thanks a lot, Professor Skinner. Your extinction procedure has made the problem twice as bad. Got any more bright ideas?" If you're going to use extinction to deal with a problem behavior, you have to let everyone involved know that the problem may get worse before it gets better.

If you become a parent, a teacher, a school counselor or do any kind of work that involves modifying other people's behavior, chances are you will see lots of extinction bursts. Actually, they need not be a serious problem as long as you persist with the extinction procedure. The trouble is that when an extinction burst occurs, people often go back to reinforcing the behavior.[11]

"That could make things even worse, couldn't it?"

Indeed it could, Belinda. If you provide reinforcement during an extinction burst, you're probably going to reinforce a higher rate of the behavior or a more intensive level of the behavior. If you put a child's tantrums on extinction, for example, then during the extinction burst you'll probably get even louder screaming and more throwing of objects than you normally get. If you then provide reinforcement, you've not only reinforced tantrumming, but louder and more destructive tantrumming.

An extinction burst is a fairly regular feature of extinction programs, but it's not the only side effect of extinction. Have you ever put money into a vending machine that was out of order? You put in your money, press the necessary button or plunger, and nothing happens. What's going on here? Yes, Carlotta?

"I'm on extinction."

You are?

"I mean, my *behavior* is on extinction.[12] Putting money in and pressing buttons usually is reinforced with food or whatever. If the machine is out of order, the behavior isn't reinforced, so it's on extinction."

Exactly right. Now, I know you've all been in this situation and you've seen other people in this situation. What happens?

"They push the buttons some more and they might put some more money in the machine. If their coin keeps falling through, they might try a different coin, or rub the coin on the floor before inserting it. I've seen people jiggle the plunger or press buttons harder or hold them down longer."

Yes. If the behavior that usually produces reinforcement doesn't work, you see all sorts of variations in the behavior. So another side effect of extinction is an increase in the variability of behavior. What does the vending machine operator do if none of this behavior works? Yes, Belinda?

"Sometimes people get angry. They start cursing at the machine; they might pound on it or kick it."

I think we've all seen that. Emotional outbursts are a common side effect of extinction. Back in the days of typewriters, it was common to see a person pound on the machine when it misspelled a word; today, people sometimes pound on their computers when the machines don't do as the operators would like—that is, when the computers "withhold reinforcement." Emotional behavior is often seen in children when their behavior is put on extinction. If a child doesn't get the dessert he asked for, he may throw the proffered food on the floor.

Emotional outbursts during extinction are usually short-lived and need not pose any special problem so long as they are not reinforced. That, of course, is precisely the problem: When emotional behavior occurs, it often *is* reinforced. The student who curses loudly and bangs his computer with a fist may be offered help by a classmate. The child who throws his dessert on the floor may become the center of attention for the entire family. So long as the target behavior is not reinforced, it will continue to decline. But if the emotional side effects are reinforced, the effort to get rid of one troublesome behavior may actually establish a new troublesome behavior.

So far we've talked about extinction side effects that you have all seen and readily recognize when they are pointed out to you. Now I want to talk about two side effects that you may have seen but not recognized as products of extinction.

Consider 4-year-old Harry: Whenever little Harry is denied anything, he throws things around the room; then he gets what he wants. This method of obtaining things becomes well-established and continues until Harry starts school, where he encounters teachers and children who no longer reinforce this repugnant behavior. Gradually, Harry learns more acceptable ways of getting the things he wants. He asks for them nicely. He says "please." He trades items. He waits his turn. These more desirable behaviors become well-established at school, and they occur sometimes at home, where they are also reinforced. Everyone says little Harry is growing up—as if the change in behavior had nothing to do with the change in consequences, but were the inevitable result of time.

Years pass, and little Harry is a young man. He falls in love with a woman and they marry. As a modern, politically correct couple, they divide the household chores: He does the cleaning, she does the cooking, and so on. Life is good for Harry and his bride, but there are a few little things that his wife does that annoy him. Why must she, for example, squeeze the toothpaste from the middle of the tube? He asks her nicely not to do it, and explains that although it is a small thing, it annoys him greatly. She agrees to mend her ways, but she forgets. One day after noticing the toothpaste tube has been smashed in the middle again, Harry confronts his wife and throws the tube of toothpaste across the room. She is rather frightened by this outburst and swears she will never squeeze the toothpaste from the middle again. The next time she commits one of her minor offenses, Harry throws something across the room. Pretty soon, Harry is throwing things around every time things are not just the way he wants them. Now, what has happened here? Yes, Belinda?

"Asking politely is on extinction, and throwing things is reinforced. So he's given up asking nicely and returned to throwing things."

Exactly so. But why did throwing things get reestablished? Why didn't he shout or sit down and cry or maybe walk out of the house? Yes, Brian?

"Because throwing things had been reinforced in the past?"

Yes! During extinction, behavior that *used* to produce reinforcement tends to reappear. This phenomenon is called resurgence[13]:

Resurgence:
The reappearance, during extinction,
of previously effective behavior.

Some of you may see a similarity between resurgence and a phenomenon described by Sigmund Freud. Any guesses? Yes, Carlotta?

"It sounds like what Freud called regression."

Yes it does. According to Freud, people sometimes revert to less mature forms of behavior. He called the phenomenon *regression*. Freud believed that the behavior that reappears must be less sophisticated, less mature, than the behavior it replaces. But Freud's ideas were based exclusively on case studies. Experimental research suggests that *any* behavior that was once effective in producing reinforcement may reappear, or resurge, if another way of obtaining reinforcement is put on extinction.[14]

Resurgence is a possible side effect of extinction for which the behaviorist must be on the lookout. If the behavior that resurges is unacceptable, it must not be reinforced or we have simply replaced one problem behavior with another. In fact, it is possible that resurgence underlies claims about symptom substitution. Who recalls what symptom substitution is? Maya?

"That's the idea that if you get rid of a symptom, some other symptom will take its place."

Just so. And you can see that if you put a problem behavior on extinction and some other problem behavior resurges, you might conclude that symptom substitution had occurred. If you withhold reinforcement for a problem behavior, old ways of obtaining reinforcement may reappear. But so long as the resurging behavior is not reinforced, it won't become a problem. It will extinguish quickly.

Now there's one more side effect of extinction you need to know about. Sometimes after the successful completion of an extinction procedure, when the target behavior is said to be extinguished, the behavior suddenly reappears without warning. This phenomenon is called spontaneous recovery:

Spontaneous recovery: The reappearance of the target behavior following its extinction.

Spontaneous recovery need not be a serious problem so long as the behavior is not reinforced when it recovers. The trouble is, the behavior often *is* reinforced. What sometimes happens is that the problem seems to have been solved—the tantrums or vomiting or whatever no longer occurs—and then suddenly it reappears. Well, when that happens, people are apt to respond. This is especially true when children are involved. If a child gets sick or starts screaming, adults tend to rush to the child to lend assistance. That often reinforces the behavior. When that happens, the extinction procedure must be repeated. Fortunately, extinction takes far less time the second time around. Still, it is far better to avoid reinforcing the target behavior when spontaneous recovery occurs.

"Dr. Cee? I'm having a little trouble seeing the difference between spontaneous recovery and resurgence."

There is definitely a similarity between them, Jamal. Both involve the reappearance of a behavior that was once effective. But there is an important difference. Does anyone see what it is? . . . Midori?

"In spontaneous recovery, the behavior that reappears is the behavior that's currently on extinction. In resurgence, the behavior that reappears is some *other* behavior that used to be reinforced."

Well done.

Now, you've just seen that there are some problems with extinction. Fortunately, these problems are largely avoided when extinction is used in combination with other procedures. One that I want to discuss today is differential reinforcement.

Differential Reinforcement Defined

Differential reinforcement is an umbrella term for several procedures in which the rate of a target behavior is changed by the combined use of extinction and reinforcement.

Differential reinforcement: Any procedure that combines extinction and reinforcement to change the frequency of a target behavior.

As this definition implies, you can use differential reinforcement to increase or decrease the frequency of a behavior.[15] However, our focus will be on the latter.

"I guess I'm dense, but I don't see how you can reduce the frequency of a behavior with reinforcement."

You're not dense, Belinda. Part of the difficulty comes from the fact that differential reinforcement is not one procedure, but several related procedures. All that they have in common is that they combine extinction and reinforcement. You'll understand differential reinforcement better when we have considered some specific kinds of differential reinforcement.

Kinds of Differential Reinforcement

DRL

Let's start with an easy question: What kind of problem are we dealing with today? . . . Midori?

"Problems where the behavior occurs too often?"

Right. Well, if we want the behavior to occur less often, why don't we provide reinforcement for the behavior when it occurs *less often*? Isn't that a clever idea? It's called differential reinforcement of low rate, or DRL, for short.

DRL:
The procedure of reinforcing the target behavior only when it occurs at a low rate.

"I still don't get it, Dr. Cee. How can you reinforce the behavior without making it occur more often?"

It does sound absurd, doesn't it, Jamal? But you're not just reinforcing the behavior, you're reinforcing the act of performing the behavior *at a low rate*.[16] There are two ways of doing that. One way is to provide reinforcement only if the behavior occurs less often than a specified number of times in a given period. The other way is to reinforce the behavior only if it occurs after a specified interval.

Let's consider the first form of DRL. Suppose you have a youngster—let's call him Mike—who eats too fast. Mike is a kind of human threshing machine, a regular food harvester. You want him to eat more slowly. What does that mean? It could mean that the fork makes fewer trips to his mouth each minute. If he's currently shoveling food at the rate of ten forkloads a minute, you might provide reinforcement only if he makes no more than four trips with the fork during a minute.

"So you're reinforcing the act of eating slowly?"

You could say that, Brian. You're reinforcing the performance of the target behavior at a lower rate.

Okay, now let's consider the second way of using DRL. You're still working with Mighty Mouth Mike, but this time you're going to record how long the intervals are between mouthfuls. On average, you find that a forkful of food finds its way into Mike's mouth every 6 seconds. After this, you provide reinforcement only when he takes food after an interval of at least 15 seconds. In other words, after he uses that fork, he has to wait 15 seconds before using it again, or he gets no reinforcer. By increasing the interval between bites, you slow down the rate of eating. You have a question, Maya?

"Yes. What do you do if he takes food before the 15 seconds are up? Like, suppose 12 seconds go by, and he takes some food. What do you do?"

You start counting seconds again. Every time he puts that fork in his mouth, the 15-second interval starts again. He does not receive a reinforcer unless 15 seconds have passed since the last time he used the fork.

"Wow. You're hard."

Well, Alfred, I might have to set a lower standard to begin with. Fifteen seconds might be too much to ask from someone who is bending that elbow every 6 seconds. But whatever the interval is, the clock starts each time Mike takes a bite of food.

The two forms of DRL are more or less equivalent. They're just different ways of reinforcing a lower rate of the target behavior.[17] Now, Mike is a hypothetical case, but cases of fast eating have been treated successfully with DRL.[18] Now let's look at another form of differential reinforcement, DRA.

DRA

DRA stands for differential reinforcement of alternative behavior. As the name implies, the idea is to put the target behavior on extinction and reinforce some alternative behavior. Here's a definition:

DRA:
The procedure of reinforcing
an alternative behavior instead
of the target behavior.

In DRA, reinforcers that were available for the target behavior become contingent on some more acceptable alternative behavior. DRA gives the person an alternative way of obtaining reinforcers.

Undesirable behavior is often an unacceptable way of achieving acceptable ends.[19] Babies who are wet, hungry, or experiencing some other form of discomfort typically react to their discomfort by crying. This behavior often induces someone to take action that reduces the infant's discomfort. Crying in such circumstances is thus reinforced. As babies acquire language, the time spent crying drops off.[20] This makes sense: If you can say "cookie" or "eat" and receive food, there is no need to scream yourself hoarse. Toddlers also become less aggressive as they master language.[21] People often attribute such changes to maturation, as if the changes were the inevitable result of aging. But what is more likely is that one way of obtaining reinforcers is replaced with a more efficient (or "grown-up") way of obtaining those reinforcers.

Edward Carr has pointed out that in many cases, abnormal behavior and normal behavior are functionally equivalent: They serve the same purpose, which is to say that they produce similar consequences.[22] When a child is hungry, crying is functionally equivalent to saying "eat" if they both produce food. If the child can obtain food by saying "eat," he will depend less on crying. It follows that we may reduce undesirable behavior by providing the person with an alternative means of obtaining reinforcers. That's what DRA does.

DRI

Suppose I asked you to walk across the room. That's easy, right? And suppose I asked you to sit in a chair. Again, it's easy. Now suppose I ask you to sit in a chair and walk across the room at the same time. To sit in a chair means to have your weight on the chair and the chair on the floor. To walk you have to be upright, with your weight directly on the floor. It's impossible to sit and walk at the same time.

Now, if I reinforce sitting, the amount of time spent sitting should increase. And if the amount of time spent sitting increases, the amount of time spent walking necessarily . . . what, Jamal?

"Decreases."

Exactly. Some kinds of behavior are incompatible: If you do one, you cannot do the other. So one way to reduce the frequency of an unwanted behavior is to reinforce behavior that is incompatible with that behavior. That's DRI—short for differential reinforcement of incompatible behavior:

DRI:
**The procedure of reinforcing a behavior
that is incompatible with the target behavior.**

The example of DRI that I've given—reinforcing sitting and not reinforcing walking—is not as silly as it sounds. A common complaint among elementary school teachers is that some of the students spend far too much time wandering around the room instead of sitting at their desks. The kids always have a good reason for leaving their seat, of course: "I have to sharpen my pencil"; "I need to ask Su Li something"; "I want to see if it's snowing outside." But the teacher would rather that they were writing or solving math problems or discussing an assignment with their study group.

It turns out that the chief reinforcer for being out of their seats is often the attention, albeit critical attention, of the teacher: "Billy, what are you doing out of your seat?" "Mary, get back to your desk!" "George!! Will you *stop* wandering around the room!"

Teachers can sometimes reduce the frequency of such meanderings by ignoring them; that is, by putting the behavior on extinction. Unfortunately, this takes a while, especially if the students have received teacher attention for wandering for some time.

DRI speeds up the process and avoids or reduces the negative side effects of extinction. As with DRA, you're creating a situation in which the youngsters can still get attention, but they get it for behavior that is incompatible with the troublesome behavior. Whereas students used to get attention by leaving their seats, now they get attention by staying in their seats: "Billy, I'm glad to see you hard at work"; "Mary, you're doing a great job of working at your desk"; "George, it certainly is nice to see you working."

Notice that there is no sarcasm in the attention the teacher provides. The teacher doesn't say, "Well, George, I'm glad to see you getting reacquainted with your desk!" Compliments are more likely to be reinforcing if they are genuine.

In a way, DRI is really just a form of DRA. The difference between them is—well, you tell me. Carlotta, what's the difference between DRI and DRA?

"In DRI, the behavior you reinforce is incompatible with the behavior you're trying to decrease; in DRA, the reinforced behavior is different from the problem behavior, but it's not necessarily incompatible with it."

Sehr gut! Now let's consider some studies that used differential reinforcement to solve a behavior problem.

Illustrative Studies

DRL: Earl, the Moving Machine

Gerald Patterson describes a case of hyperactivity treated with DRL.[23] His client was Earl, a 9-year-old boy who was having trouble in the second grade. Earl's early history may reveal the reason for his trouble. Before his adoption at age 3, he had been severely abused by his parents and grandparents. He had received a skull fracture before his first birthday, and he had recurring convulsions and some coordination problems. A neurological examination at age 4 revealed an abnormal EEG and other evidence of minimal brain damage. He tested at the borderline level of intelligence. Brain injury is a common factor in the backgrounds of many hyperactive people, and it seems likely that Earl's hyperactivity was in some way due to neurological damage.

In any case, Earl was one of those kids who seemed to be constantly in motion. He would work on an assignment for only a short period before moving around the room, sometimes pushing his desk ahead of him through the classroom. He would often hit or pinch other children without provocation. Sometimes he would throw himself into a group of children as though he were a bowling ball and they were a rack of pins. Patterson found that most of Earl's objectionable behavior consisted of talking, pushing, hitting, pinching, looking around, moving about, or "moving in location"—tapping, squirming, and handling objects.

Trying to monitor a student's behavior for 10-second intervals and provide immediate reinforcement of appropriate behavior is difficult in a classroom. Patterson found a rather clever way to do it: He used a box, about half the size of a shoe box, with a flashlight bulb and the dial of a counting mechanism. The experimenter, who sat across the room from Earl, controlled the bulb and counter. Whenever Earl managed to get through a 10-second period without talking, moving about, or crashing into someone, the lightbulb would flash, the counter would click, and Earl would have earned one M&M candy. At the end of each session, the M&M's would be divided among the students in the class. (Later on in the program, pennies were sometimes provided instead of candy.[24]) The other students were told what was going on, and they were told that they could help Earl by not disturbing him during these sessions.

It turned out that Earl was able to control his hyperactive behavior. In fact, he earned from 60 to 100 reinforcers (M&Ms or pennies) per session. Other children in the class started to provide reinforcers as well. When the experimenter announced how Earl had done, the students applauded. They would also walk by his desk from time to time and look at the counter to see how he was faring. And during recess and other breaks, students often complimented Earl by saying things such as, "You sure are doing good; you get better every day."[25] These reactions from his peers probably were reinforcing.

The result of all these reinforcers was that Earl calmed down substantially during the training sessions. In fact, Earl was sometimes one of the best-behaved students in the class. The intervention did not by any means end Earl's problems—or those he caused for his teacher and classmates. But it did demonstrate that Earl could learn to control the frenetic rate of his behavior. He could—a question, John?

"Does that mean that his hyperactivity wasn't caused by brain damage after all?"

Why do you say that?

"Well, if it was organic, he wouldn't be able to control it."

Another common misconception raises its ugly head! Just because a behavior problem has an organic origin doesn't mean it can't be dealt with by providing certain kinds of experiences. There are lots of organic disorders that respond very well to operant procedures. For instance, a person can have a stroke and lose the ability to speak or read. Operant procedures can help the person recover those lost skills. That doesn't mean that the stroke never happened. Mental retardation and autism are organic disorders, yet operant procedures help people with those disorders. We have to get away from this idea that if a behavior problem arises from an organic condition, nothing can be done about it until someone finds a medical cure. That's not so, and it's a mistake that has been very costly in terms of human suffering. All right, now for a case involving DRA.

DRA: *Malfunctioning Communication*

Edward Carr has developed a procedure for helping seriously disturbed children. He calls it *functional communication training,* but I think we can consider it a form of DRA. In one well-known study, he and Mark Durand worked with four disturbed youngsters who were accustomed to receiving reinforcement by means of disruptive behavior.[26] The researchers studied the consequences of the misbehavior and found that in some cases the reinforcer that maintained the behavior was adult attention; in other cases the reinforcer was escape from an unpleasant task. A child might scream and holler because doing so resulted in attention, or he might scream and holler because when he did so he escaped a frustrating situation.

Carr and Durand's solution to the problem behavior was to teach the youngsters more acceptable ways of obtaining these same reinforcers. Instead of receiving attention for throwing things about a room, for example, a child learned to get attention by asking, "Am I doing good work?" Instead of getting relief from a frustrating task by throwing tantrums and biting the teacher, he learned to ask for help. Following this training, *all* of the children showed better than 90% reduction in the disruptive behavior in a matter of *minutes.*

"Dr. Cee?"

Yes, Midori?

"If it's that simple, why didn't the kids figure it out on their own? Why did they have to be taught what to do?"

A fair question. Does anybody have an answer? Brian?

"Didn't you say these kids were disturbed? If they're autistic, or schizophrenic, ordinary learning experiences might not be enough. People with mental retardation need extra help in learning lots of ordinary things, like tying their shoes and using the bathroom. Some kids might need special training in learning how to get attention or deal with difficult tasks."

Exactomundo! And sometimes people don't even get those "ordinary learning experiences" you mentioned. A lot of kids who are not psychotic or retarded behave in very troublesome ways, as some of you will discover if you become teachers or parents. Often the problem is that reinforcement for more acceptable forms of behavior just hasn't been available. Children aren't going to learn to ask for food if the only time they get fed is when they scream and cry.

I said before that babies cry less as they learn to speak. But that's not some sort of law of nature; that's the result of reinforcement. If speaking doesn't work— if saying "cookie" or "eat" doesn't get the child food—we shouldn't be surprised if he continues to cry when hungry rather than asking for food. That's what often happens with neglected children, and their development suffers.

People generally do what works. That applies to babies, to ordinary kids and adults, to workers in offices and factories, and to psychiatric patients on the locked ward. DRA is a way of providing people with an alternative way of obtaining reinforcers. As the alternative behavior increases in frequency, the unacceptable behavior decreases.

DRI: Helen Talks Crazy

All right, suppose you have a psychotic patient—let's call her Helen—who talks a great deal, but what she says doesn't make a lot of sense. She talks mostly about her illegitimate child and the men she claims are chasing her. She just talks and talks and talks about these topics until people can't stand it. The behavior is so annoying that in the past 4 months, Helen has been beaten several times by other patients. If you sat next to Helen on a train, after a while you'd want to throw her off. The reinforcer maintaining this incessant nonsensical speech seems to be the attention of others, particularly nurses who nod and say things like, "Yes, I understand." Now, how could you apply DRI—differential reinforcement of incompatible behavior—in this situation? . . . Yes, Jamal?

> "I'd say that being quiet is incompatible with talking, so I'd reinforce being quiet."

Well, that would be DRI, but I think I see a problem with your plan. Does anyone else see a problem? Yes, Carlotta?

> "Being quiet is incompatible with talking, but it seems to me you want the person to talk. You just don't want her to talk crazy."

Very good. So, Jamal, what desirable behavior would be incompatible with talking crazy?

> "Uhm, talking sense? I mean, talking, but talking normally."

Exactly. So what would you do to help this woman?

> "I'd ask the nurses to pay attention to her only when what she said made sense."

Excellent! And that's just what the behaviorists involved in this case—I didn't make this one up—that's just what they did.[27] The result was a sharp decline in psychotic talk.

The researchers, Teodoro Ayllon and Jack Michael, also note that the other patients no longer hit Helen. That's an interesting point: When you help a person change her behavior for the better, there are often all sorts of positive side effects, sometimes unpredictable. In this case, one result of changing Helen's speech patterns was that the other patients stopped hitting her.

Unfortunately, after several weeks of steady decline in psychotic speech, a problem arose. The data chart looked something like this:

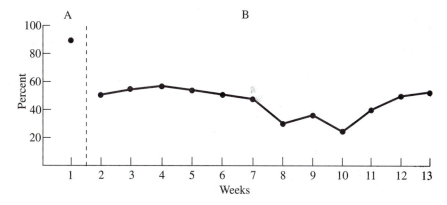

Figure 6-3. Extinction of psychotic talk. Adapted from Ayllon and Michael (1959).

Do you see the problem? How about it, John?

"It looks like the behavior became more frequent again around week 11."

Yes, it does. Do you have any idea why this might have occurred?

"Maybe the nurses started reinforcing crazy talk again."

No, the nurses seem to have stayed the course. Any other ideas? Midori?

"If it wasn't the nurses, then someone else must have provided reinforcement. Maybe the other patients."

You're on the right track. If a behavior increases in frequency, it's reasonable to assume that it has reinforcing consequences. In this case, the researchers identified outside sources of reinforcement. The main one may have been a social worker. At one point the patient told one of the nurses, "Well, you're not listening to me. I'll have to go and see Miss _____ (the social worker) again, 'cause she told me that if she would listen to my past she could help me."[28] Reinforcement may also have been provided by some visitors, including a group of volunteers who came to entertain the patients. Such inappropriate reinforcement is called . . . what is it called, Alfred?

"It's something to do with booze. Is it hooch something?"

Not quite, but you're in the right neighborhood. You just need a little prompt, a *leg* up, as it were.

"Oh, right! It's called bootleg reinforcement."

Good man. And bootleg reinforcement is a real pain in the coccyx for anyone trying to reduce the frequency of troublesome behavior. It is less problematic when extinction is combined with differential reinforcement, but it's still a problem.

Okay, we've discussed DRL, DRA, and DRI. There are other forms of differential reinforcement, but these three are probably the most frequently used. If properly applied, they will bring down the rate at which an unwanted behavior occurs in a hurry. I say, "If properly applied." Let's talk about the proper use of differential reinforcement.

Rules for Using Differential Reinforcement

Differential reinforcement is merely the combination of extinction and reinforcement, so the rules to follow are basically those we discussed earlier in considering those procedures. I'm sure you can guess the first rule. What is it, John?

"Decide what behavior you want to change—the target behavior."

Good. I'll put that on the board:

1. Define the target behaviors.

With differential reinforcement, there are generally two target behaviors. You're trying to reduce the frequency of one behavior and increase the frequency of another behavior. We're trying to reduce Earl's tendency to behave like the Tasmanian Devil, and more like a little boy; we're trying to get Helen to talk less about things that provoke assaults, and more about things that people find interesting. In some cases the two target behaviors are different rates of the same activity. For example, if Junior eats like a ravenous wolf, you can identify two rates of eating, fast and slow. You want him to do less fast eating and more slow eating.

Now, differential reinforcement combines reinforcement with extinction, so rule number two is to put the unwanted behavior (or rate) on extinction:

2. Put the undesirable target behavior (or rate) on extinction.

You've already learned about extinction, so you know that before you can use extinction, you need to identify the reinforcers that maintain the problem behavior. When you've done so, you prevent those reinforcers from following the unwanted behavior. If you are going to use DRA or DRI, you withhold reinforcement of the problem behavior; if you're going to use DRL, you withhold reinforcement of the problem *rate* of the target behavior.

While you have the undesirable behavior on extinction, you reinforce the desirable behavior:

3. Reinforce the desirable target behavior (or rate).

Actually, it's probably a mistake to speak of undesirable and desirable behavior here. Very often the behavior you want to weaken is perfectly acceptable, it just occurs at too high a rate. The "desirable" behavior may be no more desirable than the problem behavior in absolute terms. As is often the case, the difference is a matter of frequency. In any case, you put the behavior you want to weaken on extinction and reinforce the behavior you want to strengthen.

Now, we have one more rule. I'm sure you can guess what that is. What is it, Maya?

"Monitor the results?"

Right:

4. Monitor results.

Once you've implemented your intervention, you have only to take care that it is producing the desired results. You may need to make some adjustments: Bootleg reinforcement of the behavior on extinction may prove a problem, or the reinforcers you're using to strengthen the desirable behavior may not be producing much change. If so, you'll have to do some fine-tuning, but that's pretty much par for the course.

Okay, today we have discussed two procedures for reducing the frequency of behavior, extinction and differential reinforcement. Do you think you understand them? Could you pass a little pop quiz? Hmm? Well, in lieu of a pop quiz, let's have a quick review.

Review

Let's start our review with a definition of extinction. Maya?

"It means withholding the reinforcers that maintain a behavior."

Right. Extinction is a good way of dealing with problems involving . . . involving what, Carlotta?

"I guess you mean, involving behavior that occurs too often."

You guessed right; that's just what I meant. All right. We discussed four rules to follow in using extinction. What was the first rule, Maya?

"Define the target behavior."

And once you've defined the target behavior, you need to identify . . . what, John?

"The reinforcers that maintain the target behavior."

Right. The next step is . . . Jamal?

"Withhold those reinforcers."

And the last rule to remember is . . . what, Alfred?

"Monitor the results. You have to see what results you get so you can tell if the procedure is working."

Exactly right. Okay, now we talked about some problems with extinction. One had to do with uncontrollable reinforcers. Can you tell me about that, Brian?

"Some reinforcers may be outside of the behaviorist's reach. Some people who are asked to stop reinforcing the target behavior may not comply; they may continue to reinforce it. And sometimes the behavior itself might be reinforcing. Like watching television. It's hard to see how you could use extinction to reduce TV watching if the reinforcers come from watching TV."

So instead of being on extinction, the behavior continues to be reinforced. That's a problem even if the behavior isn't reinforced very often, because sometimes occasional reinforcement is enough to maintain a behavior at a high rate. Another problem with extinction is that it tends to be rather slow. Why is that a problem, Midori?

"Because if it takes a long time, people might give up on it. They might start reinforcing the behavior."

Anything else?

"Well, if someone is injuring herself or others, you couldn't just wait for the behavior to extinguish."

Exactly right on both points. So the fact that extinction may take a while can sometimes make it inappropriate.

Another problem we discussed had to do with some troublesome side effects of extinction. One of these is the sudden *increase* in the behavior that's on extinction. This sudden increase is called an . . . Alfred?

"An extinction bust?"

Close, but no balloon.

"*Burst.* An extinction burst."

That's the one. Another side effect of extinction also involves an increase. What sort of increase? Yes, Belinda?

"There's an increase in the variability of behavior. The person tries all sorts of variations of the behavior before giving up on it."

Yes. And you can see that that makes sense. Sometimes when one behavior is ineffective, a slightly different behavior will work. The tendency to vary our behavior is probably reinforced on lots of occasions, so it's not surprising that we try different things during extinction. What other side effects might occur during extinction? Brian?

"Emotional outbursts?"

Yes. When a behavior that has been reinforced many times in the past suddenly stops producing reinforcement, people are apt to get emotional. If you've ever kicked a door that wouldn't open, you've experienced an emotional outburst associated with extinction. Emotional behavior is not always a side effect of extinction, but it is something you have to be on guard against.

Two more side effects we discussed were resurgence and spontaneous recovery. They're similar, but I expect you to be able to distinguish between them. Let's take resurgence first. Jamal?

"That's the reappearance during extinction of some behavior that used to produce reinforcement."

Good. And what is spontaneous recovery, Midori?

"That's the reappearance of the behavior currently on extinction after it has dropped to a very low level."

Right. The rate of the behavior falls off and then suddenly it shoots up again, even though it hasn't been reinforced. What's the difference between these two side effects, resurgence and spontaneous recovery? Carlotta?

"Spontaneous recovery involves the target behavior, the behavior that's on extinction; resurgence involves some other behavior, a behavior that had been reinforced in the past."

Despite the problems we've discussed, extinction is a very useful procedure. However, it's usually most helpful when used in conjunction with other procedures. We talked about one of those other procedures today. What was it, Belinda?

"Differential reinforcement?"

Right. And what is differential reinforcement?

"It's a procedure that combines extinction and reinforcement to change the frequency of some behavior."

Very good. Now, do you remember Helen? She was the woman who talked so incessantly and nonsensically that the other patients hit her. The behaviorists who took on her case asked the nurses to pay attention to Helen whenever she talked sensibly, and to ignore her when she talked nonsense. What procedure is that, John?

"DRI."

Right. Can you explain why it's DRI?

"Well, the two kinds of behavior—talking sense and talking nonsense—are incompatible. If the one increases, the other necessarily decreases."

Excellent. Now, if I asked you to devise a way of changing Helen's behavior using DRA; how would you do it . . . Brian?

"I'd ignore the psychotic talk, and I'd provide attention for some alternative behavior, such as helping the nurses."

Okay. As long as talking crazy isn't reinforced, it will drop off and be replaced by the other activity. Which procedure do you think would work better in this situation, DRI or DRA? Carlotta?

"I think DRI."

Why?

"Because with DRA, you might reinforce crazy talk accidentally. Helen can talk crazy at the same time she's helping the nurses, and if she gets attention while she's helping, she's also getting attention while she's talking nonsense. You might be reinforcing both."

Good point. Now let's consider Mike, whose mouth was faster than a speeding taco. We talked about using differential reinforcement to slow his eating pace down. What sort of differential reinforcement did we talk about using? Maya?

"DRL."

Right. Now let's quickly review the rules for using differential reinforcement. Can you name all four of them, Jamal?

"The first is to define the target behaviors."

Yes. You have two target behaviors: the behavior you want to weaken and the behavior you want to strengthen. Next?

"Put the problem target behavior on extinction and the other target behavior on reinforcement."

Yes, that takes care of rules 2 and 3. And the last rule?

"Monitor the results of the intervention."

Very good. Well, we've now discussed two procedures for reducing the frequency of unwanted behavior—extinction and differential reinforcement. Neither of these procedures is generally familiar to the public. Next time we will talk about a procedure that is familiar to everyone: punishment.

◀ **Exercises** ▶

 Feed the Skeleton

I. Extinction Defined

    A. Extinction is _____ .

II. Illustrative Studies

    A. Bill's crying was extinguished by withholding _____ .

    B. Laura's vomiting was extinguished by withholding _____ .

III. Extinction Rules

    A. _____ .

    B. Identify the _____ .

    C. Withhold _____ .

    D. _____ .

IV. Problems with Extinction

    A. Inappropriate reinforcement is called _____ reinforcement.

    B. Extinction is inappropriate for some problems because it is

    _____ .

    C. The side effects of extinction include:

        1. the sudden increase in the unwanted behavior, called an extinction

        _____ .

        2. resurgence, which is _____ .

        3. spontaneous recovery, the _____ .

V. Differential Reinforcement

    A. Differential reinforcement is _____ .

    B. Kinds of Differential Reinforcement

        1. DRL stands for _____ .

            a. One form of DRL is based on _____ .

            b. Another form of DRL is based on _____ .

        2. DRA stands for _____ .

        3. DRI stands for _____ .

VI. Illustrative Studies

    A. Earl got control of his tendency to locomote when _____

    _____ .

    B. Carr treats behavior disorders by _____

    _____ .

    C. Helen's aggravating speech changed when _____

    _____ .

VII. The rules for using differential reinforcement are:

A. _____ ____ .

B. Withhold _____ .

C. Reinforce _____ .

D. _____ .

Daffy Advice:
Daphne Donchano Answers Your Questions
Can you offer better advice than Daffy?

Dear Daffy:

My little girl speaks with a lisp. People can understand her perfectly, and she is doing well academically in the third grade. The trouble is that a lot of the other children at school tease her unmercifully. She comes home crying two or three times a week. What can I do to help?

Regards,

Lisper's Mother

Dear Lisper's Mother:

When I was a little girl, there was a boy in my class who lisped badly, and we teased him constantly. That little boy is now a very successful speech therapist who probably makes more money than you and I do put together. So I say, don't mess with a system that works. This may be the best thing that ever happened to your daughter.

Matilda's Rages
Remember Matilda, the woman who wore an extra 20 pounds of clothes? Ayllon used a kind of shaping procedure to get her to shed some of the excess items. You may recall that Matilda engaged in some emotional outbursts at the beginning of the shaping process: crying, shouting, and throwing chairs around. You should now be better prepared to explain this behavior, so explain it.

"It's like, annoying, you know?"
You are a teacher. Your students' tendency to say, "I'm like," "he's like," and other "like" expressions drives you up the wall. You also recognize that this behavior is not helpful to their literary development. How do you go about using differential reinforcement to reduce the frequency of these expressions by your students?

Practice Quiz

1. Extinction and differential reinforcement are both often used to _____ _____ the rate of behavior.

2. DRA stands for differential reinforcement of _____ behavior.

3. Ayllon and Michael reduced bizarre speech in Helen by providing attention whenever she spoke rationally. This is an example of the form of differential reinforcement known as _____ .

4. The first step in using differential reinforcement is to _____ ; the first step in using extinction is to _____ .

5. The reappearance of a target behavior following its extinction is called

_____ .

6. The procedure that is most appropriate for reducing the rate of a desirable behavior is differential reinforcement of _____ .

7. Extinction is often inappropriate for injurious behavior because

_____ .

8. _____ reinforcement is inappropriate reinforcement that undermines an intervention.

9. If a teacher wants to reduce the rate at which one of her fourth-graders leaves his seat, she might use DRI by providing a reinforcer whenever

_____ .

10. The only sure way of determining whether a particular consequence maintains a behavior is to _____ .

Reprint: EXTINGUISHED TEARS
by Carl D. Williams

This famous article is an early example of the good use to which extinction can be put. It illustrates not only the effectiveness of extinction but also how readily the strength of an extinguished behavior may be reestablished by "bootleg reinforcement"—a major weakness of the procedure.

This paper reports the successful treatment of tyrant-like tantrum behavior in a male child by the removal of reinforcement. The subject (S) was approximately 21 months old. He had been seriously ill much of the first 18 months of his life. His health then improved considerably, and he gained weight and vigor.

S now demanded the special care and attention that had been given him over the many critical months. He enforced some of his wishes, especially at bedtime, by unleashing tantrum behavior to control the actions of his parents.

The parents and an aunt took turns putting him to bed both at night and for S's afternoon nap. If the parent left the bedroom after putting S in his bed, S would scream and fuss until the parent returned to the room. As a result, the parent was unable to leave the bedroom until after S went to sleep. If the parent began to read while in the bedroom, S would cry until the reading material was put down. The parents felt that S enjoyed his control over them and that he fought off going to sleep as long as he could. In any event, a parent was spending from one-half to two hours each bedtime just waiting in the bedroom until S went to sleep.

Following medical reassurance regarding S's physical condition, it was decided to remove the reinforcement of this tyrant-like behavior. Consistent with the learning principle that, in general, behavior that is not reinforced will be extinguished, a parent or the aunt put S to bed in a leisurely and relaxed fashion. After bedtime pleasantries, the parent left the bedroom and closed the door. S screamed and raged, but the the parent did not re-enter the room. The duration of screaming and crying was obtained from the time the door was closed.

The results are shown in Fig. 1. It can be seen that S continued screaming for 45 min. the first time he was put to bed in the first extinction series. S did not cry at all the second time he was put to bed. This is perhaps attributable to his fatigue from his crying of Occasion 1. By the tenth occasion, S no longer whimpered, fussed or cried when the parent left the room. Rather, he smiled as they left. The parents felt that he made happy sounds until he dropped off to sleep.

About a week later, S screamed and fussed after his aunt put him to bed, probably reflecting spontaneous recovery of the tantrum behavior. The aunt then reinforced the tantrum behavior by returning to S's bedroom and remaining there until he went to sleep. It was then necessary to extinguish this behavior a second time.

Figure 1 shows that the second extinction curve is similar to the first. Both curves are generally similar to extinction curves obtained with sub-human subjects. The second extinction series reached zero by the ninth occasion. No further tantrums at bedtime were reported during the next two years.

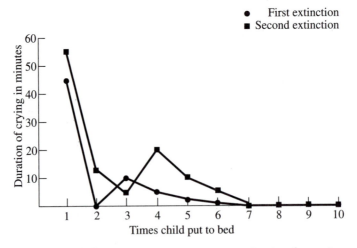

Figure 1. *Length of crying in two extinction series as a function of successive occasions of being put to bed.*

It should be emphasized that the treatment in this case did not involve aversive punishment. All that was done was to remove the reinforcement. Extinction of the tyrant-like behavior then occurred.

No unfortunate side- or aftereffects of this treatment were observed. At three and three-quarters years of age, S appeared to be a friendly, expressive, outgoing child.

Excerpted from "The Elimination of Tantrum Behavior by Extinction Procedures," by C. D. Williams. In *Journal of Abnormal and Social Psychology, 59,* © 1959 American Psychological Association.

Reprint: Exorcising a Witch
by Brad A. Alford

Introductory textbooks in behavior analysis typically describe the prototypical use of treatment procedures, rather than its many variants. Moreover, in an attempt to clarify how a particular procedure is used, the tendency is to ignore or minimize the role of other procedures that may be involved. This can give the student the impression that the procedures usually take the same form and are used more or less in isolation from one another. The truth is that most procedures for changing behavior can take a myriad of forms, and more often than not a procedure is used in conjunction with several others. See if you can spot the use of differential reinforcement (and other procedures) in this study of delusional thinking:

. . . The present study employed a single-case experimental analysis to ascertain the effects of behavioral procedures designed to directly modify chronic schizophrenic delusional beliefs while actively avoiding belief confrontation (cf. Milton, Patwa, & Hafner, 1978). Consistent with the notion that pharmacological and behavioral interventions may work synergistically in effecting improvement (cf. Bellack, 1984; Hartman & Cashman, 1983), effects of treatment were evaluated subsequent to stabilization on appropriate neural medication:

Method

Subject

The participant in this study was a 22-year-old white male whose DSM-III diagnosis was schizophrenia, paranoid, chronic (295–32). Diagnosis was obtained from careful review of the patient's clinical records, as well as from a clinical interview structured to assess presence or absence of DSM-III classification criteria. At the time of this experiment, he had a history of five previous admissions to a university medical center where he had received psychiatric treatment. For the past two years he had been continuously under observation and treatment at a state psychiatric hospital. Ongoing long-term treatment with neuroleptic medication (prolixin decanoate) had resulted in substantial improvement, according to his clinical records, and his behavior was generally stable except for hallucinatory-delusional symptoms. The primary presenting problem was the delusional belief that a "haggly old witch" often followed him wherever he went. Associated with this belief were apparent hallucinatory experiences in which the witch visually appeared to him at various times throughout the day. A second, infrequent problem reported was hearing voices which suggested that he carry out aggressive actions against others. . . . The subject himself attributed these symptoms to his viewing a horror movie entitled "Halloween" numerous times; in his words, "too many times . . . about 13 times."

Procedure

During the initial meeting with the subject, he verbalized his belief regarding the "haggly witch" following him around the hospital. The clinical interview also revealed that he occasionally thought that people from "another dimension" spoke to him, suggesting that he take aggressive actions against others. During that meeting he at first showed minimal ability to distance himself (see Beck, 1970) from the targeted cognitions as measured by self-report of strength of belief, using a percent scale from 0 to 100 (0 = certainty that the belief is invalid, and 100 = certainty that the belief is completely valid). He initially verbalized ratings as 100% certainty. However, following careful questioning, by the end of the interview he gave a rating of only 50% certainty (cf. Hole, Rush, & Beck, 1979).

Experimental design. . . . Throughout the study, a log was used to collect self-report data on the (1) frequency of delusions regarding the witch and/or voices and (2) strength of belief in the reality of these delusional experiences using the scale from 0 to 100 introduced during the initial interview. Individual sessions were held with the subject two to three times per week during both treatment as well as "baseline" phases.

Treatment phases. During treatment phases of the study, the subject was instructed to continue his recording of self-report data as before, but to write an alternative interpretation on the log immediately following the targeted delusional cognition. The subject himself was encouraged to help develop the alternative interpretations used, and he consistently favored using the alternative idea that the delusional experiences were perhaps simply due to his "imagination" (rather than to the existence of actual external phenomena). Therapy sessions focused on repeated evaluation of the belief by collaborating with the subject in considering the evidence upon which his belief was based. Strategic questioning and discussion, rather than direct confrontation, was a predominant component of these individual sessions. The subject was actively involved in critically evaluating the abnormal belief, both in therapy sessions as well as by writing out alternative realistic interpretations throughout the week on the log. Positive feedback (social reinforcement) was given for recording frequency and strength of belief, as well as for writing the alternative interpretations on the weekly log.

Baseline phases. During baseline or non-treatment phases, sessions consisted of general conversations concerning activities on the ward or other topics of interest to the subject. During these phases, social reinforcement was given simply for recording frequency and strength of belief in the targeted cognitions.

Behavioral measures. Along with the self-report measures (cf. Jacobson, 1985), an independent measure of effects of the intervention on delusional behavior was obtained from nursing staff blind to the experimental conditions. Collection of these measures was not planned prior to the initiation of the study, but were found to be an interesting part of the clinical records after the study was concluded.

In addition to prolixin decanoate given routinely, nursing staff had orders from the attending psychiatrist to give thorazine, 100 mg, p.r.n. (pro re nata, "as occasion arises") for mild agitation associated with the hallucinatory-delusional beliefs that the witch was following him. The subject would either approach (or be observed by) nursing staff in an agitated state verbalizing his belief that a witch followed him, or that he heard voices, and the p.r.n. medication would be given at that point. Conversations both with nursing staff as well as with the subject established that agitation associated with these delusional experiences was the only reason for administering the p.r.n. medication. Given these observations, it was apparent that frequency of p.r.n. medication would serve as an independent behavioral measurement of improvement as a function of treatment phases of the study. Nursing medication logs were therefore used to determine frequency of administration of thorazine p.r.n. throughout all phases of the experiment.

Results

During both treatment and non-treatment phases, the subject appeared to consistently show adequate compliance in reporting targeted delusional ideation on his weekly log. Also, during treatment phases, 100% compliance was obtained in writing out the alternative interpretations following each targeted cognition.

As can be seen in Figure 1, there appears to be a pattern of decreasing frequency as well as strength of belief in reports of delusional ideation as a function of treatment phases of the study. This pattern of improvement during treatment phases is also observed as a decrease in the administration of p.r.n. medications (thorazine, 100 mg) given by nursing staff blind to the experimental conditions (see Figure 2).

It should be noted that in Figure 2 the first baseline (A) phase is extended, compared to Figure 1, to better depict the pattern of cumulative p.r.n. medication over a period of time. A review of nursing medication logs for the three months (not entirely shown in the Figure) immediately prior to treatment showed that the

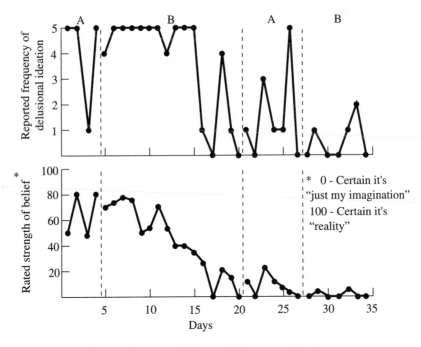

Figure 1. *Reported frequency of delusional ideation, and rated strength of belief in delusional ideation, throughout all phases of the study.*

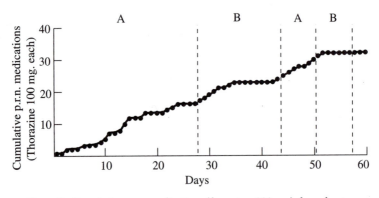

Figure 2. *Cumulative p.r.n. medications (thorazine, 100 mg.) throughout all phases of the study.*

longest the subject had gone without thorazine p.r.n. was three days. During the first treatment intervention phase, a seven-day period without thorazine p.r.n. was observed during the latter part of the treatment intervention. During and after the second treatment intervention phase, a ten-day period without thorazine p.r.n. was observed.

Discussion

Based on the results of this study, it appears that the use of the described procedures was quite effective in reducing both the frequency and strength of belief in the targeted cognitions. Additionally, need for administration of p.r.n. medication appears to have also been reduced.

Following treatment, the subject reported decreased frequency of delusional ideation. Perhaps more significantly, his rated "strength of belief" in the validity of his delusional beliefs was reduced to 0 to 5% certainty. Compared to his rating of 100% certainty at the outset of the initial interview . . . as well as to ratings of 45% to 80% certainty prior to application of the described treatment procedures, it appears that substantial improvement was clearly obtained.

Excerpted from "Behavioral Treatment of Schizophrenic Delusions," by B. A. Alford. In *Behavior Therapy, Vol. 17,* copyright 1986 Association for Advancement of Behavior Therapy. Reprinted by permission of the publisher.

◄ Recommended Reading ►

1. Buehler, R. E. , Patterson, G. R., & Furniss, J. M. (1966). The reinforcement of behavior in institutional settings. *Behavior Research and Therapy, 4,* 157–167.
   This study demonstrates that antisocial behavior often has reinforcing consequences, even in institutions where such behavior is supposedly on extinction.

2. Carr, E. G. (1977). Motivation of self-injurious behavior: A review of some hypotheses. *Psychological Bulletin, 84,* 800–816.
   Carr discusses the kinds of consequences that maintain (motivate) self-injurious behavior.

3. Epstein, R. (1985). Extinction-induced resurgence: Preliminary investigation and possible application. *Psychological Record, 35,* 143–153.
   This paper discusses the clinical relevance of resurgence.

4. Hall, R. V., & Hall, M. C. (1980). *How to use planned ignoring.* Austin, TX: Pro-Ed.
   A how-to manual on extinction, which Hall and Hall call planned ignoring.

5. Goldiamond, I. (1974). Toward a constructional approach to social problems. *Behaviorism, 2,* 1–84.
   Behavior problems are often defined in terms of behaviors that need to be weakened. Goldiamond suggests that behavior problems should be defined in terms of behaviors that need to be strengthened. Extinction and differential reinforcement are important tools in this constructional approach.

◄ **Endnotes** ►

1. There are some kinds of behavior, such as violent attacks on people or property, that are so objectionable that any occurrence is too much. In general, however, when we talk about troublesome behavior, we are talking about acts that practically everybody does now and then. To put it another way, often it's not the behavior that is troublesome but the *frequency* of the behavior.

2. Sometimes after extinction a behavior will continue to occur at a higher rate than its baseline level. This is typically because the behavior is now producing reinforcers other than those that were withheld during extinction. This means that the effects of reinforcement cannot always be entirely undone by extinction.

3. Hart et al. (1964).

4. Extinction is also sometimes referred to as *planned ignoring* (Hall & Hall, 1980). The term is often appropriate, since the reinforcer that maintains undesirable behavior is often (though certainly not always) attention.

5. Wolf et al. (1965).

6. Remember that the defining characteristic of operant behavior is that it is sensitive to its consequences. The fact that vomiting is usually a reflex does not mean that it cannot on some occasions be an operant behavior.

7. The only sure way of identifying the reinforcers that maintain unwanted behavior is to remove a suspected reinforcer for a time and observe the effects. If the target behavior occurs less often or if side effects usually associated with extinction occur, then the consequence is a reinforcer for that behavior.

8. Some textbooks say that proper use of extinction requires more than withholding reinforcement of the unwanted behavior. They argue that the reinforcers that can no longer be obtained by the target behavior should be available for other, more appropriate behavior. Thus, the child who can no longer get a parent's attention by crying may get attention by playing nicely. Although this practice greatly enhances the effectiveness of extinction, it is not a part of the extinction procedure but a distinct procedure—differential reinforcement.

9. Nevin (1988, 1993). If partial reinforcement *does* increase resistance to extinction, does that mean that we should reinforce unwanted behavior continuously for a time before putting it on extinction? Some behaviorists have suggested as much.

10. Although extinction is often a slow process, this is not always the case. In many instances involving ordinary objectionable behavior in children, ex-

tinction works quite quickly. Glenn Latham (1996), a behaviorist who does family counseling, has found that in over 90% of the cases he encounters, annoying behavior in a child will extinguish in under 2 minutes. Sometimes this includes behavior the parents have been struggling to modify for months, sometimes years.

11. Another thing that happens that can make your life difficult is that the adult becomes reluctant to try extinction again. "I tried that," the adult tells you, "it didn't work." What doesn't work is giving up on extinction during an extinction burst.

12. Just as it is inappropriate to speak of reinforcing a person, so it is inappropriate to speak of putting a person on extinction. It is *behavior* that is strengthened during reinforcement and weakened during extinction, not the person who behaves.

13. Epstein, R. (1983).

14. Epstein, R. (1985).

15. A procedure for increasing behavioral frequency with differential reinforcement is called differential reinforcement of high rate (DRH). In this procedure, a target behavior is reinforced only if it occurs at or above a certain rate. For example, a teacher might provide special praise or recognition if a student recites the alphabet correctly *within 30 seconds,* but not if he takes more than 30 seconds. Reinforcement is differentially dependent upon performing the behavior at a high rate.

16. In your reading you may encounter the term DRO. DRO originally meant "differential reinforcement of other behavior," a procedure that is now generally referred to as DRA. More recently, DRO has been used as the acronym for "differential reinforcement of zero behavior." Differential reinforcement of zero behavior means that a reinforcer is provided only if a given period of time has elapsed without the target behavior occurring. The procedure would seem to be indistinguishable from DRL.

17. The two approaches to DRL seem very different, but they are basically equivalent. In one case, we reinforce a behavior only if it occurs, say, four times a minute; in the other, we reinforce the behavior only if 15 seconds have elapsed since the last performance. In each case, the behavior must occur no more than four times a minute to produce reinforcement.

18. Lennox et al. (1987).

19. The behaviorist's job can be defined as helping people find better ways of obtaining reinforcers. In that case, DRA may be the quintessential behavior change procedure.

20. Bell & Ainsworth (1972).

21. Brownlee & Bakeman (1981).

22. See, for example, Carr (1977) and Carr & Durand (1985). Carr calls his approach functional communication training. The point is to replace an unacceptable method of obtaining reinforcers with an acceptable method of obtaining those reinforcers.

23. Patterson (1965).

24. Use of money as a reinforcer in schools may no longer be feasible: Today, children with money may be strong-armed or even shot by little thugs with handguns.

25. Patterson (1965).

26. Carr & Durand (1985).

27. Ayllon & Michael (1959). Henry Rickard and others (1960) describe a similar case. The patient was a 60-year-old man who had been hospitalized for over 20 years. He talked utter nonsense, saying things such as, "I have a fractured head and a broken nose because of spinal pressure," and "Stars have metal bottoms and exert a magnetic pressure on the earth." In one part of the study, Rickard and his colleagues attempted to decrease delusional speech by reinforcing sensible speech. Reinforcers were smiles, nods, expressions of interest, and the like. When the patient spoke nonsense, the therapist would turn away from him, gaze at the floor, look out the window, and so on. The researchers also asked the hospital staff to ignore the patient's delusional behavior but to respond favorably to rational speech. These procedures resulted in a marked increase in rational speech and a parallel decline in delusional speech.

28. Ayllon & Michael (1959).

Punishment

W<small>E HAVE BEEN DISCUSSING WAYS</small> of reducing the frequency of unwanted behavior. So far we've talked about extinction and differential reinforcement. These are both excellent procedures, but they're not the first thing most people think of when the problem is that a behavior occurs too often. What is the first thing people think of? Yes, Belinda?

"Punishment."

Yes. In general, punishment is the *first* thing the public tries, and the *last* thing a behaviorist tries.[1] But behaviorists and other people have very different ideas about punishment. Let's begin our study of punishment by talking about how people typically use the word *punishment* in everyday discourse. What does the word *punishment* mean to most people? Yes, Alfred?

"Payback!"

Yes. A fancier word for the same idea is *retribution*. Someone commits an offense, and we get even. "An eye for an eye, and a tooth for a tooth." What else comes to mind when you think of punishment? Yes, Midori?

"Things like suffering, torture, pain."

Yes. We usually think of punishment as hurting someone, in one way or another. It usually implies making someone suffer for something they've done. To a behaviorist, punishment means something very different. It does *not* mean getting even, or making someone suffer, or inflicting pain. So you will have to set aside your old ideas about punishment, and try to think about it in a new way. We'll start with some definitions.

Punishment

To begin with, we need to go back to the law of effect, which says . . . What, Midori?

"Uhm, that behavior depends on its consequences."

Right. Or, as behaviorists like to say: Behavior is *a function of* its consequences. In its more formal expression, the law of effect says:

Law of effect:
In any given situation, the probability of a behavior occurring is a function of the consequences that behavior has had in that situation in the past.

This implies that consequences can change behavior in one of two ways. And they are . . . Carlotta?

"They can strengthen the behavior, or they can weaken it."

Right. In practice, we usually equate strength with frequency, so what you're really saying is . . .

"That the consequences can increase or decrease the rate of the behavior."

Exactly! Consequences that increase, or maintain, the rate of a behavior are called . . . what's the word, John?

"Reinforcers."

Right. What is the formal definition of a reinforcer, Jamal?

"An event that, when made contingent on a behavior, increases or maintains the frequency of that behavior."

Excellent. Now, consequences that *decrease* the rate of a behavior are called *punishers*:

Punisher:
An event that, when made contingent on a behavior, decreases the frequency of that behavior.

Punishers are aversive. You will recall that an aversive event is one that people ordinarily . . . ordinarily what, Maya?

"Avoid or escape?"

Exactly. Having one's toes stepped on is, for most people, an aversive event: We will avoid it if we can, and if we can't avoid getting stepped on, we try to escape once we are stepped on.

Aversives can be used as punishers. That is, if they follow a behavior they will typically reduce the strength of that behavior. But, as was true of reinforcers, the defining property of a punisher is its effect on behavior. If a consequence makes the behavior it follows less likely to occur, it is a punisher; if it does not have that effect, it is *not* a punisher.

Now, reinforcement involves using reinforcers. What is the formal definition of reinforcement, Carlotta?

"It's the procedure of providing consequences for a behavior that increase or maintain the frequency of that behavior."

Very good. Punishment involves providing consequences that make the behavior they follow *less* likely to occur. Its formal definition is similar to that of reinforcement:

> ### Punishment:
> ### The procedure of providing consequences
> ### for a behavior that decrease the frequency
> ### of that behavior.

Please note that punishment weakens *behavior,* not *people*.[2] Everyone slips up now and then and speaks of punishing a person, but you don't decrease the frequency of a person with punishment; you decrease the frequency of the person's *behavior*. Please try to remember that.

To the behaviorist, punishment has nothing to do with retribution or justice.[3] It has to do with reducing the frequency of a behavior. In behavior analysis, a procedure qualifies as punishment only if it involves providing consequences for a behavior that reduce the frequency of that behavior.

Punishment can take many different forms. Let's consider some examples.

Kinds of Punishment

Reprimanding

The term *reprimand* has been defined in various ways, but most often it refers to providing expressions of disapproval, usually in the form of verbal remarks:

> ### Reprimand:
> ### To reduce the frequency of a target behavior
> ### by making disapproval contingent
> ### on the target behavior.

Most often the reprimand takes the form of a few words, usually expressed in a loud voice. Sometimes it takes the form of sarcasm: "Oh, that's just great"; "Now, that's a pretty mess." Sometimes the reprimand takes the form of a rhetorical question: "Are you crazy?" "Were you raised in a barn?" Often the reprimand takes the form of corrective feedback as in, "No, not like *that!*"

Reprimanding is arguably the most frequently used form of punishment. After the second grade, teachers reprimand students twice as often as they praise them.[4] One study found that teachers reprimand on average about once every two minutes throughout elementary and junior high school.[5] I suspect that what is true of teachers is true of most other groups, including parents and bosses.

Despite its popularity, reprimanding is not always effective. When you reprimand a person, you're paying attention to that person. The attention can be reinforcing, especially for children.[6] Moreover, if other people are present, the reprimand brings *their* attention. The kid who is reprimanded for being out of his seat may become the center of attention not only for the teacher but for the entire class. All that attention can be powerfully reinforcing. Nevertheless, when reprimands follow a target behavior, they do sometimes reduce the rate of the behavior, and in those instances they qualify as punishment.

Although reprimanding can be effective, it is a relatively weak form of punishment. A stronger form of punishment that is also fairly common is called response cost.

Response Cost

Response cost gets its name from the fact that if you engage in the target behavior, you have to pay a price. The behavior *costs* you something:

Response cost:
To reduce the frequency of a target behavior
by making removal of a reinforcer contingent
on the target behavior.

A familiar example of response cost is the parking ticket. You park where you shouldn't, and when you come back to your car you find a slip of paper indicating that you will have to pay a fine.[7] Similarly, the student who "acts up" in class may be denied the opportunity to go on the playground during recess. And in the same way, an employer may dock a worker for arriving late. In each case, the consequence of the behavior is that the person has to give up something reinforcing.

Response cost is a safe form of punishment that works in a wide variety of situations. Another form of punishment I want to discuss is time out.

Time Out

Time out, often abbreviated TO, is short for "time out from positive reinforcement." The term is used in various ways, but I'm going to adopt its more traditional definition:

Time out:
To reduce the frequency of a target behavior
by making removal of a person from a
reinforcing situation contingent on the target
behavior.

What this means is that when a person is in a situation in which reinforcers are readily available and he performs the target behavior, you remove him from that reinforcing situation. If the—

"Isn't that the same as extinction?"

Ah. There are a couple of differences, John. First, the extinction procedure leaves the person in the situation where the target behavior occurred, while time out removes the person from that situation. Second, extinction eliminates only those reinforcers that maintain the target behavior; time out attempts to eliminate virtually all reinforcers. Perhaps an example will help clarify the difference.

Suppose you have a 6-year-old child—let's call her Lillie. She has tantrums whenever she doesn't get her way. You determine that Lillie's tantrums are due to your tendency to give in to her demands, whatever they are, and you decide it's time to put a stop to it. One day you're trying to have a conversation with someone and Tiger Lillie wants you to focus on her exclusively. When you don't, she turns on the siren. You and your companion stuff cotton in your ears and ignore her until she finally stops screaming. What procedure is that, John?

"Extinction."

Right. It's extinction because Lillie remains in the situation where the target behavior occurred, but it is no longer reinforced. Reinforcers are still available to her; they're just not available for screaming.

Now, suppose you're in the same situation, and Tiger Lillie starts screaming. This time, you calmly get up, take her by the hand, and lead her to your utility room—the place where you keep your washer and dryer. You put her in the room, turn on the light, close the door, and leave. You go back to your companion, and when Lillie has stopped screaming and has been quiet for, say, one minute, you let her out of the utility room. This procedure is . . .

"Time out."

Right. You've removed her from the situation where the target behavior occurred, and you've put her in a situation where very few reinforcers are available.

"You've also saved your eardrums."

That's another advantage, Alfred.

"So it's like the parent who says to a kid, 'Go to your room.'"

Yes, Midori, except that sending a child to his room during time out may not accomplish much these days. Do you see why?

"Because kids' rooms often have a lot of reinforcers. They can watch TV, listen to the radio, play computer games, read books, talk to their friends on the telephone."

Right. For time out to be effective, the time out area has to be essentially devoid of reinforcing activities. So you want a place that is totally boring, like a utility room or a vacant bedroom.

"Why wouldn't Lillie just open the door and come out?"

She might, the first few times you use time out. If she leaves the time out area, you put her back. And she stays in the time out area until she has been quiet for a prescribed time period. Since Lillie is only 6, the time limit might be 1 minute. Once she is released, reinforcers are freely available to her. In other words, she isn't snubbed, glared at, scolded, lectured, or "reasoned with." If she misbehaves again, back she goes to the time out area. You have a question, Carlotta?

"Yes. How long do they stay in time out?"

I can't answer that because I don't know. Time-out periods as short as 5 seconds have been effective, but so have much longer periods.[8] I doubt if time-out periods longer than 10 minutes are usually required in a home or classroom situation.

Time out is a safe, and often very effective, procedure. But serious problem behaviors, such as those found in populations of juvenile offenders and psychiatric patients, sometimes require stronger measures. In these cases, overcorrection usually gets the job done.

Overcorrection

There doesn't seem to be a generally accepted definition of overcorrection, but here's one that will serve our purposes:

> **Overcorrection:**
> **To reduce the frequency of a target behavior**
> **by making restitution for damage done and**
> **repeated performance of appropriate behavior**
> **contingent on the target behavior.**

As this definition suggests, overcorrection has two components: restitution for the damage caused by the target behavior, and repeated performance (called *positive practice*) of appropriate behavior.[9] To understand what overcorrection means, you must understand these two components.

For instance, suppose a youngster takes a shortcut through a neighbor's property and runs through her flower garden. *Restitution* means not only replacing the damaged flowers but also making other improvements to the neighbor's property, such as weeding the garden or painting a fence.

Positive practice means repeatedly performing the appropriate behavior in the situation where the target behavior occurred. The youngster who runs through a flower bed might be required to pass the neighbor's house repeatedly—perhaps 15 or 20 times—without going on her property.[10]

Overcorrection can be very useful, but it is not without its problems. Restitution and positive practice are both very time-consuming. Also, while overcorrection often works well against severe behavior problems, it is not always the answer. Fortunately, there is one more procedure to which we may turn when all else fails.

Physical Punishment

The term *physical punishment* applies to any form of punishment in which the consequence that suppresses behavior does so because of its impact on tissues.

> **Physical punishment:**
> **To reduce the frequency of a target behavior**
> **by making brief and noninjurious contact with**
> **the skin contingent on the target behavior.**

It is important to note that the correct use of physical punishment causes neither long-lasting discomfort nor permanent damage. The teacher who boxes a child's ears may cause permanent hearing loss and even brain damage. The parent who shakes a crying infant may cause severe brain damage or death. But so far as the behaviorist is concerned, these practices are *not* forms of physical punishment; they are acts of physical *abuse*. The line between physical punishment and physical abuse is a fine one, but it is a line that no one has a right to cross.

Many parents consider physical punishment an essential tool of child rearing; most behaviorists do *not*. Behaviorists generally oppose the use of physical punishment except when the problem behavior might cause permanent injury. Even then, most approve of its use only if other procedures, such as time out and overcorrection, have failed to produce results. When behaviorists do use physical punishment, it is most often to treat self-injurious behavior.

At one time or another, most people engage in some sort of self-injurious behavior: They smoke cigarettes, they pick at a scab, they chew their fingernails to the quick, and so on. This is not the sort of behavior I have in mind when I speak of using physical punishment to control self-injurious behavior. I am thinking of a person who chews the flesh off of his fingers, of someone who hits herself repeatedly in the eyes with her fists or other objects, or of someone who bangs his head against a wall or piece of furniture. Such behavior can cause severe, permanent damage, including blindness, hearing loss, brain damage, and disfigurement. For example, I once heard about an autistic boy who chewed one of his fingers off. When the hospital staff put him in restraints so that he couldn't reach his hands, he turned his head to one side, hunched up his shoulder and started chewing. Physical punishment typically puts a stop to such behavior very quickly, even when the behavior has persisted for years.

"I don't get it."

Get what, Jamal?

"Well, these kids are hurting themselves, right? They're inflicting pain. It seems to me they would enjoy physical punishment. It should be a reinforcer for them."

That might seem logical, but it doesn't work that way. Self-injurious behavior is usually stopped or greatly reduced in a very short time with just a few applications of physical punishment.

The term *physical punishment* usually conjures up images of spankings and the like, but it can actually take a variety of forms. For example, behaviorists have used water mist very successfully to control self-injurious behavior and other serious problems.[11] The water mist procedure involves using an atomizer to spray a fine mist of water in the person's face whenever he or she engages in the target behavior.

All right. That's enough on physical punishment. The lessons—

"What? Aren't you going to say anything about electric shock? I thought behaviorists used shock all the time."

No, Alfred, they don't. It is true that shock was used in the early days of applied behavior analysis—mostly the sixties and seventies—to control serious behavior problems, such as self-injurious behavior in psychotic children. Shocks were delivered by means of a battery-powered shock stick, a kind of baton that provided a brief and harmless, though painful, shock to the skin. This is nothing at all like the electroconvulsive shock treatment that is used by psychiatrists in the treatment of severe depression. The shock stick delivers a low voltage charge to the point where it touches the skin. For some time now, other procedures, such as the water mist procedure, have pretty much replaced shock. In fact, behaviorists are usually able to treat most behavior problems without resorting to any form of physical punishment. They now get by with extinction or differential reinforcement or with milder forms of punishment such as time out and overcorrection. But if you're serious about helping people with debilitating behavior problems, you do what you have to do to help them. Sometimes, such as in the case of self-injurious behavior, that may mean using physical punishment.[12] Now, let's take a closer look at the use of punishment to solve behavior problems.

Illustrative Studies

Matilda, the Food Thief

Stealing is sometimes a problem with institutionalized patients. In the study I'm going to describe, the problem was that a psychiatric patient stole food.[13] The person involved, whom I've called Matilda, was a 47-year-old schizophrenic woman who had been hospitalized for 9 years. We talked earlier about how Teodoro Ayllon used a shaping procedure to get Matilda to shed some of the 20 pounds of excess clothing she wore. Well, in addition to wearing an entire closet of clothes, Matilda stole food. She ate not only her own food but took and ate additional food from the food counter and from other patients. She weighed over

250 pounds, which the medical staff considered bad for her health, and it is reasonable to suppose that the other patients didn't much like having food taken from their plates. The staff had dealt with the problem by prescribing a special diet and trying to persuade Matilda not to steal food. These efforts didn't work.

Ayllon began by asking the nurses to record food-related behavior in the dining room. They did this for nearly a month, and the data showed that Matilda stole food during two-thirds of all meals. Next, Ayllon asked the staff to stop trying to persuade or coerce Matilda not to steal food. Instead, they were to assign her to a particular table in the dining room where she would eat alone. (That way she couldn't easily steal food from other patients.) Further, if she approached any table other than her own or took food from the dining room counter that she was not allowed to have, the nurses were to escort her immediately from the dining hall. This meant that she got no more to eat, including the food she had been served. In other words, the cost of stealing food was that she lost food.

The result of this effort was an abrupt and dramatic drop in the frequency of stealing. Within two weeks, the behavior was essentially eliminated. I say "essentially," because there were a few isolated episodes of stealing, but the behavior was no longer a serious problem. Once the patient was no longer supplementing her diet with stolen larder, she began to lose weight. During her 9 years of hospitalization, she had never weighed less than 230 pounds. After about a year on the program, her weight was about 180 pounds and her health was considered excellent.

"What sort of punishment does this study illustrate?"

You tell me, Belinda.

"Response cost?"

Why do you say that?

"Because whenever the target behavior occurred, the consequence was that she had to give up something—food."

So you say it's response cost because stealing food cost her something. Carlotta?

"Could it be time out? When Matilda steals food, she is removed from the dining hall. Doesn't that sound like time out?"

Well, that's an interesting idea. Do you care to defend your position, Belinda?

"I don't think it's time out because Matilda wasn't taken to an area without reinforcers; she was just removed from an area where one reinforcer, food, was available."

What do you say to that, Carlotta?

"I guess I agree, but it seems to me it could be argued either way."

That's often the case. We can define terms in the classroom so that they seem very distinct from one another. But when we look at real examples, the distinctions sometimes get fuzzy. Still, in this case I have to agree with Belinda. I think removing Matilda from the dining hall was merely a convenient way of taking away her food. Besides, as Belinda pointed out, Matilda was not removed to an area devoid of reinforcers; she went back to the ward, which probably provides lots of reinforcers. Now let's see if you can figure out the kind of punishment used in this next study.

Exiled Behavior

Ronald Drabman and Robert Spitalnik used punishment to reduce disruptive behavior in a residential treatment facility for children with psychiatric disorders.[14] The kinds of problems posed by these children were similar to those of ordinary children in regular classrooms—only worse. Drabman and Spitalnik first identified the most troublesome children in each of three classes. All of the children were between the ages of 9 and 11. The researchers observed three kinds of disruptive behavior: talking out of turn; leaving one's seat without permission; and aggressive acts.

In this study, the observers were 12 trained undergraduate students, working 2 to a class. They would count instances of the target behavior for each of the selected students during a 20-second period. They then had 10 seconds to record their observations before observing for another 20 seconds. They did this, observing for 20 seconds, recording for 10 seconds, over and over for the entire 55-minute class period. By the way, what sort of recording method is this? John?

"Interval recording?"

Right. It turned out that of the three kinds of behavior, being aggressive and leaving one's seat were the most damaging to the conduct of the class, so the researchers decided not to try to change the tendency to talk out of turn. Talking out therefore served as a kind of control activity. Do you know what I mean by that, Midori?

"You mean that if they tried to change aggressive behavior and being out of their seats, they could compare the results they got with changes in talking out."

That's correct. Why would they want to make that comparison?

"Well, it would help rule out the possibility that any changes they saw in behavior were due to something other than their intervention. If there's a reduction in aggressive acts and running around but no improvement in talking out, that suggests that the intervention worked."

Very good, Midori. The punishment procedure worked like this: Each time one of the children engaged in one of the target activities, an observer would secretly signal the teacher to remove the child from the class. The teacher would then say, "John (or whatever his name was), you have misbehaved. You must leave this class." The teaching assistant would then escort the child to a small, empty, sound-resistant room normally used for music practice. Once the teacher had announced the punishment, the child was destined for the quiet room. There was no discussion of the matter, no explanations, no arguments, no "second chances." If the child misbehaved, he went to the quiet room. Period.

The criterion for punishment varied with the misbehavior. Any instance of aggressive behavior resulted in eviction, but leaving a seat was treated more liberally. Students were not punished for being away from their seat unless the behavior occurred in each of 3 consecutive 20-second observation periods.

Now, during the first part of the study, the researchers made observations of the target behaviors but didn't attempt to punish them. They did this for 11 days to obtain . . . to obtain what, Midori?

"A baseline?"

Right. Then the intervention period lasted 16 days. When the researchers looked at the results of the experiment, they found that the procedure had had a very pronounced effect on the target behaviors. During the initial baseline period, aggressive acts occurred in an average of 2.8% of the 20-second observation intervals. Now, 2.8% of the observation intervals may not sound like a lot of aggressive behavior, but that works out to several aggressive acts each class period. It's hard to conduct a class with that much disruptive behavior going on, even if all the other students act like angels.

The punishment procedure sharply reduced the frequency of aggressive behavior. Aggressive acts fell to an average of only .37% of observation intervals. Even the most aggressive student committed an aggressive act only about once in an hour. Data for out-of-seat behavior showed similar results.

What sort of punishment does this study illustrate? Jamal?

"Time out."

You seem very confident of your answer. Are you sure the procedure isn't extinction? Or maybe response cost?

"No. It's not extinction because the kids didn't remain in the area where reinforcers were available. And it's not response cost because nothing was taken away from them. It's time out."

Your confidence is well placed—it is time out.

Ruminating Baby

The idea of punishing a baby is offensive to most people. This is probably because of our tendency to equate punishment with retribution. Babies are too young and innocent to be held responsible for any wrong they might do, so punishment of any sort seems inappropriate and cruel. But remember that when behaviorists speak of punishment they are *not* concerned with retribution. For the behaviorist, punishment is a procedure for reducing the frequency of unwanted behavior. Viewed in this way, punishing a baby can be justified *if* the target behavior is injurious to the baby *and* no other procedure (such as reinforcement or extinction) is likely to be effective. I can see that some of you aren't buying this; well, I'll describe a study and you decide whether the use of punishment was justified.

The problem was rumination in a 6-month-old girl.[15] Rumination is not a very pleasant topic: It is the regurgitation of food into the mouth. I'm not sure anyone knows exactly why people ruminate, but they typically do so without signs of disgust or discomfort, and it appears to be operant behavior. Apparently the return of food to the mouth is, for these individuals, intrinsically reinforcing. The practice occurs mainly in infants and the retarded.

In this case the victim was a baby. She received baby formula every 4 hours, but immediately after eating began ruminating. She would open her mouth and move her tongue backward and forward until the formula reappeared. She would do this for 20 to 40 minutes until she had regurgitated all of the formula. The girl did not cry or show other signs of discomfort during this process.

Rumination is a serious health problem and can be fatal. In this case, the baby was dehydrated and lethargic and had lost weight. The rumination had become life-threatening.

Thomas Sajwaj and his colleagues decided to try squirting a small amount of lemon juice into the baby's mouth each time she made the tongue movements that preceded rumination. The hope was that the lemon juice would be sufficiently aversive to suppress the tongue movements that caused food regurgitation.

Fortunately, Sajwaj's hope was fulfilled: Lemon juice, made contingent on tongue movements, resulted in a sharp decline in this behavior and, consequently, there was less rumination. The researchers discontinued treatment briefly to see if the rumination would reappear. It did. The researchers reinstituted the lemon juice treatment and, after a total of 12 days of treatment, all rumination ceased. The child gained weight and was released from the hospital. Six weeks after her release, the parents noticed two instances of rumination. The lemon juice treatment was applied again, and there was no further recurrence of the problem.

Now, the idea of squirting lemon juice into an infant's mouth is not pleasant, and this is the kind of thing that critics of behavior analysis like to point to in their attacks. "Here is a defenseless, *sick* baby and these behaviorists are squirting lemon juice into her mouth!" Well, what's the alternative? Pick up the baby when she ruminates and comfort her? That is more likely to reinforce the behavior than reduce its frequency. Shall we reason with her? Explain to a 6-month-old baby that ruminating is harmful? Or perhaps we could just stand by and watch her starve to death? Some people would advocate that: "If she chooses to ruminate and dies, that is her right." I'm sorry, I can't accept that. You have to reach your own conclusion, but to my mind, people like Sajwaj and his colleagues are heroes. They very probably saved this baby's life because they were willing to use a procedure that, though controversial, worked.

What sort of punishment is squirting lemon juice into a person's mouth? What do you say, Brian?

"I'd have to say it's physical punishment."

Why would you have to say that?

"Because there's contact with tissue."

Good, good. What if they had used sulfuric acid? Would that have been physical punishment?

"No."

Why not?

"Because sulfuric acid would do serious damage to the skin. It would be abuse, not punishment."

Outstanding! I thought I might trip you up with that question, but I see you're really on your toes. Remember that physical punishment involves brief and non-injurious contact with the skin. Long-lasting contact, or contact that causes injury, is not physical punishment; it's physical abuse.

The lesson to be learned from the studies of punishment we have considered is that punishment can be helpful in dealing with certain kinds of behavior problems. This is true, however, only if the procedure is properly used. Let's talk about the rules for using punishment correctly.

Rules for Using Punishment

Okay, what's the first rule going to be? Jamal?

"Define the target behavior."

Ah! I've fooled you a bit, actually it's:

1. Define the target behaviors.

Notice the plural *behaviors*. The reason is that, in general, you do not try merely to punish an unwanted behavior but to reinforce a more acceptable alternative behavior. So when you use punishment, you need to identify two target behaviors: the behavior you want to weaken, and the behavior you want to strengthen.

Most of the time, the reinforcers that maintain a person's behavior are perfectly acceptable. There is nothing wrong with wanting attention, or food, or praise, or most of the other events that often reinforce behavior. The problem is that sometimes people obtain acceptable reinforcers by unacceptable means. You not only need to reduce the frequency of behavior that is currently being reinforced, you also need to provide another way of obtaining those reinforcers.

So, if you plan to use a punishment procedure, you need to identify the target behavior that is to be punished *and* the target behavior that is to be reinforced. Having done that, you are ready to:

2. Select appropriate punishers.

Once you've decided exactly what behavior you want to punish, you have to decide how to punish it. You'll want to have one or more punishers at your disposal, but which ones? What criterion do you use in selecting punishers?

A good rule of thumb is to use the mildest punisher that will reduce the rate of the target behavior. If a quiet word of criticism will do the job, you shouldn't shout a reprimand; if a $2 fine will stop people from parking illegally, don't use a $200 fine; if a 5-minute time out works, don't require 50 minutes.

Shaking a child is *out of the question*: It can cause whiplash injuries, spinal injuries, and brain damage; it can even kill small children. Striking a person, especially a child, above the shoulders is seldom, if ever, justified; it is too easy to cause injury, and there are better alternatives.

However, it is not enough to say, "Use mild punishers." There is a danger in choosing a punisher that is too mild. I wonder, can you guess what that danger is . . . yes, Carlotta?

"I suppose, if you used a weak punisher, the person might get used to it."

Can you give me an example?

"Well, a teacher might put a student in time out for 30 seconds. It might not have any effect on the student's behavior, so then the teacher might increase it to 1 minute. Well, a minute is not much different than 30 seconds, so it might not have much effect either. So then the teacher might increase the time-out period to 3 minutes, then to 4, 5, and so on."

What does that procedure remind you of, Brian?

"Shaping?"

Yes, shaping. A parent may begin with a very mild form of punisher, such as a mild slap, and then use progressively stronger blows. Sometimes the parent ends up using considerable force and causing serious injury. Our society does much the same thing in a very systematic way in treating crime. We make it very difficult to get convictions, and then when we get a conviction, we begin with very mild forms of punishment and gradually increase its severity. If you wanted to design a judicial system that would ensure that most criminals would continue to commit crimes, you couldn't do much better than the system we have.

Well, I'd better get down from my soap box. Just remember that in selecting a punisher, the key thing is to choose the mildest consequence that is likely to do the job. And if you have to increase the intensity of the punisher, try to increase it to an effective level. Be wary of gradually shaping up tolerance for increasingly stronger consequences. Okay. Once you've selected a punisher, you're ready to begin using it. To use it properly you have to . . .

3. Make punishment immediate and certain.

Can you tell me what that means, Jamal?

"Well, it means that for punishment to be effective, the punisher has to follow the target behavior very closely . . ."

Yes. go on.

"And it has to be very likely that if the behavior occurs, it will have punishing consequences."

Right. That's—

"This all sounds very familiar, Dr. Cee."

Well, Alfred, that's probably because we said the same things about the use of reinforcement: The reinforcer had to be immediate and certain. Why do you think the timing of the punisher is so important, Maya?

"Probably because if there's a delay between when the target behavior occurs and when the punisher occurs, then some *other* behavior may occur and be punished."

Right. Delays allow time for other behavior to occur, and that behavior may be punished rather than the target behavior. So timing is important. Making punishment certain is also important. In general, punishment is effective to the extent that the target behavior is likely to result in aversive consequences. That doesn't mean, however, that it's a good idea to use lots of aversives; the aversives must be contingent on the occurrence of the target behavior. It means that the greater the probability that a punisher will occur after the target behavior, but not otherwise, the more rapidly the frequency of the behavior will decrease. Best results are usually obtained when the punisher is almost certain to occur after the target behavior, but not otherwise.

The need for immediacy and certainty may seem rather obvious, but this rule is often ignored. Can you give me an example you've seen of someone providing delayed punishment, Alfred?

"Well, the other day I was hanging out in the mall, and I saw this kid who was being a real pain in the bazonga. And I heard the mother say, 'You just wait til I get you home!'"

What do you suppose she meant?

"I think she meant she was going to kick his butt when they got home."

Yes. And such delayed use of punishers is usually ineffective.[16] What about certainty? Can someone provide an example of someone failing to make punishment certain? Yes, Maya?

"Sometimes parents ignore or reinforce an annoying behavior several times before they punish it. And sometimes they punish a behavior if they're upset about something, but not if they're feeling okay."

Yes. And for punishment to get good results, there has to be a consistent relationship between the behavior and the aversive consequence. The teacher, parent, or therapist must make it clear that the punisher will occur if the target behavior occurs.

Okay, the fourth rule for using punishment is:

4. Use extinction and differential reinforcement.

Punishment of inappropriate behavior should always be used in conjunction with extinction and reinforcement. What behavior should you have on extinction during a punishment program? Yes, Midori?

"The behavior you're trying to punish?"

Why?

"It seems to me the behavior must get the person something, or it wouldn't occur. Like, if a kid is having tantrums, the tantrums must have some sort of reinforcing consequence: attention, toys, food, or something. So if you start punishing the tantrums, but they're still producing attention or whatever, then the punishment is going to be less effective."

Well done. If a behavior occurs regularly, it's a pretty safe bet that it has reinforcing consequences. To get the most out of punishment, you have to prevent the target behavior from being reinforced. Suppose you don't put the target behavior on extinction, but you get a pretty good reduction in the behavior from punishment. What happens when you discontinue punishment? John?

"Well, if the target behavior is still being reinforced, then when you stop punishing, it's going to increase in frequency again."

Of course. Sometimes you'll hear someone say that punishment effects are only temporary. "Punishment worked," they'll say, "but as soon as we stopped punishing, the misbehavior increased again." This does happen *if* the behavior is still being reinforced. So it's never enough to punish; you also have to prevent the behavior from being reinforced.

"What if you can't withhold the reinforcer?"

That's a very good question, Maya. How would you answer it?

> "I guess you'd have to continue using punishment as long as the behavior was being reinforced."

Yes. If you can't prevent the unwanted behavior from being reinforced, you're going to have to continue the punishment program. And you're going to have to try to make the punishers stronger than the reinforcers.

I said that a punishment program should include both extinction and differential reinforcement. How would you use differential reinforcement, John?

> "Hmm. Well, I guess you'd try to provide the reinforcers the person is getting from the target behavior, and provide them for doing something else."

Good answer. The something else could be a behavior that is incompatible with the target behavior, or it might just be some alternative activity. So, for example, if your 2-year-old holds his breath until he turns blue any time you deny him something, you might show him a more acceptable way of getting what he wants.

We've talked about punishment as an independent procedure, and so it is; but by itself it is of limited effectiveness. Why is that? Yes, Brian?

> "I've heard it said that punishment just teaches us what *not* to do."

That's it, exactly. Dealing with behavior problems seldom means just getting rid of some annoying behavior. It also means increasing the frequency of desirable behavior. Most of the time, you can't do that with punishment. You have a child who obtains attention by having terrible tantrums. You may get rid of the tantrums with punishment, but you haven't taught the child appropriate ways of obtaining attention. So when you provide punishment for one behavior, you must also provide reinforcement for another.

When punishment is used in conjunction with extinction and differential reinforcement, it is extremely powerful and results in very rapid changes in behavior.

Now, the last punishment rule is the same as it always is . . . Maya?

> "Monitor results?"

Right.

5. Monitor results.

You must never assume that the procedure you use is having the intended effects. The fact that you *intend* to decrease the frequency of an unwanted behavior does not mean that you will get that result. The only way you can tell whether you are using punishment is to look at the effects you are having on behavior. And the only way you can do that is by monitoring behavior in some systematic way. If the target behavior declines, you have succeeded in punishing it; if it does not, no matter what you have been doing, you have not been providing punishment.

Now, punishment is just as complicated and difficult to use effectively as reinforcement. In addition, there are other problems with punishment as a therapeutic or instructional tool.

Problems with Punishment

Anyone who takes an unbiased look at the literature on punishment has to conclude that it can be very effective. But there is a strong case to be made against punishment.

Inappropriate Use

We've already talked about this to some extent. You must always remember that from the standpoint of behavior analysis, punishment is about reducing the frequency of a specific target behavior; it is not about hurting people or about retribution. It is about changing the rate of behavior. People who forget that often punish inappropriately. They use far stronger forms of punishment than are necessary; punish long after the target behavior occurs; provide punishers noncontingently; and may even reinforce the behavior they are attempting to punish.

Moral Objections

Some people object on moral grounds to the use of aversive consequences of any sort to change behavior. People are particularly likely to object to the use of punishment with children or with those whose behavior is considered involuntary or the result of "mental disturbance."

As you've probably guessed, I find punishment objectionable myself. So do most behaviorists. But I refuse to reject punishment categorically as a means of changing behavior. To me, the question is always, "What is the alternative?" If the alternative to using punishment is worse than the punishment, then as far as I'm concerned, punishment is justified. Hitting someone in the face with your fist is never justified. On the other hand, spraying a person in the face with a water mist is justified if the alternative is to let him poke his eyes out or keep him in a straitjacket to prevent him from doing so.

Most people will probably agree that punishment is acceptable if the alternative to punishment is worse than the punishment. Where we disagree is in deciding when the alternative is worse than the punishment. That's a personal value judgment. You will have to decide for yourself when certain forms of punishment are morally acceptable.

Negative Side Effects

One side effect of punishment is that it produces undesirable *emotional reactions,* particularly fear and anger. Fear may take the form of efforts to escape or avoid anything associated with punishment. This is understandable, since escaping or avoiding an aversive event is going to be negatively reinforced.

So, if we use punishment to suppress a person's behavior, that person is likely to escape or avoid the punishment if he can. For instance, suppose you have something cooking on the stove and your 3-year-old tries to grab the pot handle. You yell, "No!" and then give her a swift slap on the behind with the flat of your hand. But the next time you see her do something that could be very harmful and yell, "No!" she may run off as you approach to deliver the *"coup de derriere."*

"The kootie what?"

Coup de derriere, Alfred. The blow to the rear end. The opposite of a *coup de état.* It's a joke. . . . Anyway, if you use punishment, you can't expect those whose behavior you punish to be glad to see you coming, particularly if you use some form of physical punishment. Murray Sidman, a behavior analyst who is an expert on punishment—and one of its severest critics—likes to say that people who *use* shocks *become* shocks.

"You become a conditioned punisher, because you're paired with a punisher?"

That's right, Brian. And if the person cannot get away from you, he may attack you. Even very small children will hit, bite, or kick their parents as they attempt to punish them. And, if the parent backs off, the parent has very likely reinforced . . . what, Maya?

"Aggressive behavior."

Yes. If you see a kid kicking and screaming when a parent tries to punish him, it's a fairly safe bet that he has been able to escape punishment in the past through such behavior.

The fact that fear and aggression are sometimes by-products of punishment is a strong argument against punishment. As a teacher, a parent, or a therapist, you want to have a cordial relationship with the person. You don't want the person to be afraid of you or hate you.

However, strong emotional reactions are primarily problems with physical punishment. Reprimands, response cost, time out, and overcorrection may provoke some emotional outbursts, but these tend to be mild and short-lived. Even with physical punishment, emotional outbursts are usually not enduring problems—provided the emotional behavior is not reinforced. Nevertheless, punishment can produce emotional behavior, and anyone who uses punishment needs to know that.

A second possible side effect of punishment, especially physical punishment, is *abuse.* We often use punishment to reduce behavior that we find annoying. The punishment allows us to escape that annoyance, so the use of punishment is negatively reinforced. The danger is that we may use punishment more and more until we are using punishment when other procedures would be more appropriate. In some homes, practically the only way in which adults interact with children is to provide some sort of punishment. Often this means that the only time the kids are touched is when someone hits them.

It seems like practically every week I see an article in the paper about a parent or guardian who has killed or seriously injured a child in the process of providing what the adult called "discipline." Often what happens is that a child cries for a prolonged period. Perhaps she has a middle-ear infection, or she is teething or colicky. Sometimes babies and very young children with such complaints will cry for hours on end. The exasperated parent may slap or shake the child to stop the crying, and the result may be a dead or seriously injured baby.

Another scenario in which punishment becomes abuse involves an adult who does nothing about misbehavior except offer threats. The child's behavior gets worse and worse, and finally the adult assaults the child in a rage. Parents have hit their children with belts, whips and boards, burned them with cigarettes, cut them with knives, kicked them with boots. You name it, it's been done.[17] And often it is done in the name of discipline or punishment. It is neither discipline nor punishment; it is abuse. And it's terribly wrong.

When physical punishment is used in a therapeutic setting, such as a hospital or clinic, all sorts of safeguards are taken to prevent punishment from devolving into abuse. There are rules about the circumstances under which punishment is used, who will deliver it, how strong it will be, and so on. The possibility of abuse under such circumstances is remote. But in other settings, such as the home and school where such safeguards are not in force, abuse is a strong possibility.

A third unwanted side effect of punishment is *imitation* of the use of punishment. If I get what I want by slapping you, there is a risk that you will slap others to get what you want. Numerous studies have shown that parents who use physical punishment with their children a great deal generally have children who are physically aggressive toward others.[18]

Again, this seems to be more of a problem in the home and the school than in the hospital and the clinic. When physical punishment is used by behavior analysts in institutional settings, the therapists are careful not to reinforce any imitative aggression that may occur. In the home and school, however, it may be impossible to prevent the reinforcement of imitative aggressive acts.

These side effects of punishment are certainly undesirable, and some people use them to build a case against any use of punishment. However, it is well to remember that these negative side effects stem primarily from the misuse of physical punishment. Reprimands, time out, response cost, and overcorrection do not usually arouse strong fear or anger, nor do they lead to physical injury. And if someone imitates our use of them, that's not likely to be particularly troublesome. It's physical punishment that is most likely to produce negative side effects.

It's also worth noting, however, that punishment can have positive as well as negative side effects. Even physical punishment can produce benefits other than the suppression of unwanted behavior. For instance, K. L. Lichstein and Laura Schreibman examined side effects in ten studies using shock in the treatment of autistic children.[19] The children became more sociable, more cooperative, more affectionate, and were more likely to make eye contact and smile. It's hard to believe that punishment, especially physical punishment, can have such side effects, but people with severe behavior disorders often seem happier after their most inappropriate behavior has been suppressed with punishment. In fact, there is evidence that punishment is more likely to produce positive side effects than negative ones.[20]

Even so, punishment is a risky procedure that must be used cautiously, sparingly, reluctantly. Earlier, I said that punishment was often the first thing people think of when they want to change behavior. When *you* face a behavior problem, make it a rule to consider punishment *last*. The debate—yes, Brian?

"Suppose you do decide to use punishment. Which form of punishment should you use?"

That's a good question, for which I lack a good answer. I'm afraid there isn't any simple rule you can follow in selecting a form of punishment. The one thing I can suggest is that you use the mildest form of punishment that is likely to work. In particular, don't use any form of physical punishment if some other kind of punishment is likely to produce satisfactory results. And always, *always* make punishment the last solution that you consider.

Review

To begin today's review, Jamal, how about telling me what punishment is?

"That's doing something that reduces the frequency of a behavior."

Sorry, Jamal, that's not good enough. Try again. Try beginning with, 'Punishment is the *procedure* . . .'

"Hmm. Punishment is the procedure . . . of providing a consequence that reduces the frequency of a behavior."

Good. Now, what about the word *punisher*, Maya?

"That's the consequence that you use in the punishment procedure. It's a consequence that weakens the behavior it follows."

Right. We discussed five kinds of punishment. The first was reprimanding. Reprimands are . . . Brian?

"Expressions of disapproval, such as when you said Jamal's answer wasn't good enough."

Yes, that was a mild reprimand. To qualify as punishment, reprimands have to . . . what?

"They have to be contingent on a target behavior and they have to reduce that behavior."

Good. The second form of punishment we discussed was response cost. What's that, Belinda?

"That's the removal of a reinforcer contingent on a target behavior."

Number 3 was time out. Tell me what time out is, Carlotta.

"That's the removal of a person from a reinforcing situation contingent on a target behavior."

Right. And overcorrection . . . Brian?

"That's requiring restitution and repeated practice of appropriate behavior contingent on the target behavior."

What does *restitution* mean?

"It means the person has to undo or make amends for the damage the target behavior has caused."

Good. The fifth kind of punishment we discussed was . . . what, Alfred?

"Physical punishment."

Correct. And physical punishment is . . . ?

"That's where you provide contact with the skin contingent on a target behavior."

Yes, but I had some modifiers describing that contact with the skin. It had to be . . .

"Brief. Short-lived. And the other modifier was noninjurious."

Right. Physical punishment is brief and noninjurious contact with the skin. If it's not brief, or if it causes injury, then what you're doing is not punishment, it's . . . what is it, Alfred?

"Abuse?"

Exactly. It's abuse. *Punishment,* as the behaviorist uses the term, is not abuse.

Now, we discussed five rules for using punishment. Let's see if you can recall them. The first was to define . . . yes, John?

"Define the target behaviors—the behavior you want to occur less often and the behavior you want to occur more often."

Good. And the second was to . . . Jamal?

"Select appropriate punishers."

Yes. You need to identify consequences that are likely to suppress the behavior. And the third rule . . . Brian?

"Make the punishment immediate and certain."

Right. Delayed, unlikely consequences have weaker effects than immediate, likely consequences do. What was rule number 4, Maya?

"When you use punishment, you also need to use extinction and differential reinforcement."

Yes, you need to make sure the behavior you're punishing is not also being rein-forced. And you need to make the reinforcers that were obtained by the punished behavior available for some more appropriate behavior. The last rule for using punishment? Jamal?

"Monitor results."

Yes. You must always monitor the behavior to see what results you are getting. Even if you are using a procedure that has worked repeatedly in the past, you can't assume that you are getting the desired results this time. You must monitor behavior, especially the target behavior.

Punishment is a controversial procedure, and with good reason. It is likely to be used incorrectly, and some people object to it on moral grounds, even when it is used correctly. And it can have negative side effects. What was one negative side effect we discussed, Belinda?

"Emotional outbursts."

Yes. Punishment tends to elicit emotional reactions, especially fearful and aggres-sive behavior. Often the reactions are mild, but sometimes they are intense and cause serious problems.

Another side effect we talked about was . . . Jamal?

"Abuse. Like when a parent decides to give a child a spanking and overdoes it."

Yes, and the child ends up in the hospital or the morgue. Abuse is most often a problem with physical punishment, but other forms of punishment can be abused—such as when a person is put in time out for hours at a time. A third negative side effect of punishment is that the person whose behavior is being punished tends to . . . do what, John?

"To imitate the person using punishment."

So if you use punishment a lot with your kids, . . .

"Then my kids will probably use punishment a lot themselves."

Yes. When a parent, teacher, employer or other person uses a particular proce-dure for changing behavior, the person is also modeling that procedure. And if it works, people are likely to imitate it. Punishment usually gets results, so if a par-ent uses punishment a lot, so will their kids. If a teacher uses punishment, so will her students.

Which kind of punishment is most likely to produce negative side effects? Brian?

"Physical punishment."

Right. So we have to be particularly careful about using physical punishment. That's the kind of punishment that is most likely to get us into trouble.

Well, that concludes our prerelease review of punishment. You're free to go.

◀ Exercises ▶

Feed the Skeleton

I. Punishment

   A. The idea that behavior is a function of its consequences is called the

      _____ .

   B. A punisher is an event that _____

      _____ .

   C. Punishment is the procedure of _____

      _____ .

II. Kinds of Punishment

   A. Reprimanding means _____

      _____ .

   B. Removing a reinforcer following a target behavior is called _____

      _____ .

   C. Removing a person from a reinforcing situation is called _____

      _____ .

   D. Overcorrection involves _____ and

      _____ .

   E. Physical punishment involves contact with the skin that is

      _____ and _____ .

III. Illustrative Studies

   A. When Matilda stole _____ , it was taken away from her.

   B. Drabman and Spitalnik used _____ to reduce the frequency of aggressive acts in students with psychiatric disorders.

   C. Sajwaj and his colleagues squirted lemon juice into the mouth of a baby to reduce the frequency of life threatening _____

      _____ .

IV. Punishment Rules

   A. _____ .

   B. Select appropriate _____ .

   C. Make punishment _____ and

      _____ .

   D. Use _____ and _____ .

   E. _____ .

V. Punishment Problems

   A. One problem with punishment is that it may be used _____

      _____ .

B. Some people object to the use of punishment on _____
_____ grounds.

C. Punishment can have negative side effects, including _____
_____ reactions, _____ , and
_____ .

Daffy Advice:
Daphne Donchano Answers Your Questions

Dear Daffy:
    Me and the guy in the neighboring cell want you to settle an argument about the death penalty. I say it's a form of punishment, but Dopey says it ain't. Who's right?
                                            Two on Death Row

Dear Two:
    Sounds like you're both gonna find out the hard way!

Is capital punishment *really* punishment?

Overcoming Mental Conflicts

In the Ayllon study, the nurses attempted to persuade their patient to diet. There were good medical reasons for the patient to lose weight, and the fact that the patient's behavior was not changed by these arguments was interpreted by the staff as evidence of her mental illness. Is this interpretation valid? How does the data from the study affect that interpretation?

Throwing in the Towel

In addition to stealing food, the patient treated by Ayllon also collected towels and stored them in her room. Again, efforts to reason with the patient were unsuccessful, and the staff had to enter the patient's room twice a week to remove towels. To obtain a baseline on this behavior, the staff entered the patient's room three times a week (when she was not there) and counted the towels. The record showed that the number of towels ranged from 19 to 29, despite the fact that towels were being removed twice a week.

    Ayllon's suggested intervention was to ask the nurses to stop removing towels and to begin giving the patient extra towels. From time to time during the course of the day, a nurse would take a towel to the patient's room and hand it to her without comment. The first week they gave the patient an average of 7 towels a day; by the third week they were giving her 60 a day.

    The procedure was remarkably successful. At first, the patient was happy to have the extra towels. When given an extra towel she would say something like, "Oh, you found it for me, thank you." By the second week, her reaction was more likely to be, "Don't give me no more towels. I've got enough." The third week she was heard to say, "Take them towels away . . . I can't sit here all night and fold towels." And by the fourth week, a typical comment was along these lines: "Get these dirty towels out of here!"

When the number of towels in the patient's room reached 625, she began to remove them, and at this point she was given no more. Gradually her stockpile of towels fell until it leveled off at about 1.5 towels. The patient's behavior was monitored for over a year after the intervention ended. Not once during that time did she return to hoarding towels, nor did any other problem behavior arise to take the place of hoarding.

This unconventional study raises some interesting questions: The nurses who treated this patient had undergone traditional psychiatric training. What sort of explanation do you suppose the nurses would have given for this patient's hoarding? What predictions might they have made about the effects of Ayllon's treatment? Were those predictions fulfilled? And, finally, was this a punishment procedure?

Practice Quiz

1. A _____ is an event that decreases the frequency of the behavior it follows.

2. In _____ , the person is removed from a reinforcing situation when he or she performs the target behavior.

3. In response cost, performance of the target behavior results in _____ _____ .

4. Using a very weak punisher and gradually increasing the strength of the punisher can be a mistake since it can result in _____ _____ .

5. It is essential that punishers be delivered while the target behavior is occurring or immediately afterward. Otherwise, _____ _____ .

6. Punishment should never be used alone. It should be used in conjunction with extinction and _____ .

7. Drabman and Spitalnik reduced the frequency of aggressive acts in children with psychiatric disorders by _____ .

8. A retarded man in your care gets angry in the dining hall and throws his food onto the floor. You decide to punish this behavior by requiring him to clean up the mess and to clean all the tables in the dining hall that are not being used. You are using the overcorrection procedure called _____ _____ .

9. Sajwaj squirted _____ into the mouth of a baby to suppress rumination.

10. Reprimanding is typically intended to punish behavior, but sometimes _____ it.

Mini-Essay: QUESTIONING PUNISHMENT

Before using any form of punishment, but especially before using physical punishment, one should always ask these three questions:

First: Is the punishment procedure likely to be effective? If an aversive contingency is not likely to suppress the target behavior, there is little point in using it. Remember, the purpose of punishment is not retribution; it is to reduce the frequency of a behavior. If it will not do that, then you are considering abuse, not punishment.

Second: Are the positive effects of the procedure likely to be greater than its negative effects? Punishment can severely reduce the frequency of a problematic behavior; but it can also arouse fear and provoke aggression. Punishment might get rid of an unwanted behavior, but if it drastically undermines your relationship with the person you're trying to help, it may do more harm than good. You have to consider both the benefits and the costs of using punishment.

Third: Are you sure there are no satisfactory alternatives to punishment? Extinction and the various forms of differential reinforcement are useful ways of reducing the frequency of problem behavior. If the unwanted behavior can be eliminated with one of these procedures without the risk of someone being seriously injured, then the gentler procedure should be used. So, do you really need to use punishment?

Unless you can answer yes to all three questions, you should not use punishment.

Reprint: TIME OUT FOR HALLUCINATIONS
by Steve N. Haynes & Pamela Geddy

Hallucinations are usually defined as sensory experiences without an appropriate external stimulus. For example, patients sometimes report hearing voices when there is no one speaking, seeing people who are not present, smelling flowers when no flowers are around, or feeling bugs crawling on the skin in the absence of bugs. If hallucinations are defined as inappropriate behavior (or as behavior that is inappropriate, given external events), then it may be possible to reduce their frequency by changing the consequences of that behavior. In this study, Haynes and Geddy attempt to do just that with time out.

Behaviors assumed to be indicative of hallucinations are often observed in chronic hospitalized psychotics. An individual exhibiting hallucinations appears to be making verbal, facial and/or gestural responses to an unobservable stimulus. Psychotic hallucinatory behaviors are incompatible with adequate social functioning and responsiveness to environmental stimuli (Davidson, 1969). Therefore suppression of hallucinatory behaviors may facilitate the development of more effective social behaviors.

Time-out from positive reinforcement (TO) is a behavior modification technique in which positive reinforcers are withdrawn for a period of time following a target response. Bostow and Bailey (1969) found that brief periods of isolation contingent on abusive talk by an institutionalized retarded adult was effective in reducing the rate of that response.

As disruption of and withdrawal from the normal social environment is characteristic of psychotics, it is unclear whether isolation, which entails time-out from the reinforcers mediated by social contact, can be an effective punishing stimulus with psychotics. It has also not been demonstrated that contingent isolation can serve as a punishing stimulus for hallucinations which has been hypothesized to be a function of reduced sensory input (McReynolds, 1960). In the present study, short duration TO (isolation) was made contingent on the hallucinatory behaviors of a chronic hospitalized psychotic within an own-control replication paradigm.

Method

Subject

The subject was a 45-year-old female schizophrenic who had been in a state hospital for 22 years. The patient's typical day was spent in a ward day-room where she would manifest verbal behavior varying from quiet talking and mumbling to loud and disruptive yelling. These verbal behaviors did not appear to be in response to any identifiable stimulus and were incomprehensible approximately 75% of the time. The patient was never observed to initiate contact with other patients or staff members and only seldom responded to contact initiated by others.

Response

Any verbal behavior which was not in response to a stimulus from an environmental source or directed toward an external stimulus was considered a target response or hallucinatory behavior.

Observations

Observations of the subject's hallucinatory behaviors occurred on the ward during 10-min sessions. Each observation session was divided into 60 10-sec periods and the subject's specific verbal responses during each period were coded. A maximum of two responses were coded for each 10-sec period.

Time-Out Stimulus

The time-out stimulus was isolation in a small (5 X 5 m) room. The room was lighted and had one window but was devoid of any furniture except a chair.

Procedure

There were two baseline phases and two treatment phases within an own-control replication paradigm. The only variable manipulated between these conditions was the application or omission of TO contingencies to hallucinatory behaviors. Attempts were made to minimize the possibility of differential reinforcement of alternative behaviors (e.g., reinforcing attending to environment, social responsiveness).

Baseline. During this phase no contingencies were programmed. Nine behavioral observations occurred over a 15-day period.

Time-Out I. During this phase the staff placed the patient in the isolation room for 10 min immediately after the commencement of her hallucinatory behavior. Because of the high frequency of the target response TO did not follow every hallucinatory behavior.

When TO was to be administered, a staff member approached the patient and said, "You have to go to room _____ because you were talking to yourself." The staff member would then turn and without further comment lead the patient to the TO room and close the door. A timer was then set and the patient remained in the room for 10 min and until she had been quiet for 30 sec. The TO phase remained in effect until the rate of hallucinatory behavior became stable. This phase of the study lasted 21 days with 12 intermittent behavioral observations occurring during this time.

Recovery. During this phase all TO contingencies were withdrawn. This condition was maintained until recovery to the baseline rates was demonstrated. The recovery phase lasted 5 days with behavioral observations occurring on all 5 days.

Time-Out II. This phase was a replication of Time-Out I conditions. Ten behavioral observations occurred intermittently over a 14-day period.

Results

Reliability

Reliability was assessed by adding a second observer who recorded the patient's behavior concurrently with the first observer. Reliability was assessed six times throughout the study and was calculated by dividing the number of 10-sec periods in which total agreement occurred as to the presence or absence of a hallucinatory behavior by the total number of 10-sec periods. Interobserver agreement varied between 90 and 98% with an average agreement of 95%.

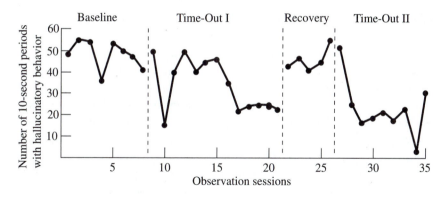

Figure 1. *Number of 10-second periods in which hallucinatory behavior occurred during Baseline, Time-Out I, Recovery, and Time-Out II phases. Each observation session lasted 10 minutes.*

Behavioral Observations

The observers were unable to discover any naturally occurring environmental consequence which may have functioned as a maintaining contingency for hallucinatory behaviors. Staff attention did not appear to follow this behavior nor did it appear to function as a response to avoid other people. Although not experimentally manipulated, the rate of hallucinatory behaviors did not vary as a function of the patient being alone or in the presence of others.

Effect of Time-Out

During Time-Out I and II, time-out was administered an average of 4.3 times per day. Figure 1 shows that the introduction of time-out contingencies effected a notable decrease in the rate of hallucinatory behaviors.

Removal of the time-out contingencies in the Recovery phase resulted in almost immediate recovery to rates comparable to Baseline. Reintroduction of time-out contingencies in the replication phase resulted in a reduction in the rate of hallucinatory behaviors comparable to that effected in the last five sessions of Time-Out I.

Discussion

The reduction in the rate of hallucinatory behaviors as a function of contingent short-duration time-out indicates that brief isolation, used as the TO stimulus, served as a punishing stimulus. The resulting response suppression does not support the contention that removal from social situations may be reinforcing for withdrawn psychotic patients. It is possible, however, that isolation possesses punishing properties (e.g., activity restriction, sensory monotony) in addition to those inherent in the withdrawal of reinforcers which may account for the observed effect.

Hallucinatory behaviors may belong to a class of behaviors which are often emitted in the absence of external reinforcements (e.g., masturbation, thumbsucking). From this perspective, what is impressive about the environment of the patient was the lack of negative contingencies following her hallucinatory behaviors. These behaviors occurring in the natural social situations would probably meet with intermittent punishment. That such contingencies did not occur on the ward may account in part for the emission of these responses—especially in the absence of alternative, more reinforcing behaviors in the patient's repertoire.

The results of this study support those of Baer (1961, 1962) who found that withdrawal of any reinforcer may affect a decrease in the rate of a response even when the reinforcer has not functioned as a reinforcer for that particular response. The inability to identify a reinforcer maintaining hallucinatory behavior did not preclude the ability of TO to affect a decrease in response rate.

The partial rather than complete suppression of the target response would be expected as a function of the intermittent schedule of TO. The partial suppression may also be a function of the nonreinforcement of alternative behaviors which has been shown to be a significant factor in determining the degree and permanence of rate reduction (Azrin and Holz, 1966).

In an additional application of TO to the modification of hallucinatory behaviors with another patient on the same ward using a similar replication paradigm, the frequency of these behaviors declined from a rate of 4.0 per observation period during baseline observation to 1.5 after the application of TO contingencies. Observations were made for 5 min every 2 hr from 8:00 AM to 6:00 PM.

Excerpted from "Suppression of Psychotic Hallucinations Through Time-Out," by S. N. Haynes and P. Geddy. In *Behavior Therapy, Vol. 4,* copyright 1973 Association for Advancement of Behavior Therapy. Reprinted by permission of the publisher.

‹ Recommended Reading ›

1. Bandura, A., & Walters, R. H. (1959). *Adolescent aggression.* New York: Ronald Press.
   This study found heavy reliance on punishment by parents to be a common factor in the backgrounds of aggressive adolescents.

2. Carr, E. G., Robinson, S., & Palumbo, L. W. (1990). The wrong issue: Aversive versus nonaversive treatment. The right issue: Functional versus nonfunctional treatment. In A. Rapp & N. Singh (Eds.), *Perspectives on the use of nonaversive and aversive interventions for persons with developmental disabilities.* Sycamore, IL: Sycamore Press.

Carr et al. suggest that the question of whether to use punishment (and other aversive procedures) might never arise if other procedures were used in a timely fashion.

3. Castrale, E. G., & Cunio, T. F. (1995). Negative rewards for positive behaviors. *Phi Delta Kappan, 77* (4), 320–321.
   Companies often reward worker achievements with a certificate, a cash bonus, a bigger office, a larger budget, more assistants, or an expense-paid trip to some nice vacation spot. In education, things are different.

4. Hart, B., & Risley, T. R. (1995). *Meaningful differences in the everyday experience of young American children.* Baltimore: Paul Brookes.
   Punishment is not the focus of this book, but the study described does reveal important differences in the use of punishment by parents, and these differences are associated with differences in the intellectual and academic success of children.

5. Sears, R. R., Maccoby, E. E., & Levin, H. (1957). *Patterns of childrearing.* Evanston, IL: Row, Peterson.
   A classic work on the effects of different parenting styles on children. Heavy use of punishment by parents was associated with aggressiveness in children.

6. Sidman, M. (1989). *Coercion and its fallout.* Boston, MA: Authors Cooperative, Inc.
   Sidman is a prominent researcher in the use of aversives, including punishment. This book sets forth a strong case against the use of punishment for training and therapy.

◄ Endnotes ►

1. Our society is strongly inclined to use punishment. For instance, a survey of American mothers found that 42% had spanked their *toddlers* in the previous week (Socolar & Stein, 1995). I emphasize the word *toddlers* because we're talking about hitting little kids—preschoolers. Behavior analysts have led the way toward more humane methods of changing behavior, but few people have followed them.

2. Notice that the definitions of *reinforcement* and *punishment* are not quite parallel. Reinforcement speaks of maintaining the rate of a behavior, but punishment does not. The reason is that only reinforcement maintains a behavior. If there are no reinforcing consequences for a behavior that is being punished, the rate of the behavior will fall to zero, or nearly zero, and stay there. One complaint that is sometimes made against punishment is that the effects are temporary: When you stop punishing the behavior, its rate

increases. But this is true only if the behavior is being reinforced. No reinforcement, no maintenance.

3. It might avoid confusion if behaviorists dropped the term *punishment* entirely and used some other word. One that has been suggested is *deceleration*; the term has not caught on, but it has the virtue of suggesting that what is important is the effect the procedure has on behavior.

4. White (1975). Another study (Madsen et al., 1970a) found that 77% of the interactions of elementary school teachers and students were negative in tone.

5. White (1975).

6. Madsen et al. (1970b). The effectiveness of reprimands depends on a number of variables (Van Houton & Doleys, 1983). These include the verbal content of the reprimand, accompanying nonverbal cues (such as frowns and body posture) and how often they are used. For instance, reprimands may be more effective when the person doing the reprimanding stands close to the person being reprimanded (O'Leary et al., 1970; Van Houton et al., 1982).

7. Even though you don't have to pay the fine right away, the ticket itself may be an effective punisher since it often comes relatively soon after illegally parking.

8. Matson & DiLorenzo (1984).

9. Foxx & Azrin (1973). The two components of overcorrection are often used independently. A target behavior may result in restitution alone or in positive practice alone. Because of this, MacKenzie-Keating and MacDonald (1990) have suggested that the term *overcorrection* be abandoned and restitution and positive practice considered on their own merits.

10. Foxx & Bechtel (1983).

11. Dorsey et al. (1980).

12. See, for example, Lindscheid et al. (1990) and Carr and Lovaas (1983) for discussions of the use of shock in the treatment of severe behavior problems.

13. Ayllon (1963).

14. Drabman & Spitalnik (1973).

15. Sajwaj et al. (1974). Incidentally, I should add that before this study, lemon juice had never been used in the treatment of rumination—or in the treatment of any other problem, as far as I know. There was no guarantee that the procedure would work, and, had it not worked, there is little doubt that the behaviorists involved would have come in for severe criticism.

16. See, for example, Walters (1964).

17. See Gursky (1992).

18. Bandura & Walters (1959); Sears et al. (1957); Hart & Risley (1995).

19. Lichstein & Schreibman (1976).

20. Lichstein & Schreibman (1976).

Discrimination Training

Last time we talked about punishment. What is punishment, Belinda?

"It's the procedure of providing consequences for a behavior that make the behavior less likely to occur."

Yes. Punishment is one procedure for reducing the frequency of a target behavior. Another is . . . John?

"Extinction."

Right. And another is . . . Maya?

"Differential reinforcement."

Yes, so we discussed three procedures for reducing the frequency of behavior. And if we want to *increase* the frequency of a target behavior, we use . . . Jamal?

"Reinforcement?"

Of course. And if the behavior doesn't occur, then we can provide hints to evoke behavior so that it might be reinforced. That's called . . . what is that called, Alfred?

"Prompting?"

Yes. You prompt the behavior, reinforce it, and gradually fade the prompt. If the target behavior isn't in the person's repertoire, we can reinforce successive approximations of the behavior. That's called . . . what is that called, Midori?

"Shaping."

That's right. And if the target behavior is a sequence of acts, we can use the procedure called . . . what, Carlotta?

"Chaining."

Right. Now, all the procedures we've discussed so far in this course are designed to either increase or decrease the frequency of a target behavior. That's appropriate, since we said that solving a behavior problem usually requires changing the frequency of some behavior. But sometimes the problem isn't as simple as that. Sometimes the problem isn't simply that the rate of the behavior is too high or too low; sometimes the problem is that the rate of the behavior is too high in one kind of situation and too low in another kind of situation. In these cases, we must increase the frequency of the behavior in those situations in which the rate is too low, and decrease the frequency in those situations in which the rate is too high.

For example, when you learn to drive a car, you have to learn to press various floor pedals: the gas pedal, the brake pedal, and the clutch. But it isn't enough just to press the pedals more often; slamming the gas pedal to the floor when a traffic light turns red can have very negative—even fatal—consequences. So learning to drive a car means learning to perform certain acts under certain circumstances and learning to avoid performing those acts under other circumstances. The behavior of pressing the gas pedal has to be likely in certain circumstances and unlikely in other circumstances. The tendency for behavior to occur in one situation, but not in another, is called stimulus discrimination.

Stimulus Discrimination

Stimulus discrimination refers to the tendency for behavior to occur more frequently in one situation than in another.

> ### Stimulus discrimination:
> ### The tendency for behavior to have different
> ### frequencies in different situations.[1]

Discriminating between two situations requires that the situations differ in some detectable way. Students more often dress formally for job interviews than they do for my class. They discriminate between the two situations. They can do so because there are discernible differences between the two situations: I am meeting with you in a classroom, whereas a job interviewer would ordinarily meet with you in some other location, such as an office. If you were seeing me about a job, you might have to make an appointment, wait in line, and then meet with me one-on-one. As it is, you meet with me as part of a group, and you don't have to make an appointment or wait in line. There are lots of features of the two situations that allow you to discriminate between them. The differences in situations that allow us to discriminate between them are called discriminative stimuli:

> ### Discriminative stimulus:
> ### Any event in the presence of which a target
> ### behavior is likely to have consequences
> ### that affect its frequency.

Since the consequences associated with a discriminative stimulus can be those that either strengthen or weaken behavior, it follows that there are two kinds of discriminative stimuli. I'll put their symbols and definitions on the board:

> ### S^D:
> ### An event in the presence of which the target
> ### behavior is reinforced.

S^Δ:

An event in the presence of which the target behavior is not reinforced.

"I assume the first one is pronounced "ess-dee," but how do you pronounce that other one?"

"Ess-dee" is correct, John. The second one is pronounced *"ess-delta."* The little triangle is the Greek letter *delta,* which is the Greek version of our letter *D.* So you see, both kinds of discriminative stimuli áre designated by the letter *D,* for *discriminative.* In one case the *D* is the English letter, in the other case it's the Greek letter. Can anyone tell me why we have to use different symbols for the two kinds of discriminative stimuli? Yes, Brian?

"So we can *discriminate* between them. If you used S^D for both kinds, we wouldn't know what sort of consequence the behavior would have."

Right. So the letters *D* and Δ are examples of . . . ?

"Discriminative stimuli."

Right again. It is sometimes said that discriminative stimuli signal the availability of reinforcement. This is true in a mathematical sense: An S^D indicates a high probability of reinforcement of the target behavior; an S^Δ indicates a low probability of reinforcement of the behavior.[2]

"So a person discriminates because the signals tell him the behavior will or won't be reinforced, is that it?"

No, Alfred, I'm afraid that isn't it. Suppose you dress differently for a job interview than you do for my class. You discriminate between the two situations. You're suggesting that you discriminate *because you understand that the two situations call for different attire.* You probably *do* understand that, but that understanding doesn't explain the behavior; it's just more behavior to explain. Remember, our goal as behaviorists is to identify functional relations between behavior and physical events. Discriminative stimuli are antecedent events that are correlated with certain kinds of consequences. S^{D}s are correlated with reinforcement; S^{Δ}s are correlated with extinction or punishment. It is these functional relations among antecedents, behavior, and consequences that explain behavior, including discriminations.

"I knew that. I was just trying to see if your readers were paying attention."

Thank you, Alfred. Your pedagogical efforts are appreciated.

"Is the S^D like the stimulus in a reflex?"

That's a good question, Maya. No, it isn't. We're still talking about operant behavior, and operant behavior is not reflexive. An S^D is said to "set the occasion for" a particular behavior, but it doesn't induce it in quite the mechanical sense that a rap on the knee evokes the knee-jerk reflex. However, if a target behavior occurs during or following the appearance of an S^D and is reinforced, presenting the S^D will greatly increase the likelihood of the target behavior occurring again.[3]

All sorts of things can serve as discriminative stimuli. A parent saying "Da-da" is an S^D for the baby to say, "Da-da." The symbol "8" is an S^D for saying "eight," and "8 + 3 =" is an S^D for saying "eleven." The positions of the hands on a clock can be an S^D for eating, going to class, leaving work, or going to bed.

Nonverbal behavior often serves as discriminative stimuli for social interactions. If you go on a date, you may detect subtle hints that efforts at familiarity will, or will not, be reinforced. These nonverbal cues are discriminative stimuli. When a person describes a meeting with someone as producing "good vibes," he's talking about the discriminative stimuli detected. When—

"But how come these discriminative stimuli are so often wrong?"

What do you mean, Alfred?

"Well, like, I have this friend. He went on a date. Everything seemed to be going pretty well, so he started, well . . . getting familiar. He put his arm around her or something. At first she laughed and said something like, 'Don't do that.' Well, I thought . . . I mean, *he* thought she was just being coy, and really wanted him to go ahead. So he went ahead. Next thing he knew, she was calling him all kinds of names . . ."

So? What's the problem?

"Well, if she didn't want him to make advances, why did she provide S^Ds for making advances?"

Ah. I guess the question is, did she? Anybody have any thoughts on the matter? Yes, Midori?

"I've been in that situation. Some guys just don't get the message. You just about have to hit them on the head with a lead pipe."

So, you're saying the problem is that Alfred's friend didn't respond appropriately to the discriminative stimuli. That's certainly a possibility. There's a book called *That's Not What I Meant* that is about miscommunication between people, especially between the sexes.[4] The author is talking partly about discrimination failures.

There are lots of discrimination failures, instances in which behavior occurs in inappropriate situations despite the presence of discriminative stimuli.[5] Traffic signs tell us to stay to the right, slow for a curve, yield to oncoming traffic, yet sometimes people stay to the left, maintain their speed on a curve, and ignore oncoming traffic. Why do discrimination failures occur? The main reason is lack of training. If Alfred's friend doesn't know when "No" means *no*, it may mean that he hasn't had sufficient experience with "No" as an S^Δ in dating situations.

"Yeah, he needs to get his face slapped more often."

Well, Midori, it may not require such strong measures, but some sort of appropriate consequence is required. Whether a person discriminates appropriately has to do with the training he has received—which brings us to the problem of discrimination training.

Discrimination Training

Discrimination training is a set of procedures for establishing discriminations:

> ### Discrimination training:
> ### Any procedure that results in a target behavior having different frequencies in different situations.[6]

Usually, discrimination training involves reinforcing a behavior in the presence of an S^D, and not reinforcing it in the presence of an S^Δ. There are, however, various ways of going about this. One is called simultaneous discrimination training.

Simultaneous Discrimination Training

In simultaneous training, a person is presented with a choice. For example, we might present a child with an apple and a banana, side by side, and say, "Point to the apple."[7] If the youngster points to the apple, we would provide some sort of reinforcer. We might say something like, "Good," or "That's correct," and we might also provide some treat, such as a piece of apple. If he makes the wrong choice, we would ignore the answer or provide a mildly punishing consequence such as, "No, that's wrong."[8]

When you are confronted with an apple and a banana and asked to point to the apple, pointing is reinforced only if you point to the apple. So, the apple is . . . is what? Jamal?

"The S^D?"

Yes. And that means that the banana is . . .

"The S^Δ."

Right again. Now, the procedure just described constitutes one training trial. After it, we would shield the fruit from view, perhaps with a piece of cardboard, for a few seconds. During this time we might alter the position of the two items. (That way the apple would be on the child's left on some trials, and on his right on other trials.) Then we would remove the shield, ask the child to point to the apple, and provide consequences appropriate to his choice. Why is it important to vary the position of the S^D and S^Δ? Maya?

"Because if the apple is always on the left, then pointing to the left is reinforced."

So? What's wrong with that?

> "The behavior you want to reinforce is pointing to the apple, not pointing to
> the item on the left."

Excellent. If the apple were always on the left, say, then the child might not have
learned to discriminate between the apple and the banana; he might have simply
learned to point to the object on the left. If you put a carburetor from a 1947
Oldsmobile on the left and said, "Point to the apple," he might point to the
carburetor.

Once the child is able to discriminate between an apple and a banana, we
might present him with a choice between an apple and an orange on several trials. When this discrimination is mastered, the choice might be between an apple
and a pear, and so on. In each case, two alternatives are presented, the child is
asked to point to the apple, and the trainer provides consequences depending on
how the child performs.

Simultaneous training need not be limited to two choices. You might present
a child with an array of items: an apple, a banana, a pear, and a mango, for example. One of the items would always be an apple, and the child would be asked to
point to that item. Selecting the one apple out of three or four items is more difficult than selecting between two items, so we would probably begin with a discrimination between two items and increase the number of alternative items
gradually. In any case, simultaneous training always involves items presented at
the same time.

Successive Discrimination Training

In successive training, the discriminative stimuli are presented one after the
other. For example, in training a preschooler to discriminate between an apple
and a banana, we would present one of the fruits and say, "What's this?" After the
child answers, we would provide an appropriate consequence. Then we would
put the fruit behind the screen, and offer it or the alternative item again and say,
"What's this?"

> "What if she doesn't know the answer?"

That's quite likely, John, otherwise she wouldn't need the training. At first, you
may have to prompt the answer. You show her the banana, for example, and say,
"What's this? . . . Say, 'banana.'" On the next trial, you might show the apple and
say, "What's this? . . . Say, 'apple.'" When a prompt regularly elicits the correct
response, you would begin to . . . to do what, Midori?

> "To fade it. You'd say, 'What's this? . . . Say, *ba-nan* . . .' You'd gradually reduce
> the prompt."

Very good. Eventually the question, "What's this?" would elicit the appropriate
replies.

The successive procedure represents a more difficult task than the simultaneous procedure, since in the successive procedure the alternative item is not

available for comparison. It is therefore often a good idea to begin training with the simultaneous procedure and then move on to the successive procedure.

Errorless Discrimination Training

In simultaneous and successive procedures, the person undergoing training inevitably makes a number of errors. These mistakes include failing to perform the target behavior in the presence of the S^D, and performing the target behavior in the presence of the S^Δ. For example, a person who's learning to identify birds may be required to discriminate between eagles and other birds. This means, in part, saying "eagle" when shown a photograph of an eagle and *not* saying "eagle" when shown a picture of any other kind of bird. However, on some trials, our student may say nothing when shown the photograph of an eagle, and he may say "eagle" when presented with the photograph of a duck. Such errors are common during discrimination training.

Errors are thought to be problematic, partly because they can arouse emotional reactions that interfere with learning. Herbert Terrace developed a procedure for establishing discriminations essentially without errors. The procedure is called, appropriately enough, *errorless discrimination training*. Errorless discrimination training is a variation of simultaneous training. The S^D is presented in the usual manner, and appropriate behavior in its presence is reinforced. The S^Δ, however, is presented in very, very weak form, so that it evokes no reaction at all. Gradually, the strength of the S^Δ is increased.

"That sounds like fading in reverse."

It is fading in reverse, Carlotta. In fading, a prompt is presented in weaker and weaker form. In errorless discrimination training, the S^Δ is presented in stronger and stronger form. The idea is that if the S^Δ is extremely weak, the target behavior won't occur: Our birding student won't say "eagle" when shown a duck if the photograph of the duck is so faint that he can hardly see it. He will, however, say "eagle" when shown a photograph of an eagle. The picture of the eagle is the S^D, and it's presented at full strength.

Gradually, the strength of the S^Δ is increased until finally the S^D and the S^Δ can be presented at full strength and the person will behave appropriately. In the case of our birder, he'll say "eagle" when shown an eagle but not when shown a duck. And this discrimination is achieved with few or no errors.

Any of these procedures—successive, simultaneous, and errorless—can be used to produce a discrimination. They can be used by parents and teachers to teach elementary academic skills to ordinary students; by special education instructors working with people who have learning problems, such as dyslexia; by trainers teaching new work skills to employees; and by clinicians trying to teach psychotic patients to behave appropriately in different situations. Let's consider a couple of illustrative studies.

Illustrative Studies

Getting the Message

Effective social interaction depends on the ability to interpret nonverbal cues provided by other people. People "say things" not only with words but with facial expression, posture, and other nonverbal cues. Correctly interpreting these nonverbal cues requires making discriminations: We learn that a smile indicates pleasure or satisfaction, a frown means displeasure or confusion, and so on. Some people become quite good at these discriminations, and can "read" very subtle signals; others are quite inept at the task and often find themselves misinterpreting what another person is feeling. Can people who are not very skillful at interpreting nonverbal messages learn to improve their skill? Rachel Azrin and Steven Hayes decided to find out.[9]

Before the training, Azrin and Hayes asked college males to view videotapes of women interacting casually with men for 1 minute. After viewing each tape, the men rated the degree of interest the woman displayed in the man with whom she was talking. (Incidentally, only the women were visible on the tapes; the men were out of camera range. In addition, the audio was turned off, so the ratings of interest were based entirely on nonverbal behavior.) The women on the tapes also rated their interest in the men with whom they spoke. These self-ratings were taken as the standard against which the ratings of the men could be compared. The idea was that if a woman rated her interest in a man as 2 (very little interest) but the student viewing the tape thought her interest rated a 7 (strongly interested), then that student is misreading signals.

After the pretesting (which also included some role playing), the students began training. The training was similar to the videotape pretesting except that the students got feedback about their ratings: The students would watch a tape, rate the level of interest the woman showed in the man, and then hear how the woman rated her interest in the man. This procedure was repeated until the students had seen and rated 24 one-minute tapes. After the training procedure, the researchers repeated the pretest procedures again to get a posttraining measure.

Now, the assumption is that the feedback about the woman's rating will . . . will what, Jamal?

"Will reinforce accurate ratings?"

Yes. If a student guesses that a woman's interest is low and he learns that he's right, that should be reinforcing. If he guesses wrong, that tells him he has to modify his behavior. This sort of feedback is often very effective in changing behavior, and it was effective in this study. As the training proceeded, the men got better at discriminating between nonverbal cues that signal interest and those that signal lack of interest. The researchers compared these students with others who had been through the same training procedure *except* that they had not received feedback. The two groups of students—those who got feedback about their ratings and those who did not—were about equally skilled at rating women's interest early in the training. Over the course of the training, however, the two groups drifted apart: Those who got feedback got better, while those who didn't get feedback didn't improve.

"In other words, practice at watching videotapes didn't have any effect?"

That's right, Midori. The feedback was essential. It's interesting to note that the training procedure did not identify the specific discriminative stimuli the students had to discriminate. Nobody said to the students, "Notice that the woman was gnashing her teeth; that suggests she doesn't like the man she's with." Nobody said, "This woman conveyed her strong interest in the man by smiling and making eye contact." Yet, even without such instruction, the students made a lot of progress. All they needed was the opportunity to rate nonverbal behavior and get feedback about the accuracy of their ratings.

So, discrimination training can be used to teach social skills to college students. Can it also help people with serious behavior disorders? Let's consider another study.

Promptness Counts

Psychotic patients often engage in behavior that interferes with their own treatment, makes life difficult for their caregivers, and adds to the expense of their care. A group of schizophrenic women in a psychiatric hospital provide an example.[10] Instead of proceeding directly to the dining area for meals, they trailed in slowly. It took several attendants half an hour to round them up and get them into the dining room.

Faced with this problem, Teodoro Ayllon and Eric Haughton decided to use a kind of discrimination training procedure to change the patients' behavior. They asked the staff to discontinue all efforts at getting patients into the dining room. Instead, they rang a dinner bell, and any patient who arrived at the dining room within 30 minutes after the bell sounded would be admitted. Anyone who showed up at the dining hall after the 30-minute deadline was to be turned away.

The first time the new procedure was in effect, only a few patients made it to the dining hall in time to eat. Gradually, however, more and more of them made it on time until they were all getting their meals. At this point Ayllon and Haughton gradually reduced the interval between the bell and the closing of the dining room doors. Soon, when the dinner bell rang the patients went directly to the dining hall without delay.

"Dr. Cee?"

Yes, Belinda?

"That doesn't seem like the other examples of discrimination training you've given us."

I know, but I think it does qualify as discrimination training. Can you tell me what the S^D was?

"The bell?"

Right. Approaching the dining hall within a certain time after the bell rang was reinforced—the patients got to eat. Approaching the dining hall after a certain length of time was not reinforced—the patients were turned away. What was the S^Δ?

"The absence of the bell?"

Yes. Approaching the dining hall before the bell rang or long after it had rung got the patients nothing. One thing that makes this case different from others we've discussed is that Ayllon and Haughton not only introduced discriminative stimuli, they also changed the nature of the behavior that was reinforced. They defined the target behavior not as arriving at the dining hall but as arriving at the dining hall *within a specified time*. Put another way, the S^D signaled that food was available for approaching the dining hall, but only if the behavior occurred soon after the bell.

You can see from these illustrative studies that discrimination training is a very useful tool in dealing with behavior problems. To get the most out of this tool, however, it's necessary to follow certain guidelines. I'll list them on the board:

Rules for Discrimination Training

1. Define the target behavior.

By now you know the importance of defining the target behavior. In discrimination training, defining the target behavior means deciding what you want the person to do in the presence of the S^D, but not in the presence of the S^Δ. The behavior might be as simple as pointing to something or stating its name. Or it might be as complicated as selecting the right kind of wines to accompany a variety of dinner menus.

2. Select appropriate discriminative stimuli and their consequences.

To do discrimination training, you have to identify two or more situations that can be discriminated in some way. The differences that permit discrimination are the S^D and S^Δ. In the initial stages of training, it is important that the S^D and S^Δ be sharply different in some way, so that the person being trained is almost certain to be successful. Why is it important that the person be successful? Jamal?

"You have to be able to reinforce the behavior, and you can't reinforce it if it doesn't occur."

Exactly. In addition, failing is usually punishing. So if the discrimination is too difficult, the person is punished for trying.[11] That means the person is less likely to try again. If you want someone to learn a discrimination, you have to ensure that their efforts are reinforced. That means using S^Ds and S^As the person is able to discriminate.

So, if you are teaching a preschooler to discriminate apples from other fruits, you might make the first S^Δ a banana, since bananas are very different from apples. They differ markedly in shape and color. When this discrimination is learned, you might replace the banana with a grape. The shapes are similar, but there are marked differences in color and size. Then you might try an orange. The size and shape are similar to an apple, but the color is different. Then you might use a mango. The size, shape and color are similar to the apple, but not quite the same. In other words, you go from easy discriminations to more difficult ones. Along the way, the person you're training is able to be successful most of the time.

3. Present the S^D and S^Δ with appropriate consequences.

I've explained that there are different ways of presenting the S^D and S^Δ. Which you use will depend on the situation. If you're working with a preschooler or a mentally retarded older child or adult, you will probably want to begin with the simultaneous procedure. On the other hand, if you're teaching normal first-graders the letters of the alphabet, you can present the letters one after another and ask the students to call out each letter's name.

There's nothing wrong with moving from one procedure to the other as your needs vary. For instance, suppose you're using successive presentation to teach the letters of the alphabet, and you find that several students have a tendency to confuse some letters—that is, they fail to discriminate between them. You hold up the letter *b*, and they say, "dee." You hold up the letter *d*, and sometimes they say, "bee." Lowercase *b*'s and *d*'s are often confused by students in the early grades. So are certain other letters.

"My mother used to say, 'Mind your *p*'s and *q*'s.'"

Yes, Carlotta, that expression might come from the failure to discriminate those lowercase letters. A failure to discriminate indicates the need for additional or improved discrimination training.

If the desired behavior is not forthcoming, you must prompt it. Early on, prompting might take the form of instructions; later, it might take the form of a hint, such as "Touch the one that is round." It might take the form of modeling; you might, for example, point to the apple yourself. Or it might take the form of a physical prompt; you might take the child's hand and point it toward the apple.

Once the desired behavior occurs regularly with the aid of a prompt, you then begin fading the prompt. You want the preschooler to point to the apple without any help from you, so you must fade that help.

When the target behavior occurs, you must provide appropriate consequences. Appropriate consequences means primarily reinforcement for correct performances. Punishing errors can speed up the learning process, but you have to be careful about this. As you know, strong punishment in particular is apt to create problems and should be avoided unless the unwanted behavior is dangerous. Generally, the best procedure is to reinforce successes and ignore failures or provide punishment in the form of a mild reprimand. Often praise or simple positive feedback are sufficient reinforcers, but sometimes hugs, small pieces of food, or tokens that can be exchanged for toys or special privileges are useful. In discrimination training, as in the early stages of learning any new behavior, it's very desirable to reinforce each correct performance.

And of course the last rule is . . . what, Maya?

"It must be, monitor results."

It must indeed:

4. Monitor results.

As always, you must monitor performance so that you can tell how well the training procedure is working. It's usually helpful to tally the successes and plot them on a frequency graph. If progress slows or levels off, the graph will reveal that.

Well, I think that covers the guidelines for discrimination training. Any questions before we proceed to the next topic? Yes, Brian?

"How many training trials do you provide?"

A general rule of thumb is to continue the training sessions until the person reliably performs the behavior in the presence of the S^D but not in the presence of the S^Δ.

"What does *reliably* mean?"

I was rather hoping you would let me slip by with that bit of vagueness. I don't think there's any hard and fast definition of *reliably* as it applies to discrimination training. If you're using simultaneous presentation with a single S^D and a single S^Δ, your pupil can get the correct answer half of the time by chance, so reliably necessarily means success on something more than 50% of the trials. How much more? What are you willing to settle for? Do you want correct choices 100% of the time? Is 80% of the time satisfactory? Your decision probably depends on a number of factors: the age and limitations of the person being trained; the difficulty of the discrimination; the importance of errors; the—

"What's that bit about the importance of errors? What do you mean?"

Well, Jamal, if you're teaching a preschooler to discriminate between oranges and tangerines, you might be satisfied when he chooses correctly 80% of the time. But suppose that you are teaching a graduate biology student to identify peregrine falcons. The student is going to be doing field counts to get an estimate of the number of peregrine falcons in the study area. For the research project to be successful, you must have an accurate census. To the extent that the student counts other sorts of birds as peregrines or counts peregrine falcons as other species of birds, the data are flawed and conclusions drawn from them may be invalid. Since the consequences of errors in this situation are rather serious, you might want a very high accuracy level—perhaps 98% if you can achieve it. There are even some situations in which you would want to have nearly 100% accuracy. I wonder, can anyone think of such a situation? . . . Yes, Maya?

> "If I discovered a growth and went to a doctor, I'd want to be sure she could discriminate accurately between a malignant growth and a benign one. If she says, 'Oh, that's nothing. Forget about it,' I'd like to believe that she's right."

That's a good example. And if she takes a biopsy and the pathologist examining the specimen doesn't discriminate correctly between malignant and benign, you could either have unnecessary treatments, such as surgery and chemotherapy, or a life-threatening disease could go untreated.

> "Well, doctors and pathologists probably go through pretty rigorous discrimination training, right?"

You sound a little nervous, Alfred. I wish I could reassure you, but I don't think doctors go through the sort of discrimination training I would want them to have. They do residencies in which they have opportunities to make discriminations, and their judgments are often checked by more experienced residents or staff physicians, so that their performance on most "trials" are reinforced or punished. But the training seems rather hit or miss to me. A person doing a residency in dermatology, for example, might see several cases of malignant melanoma, but there might be certain forms of the disease that she would never see during her training except in textbook photographs. The result is that doctors are to some extent trained by their patients.

> "Like they say, doctors bury their mistakes."

I'm afraid so, Alfred. Anyway, you can see that the level of accuracy needed for a particular discrimination will vary. In general, I would say most behaviorists would consider 80% accuracy in discrimination the minimum for success in most situations. When a satisfactory level of discrimination has been achieved, we say that the behavior is under stimulus control.

Stimulus Control

When discrimination training has been effective, the behavior is said to be under stimulus control. I'll put a definition on the board:

> ### Stimulus control:
> ### The tendency for the target behavior to occur in the presence of the S^D, but not in the presence of the S^Δ.

The term *stimulus control* means that a desired level of discrimination has been achieved.

In applied behavior analysis, stimulus control usually refers to the tendency for a particular behavior to occur in situations where it is appropriate and not in situations where it is inappropriate. If you are a good driver, you discriminate appropriately between red lights and green lights. This is actually a double discrimination: you press the break pedal at red lights but not at green ones; you press the gas pedal at green lights but not at red ones. The pedal pressing behaviors are influenced by particular features of the situations, hence the term *stimulus control.*

Notice that it is not the person who is under stimulus control, but a particular behavior. Stimulus control does not mean that a person has been robotized and must do as the situation dictates. If you are driving someone to the hospital for emergency care, and you can see that there are no vehicles or pedestrians near the intersection, you may continue to press the gas pedal. Similarly, if you see someone on another road entering the intersection, you may press the brake pedal even though the light is green. Stimulus control does not mean that our behavior is dictated by a situation. It merely means that the probability of a behavior is predictably affected by certain antecedent events. There is a strong likelihood that you will press the gas pedal when a traffic light turns green, and there is a strong likelihood that you will press the break pedal when the light turns red.

As this example implies, stimulus control is a routine part of our lives, and it is typically a great boon. Unfortunately, naturally occurring discrimination training sometimes results in inappropriate stimulus control. In fact, many of the most common behavior problems involve inappropriate stimulus control.

For instance, it sometimes happens that a student is a little angel in one teacher's class but a little devil in another teacher's class. When the teachers compare notes, they can't believe they're talking about the same child. In fact, you may recall a time when your entire class behaved very well when with one teacher, and very badly when with another teacher. These are instances of stimulus control. What might account for this particular difference in behavior? Yes, Midori?

"One teacher might reinforce good behavior, while the other teacher might ignore it."

Very likely. Let's suppose that Mr. Smith reinforces good behavior, while Mr. Jones ignores it. (To keep matters simple, we won't concern ourselves with the consequences of misbehavior.) It's not surprising that students soon behave very differently in the two classes—after all, the consequences for good behavior are very different in the two situations. But what are the discriminative stimuli in this situation? What is the S^D and what is the S^Δ? How about it, Carlotta?

"I'd say the S^D is Mr. Smith, and the S^Δ is Mr. Jones."

So you think the sight of Mr. Smith is an S^D for behaving well, and the sight of Mr. Jones is an S^Δ for behaving well. Suppose you had to substitute for one of the teachers. Would you rather substitute for Mr. Smith, or for Mr. Jones?

"Mr. Smith."

But why? After all, it's the same students in either case. And neither Mr. Smith nor Mr. Jones is present.

"I just have a feeling they'd behave better in Mr. Smith's class."

I think you're right. Can anyone explain why? Yes, Carlotta?

"The teachers aren't the only thing that makes the two situations different. Good behavior is reinforced in Mr. Smith's classroom, so the room might be an S^D for behaving well. The subjects they teach are different, too. If Mr. Smith teaches math and Mr. Jones teaches history, then doing math problems might be an S^D for behaving well, while doing history lessons might be an S^Δ for good behavior."

Excellent, Carlotta. In laboratory studies of discrimination training, the discriminative stimuli might be very simple. The S^D might be a light that is on; the S^Δ might be a light that is off. Outside the laboratory, things are much more complicated. Two situations might differ in a number of ways—some of them obvious and some of them subtle. Any one or all of those differences might serve as discriminative stimuli.

The example of Mr. Jones involves inappropriate stimulus control. Sometimes a problem reflects a lack of stimulus control. If you go shopping, you'll see youngsters engage in various kinds of behavior despite instructions from a parent to stop. "Don't do that, Eddy. . . . Eddy, what did I tell you? . . . Eddy, stop that. . . . Eddy, do you want a spanking? . . . Eddy! Are you deaf?!" Often the parent exclaims in exasperation, "I can't do anything with him. He just won't listen." Asked to explain such behavior, the parent may suggest that "All kids his age are like that. It's a stage they go through." If you point to other children Eddy's age who do not behave in this way, the parent may place the blame on genetics: "He gets it from his father; he's a blockhead, too."

Discrimination training provides a better explanation. When a child ignores parental requests, it's often because those requests have not been established as discriminative stimuli. "Don't do that" is meant to be an S^Δ for engaging in an ongoing behavior. "Come here" is meant to be an S^D for approaching the parent in a timely fashion. So why is it that such statements do not always act as discriminative stimuli? Yes, Maya?

"The parent probably hasn't provided appropriate consequences for the behavior."

Exactly right. To establish stimulus control, we must provide appropriate consequences. It isn't enough to say, "Come here." We must say that and then reinforce the behavior when it occurs. Reinforcement might take the form of a hug, a smile, or a few kind words. It can take any number of forms, but there must be some sort of reinforcer or "Come here" will not become an S^D for approaching. In all too many cases, the only time a parent says, "Come here" is when the child is to be spanked.

"This is all very interesting, but I'm planning on being a teacher. Is the concept of stimulus control of any use in teaching academic content?"

Well, Maya, a good deal of academic instruction has to do with learning concepts, and a concept is a kind of discrimination. For example, understanding the concept tree means being able to discriminate between trees and other items, including bushes and reeds—some of which resemble trees very closely. Concepts are efficiently taught through discrimination training.

For instance, if you want to teach children the concept square, you must do more than talk about the features that identify squares; you must provide your students with the opportunity to identify squares from among other items. You might, for example, present a square and a circle, ask the students to pick the square, and provide feedback about their choice. The discriminations required would get more and more difficult, with the final S^Δ being perhaps a rectangle that is nearly square.

Common geometric forms are fairly easy concepts to teach, but other concepts are more difficult. The difficulty often is due to the fact that the differences that separate the S^D from various S^Δs are very subtle. All of you know, or think you know, what a horse is, and most of you can discriminate between a horse and a giraffe or a zebra. But I suspect that some of you might make errors when asked to discriminate between a horse and a mule. They are two different critters—two different concepts—but the differences between them are relatively small, and that makes them hard to discriminate. Discriminating between a male bald eagle and a female bald eagle is even more difficult; the only difference the bird watcher can detect is that the female bird is a little larger than the male.

Well, enough about eagles and mules; time to wrap up this lesson with a short review.

Review

Let's start with stimulus discrimination. Can you define it for us, Jamal?

"That would be the tendency for a behavior to occur more often in one situation than in another."

Yes, all right. The behavior has different frequencies in different situations, so we say the person discriminates between the situations. What distinguishes the one situation from the other? Midori?

"They're different. . . . There are features of the situation that are different."

And what do we call these "features that are different"?

"Discriminative stimuli?"

Right. There are two kinds of discriminative stimuli. They are called . . . what, John?

"S^Ds and S^Δs."

That's right. And what is an S^D? Carlotta?

"That's an event in the presence of which the target behavior will be reinforced."

Yes. Behaviorists sometimes say that an S^D is something that signals the availability of reinforcement for a particular behavior. The other kind of discriminative stimulus is . . . Alfred?

"No, it's not called Alfred; it's called S^Δ."

Thank you for correcting me, Alfred. So, what is an S^Δ, Alfred?

"That's an event in the presence of which the target behavior is unlikely to be reinforced."

Exactly so. Some behaviorists like to say an S^Δ is something that signals that reinforcement is unavailable for a particular behavior.

Discriminations are established by means of discrimination training. Discrimination training is any procedure that results in . . . in what, Brian?

"In a target behavior having different frequencies in different situations."

That's right. Can you give me an example?

"Well, I took a course in botany once. When I started I could tell an oak tree from a maple . . ."

You could discriminate oak and maple trees. Yes, go on.

"But I couldn't tell one oak from another or one maple from another. By the end of the course, I could identify a half-dozen kinds of oak—"

You could discriminate among a half-dozen oak species . . .

". . . and I could *discriminate* three or four kinds of maples."

That's a good example, but are you really talking about differences in the frequency of behavior?

"Sure. Show me a leaf from a white oak and I will say white oak every time. I won't say red oak or scrub oak or sugar maple."

All right, fine. We talked about different kinds of discrimination training. What are they, Belinda?

"Simultaneous and . . ."

And . . . ?

"Successive?"

And . . . ?

"And errorless."

Right. How does simultaneous discrimination training work?

"That's where you present the person with a choice. You might show a child pictures of a car and a truck and say, 'Point to the truck.'"

Good. And how would you do the same thing using the successive procedure?

"I'd present the picture of a truck and say, 'What's this?' and provide an appropriate consequence, depending on their answer. Then I'd present the other figure and ask them to identify it."

What about errorless training?

"That's like simultaneous training except that you present the S^Δ in very weak form and gradually increase its strength."

Good. We talked about some rules for doing discrimination training. Can you remember the first one, Jamal?

"It's the same as it always is: Define the target behavior."

Yes, we always start by defining exactly what behavior we're trying to change. Next you select . . . John?

"You select the discriminative stimuli and consequences you're going to use in training."

Right. And, then you're ready to . . . to do what, John?

"Present the S^D and S^Δ and the appropriate consequences."

That's right. And the last rule to remember . . . Belinda?

"Monitor results."

Exactly. You always monitor results. Behaviorists are data-driven: What they do is dictated by the results they get.

Once you've done discrimination training, if you're very successful you end up producing something called stimulus control. What's that, Brian?

"Stimulus control is the tendency for the target behavior to occur in the presence of the S^D but not in the presence of the S^Δ."

Yes, stimulus control is the product of effective discrimination training. When you have good stimulus control, the behavior occurs reliably in the presence of the S^D and does not occur in the presence of the S^Δ. If you're flying in an airplane, you want a pilot whose behavior is under excellent stimulus control. You don't want a pilot who has to prompt appropriate behavior by reciting a mnemonic or saying to himself, "Let's see, push the right rudder to go right . . ."

So, discrimination training plays an important role in our lives: With a bit of practice, we hit the delete key on the new keyboard and avoid getting the unwanted help file; the child learns that she may call Mrs. Smith the balloon lady but *not* when Mrs. Smith is present; and the tourist soon drives only on the left where that is the law. Discrimination learning is a natural phenomenon. Discrimination training can speed up the process and can prevent much wasted effort.

Now I think I'll end this lesson by providing the S^D for leaving. Goodbye.

◄ Exercises ►

Feed the Skeleton

I. Stimulus Discrimination
  A. Stimulus discrimination is the tendency for b_____ to have different f_____ in different s_____ .
  B. Discriminative stimuli are events in the presence of which a b_____ is likely to have c_____ that affect its f_____ .
  C. There are two kinds of discriminative stimuli. Their symbols are _____ and _____ .

II. Discrimination Training
  A. Discrimination training is a procedure that results in a b_____ having different f_____ in different s_____ .
  B. In the simultaneous procedure, the discriminative stimuli are presented _____ .
  C. In the successive procedure, the discriminative stimuli are presented _____ .
  D. In errorless discrimination training, the S^Δ is presented _____ .

III. The rules for discrimination training are:
   A. _____ .
   B. Select _____ and their _____ .
   C. Present the _____ with appropriate _____

   _____ .
   D. _____ .

IV. Stimulus control is the tendency for a _____ to occur in
   the presence of the _____ but not in the presence of the _____ .

A Difference of Opinion

Remember Mr. Smith and Mr. Jones, the schoolteachers? They are both out sick
one day, and a substitute teacher, Mr. Gable, is called in to take their classes. The
school principal looks in on Mr. Gable while he is teaching Mr. Smith's class, and
the vice principal looks in while he is teaching Mr. Jones's class. At the end of the
day, the principal and vice principal compare notes, and they can't believe they're
talking about the same substitute teacher. One thinks the substitute did an outstanding job; the students were well behaved and the lesson went well. The other
thinks the substitute did a terrible job; there was so much misbehavior, she says,
that the substitute didn't even get through the lesson. Can you account for this
difference in judgments about Mr. Gable?

Guns R Us

You are an advisor to the mayor of a large American city. In the past year, three
children under the age of 12 have been shot by police officers when the children
pointed realistic-looking toy guns at the officer or another person. The public is
outraged by the killings and call the police trigger-happy. Yet there have been
instances in which the police were shot by children as young as 9. What advice
do you give the mayor?

What Cats See

Describe an experiment to determine whether cats see colors. Your experiment
should not involve injuring the cat in any way.

Invisible Trains

Every year, drivers are killed by trains at railroad crossings. This happens despite
the fact that there are warning signs indicating that a train may be coming. Why
don't people look before crossing the tracks?

Practice Quiz

1. If a behavior regularly occurs in the presence of an S^D, but not in the presence of an S^{Δ}, then the behavior is under _____ .

2. If you want a person to make a minimum number of errors while establishing a discrimination, you should use _____ discrimination training.

3. An S^Δ indicates that the target behavior _____ .

4. One type of discrimination error consists of failing to perform the target behavior in the presence of the _____ .

5. There are two kinds of _____ stimuli: S^D s and S^Δ s.

6. In _____ discrimination training, the discriminative stimuli are presented side by side.

7. Ayllon and Haughton used a discrimination procedure to get psychiatric patients to report to the dining hall in a reasonable amount of time. The S^D for going to the dining hall was _____ .

8. The last step in discrimination training is to _____ .

9. S^Δ is pronounced _____ .

10. In _____ discrimination training, the discriminative stimuli are presented alternately.

Reprint: ATTENTION
by B. F. Skinner

Skinner has a way of turning "common sense" on its ear. To most people, attending to something means focusing on it, tuning it in. We say that we "direct our attention" to an item, and we explain errors with the excuse, "I wasn't paying attention." Common sense tells us that attending is a quintessentially cognitive activity, one that must be part of almost any operant behavior. Well, read on.

The control exerted by a discriminative stimulus is traditionally dealt with under the heading of attention. This concept reverses the direction of action by suggesting, not that a stimulus controls the behavior of an observer, but that the observer *attends* to the stimulus and thereby controls it. Nevertheless, we sometimes recognize that the object "catches or holds the attention" of the observer.

What we usually mean in such a case is that the observer continues to look at the object. An animated billboard is dangerous, for example, if it holds the attention of a motorist too long. The behavior of the motorist in attending to the sign is simply the behavior of looking at it rather than at the road ahead of him. The behavior involves conditioning, and, in particular, the special conditioning of the discriminative operant. The variables are not always obvious, but they can usually be detected. The fact that people read billboards instead of looking at the surrounding countryside show how effectively reading is usually reinforced—

not only by billboards, but by stories, novels, letters, and so on. Powerful reinforcements are arranged by thousands of writers in every field of the written or printed word. . . .

A steady orientation of the eyes is not the only possible result. The behavior of a lookout in the dark or a heavy fog is an example of looking with orientation to the whole visual field. The behavior of searching the field—or responding to every part of it in some exploratory pattern—is the behavior which is most often reinforced by the discovery of important objects; hence it becomes strong. We can usually observe that the behavior with which a child looks for a misplaced toy is specifically conditioned. If some patterns of looking are reinforced by the discovery of objects more often than others, they emerge as standard behavior. . . .

But attention is more than looking at something or looking at a class of things in succession. As everyone knows, we may look at the center of a page while "attending to" details at the edges. Attempts to account for this in terms of "incipient eye movements" have failed; and in any case no comparable orientation appears to occur in attending to features of an auditory pattern. Thus, when we listen to a phonograph recording of a symphony while attending particularly to the clarinets, it is apparently not possible to demonstrate any special orientation of the ear. But if attention is not a form of behavior, it does not follow that it is, therefore, outside the field of behavior. Attention is a controlling *relation*—the relation between a response and a discriminative stimulus. When someone is paying attention he is under special control of a stimulus. We detect the relation most readily when receptors are conspicuously oriented, but this is not essential. An organism is attending to a detail of a stimulus, whether or not its receptors are oriented to produce the most clear-cut reception, if its behavior is predominantly under the control of that detail. When our subject describes an object at the edge of the page even though we are sure he is not looking at it, or when he tells us that the clarinets have fallen a beat behind the violins, we need not demonstrate any spatial arrangement of stimulus and response. It is enough to point to the special controlling relation which makes such a response possible. . . .

When we enjoin someone to pay particular attention to a feature of the environment, our injunction is itself a discriminative stimulus which supplements the stimulus mentioned in controlling the behavior of the observer. The observer is conditioned to look at or listen to a particular stimulus when he is told to "pay attention" to it because under such conditions he is reinforced for doing so. People generally say "watch that man" only when that man is up to something interesting. They generally say "Listen to the conversation in the seat in back of you" only when something interesting is being said.

Just as we may attend to an object without looking at it, so we may look at an object without attending to it. We need not conclude that we must then be looking with an inferior sort of behavior in which the eyes are not correctly used. The criterion is whether the stimulus is exerting any effect on our behavior. When we stare at someone without noticing him, listen to a speech without attending to what is said, or read a page "absent-mindedly," we are simply failing to engage in some of the behavior which is normally under the control of such stimuli.

From "Attention," by B. F. Skinner, in *Science and Human Behavior.* Copyright 1953 Macmillan. Reprinted with permission.

◄ Recommended Reading ►

1. Azrin, N. H., & Powell, J. (1968). Behavioral engineering: The reduction of smoking behavior by a conditioning apparatus and procedure. *Journal of Applied Behavior Analysis, 1,* 193–200.
   An attempt to help smokers get "stimulus control" over cigarettes.

2. Powers, R. B., Cheney, C. D., & Agostino, N. R. (1970). Errorless training of a visual discrimination in preschool children. *The Psychological Record, 20,* 45–50.
   Errorless discrimination training goes to school.

3. Salzinger, K. (1991). *Human error.* Paper presented at a meeting of the American Psychological Association, San Francisco, CA.
   Salzinger analyzed accidents and found that many can be understood in terms of stimulus control failures. The possibility is raised that catastrophes could turn on whether the safe and unsafe positions of a dial are easily discriminable.

4. Skinner, B. F. (1953). Operant discrimination. In *Science and Human Behavior* (pp. 107–128). New York: Free Press.
   Skinner discusses attention and other matters from the standpoint of discrimination.

5. Terrace, H. S. (1963). Discrimination learning with and without "errors." *Journal of the Experimental Analysis of Behavior, 6,* 1–27.
   Terrace demonstrates errorless discrimination training in pigeons. This is the classic paper on errorless discrimination.

◄ Endnotes ►

1. Many authors define discrimination in terms of the probabilities rather than the frequencies of behavior. Since probability is measured by its frequency (the number of occurrences in a unit of time), the terms are functionally equivalent.

2. Some authors use S+ and S− to designate the two kinds of discriminative stimuli. The trouble with these terms is that they are easily confused with S^+ and S^-, which are commonly used to indicate reinforcers and punishers,

respectively. The differences between S+ and S$^+$ and between S– and S$^-$ are subtle—i.e., they are hard to discriminate.

3. An S^D is similar to a prompt. In fact, some authors define a prompt as a kind of S^D (e.g., Grant & Evans, 1994). However, the word *prompt* is usually reserved for events used to evoke a target behavior when the discriminative stimuli that are ordinarily available are ineffective. For example, if I see you sitting in a chair in the student center, apparently deep in thought, I may say, "Hello." Ordinarily that would evoke a similar reply, such as "Hi." If, however, you do not reply but continue staring blankly into space, I may become concerned. At that point I will attempt to prompt a reply, first by saying "Hello" again, only louder, then perhaps by saying, "Are you all right?" If I still don't get a reply, I may put a hand on your shoulder and give you a light shove. Such prompts are so reliably effective that if I don't get a reply, I may call the paramedics.

4. Tannen (1986).

5. It used to be that if a student failed to discriminate between certain letters properly, teachers would say the child needed more instruction and practice. Today the same behavior is often taken as a sign of neurological disorder and the child is labeled dyslexic—even though there is often no independent evidence of neurological disorder. The dyslexia label is then sometimes used as an excuse for poor performance. "He's dyslexic. We can't expect him to spell correctly." Labels not only don't solve problems, they sometimes create them.

6. Discrimination training is sometimes defined as any procedure that increases the probability of a target behavior occurring in the presence of an S^D, and decreases the probability of its occurring in the presence of an S$^\Delta$.

7. A variation of the simultaneous procedure is called *matching to sample*. In this procedure, the item to be identified is presented in one position, say to the left, and the person is to identify the identical item from two items in a different position, say on the right. For example, we might put an apple on the child's left and an apple and a banana on the child's right. The apple to the left is held up or pointed to by the trainer, who says something like, "Show me the apple." When the child points to one of the two items to his right, the trainer provides the appropriate consequences.

8. Discrimination training that includes strong aversives can be highly effective. However, punishment is seldom necessary for effective discrimination training. In addition, the use of punishment in discrimination training incurs substantial risks; we considered these earlier when discussing punishment. The essence of effective discrimination training is reinforcement for the target behavior in the presence of the S^D, and the absence of reinforcement in the presence of the S$^\Delta$.

9. Azrin & Hayes (1984).

10. Ayllon & Haughton (1962).

11. People are fond of saying, "We learn from our mistakes." We do learn from our mistakes, but the lesson learned is often not what others would have us learn. We learn we are "not good at math" (or art, writing, spelling, science, etc.). We learn that certain activities are frustrating and lead to parental, teacher, employer, or spousal criticism. We learn to avoid those situations (courses, teachers, jobs, etc.) at which we regularly fail. We learn from our mistakes, but as a rule we learn far more useful things from our successes.

Generalization Training

So far, we have discussed a number of behavior analytic procedures: reinforcement, prompting and fading, shaping, chaining, extinction, differential reinforcement, punishment, and discrimination training. These are the fundamental tools for changing behavior.

"So the course is over? We're free to go?"

Not quite, Alfred. There's a bit more to solving behavior problems. And today I want to discuss part of that bit. I'll introduce today's topic with an example.

Suppose you are a counselor in a middle school. An 11-year-old named Julie has been sent to you for counseling because of her repeated conflicts with other students. Julie normally works well by herself, but if one comment characterizes her, it would be "Does not work well with others." In fact, she is known as Muley Julie among the other students because she always insists on doing things her way. Any time the students work together in pairs or in small groups, the other students groan if they get "stuck with" Muley Julie. The students with whom she works either agree to do things exactly as Julie wants, or they resist and there is a terrible row. Julie's teacher has asked you to provide counseling.

Your plan is to teach Julie how to work with others by working with her yourself. You decide to use a computer game as the activity. The game is one of the find-the-treasure types that provide a series of choice points at which you must decide which way to go, what doors to open, what questions to ask, and so on. The two of you play the game at the end of each school day for 20 minutes while Julie is waiting for her bus. You play the game in the normal way, except that you make a point of praising any concessions or signs of compromise you see in Julie. When these are not forthcoming, you attempt to prompt them by saying things like, "How about letting me choose the door this time?" If she agrees, you thank her and compliment her for playing well. During play, you keep count of the number of times she makes concessions, and after a few days you begin to see improvement. After three weeks, she plays as cooperatively as a career diplomat. You're feeling very pleased with yourself until you get a chance to see Julie's teacher and find that there has been no change in Julie's behavior in the classroom. "I'm glad you two are having fun playing computer games," the teacher says sarcastically, "but Julie's still muley in my classroom."

Clearly the teacher thinks you failed. What do you think? Yes, Midori?

"I think the teacher is right. The problem is Julie's failure to cooperate with students in the classroom. That hasn't changed."

True enough. Did you want to comment, John?

"I agree the problem hasn't been solved. But Julie's behavior has been changed for the better, so the effort wasn't a total failure."

That's a good point. In one sense, your efforts have been a complete success: A behavior that occurred very infrequently at the beginning of your training program—making concessions—later occurred much more often. Yet, in another sense, your efforts were a complete failure: Julie still doesn't work or play well with other students in the classroom. It is not enough to change a target behavior; the effects of training must generalize.

Generalization

Generalization is the tendency for the effects of training to transfer or spread:

Generalization:
The tendency for the effects
of training to spread.

There are two kinds of generalization: stimulus generalization and response generalization.

Stimulus generalization refers to the tendency for the effects of training to spread across situations:

Stimulus generalization:
The tendency for the effects of training
in one situation to spread to other situations.

Note that this definition speaks of the spread of the effects of training—any sort of training. I mention this because sometimes students get the idea that stimulus generalization is something that happens only after reinforcement.[1] That is not the case. In fact, it doesn't matter what sort of training we're talking about: If training changes a behavior, and the change in behavior carries over to another situation, then you've got stimulus generalization.

So, then, if you reinforce a target behavior in one situation and the behavior also occurs more often in another situation, then the effects of reinforcement have generalized. And if you put an undesirable behavior on extinction and the behavior declines not only in the training setting but elsewhere as well, then the effects of extinction have generalized. And if you suppress a dangerous behavior by punishing it and the behavior is suppressed in settings where punishment did not occur, then the effects of punishment have generalized. If the effects of training—

whatever the training and whatever the effects—carry over to situations where there was no training, that's stimulus generalization.

Now, in our hypothetical example, Julie behaved in an uncooperative manner when she first began to play the computer game, but with training her behavior changed *in that situation*. The reinforcement procedure worked—cooperative behavior increased. But the effects of training did not generalize to the classroom, a different situation—

"So why isn't it called situational generalization?"

A fair question, Carlotta. That might be a better term. However, generalization was first studied scientifically in laboratories. In laboratory research, the training situation is kept as simple and uniform as possible to rule out the unwanted influence of extraneous variables. So, in a laboratory study of generalization, a pigeon might learn to peck a disk in a very simple experimental chamber.[2] For example, a bird might receive food each time it pecked a disk illuminated by a red light. Then, to study generalization, the light behind the disk might be turned out. Everything else in the experimental chamber would remain the same except for that one aspect of the situation, that one stimulus. And what happens is that the bird's behavior changes somewhat with that change in stimulus. So, researchers spoke of *stimulus* generalization.

In applied behavior analysis, the situations in which training occurs—called training situations—are generally far more complicated and variable than those found in a laboratory. So are the situations—called test or target situations—in which we look for generalization. However, the differences can be described in terms of the stimuli present in the various situations, so stimulus generalization is still an appropriate term. You just need to keep in mind that when we talk about stimulus generalization in applied settings, we're talking about a complex array of stimuli—a situation.

Situations can differ from one another in a variety of ways. Two rooms may be identical, for example, except that one may have a painting on the wall and the other may not. Or the two rooms may differ in size, shape, color of walls, lighting, type of floor covering, style of furniture, and so on. Atmospheric conditions may differ. Training may take place indoors where it is air conditioned, but the target behavior may occur outdoors where it is hot and humid. There may be differences in the presence of people. A person may learn to participate in a conversation with one other person, but many of the situations in which he finds himself may involve group discussions.

Laboratory research has consistently shown that generalization varies with the degree of similarity between the situation in which training occurred and other situations.[3] The more alike two situations are, the more likely training effects are to carry over. For example, if a pigeon learns to peck a disk illuminated by a red light, it will peck very nearly as often when the disk is dark orange. It will peck at a lower rate if the disk is pale orange, and at a still lower rate if the disk is yellow.[4]

Much the same thing occurs with humans in more complicated settings. For instance, if Julie's teacher had played the computer game with her in your office, it's likely that she would be almost as cooperative as she had been with you. The adults would be different, but otherwise the situations would be similar. If you had one of Julie's classmates play the game with her in your office, she's apt to be less cooperative. The reason is . . . what is the reason? Jamal?

> "The teacher is an adult, so she's similar to the counselor she played with during training. A classmate is a child, so there's more difference in the two situations."

Exactly right. And if the teacher has the students pair off and play the game in her classroom, then you've got a situation that is very different from the one in which training occurred, so you probably shouldn't expect much generalization of training. And if they pair off and play a different sort of game, Julie's apt to show even less evidence of training.

Okay, so much for stimulus generalization.[5] Now let's talk about response generalization. Response generalization refers to the tendency for training to spread from one behavior to another:

Response generalization:
The tendency for the effects of training
one behavior to spread to other behaviors.

Again, this term comes from laboratory research with animals. For example, training a pigeon to peck a disk on a wall might increase its tendency to peck at disks on the floor. Pecking at a disk on the wall and pecking at a disk on the floor are not the same behavior; they involve very different topographies. Any time training one behavior affects the performance of other behaviors, response generalization has occurred.

Muley Julie can help illustrate response generalization in people. After teaching Julie to cooperate in playing the computer game, you might find that she not only cooperated more but was also more likely to smile and say "Thank you." Even though you hadn't reinforced smiling or saying "Thank you," you might see an increase in these behaviors as you reinforced cooperativeness. The effects of training have generalized from one behavior to another.

Response generalization is often important in solving behavior problems. As a rule, such problems are not solved merely by changing the frequency of one specific form of behavior. In Julie's case, for instance, you don't want merely an increase in the tendency to say, "Okay. It's your turn now." Being cooperative means more than just saying those few words. You're looking for an increase in a variety of cooperative behaviors. You want her to let others have a turn, but you also want her to compromise, to share toys, to let someone else have his way once in a while, to—

> "I'm not sure I see the difference between response generalization and stimulus generalization. When you talk about compromising, sharing toys, letting someone else have his way, aren't you talking about different situations?"

You could say so, John. The fact is, stimulus generalization and response generalization are often hard to separate because different behaviors occur in different situations. Interacting with other people means one thing when you're at a formal dinner party hosted by the president of your college; it means something quite different when you're at a beach party with your college friends. Different situations; different forms of behavior. But you can also get different forms of behavior in the *same* situation. You might think of the difference between stimulus generalization and response generalization this way: With stimulus generalization, the critical change is in the situation; in response generalization, the critical change is in the behavior. Now, let's consider some applications.

Illustrative Studies

Crystal Learns to Speak Up

Crystal was an extremely shy 4-year-old. She passed most of the developmental tests for her age, but her speech skills were delayed and she spoke so softly she could hardly be heard. Crystal's teachers believed that her soft voice was interfering with her academic and social development, yet there was nothing physically wrong with Crystal that would account for her behavior. Louie Fleece and his colleagues designed an intervention program to get Crystal to speak more loudly.[6] What basic procedure do you suppose they used? Carlotta?

> "Shaping?"

That's right. They planned to reinforce slight increases in the volume at which Crystal spoke. They did this in a rather clever way: They designed a lighting display that looked something like a miniature Christmas tree. The lights were wired up to some hardware so that when Crystal spoke, the lights on the display would come on. The researchers hoped that making the lights come on would reinforce speaking. A teacher asked Crystal to recite nursery rhymes. Crystal would recite a rhyme, and if she spoke loudly enough, the tree lights would come on. She met with her teacher for this training about twice a week for 15 minutes at a time. If she managed to "light up the tree" in one training session, the teacher would modify the hardware so that she would have to speak slightly louder the next time to get the same result.

In addition to this training, Crystal and other students were asked to recite a nursery rhyme before the class of about 6 to 10 students. They did these recitations about twice a week an hour or so after Crystal's training session. Thus, the intervention includes a shaping procedure outside of the class and a practice exercise in the class. This practice exercise provides both a way of monitoring the effects of the training program and of reinforcing generalization of improvements made in the training sessions.

Observers rated the audibility of children's speech as they recited rhymes in class. The rating scale ran from zero, meaning a volume so low the child couldn't usually be heard, to 20, meaning the child was screaming. Normal volumes for children fell between 9 and 11. Here is a graph showing how loudly Crystal recited in the classroom over the course of the study:

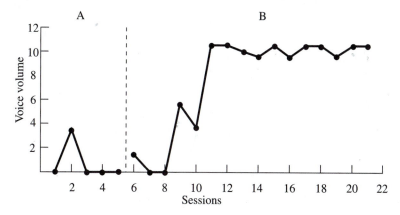

Figure 9-1. *Speaking volume. Crystal's average voice volume levels in the classroom. Adapted from Fleece et al. (1981).*

What do these data show you, Jamal?

"It looks like she generally couldn't be heard during the baseline, and for the first few training sessions. Then she really started making progress and steadily improved until she got to a normal speaking volume."

Very good. It's interesting that there was very little progress during the first few sessions; I don't know why that happened. But you can see that she really did progress rapidly after that.

Now, this study is a little unusual in that the researchers don't report the data obtained in the training sessions; instead, they report the generalization data they got in the classroom. They were clearly interested primarily in generalization of the target behavior to the classroom. By having Crystal recite rhymes in class, they not only were able to monitor generalization, but they also provided opportunities in which speaking more loudly might be reinforced. Having her recite nursery rhymes in the training sessions and in the class probably helped get generalization. It's also worth noting that the researchers used a number of different nursery rhymes. The more variations of the target behavior that are reinforced in training, the more likely generalization is to occur.

The effort was a great success, and I'm sure Crystal was helped a lot. At the end of the school year, it was recommended that she be removed from the special education program and placed in a regular class. That might not have happened if she had continued to speak in a whisper.

Crystal was a fairly normal little girl. Getting her to speak louder and getting that behavior to generalize to the classroom is not much of a challenge as behavior problems go. Let's turn now to something more difficult.

Learning to Bus Tables

We've seen that, with the proper training, people with severe handicaps can often acquire the skills they need to live happier, more fulfilling lives. People with mental retardation, for example, can often learn to perform useful job skills. A major problem in preparing them for work, however, is that the nature of the work often varies tremendously from moment to moment. Busing tables in a restaurant is an example.

Busing tables is an apparently simple, repetitive task. Even people with severe retardation can collect dishes and silverware from a table, pick up trash in the area, straighten chairs, wipe the table clean, throw trash and garbage in a receptacle, and return the dishes and silverware to the kitchen. But in practice there is more to the job: The worker must first decide whether or not a table should be bused. If, for example, a diner leaves the table to visit the restroom and returns to find that her food has been removed, the worker has not made a useful contribution in busing her table. So, training a person with mental retardation to bus tables must mean training him to bus tables in certain circumstances, but not others. How would you go about training something like that? Yes, Carlotta?

"Could you use discrimination training?"

How do you mean?

"Well, you could identify certain features that indicate whether a table should be bused. Then use those as discriminative stimuli in training."

Excellent idea. That's just what Robert Horner and his colleagues did in training four men with mental retardation to bus tables in a university cafeteria-style restaurant.[7] The four men had IQs between 18 and 46 and ranged in age from 17 to 21. They could dress themselves, follow simple instructions, and could use a few words, including *yes* and *no*.

Horner and colleagues identified five variables that helped to determine whether a table should be bused: presence of people at the table; whether people were eating; the condition of food on the dishes (for example, is the food untouched?); the presence of garbage; the location of dishes and garbage. These were the discriminative stimuli that, in combination, indicated whether or not a table should be bused.

Training consisted of a trainer modeling and prompting busing skills and providing feedback about each man's performance. Since successful performance of busing duties required busing when busing was appropriate and *not* busing when busing was inappropriate, and since each of these situations could be represented in a variety of ways, the training provided a wide variety of situations similar to those that would be encountered on the job. In addition to manipulating the five variables identified, the researchers also varied the location of tables used in training.

These efforts paid off. By the end of the program, the four men were busing tables correctly 80 to 100% of the time. This was so even though the researchers tested for generalization in two restaurants not used in training. This study demonstrates that it is possible to train very effectively for generalization of skills if you follow a few simple rules.

Rules for Increasing Generalization

Generalization is a naturally occurring phenomenon. However, in attempting to solve behavior problems, people often expect too much of naturally occurring generalization.

Stimulus generalization failures, for example, are common. When little Dorothy is seen hitting her brother Paul in the living room, her parents pull her aside and explain why the behavior is unacceptable. "You mustn't hit Paul with a baseball bat," they say. "It isn't polite." Dorothy nods her understanding and may, if the adults insists on it, swear never to commit the offense again. Later the parents are astonished when Dorothy is seen in the front yard pounding away on poor Paul. Similarly, the English teacher who gives a lesson in the punctuation of parenthetical expressions, complete with practice exercises, may find the students punctuating correctly nearly 100% of the time. She is confident that the students "really understand" the punctuation of parenthetical expressions, and she is bitterly disappointed when she assigns an essay and finds parenthetical expressions all over the place without correct punctuation. In the same way, the corporate trainer who shows a group of employees how to operate a machine in a classroom is puzzled when he finds the workers fumbling and bumbling along when they attempt to operate the same machines in the factory.

Response generalization failures are also a problem. If little Dorothy no longer hits poor Paul with a baseball bat but continues pummeling him with her fists, her parents may conclude that their training efforts were not entirely successful.

"So will Paul, I bet."

Very likely, Alfred. And if students learn to punctuate parenthetical expressions on exercise sheets and in essays, the teacher might expect that they would also punctuate appositives correctly, since they are, after all, really just short parenthetical expressions. But the teacher may well be disappointed. Similarly, the person who trains employees to start up a machine correctly may be surprised to find that they do not automatically shut it down correctly, even though the procedures are the same but in reverse order.

Everywhere we look we can see examples of training effects that do not generalize. What are we to do about this? Maya?

"Maybe you could do something during training to increase generalization?"

Maybe you could. That something is often called generalization training. Generalization training is something of a misnomer, since it is not a separate kind of training. It simply means conducting training in such a way as to increase the likelihood of getting generalization. Although there are lots of suggestions for improving stimulus and response generalization, three rules of thumb are especially helpful:

1. Define the target behavior so as to include many variations.

If you want to get a change in many different forms of a behavior, then you have to include many different forms of the behavior in your training. If, for example, you want a student to spend more time studying, you might reinforce studying. But how do you define studying? You have to define the target behavior clearly, but a number of different acts may qualify as studying: reading, making notes, working on practice exercises, reviewing a chapter, going through flash cards, and so on. Studying involves all sorts of behavior. So if you want to get the reinforcement effects to generalize to behaviors that are not reinforced during training, reinforce several different forms of studying behavior. If all you reinforce is note taking, don't be surprised if the only change you get in natural settings is an increase in note taking.

Similarly, if you are trying to get an extremely shy person to be more outgoing, you will reinforce social interactions. But don't just reinforce one sort of social interaction, such as chatting with other students about school. Reinforce several kinds of social interaction: approaching people about dates; participating in debates; going to church; talking to people at bus stops; making comments in class; and so on. The more different kinds of social behavior you reinforce, the more likely you are to get new forms of social behavior in natural settings.

These examples involve reinforcement, but the advice applies regardless of the training procedure used. For example, if you decide to put a child's aggressive behavior on extinction, then you want to define aggressive behavior so that a variety of forms of aggression will qualify: Hitting, biting, kicking, shoving, name calling, and so on. If several forms of aggressive behavior are put on extinction, other forms of aggressive behavior are also likely to decline in frequency.

2. Make the training situations resemble natural situations.

The greater the similarity between the setting in which training occurs and the setting in which the desired behavior change is to occur, the greater the generalization.

Notice that the rule refers to training situations—plural. Since the target behavior usually occurs in a variety of situations, it is helpful to do the training in a variety of situations. If Julie's cooperative behavior is reinforced in the guidance counselor's office, we may get an increase in cooperative behavior in other offices, but we're less likely to get an increase in classrooms and playgrounds. The latter settings are very different from offices. So, if at all possible, you ought to conduct training in a variety of settings that resemble the natural settings in which the behavior change is to occur. Then—

"Why not just do the training in the natural setting, the situation where the problem occurs?"

That's a good question, Belinda. For example, we might find a way to reinforce Julie's cooperative behavior in the classroom or on the playground. And you're quite right: If you can change the behavior in natural environments where it is a problem, then you shouldn't have to worry about generalization. However, there are two reasons you can't always do this. Can anyone think of one? Brian?

"It might be inconvenient or impractical to work in the situation where the problem occurs."

Quite right. Teachers are understandably reluctant to have someone intervening in their classrooms, for example, especially if it means taking time away from instruction. Shop foremen, on-line supervisors in a factory, and middle managers in a corporation often feel the same way. Similarly, nurses and doctors are not always enthusiastic about dealing with behavior problems on the ward.

Part of this resistance has to do with the widespread tendency to think of problem behavior as originating inside the person. Julie's teacher probably thinks of Julie as defective in some way, in need of repair. The counselor's job, as the teacher sees it, is to "fix Julie." Take her away somewhere, say something wise to correct whatever is wrong with her psyche, and then she will behave differently in the classroom. It's often as though the teacher might say, "It's nothing to do with me or my class. It has to do with something inside the student." The same view is often shared by managers and supervisors. "Frank is late for work two or three times a week. Evidently he has some psychological problem such as a lack of motivation. I'll send him to the company psychologist. Maybe talking about it will help."

I hope that by now you have learned that, with the possible exception of some organic diseases, behavior problems can rarely, if ever, be said to *originate* within the individual. They originate, by and large, in the history of antecedents and consequences of the behavior. Nevertheless, people often resist attempts to deal with behavior problems in the situation where the problem behavior occurs.

So, as a practical matter, it's not always possible to do the training in the natural environment. What other reason might there be for training outside the natural environment? Yes, Midori?

"Could it have to do with the fact that there are so many different natural environments?"

It could indeed. Julie's lack of cooperation is a problem in the classroom, but it may also be a problem on the playground, in the gym, at home, at summer camp, in Sunday school, and in many other settings. It could be a problem practically everywhere Julie goes. You might get a teacher's permission to work with Julie on the playground, in the gym, and even in the classroom. But it's just not possible to work with Julie in every situation where she might be uncooperative.

So, while training in natural settings is usually desirable, it isn't always practical or possible. It is often necessary to train for generalization in contrived settings. To get generalization, it is important to make these settings resemble natural situations as much as possible.

Making a training situation resemble a natural setting implies that you're going to use a variety of training situations. Natural settings are going to vary greatly, so if you're going to make the training situation resemble the natural situation, the training situation also has to vary greatly. If you're training police officers, for example, you've got to alter the training environment repeatedly so that the training situation is likely to resemble the situations encountered on the job. If you're training them to handle domestic disputes, for instance, the training situations should include married couples quarreling over money, divorced couples fighting about custody of the kids, drunken brothers shouting about ownership of property, a father and adolescent son going at each other with knives, a daughter threatening to shoot herself because her mother won't let her stay out at night, and so on. You can't—

"How would you identify all the different kinds of situations you would need to include in training?"

That's a good question, Brian. How would *you* do it?

"Could you look at the police reports and identify the different kinds of situations? You might classify them according to the people involved, such as family members, friends, and neighbors; whether alcohol or other drugs are involved; what the dispute is about, such as property, sex, drinking, who controls the remote; and the presence of weapons—guns, knives, baseball bats, fists."

That sounds good, Brian. Then what?

"Well, then you could work up a taxonomy of domestic disputes. There would be situations including drunken husbands quarreling with their wives about money but without physical violence; there would be drunken wives throwing china at their husbands because of suspicions about infidelity; and so on. Then, in your training program, you could make sure that the officers had training in all of these situations—or at least several of them."

Yes, you probably couldn't provide training with every different situation in your taxonomy. But you could probably identify ten situations to use in training that would resemble most of the situations an officer would encounter in the field.

Okay, let's say you've followed the first two rules in your training. You've defined the target behavior in such a way as to include a variety of forms of the behavior and you've trained those various forms, and your training has included a variety of different situations that resemble natural situations. How do you know if you've done enough? Yes, Midori?

"You'd have to monitor the behavior in the natural settings."

Right. And that's rule number 3:

3. Monitor the target behavior in natural settings.

At the very least you want to get regular feedback from a teacher, parent, foreman, or other person in a position to observe the target behavior. Ideally, you should observe the target behavior in a variety of natural settings and record data. When you see a satisfactory change in behavior in various natural settings, you'll know the training is working.

So, in Julie's case, you might get the teacher to record the number of times Julie was uncooperative in a particular activity. Then you might look out on the playground a few minutes each day to record instances of uncooperative behavior. And you might ask the gym teacher to record instances of uncooperative behavior. If the evidence is that the problem is receding on all fronts, you might consider the training effort a success. But if uncooperative behavior is still occurring, say on the playground, then you will need to modify the training to resemble playground activities and situations more.

In summary, then, generalization training means doing three things: First, it means defining the target behavior to include various forms. Several of these variations would then be reinforced, put on extinction, punished, or whatever. Second, it means making the training situation resemble natural settings as much as possible. Third, it means monitoring the target behavior in as many natural settings as is practical.

"Aren't there going to be situations you can't anticipate?"

I'm sorry, Carlotta, but I'm not sure I know what you mean.

"I can see how you can train for generalization to natural settings that you know about, but new situations can arise. I don't see how you can train for generalization to those situations."

For example?

"Well, suppose next year Julie joins the Girl Scouts. Then she might be required to cooperate in new kinds of situations."

A possibility, Carlotta. So?

> "So how are you going to train for generalization to situations you can't know are going to arise?"

That's a good question. The assumption you have to make is that if you make the training situation resemble a variety of natural situations, the chances are that any unanticipated situation will resemble those for which she was trained. If the assumption is valid, you should get generalization in those unanticipated situations.

> "Is the assumption valid?"

My guess is that it is, but there are no guarantees. Certainly there are generalization failures. One common example is the teacher who teaches students how to punctuate parenthetical expressions and then finds that they don't apply the skill when writing essays. She has instructed them, she has modeled the skill by doing sample problems on the board, she has prompted the students to punctuate the sentences with parenthetical expressions and she has reinforced correct performance. And she has gotten improved performance from the students. Yet when she asks the students to write an essay, she finds parenthetical expressions without the proper punctuation. What is she doing wrong? Jamal?

> "She's only teaching them to perform the skill in one situation."

Describe that situation.

> "Well, she gives the students a sentence with a parenthetical expression and says, 'Punctuate this.'"

Wait a minute. She also gives them a practice sheet with a number of practice sentences.

> "Yeah, but it's the same thing: 'Here's a sentence with a parenthetical expression; punctuate it.' 'Here's another sentence with a parenthetical expression; punctuate it.'"

So are you saying it's a waste of time for teachers to assign practice sheets?

> "No, the students probably need the practice. Each sentence is different, and they're getting training in punctuating parenthetical expressions in different sentences. That's good."

Why is that good?

> "Because it should increase the likelihood of the behavior generalizing to new situations."

Then why don't the students use what they learn when they write essays?

> "Because there's too much difference between the training situation—the lesson and the practice exercises—and the new situation—the essay writing."

What sort of difference?

"Well, for one thing, during the training, the student punctuates sentences someone else has written; in the test situation, the student has to punctuate sentences he has written."

Any other differences?

"In the training situation, the sentences aren't connected; in the test situation, the sentences are part of an essay. Also, in the training situation, the student knows there is a parenthetical expression in each of the sentences, since that's what the lesson was about. But in the test situation, that's not the case because the student writes the sentences himself."

So the teacher provides a prompt for searching out and punctuating parenthetical expressions in the punctuation exercise, but there's no comparable prompt in the essay situation. What do you propose the teacher do?

"I think that after the students have done the practice sentences, the teacher needs to give them training with essays. She would give them essays that have lots of parenthetical expressions, but no punctuation. The teacher could put an essay on an overhead projector and say, 'Okay, Ferdinand, how would you punctuate the first sentence?' She wouldn't tell them if there was a parenthetical expression in the sentence."

That's a really neat idea. Is it yours?

"Not really. I had an English teacher in high school who used to do that."

So your teacher found a way of making the training situation resemble the essay writing situation. Excellent. What else could the teacher do? John?

"Could she have the students make up sentences that include parenthetical expressions and punctuate them?"

Yes, that's an idea. That would make the training situation similar to the test situation, since the student is making up sentences in both cases.

All right, let's take another sort of example. Suppose you work in a home for people with developmental disorders. One of the residents, a young man named Howard, is a hand-mouther: He's always got one of his hands in his mouth, and he usually has some minor lacerations on his hands from biting himself. You've been using DRL—what's DRL, Maya?

"Differential reinforcement of low rate. It means you reinforce the behavior only if it occurs infrequently."

That's right. So you've been using DRL to reduce the rate of hand mouthing. From time to time during the day, you monitor Howard's behavior. If he meets the criterion for reinforcement, you go over to him and compliment him for not putting his hand in his mouth. Then you chat with him for a minute about his favorite comic book hero, or you do something else you know is reinforcing. Your data reveal a steady decline in the frequency of hand-mouthing, and you have very gradually increased the requirement for reinforcement from 2 minutes without hand mouthing to 20 minutes. But while Howard's behavior on the ward is much improved, you've noticed that his hands still show signs of biting. You do some investigating, and you find that Howard is continuing to mouth when he goes outdoors each day. How are you going to deal with this problem? Belinda?

"It seems to me the simplest thing would be to use the same training procedure when Howard is outside."

That makes sense. But suppose you're unable to do that. Your duties require that you remain on the ward. And there are too few staff to ask someone else to implement your training program outside. You've got to do the training on the ward in such a way that the effects will generalize to the outdoor setting. How are you going to do that?

"I don't know. You can't bring the outdoors inside."

Alfred, did you have a suggestion?

"Yeah. Have him sit by an open window."

I know some of you think Alfred's suggestion sounds laughable. In fact, judging by Alfred's sheepish grin, I think he meant it as another of his jokes. But the idea has some merit. After all, what's the difference between the two situations, indoors and outdoors? It's sunlight versus lamplight, fresh air versus stale air, birds singing versus people talking, trees and grass versus walls and tile floors. If you sit by an open window, your environment is somewhere between being outdoors and being indoors. So Alfred's idea might be worth trying. At any rate, Alfred, you're on the right track. What else can you do to improve generalization?

"Well . . . I guess I'd find ways of making the ward more like the outdoors. If there's a sun room on the ward, for example, I'd have him sit there and I'd reinforce the target behavior. And I guess having him sit by an open window might not be so crazy after all. We could sit there and look out on the grounds. And I could implement the training program while he's looking at the trees and the squirrels and the people strolling by."

Good. You're on the right track. Now, before I let you go, let's review today's main ideas.

Review

The lesson today has been about generalization. What is generalization, John?

"It's the tendency for the effects of training to spread."

Exactly right. And what are the two kinds of generalization?

"Stimulus generalization and response generalization."

Right again. Can you define stimulus generalization for me, Maya?

"That's the tendency for the effects of training to spread across situations."

Hmm. What does "across situations" mean?

"Okay, you do the training in one situation, and if the change in behavior occurs in another situation, that's stimulus generalization."

All right. So stimulus generalization is the tendency for the effects of training to spread from . . .

"From the training situation to other situations."

Right. And response generalization is . . . Carlotta?

"That's the tendency for the effects of training one behavior to spread to other behaviors."

Good. Now, I said that generalization was a natural phenomenon. If you do training, you're likely to get some generalization. But you might not get as much generalization as you'd like. To get more generalization, you . . . do what, Brian?

"You do generalization training."

And what does that mean?

"It means you do the training in a way that will increase generalization."

Right. And what does that mean, Alfred?

"Well, you can define the target behavior so that you include different forms of the behavior."

Good. What's another thing you can do, Midori?

"You can make the training situation resemble natural settings."

Right. And what else can you do to improve generalization—Jamal?

"You can monitor the target behavior in its various forms in a variety of settings."

Yes. Now, one final comment: You've learned something about strengthening and weakening behavior. You know, in principle, how to increase the frequency of desirable behavior and how to decrease the frequency of undesirable behavior. You can define reinforcement, extinction, shaping, and the various other terms we've covered. But can you reinforce behavior? Can you put it on extinction? Can you shape new behavior? Could you, if you were actually faced with a behavior problem, solve it? What do you think? Alfred?

"Sure. Why not?"

Can anyone answer Alfred's question? Yes, Brian?

"I'd say that defining shaping is very different from shaping behavior, and being able to do one doesn't mean you can do the other."

Yes. They're different activities, aren't they? And training in one does not necessarily generalize to the other.

If you think of behavior as something that is generated in a person's head, then you might expect that if a person *understands* shaping—that is, if he is able to define it, to give examples of it, and so on—then he would be able to *use* shaping properly. But if we think of behavior as the product of a learning history, then we aren't surprised when a person who is skilled at talking about shaping behavior isn't particularly skilled at shaping behavior.

The point of today's lesson is that generalization training must be part of the solution to a behavior problem or the problem isn't likely to be solved. In fact, when efforts to change behavior are unsuccessful, the complaint is likely to be, "Sure, he behaves better where you worked with him, but elsewhere he's still a mess." This is a clear indication that the person trying to change the behavior (therapist, teacher, counselor, parent, supervisor, etc.) has neglected to train for generalization. Such failures are surprising only if you accept the traditional view that says solving behavior problems means changing something inside the person. Once you understand that behavior problems are always the result of dynamic interactions between the person and his environment, you know that generalization failures are to be expected—unless you train for generalization.

Well, that's all I want to do on generalization. Until next time, have fun with the handouts. They'll help what you've learned generalize.

◀ Exercises ▶

Feed the Skeleton

I. Generalization
   A. Generalization is the tendency for the effects of _____
   _____ .

   B. Stimulus generalization is the tendency _____ .
   C. Response generalization is the tendency _____ .

II. Behaviorists encouraged generalization:
   A. in Crystal by _____ .
   B. in a group of mentally retarded men by _____ .

III. Rules for increasing the likelihood of generalization include:
   A. Define the target behavior to include _____ .
   B. Make the training situation resemble the _____ .
   C. Monitor the target behavior in _____ .

Generalized Imitation

One of the best illustrations of the importance of generalization is generalized imitation. Humans learn to imitate early in life. This comes about because imitating behavior is reinforced. The proud father says to his baby, "Say, 'Da-da,'. . . Da-da . . . Da-da." Any sort of effort on the part of the infant is reinforced with smiles, laughter, hugs and bounces, and so on. Gradually, the appropriate behavior is shaped. However, in addition to reinforcing successive approximations of the proper word, the parent is also reinforcing the tendency to imitate. The child who learns to imitate the father's, "Da-da," is then more likely to imitate the mother who says, "Say 'Ma-Ma.'" Imitation of other words (milk, dog, car, hot, etc.) soon follows, as does the imitation of acts other than speech.

Now, here is your problem: Is generalized imitation an example of stimulus generalization or response generalization?

Which Way to the Men's Room?

One of the problems adults with retardation face in trying to live outside of institutions is the tremendous variability in the situations they encounter. A case in point is finding a public rest room. The men's room may be identified in any number of different ways. The sign on the door may say *Men*, or it may say *Gentlemen, Gents, Boys,* or *Guys.* In public places with special theme decor, the label may be downright bizarre. In a restaurant with a western theme, for example, the men's room may be identified by the word *Cowboys, Cowpokes, Buckaroos,* or even *Bulls.* Many adults who are not the least bit retarded may hesitate at a door with a sign that reads, *Bulls.*

It is precisely such difficulties that keep many people with mild retardation from living on their own without supervision. How can you train adults with retardation so that they can find the men's room even when it is identified by a sign they have never seen before?

Generalized Speech

You can see generalization in speech. At first, children use the present tense regardless of when an event took place. Reminiscing about an accident that took place yesterday, they might say, "I cry." Soon they learn to form the past tense by adding *ed*, and their comment becomes, "I cried." But this new behavior generalizes to situations in which it is inappropriate. Asked why he cried, he may say, "Because I run*ed* and fall*ed* down and hurt*ed* myself."

Such inappropriate generalization may bring a smile to your face, but the same sort of error can be seen in adults. A person measuring a cabinet might say, "Its *heighth* is five feet." There is no such word as *heighth*. The correct term is *height*.

How might saying *heighth* be accounted for in terms of generalization? Spare no effort in coming to an answer. (Search the length and breadth and depth of the world, if necessary.)

At the Dog Pound

Thousands of unwanted dogs are destroyed in animal shelters each year. One idea for getting more of these animals adopted is to train them to obey one or two ordinary commands and perform a trick. There is some evidence that the practice does improve adoption rates (Pryor, 1996). But if the behavior learned in the shelter does not generalize to the dog's new home, then what? Will the dog be returned to the shelter or mistreated because it no longer performs? The possibility is worrisome. What procedures can you suggest for reducing the likelihood of this happening?

Practice Quiz

1. Generalization is the tendency for the effects of _____ to spread.

2. In _____ generalization, training results in the target behavior occurring in different situations.

3. In _____ generalization, training results in different variations of the target behavior.

4. To increase generalization, it is important that the training situation resemble _____ situations.

5. A baby who calls all men "Da-da" is displaying _____ generalization.

6. In generalization training, the goal is for the behavior to occur in the _____ situation.

7. Crystal learned to speak more loudly in a training session, and this generalized to _____ .

8. To increase generalization, it is important to define the target behavior so as to include many _____ of the target behavior.

9. The tendency to imitate models we haven't seen before is called _____ imitation. (If you don't know the answer, shame on you for not doing the second exercise.)

10. Generalization is the opposite of _____ , a topic we covered earlier in the course.

Reprint: A Technology of Generalization
by Trevor F. Stokes & Donald M. Baer

Behavior analysis attempts to develop tools for changing behavior. But changing one particular behavior in one particular situation is of limited practical value. To solve a behavior problem, the changes produced must generalize to other situations and other behaviors. We need to develop tools for getting changes in behavior to generalize. In this classic article, two behaviorists outline the beginnings of just such a technology.

. . . Generalization has been and doubtless will remain a fundamental concern of applied behavior analysis. A therapeutic behavior change, to be effective, often (not always) must occur over time, persons and settings, and the effects of the change sometimes should spread to a variety of related behaviors. Even though the literature shows many instances of generalization, it is still frequently observed that when a change in behavior has been accomplished through experimental contingencies, then that change is manifest where and when those contingencies operate, and is often seen in only transitory forms in other places and at other times.

The frequent need for generalization of therapeutic behavior change is widely accepted, but it is not always realized that generalization does not automatically occur simply because a behavior change is accomplished. Thus, the need actively to *program* generalization, rather than positively to expect it as an outcome of certain training procedures, is a point requiring both emphasis and effective techniques (Baer, Wolf, and Risley, 1968). That such exhortations have been made has not always ensured that researchers in the field have taken serious note of and, therefore, proceeded to analyze adequately the generalization issues of vital concern to their programs. The emphasis, refinement, and elaboration of the principles and procedures that are meant to explain and produce generalization when it does not occur "naturally" is an important area of unfinished business for applied behavior analysis.

The notion of generalization developed here is an essentially pragmatic one; it does not closely follow the traditional conceptionalizations (Keller and Schoenfeld, 1950; Skinner, 1953). In many ways, this discussion will sidestep much of the controversy concerning terminology. Generalization will be considered to be the occurrence of relevant behavior under different, non-training conditions (i.e., across subjects, settings, people, behaviors, and/or time) without the scheduling of the same events in those conditions as had been scheduled in the training conditions. Thus generalization may be claimed when no extratraining manipulations are needed for extratraining changes; or may be claimed when some extra manipulations are necessary, but their cost or extent is clearly less than that of the direct intervention. Generalization will not be claimed when similar events are necessary for similar effects across conditions.

A technology of generalization programming is almost a reality, despite the fact that until recently it had hardly been recognized as a problem in its own right. Within common teaching practice, there is an informal germ of a technology for generalization. Furthermore, within the practice of applied behavior analysis (especially within the past 5 yr or so), there had appeared a budding area of "generalization-promotion" techniques. The purpose of this review is to summarize the structure of that generalization literature and its implicit embryonic technology. Some 270 applied behavior analysis studies relevant to generalization in that discipline were reviewed.* A central core of that literature, consisting of some 120 studies, contributes directly to a technology of generalization. In general, techniques designed to assess or to program generalization can be loosely categorized according to nine general headings: . . .

1. Train and Hope

In applied behavior analysis research, the most frequent method of examining generalization, so far, may be labelled *Train and Hope*. After a behavior change is effected through manipulation of some response consequences, any existent generalization across responses, settings, experimenters, and time, is concurrently and/or subsequently documented or noted, but not actively pursued. It is usually hoped that some generalization may occur, which will be welcomed yet not explicitly programmed. . . .

2. Sequential Modification

These studies exemplify a more systematic approach to generalization than the Train-and-Hope research. Again, a particular behavior change is effected, and generalization is assessed. But then, if generalization is absent or deficient, procedures are initiated to accomplish the desired changes by systematic sequential modification in every nongeneralized condition, *i.e.*, across responses, subjects, settings, or experimenters. . . .

3. Introduce to Natural Maintaining Contingencies

Perhaps the most dependable of all generalization programming mechanisms is one that hardly deserves the name: the transfer of behavior control from the teacher-experimenter to stable, natural contingencies that can be trusted to operate in the environment to which the subject will return, or already occupies. To a certain extent, this goal is accomplished by choosing behaviors to teach that normally will meet maintaining reinforcement after the teaching (Ayllon and Azrin, 1968). . . .

4. Train Sufficient Exemplars

If the result of teaching one exemplar of a generalizable lesson is merely the mastery of the exemplar taught, with no generalization beyond it, then the obvious route to generalization is to teach another exemplar of the same generalization lesson, and then another, and then another, and so on until . . . generalization occurs sufficiently to satisfy the problem posed. . . .

---

*Ninety percent of the literature reviewed was from five journals: *Behavior Research and Therapy*; *Behavior Therapy*; *Journal of Applied Behavior Analysis*; *Journal of Behavior Therapy and Experimental Psychiatry*; and *Journal of Experimental Child Psychology*. Seventy-seven percent of the literature reviewed has been published since 1970.

. . . Stokes, Baer, and Jackson (1974) . . . established that training and maintenance of retarded children's greeting responses by one experimenter was not usually sufficient for the generalization of the response across experimenters. However, high levels of generalization to over 20 members of the institution staff (and newcomers as well) who had not participated in the training of the response were recorded, after a second experimenter trained and maintained the response in conjunction with the first experimenter. . . .

5. Train Loosely

One relatively simple technique can be conceptualized as merely the negation of discrimination technique. That is, teaching is conducted with relatively little control over the stimulus presented and the correct responses allowed, so as to maximize sampling of relevant dimensions for transfer to other situations and other forms of the behavior. A formal example of this most often informal technique was provided by Schroeder and Baer (1972), who taught vocal imitation skills to retarded children in both of two ways, one emphasizing tight restriction of the vocal skills being learned at the moment (serial training of vocal imitations), and the other allowing much greater range of stimuli within the current problem (concurrent training of imitations). The latter method was characterized repeatedly by greater generalization to as-yet-untaught vocal imitation problems, thus affirming "loose" teaching techniques as a contributor to wider generalization. . . .

6. Use Indiscriminable Contingencies

. . . In generalization, behavior occurs in settings in which it will not be reinforced, just as it does in settings in which it will be reinforced. Then, the analogue to an intermittent schedule, extended to settings, is a condition in which the subject cannot discriminate in which settings a response will be reinforced or not reinforced. A potential approximation to such a condition was presented in a study by Schwarz and Hawkins (1970). In that experiment, the behavior of a sixth-grade child was videotaped during math and spelling classes. Later, after each school day had ended, the child was shown the tape of the math class and awarded reinforcers according to how often good posture, absence of face-touching, and appropriate voice-loudness were evident on that tape. Although reinforcers were awarded only on the basis of behaviors displayed during the math class, desirable improvements were observed during the spelling class as well. In that reinforcement was delayed, this technique must have made it difficult for the child to discriminate in which class the behaviors were critical for earning reinforcement. . . .

7. Program Common Stimuli

The passive approach to generalization described earlier need not be a completely impractical one. If it is supposed that generalization will occur, if only there are sufficient stimulus components occurring in common in both the training and generalization settings, then a reasonably practical technique is to guarantee that common and salient stimuli will be present in both. . . .

. . . Walker and Buckley (1972) programmed generalization of the effects of remedial training of social and academic classroom behavior by establishing common stimuli between the experimental remedial classroom and the children's regular classroom by using the same academic materials in both classrooms. . . .

8. Mediate Generalization

Mediated generalization is well known as a theoretical mechanism explaining generalization of highly symbolic learnings (Cofer and Foley, 1942). In essence, it requires establishing a response as part of the new learning that is likely to be utilized in other problems as well, and will constitute sufficient commonality between the original learning and the new problem to result in generalization. The most commonly used mediator is language, apparently. . . .

A sophisticated analysis of mediated generalization was conducted by Risley and Hart (1968), who taught preschool children to report at the end of play on their play-material choices. Mention of a given choice was reinforced with snacks, which produced increasing mentioning of that choice, but no change in the children's actual use of that play material. When reinforcement was restricted to *true* reports of play-material choices, however, the children then changed their play behavior (the next day) so that when queried about their play, they could truthfully report on their use of the specified play material and earn reinforcement. . . .

9. Train "To Generalize"

If generalization is considered as a response itself, then a reinforcement contingency may be placed on it, the same as with any other operant. . . . A more formal example of the technique was seen in a study by Goetz and Baer (1973), in which three preschool children were taught to generalize the response of making block forms (in blockbuilding play). Descriptive social reinforcement was offered only for every different form the child made, *i.e.*, contingent on every first appearance of any blockbuilding form within a session, but not for any subsequent appearances of that form. Thus, the child was rewarded for moving along the generalization gradient underlying block-form inventions, and never for staying at any one point. In general, the technique succeeded, in that the children steadily invented new block forms while this contingency was in use. . . .

Conclusion

The structure of the generalization literature and its implicit embryonic technology has been summarized. . . .

This list of generalized tactics conceals within itself a much smaller list of specific tactics. These specific tactics can be presented as a small picture of the generalization technology in its present most pragmatic form, not only to offer a set of what-to-do possibilities, but also to emphasize how very small the current technology is and how much development it requires:

1. Look for a response that enters a natural community; in particular, teach subjects to cue their potential natural communities to reinforce their desirable behaviors.

2. Keep training more exemplars; in particular, diversify them.

3. Loosen experimental control over the stimuli and responses involved in training; in particular, train different examples concurrently, and vary instructions, S^Ds, social reinforcers, and backup reinforcers.

4. Make unclear the limits of training contingencies; in particular, conceal, when possible, the point at which those contingencies stop operating, possibly by delayed reinforcement.

5. Use stimuli that are likely to be found in generalization settings in training settings as well; in particular, use peers as tutors.

6. Reinforce accurate self-reports of desirable behavior; apply self-recording and self-reinforcement techniques whenever possible.

7. When generalizations occur, reinforce at least some of them at least sometimes, as if "to generalize" were an operant response class. . . .

Excerpted from "An Implicit Technology of Generalization," by T. F. Stokes and D. M. Baer. In *Journal of Applied Behavior Analysis, Vol. 10.* Copyright 1977 Society for Applied Behavior Analysis. Reprinted with permission.

◄ Recommended Reading ►

1. Brown, W. H., & Odom, S. L. (1994). Strategies and tactics for promoting generalization and maintenance of young children's social behavior. *Research in Developmental Disabilities, 15,* 99–118.
   A review of the research literature turned up strategies for improving generalization and maintenance of training effects in disabled children.

2. Carr, E. G., Levin, L., McConnachie, G., Carlson, J. I., Kemp, D. C., & Smith, C. E. (1994). *Communication-based intervention for problem behavior: A user's guide for producing behavior change.* Baltimore: Paul H. Brookes Co.
   In this how-to guide, Carr and company devote an entire chapter to generalization. They not only discuss generalization "programming" but also analyze generalization failures. This book is an excellent resource for anyone who plans to work with people who have serious behavior problems.

3. Jewett, J., & Clark, H. B. (1979). Teaching preschoolers to use appropriate dinnertime conversation: An analysis of generalization from school to home. *Behavior Therapy, 10,* 589–605.

Training at school helped improve the conversation skills of preschoolers at home.

4. Kirby, K. C., & Bickel, W. K. (1988). Toward an explicit analysis of generalization: A stimulus control interpretation. *The Behavior Analyst, 11,* 115–129. The authors suggest that generalization training is really a matter of establishing stimulus control.

5. Thorndike, E. L. (1911). *Animal intelligence: Experimental studies.* New York: Hafner.
Though this classic work deals only with animals, Thorndike's observations on generalization led the way toward our current understanding of the generalization of human behavior.

◄ Endnotes ►

1. Stimulus generalization is sometimes defined as the tendency of behavior that is *reinforced* in one situation to occur in other situations. This definition has a serious flaw: What are we then to call the tendency of behavior that is extinguished (or punished) in one situation to occur less often in other situations?

2. The experimental environment typically used for laboratory research is often called a Skinner Box, since Skinner designed the prototype and demonstrated its value to basic research. However, Skinner preferred the term *operant chamber.* This term is often used, but it is somewhat misleading since the chamber is not necessarily restricted to the study of operant behavior.

3. Guttman (1963); Guttman & Kalish (1956).

4. Guttman & Kalish (1956).

5. Our topic is the generalization of operant behavior, but respondent behavior also generalizes. You are probably familiar with the famous case of Little Albert, reported by John Watson and his colleague Rosalie Rayner in 1920. Watson and Rayner paired a white rat with a loud noise and soon induced Albert to fear the rat. In doing so, Watson and Rayner demonstrated that phobias may be the products of Pavlovian conditioning. Once Albert was afraid of the rat, Watson and Rayner tested the effects of a rabbit, cotton wool, and a Santa Claus mask—objects that resembled the white rat to some degree. Even though these items had never been paired with a loud noise, Albert was afraid of them. In other words, the effects of the training with the white rat had generalized to similar objects.

6. Fleece et al. (1981).

7. Horner et al. (1986).

Maintenance

GREETINGS! AND CONGRATULATIONS on having made it this far into the course! I realize that continuing to be a character in a textbook must be a strain; there are, after all, lots of more exciting things for fictional characters to do.

"Are you feeling all right, Dr. Cee?"

Yes, Maya. I'm fine. . . . Now, last time we talked about generalization training. What is generalization? Carlotta?

"That's the tendency for the effects of training to spread."

Right. And you learned that there are two kinds of generalization called . . . called what, John?

"Stimulus generalization and . . ."

Yes?

". . . and response generalization."

Exactly. Now, let's suppose I'm working with an adolescent who is rather schizoid. He has difficulty dealing with other people in ordinary social situations. For example, if someone says "Hello," to him, he tends to look away. In talking with him, I find that he really would like to interact with other people, but he just doesn't know how to go about it. My intervention consists of teaching him to respond to greetings such as, "Hello. How are you?" All of his training has been done in the psychiatric hospital where he is a patient. Now I take him for a walk on the hospital grounds and arrange to have a couple of people pass by him and say, "Hello" or "Hi." These are people he hasn't met before.

What happens is that he responds to the first greeting by saying, "Howdy. Nice day, ain't it?" He replies to the second greeting by saying, "Hola! Como esta?" (He studied Spanish in high school, and the person greeting him is Hispanic.) He has not said either of these things in his training sessions. Now, what kind of generalization does this example illustrate? Yes, Midori?

"Is this a trick question?"

Very possibly. Why do you ask?

"Because he's responding to greetings with comments he wasn't taught to say. That's response generalization."

Good, good. Go on.

"But you've taken him to a situation that's different from where the training took place, and the effects of training still show up. So that's stimulus generalization."

Excellent.

"So it *was* a trick question: The example shows both stimulus generalization and response generalization."

Indubitably. And you were very astute to recognize that. Now, how do you suppose I got these brilliant results? Jamal?

"You might have gotten the response generalization by teaching him several kinds of greetings, rather than just a few."

Good, good. How did I get generalization to new situations—responding to people he never met in a place he hadn't been?

"You probably did the training in a number of different places and involved several different people."

Exactly. By doing things of that sort, I got the behavior to generalize from one behavior to another and from one situation to another. Today our topic is maintenance, which has to do with getting behavior to generalize from one *time* to another. We will attempt to answer the question, "How can we get changes in behavior to persist over time?" This is sometimes called the maintenance problem. There are two basic solutions to the maintenance problem: maintenance schedules and maintenance training.

Maintenance Schedules

Before we get into the use of maintenance schedules, you need to know a bit about the basic kinds of reinforcement schedules.

Reinforcement Schedules

A reinforcement schedule is a kind of rule about how reinforcers are to be provided:

Schedule of reinforcement: A rule governing the delivery of reinforcers.

There are many different kinds of reinforcement schedules, but we will discuss the three main types.[1] These are ratio, interval, and duration schedules.

Ratio schedules are based on the number of times the behavior occurs. They are called ratio schedules because the rule for delivery of a reinforcer specifies a ratio of performances of the target behavior to each reinforcement. There are two kinds of ratio schedules, fixed and variable. In a fixed ratio schedule, the rule is:

Fixed ratio schedule:
Provide a reinforcer after the target behavior
has occurred n number of times.

In fixed ratio (or FR) schedules, the target behavior must occur a certain number of times before it is reinforced. If the behavior is on an FR-1 schedule, the ratio of the number of occurrences of the behavior to reinforcement is 1 to 1. In other words, a reinforcer is delivered each and every time the target behavior occurs. This particular schedule, FR-1, is also called *continuous reinforcement* and is sometimes abbreviated CRF.

CRF is a schedule in which the target behavior is reinforced each time it occurs; schedules that reinforce some occurrences of the target behavior but not others are called *intermittent* schedules.

An intermittent FR schedule requires that the target behavior occur a fixed number of times before it is reinforced. If a behavior is on a fixed ratio 2 (FR-2) schedule, for instance, the behavior has to occur twice before it is reinforced; if it's on an FR-10 schedule, it has to occur 10 times for each reinforcement, and if the behavior is on an FR-100 schedule, it has to occur . . . how often, Alfred?

"A hundred times for each reinforcement."

Right. Fixed ratio schedules require a fixed number of performances for reinforcement. Variable ratio schedules are identical to fixed ratio schedules except that the number of instances of behavior required for reinforcement varies around some average. The rule for variable ratio (VR) schedules is:

Variable ratio schedule:
Provide a reinforcer after the target behavior
has occurred a number of times, with the
number varying around an average of n.

In a VR-5 schedule, for example, the behavior might be reinforced after occurring three times, then after seven times, eight times, two times, four times, and so on. The number of occurrences required for any given reinforcement may vary from 1 to perhaps 10 times, but on average the ratio of occurrences to reinforcements will be 5 to 1.

So, who can tell me the difference between an FR-20 schedule and a VR-20 schedule? Maya?

"In an FR-20 schedule, the person has to perform the target behavior 20 times for every reinforcement. In a VR-20 schedule, the number of times the person has to perform the target behavior varies but on average the ratio is 20 to 1. Is that it?"

Yes, that's it.

In ratio schedules, reinforcement is based on the number of times the behavior is performed. In interval schedules, reinforcement is based on the length of the interval between reinforcements. These schedules are called interval schedules because the rule for delivery of a reinforcer specifies an interval between reinforcements of the target behavior. There are two kinds of interval schedules, fixed and variable. In a fixed interval schedule, the rule is:

Fixed interval schedule:
Provide a reinforcer the first time the target behavior occurs after an interval of n length since the last reinforcement.

In fixed interval (or FI) schedules, a fixed amount of time must elapse since the last reinforced performance; only then does the behavior qualify for reinforcement again. If the target behavior is on an FI-1 minute schedule, for instance, then after the behavior is reinforced, a minute must elapse before the behavior will be reinforced again. Performing the target behavior does not produce reinforcement until the minute has elapsed.

If a behavior is on an FI-2 minute schedule, performing the target behavior produces no reinforcement until 2 minutes have elapsed; if the behavior is on an FI-10 minute schedule, reinforcement is unavailable until . . . John?

"Until 10 minutes have gone by."

Right. One thing—

"The behavior still has to be performed, though, right?"

Excuse me, John?

"The reinforcer isn't delivered just because the time has elapsed, is it?"

Oh, right. And that's an important point: An interval schedule sets two requirements for reinforcement: A certain amount of time must elapse since the last reinforcement, and the target behavior must occur. So, after the interval has elapsed, the *next* time the behavior occurs, it is reinforced.[2]

Variable interval schedules are identical to fixed interval schedules except that the length of the interval between reinforcements varies around some average. The rule for variable interval (VI) schedules is:

Variable interval schedule:
Provide a reinforcer the first time the target behavior occurs after an interval, with the interval varying around an average of n length.

In a VI-5 second schedule, for example, the behavior might be reinforced after an interval of 2 seconds, then after an interval of 7 seconds, 8 seconds, 2 seconds, 4 seconds, and so on. The average interval is 5 seconds, but the interval between any two reinforcements may vary from one to perhaps 10 seconds. Now, who can tell me the difference between FI and VI schedules? Belinda?

> "Uh, let's see. FI and VI. The difference is that, in FI schedules, the interval during which the behavior isn't reinforced is always the same, it's fixed; in VI schedules, the interval varies around some average."

Good. Ratio schedules are based on the number of times the target behavior occurs. Interval schedules are based on the time between reinforcements. And duration schedules are based on how long the behavior must occur without interruption. They are called duration schedules because they specify the duration of the behavior. There are fixed duration schedules and variable duration schedules.

In a fixed duration (FD) schedule, an activity must be engaged in continuously for a specified period:

> ### Fixed duration schedule:
> #### Provide a reinforcer after the target behavior has been performed continuously for a period of <u>n</u> length.

Fixed duration schedules are very common. A typical example is the child who is required to practice playing the piano for a period of 30 minutes, at the end of which time his mother brings him his favorite snack. The reinforcer is earned by continuing to perform the activity, piano playing, for the specified period.

In a variable duration (or VD) schedule, the requirement for reinforcement is the same as in an FD schedule except that the period during which the behavior must occur varies around an average:

> ### Variable duration schedule:
> #### Provide a reinforcer after the target behavior has been performed continuously for a period, with the period varying around an average of <u>n</u> length.

Suppose the mother in our example requires that her son practice the piano, but she is inconsistent about how long he must practice on any given day. One day she brings him his snack after only 15 minutes of practice; the next day he practices 45 minutes before receiving the snack; the next day, the snack comes after 20 minutes; and so on. The average practice period is 30 minutes, but the practice period on any given day may vary from, say, 10 to 50 minutes. That's a variable duration schedule.

The difference between an FD schedule and a VD schedule is . . . is what, John?

"The difference is that the time you have to perform the behavior is always the same in FD schedules, but in VD schedules it varies around an average."

Sehr gut! Okay, we have discussed three kinds of reinforcement schedules: ratio, interval, and duration. There are other kinds of schedules, but these are the ones you are most likely to encounter in the behavior analysis literature. One reason that reinforcement schedules are of interest in applied behavior analysis is because of their value in maintaining behavior for long periods. One solution to the maintenance problem, then, is to put the behavior on a maintenance schedule.

Maintenance Schedules

A maintenance schedule is simply a reinforcement schedule used to maintain a target behavior:

> ### Maintenance schedule:
> ### A reinforcement schedule that maintains
> ### a target behavior at a desired rate.

Not all schedules are equally useful as maintenance schedules. Fixed interval schedules, for example, tend to produce a low rate of performance that rapidly increases as the nonreinforcement interval nears its end. This results in a scallop-shaped cumulative record that looks like this:

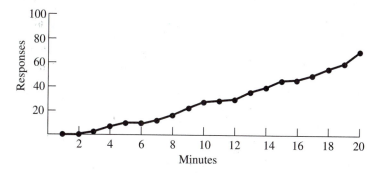

Figure 10-1. Fixed interval performance. Cumulative record shows the scalloped curve typical of fixed interval schedules. (hypothetical data)

You've probably seen this sort of pattern many times. If you have had an instructor who gave a quiz every Friday, you probably didn't study much for his class over the weekend, but as the week wore on, you studied more. By Thursday evening, you were probably hitting the books pretty hard. You may have cursed yourself every Thursday for procrastinating until the last minute, but it's likely that the reinforcement schedule was at least partly responsible for your behavior: There was no particular benefit for studying early in the week, but studying on Thursday was followed the next day by doing well on the quiz.[3]

The scalloped FI pattern can be avoided with a variable interval schedule. If you've ever had an instructor who gave unannounced quizzes an average of once a week and who was as likely to give a quiz on one day as the next, you probably studied at a fairly steady rate throughout the week.

Even variable interval schedules leave something to be desired, however. They require keeping track of the interval and varying its length systematically around an average. That's time-consuming, and can be difficult.

Duration schedules provide an alternative. You need only monitor the behavior to ensure that it occurs continuously for the prescribed period. However, since there is no requirement that the target behavior be performed at a given frequency, the tendency is for the behavior to fall to the minimum that qualifies for reinforcement. This can be seen sometimes in sales clerks and other employees who are paid solely based on the number of hours they "put in." They sometimes behave as though they have earned their pay merely by showing up. Their supervisors often complain about "the decline of the work ethic," but what they are seeing is largely accounted for by the reinforcement schedule.

FR schedules are often used in the workplace, where they are usually referred to as piece work. For example, a worker may be paid so much for each widget he produces, or for every box of widgets he packs, or for every box of widgets he sells. Sometimes the worker is paid a base salary but can earn a bonus if he produces, boxes, or sells more than a certain number of widgets a week.

FR schedules are somewhat problematic in many settings because it's not always convenient, or even possible, to keep an accurate count of the number of times a behavior is performed. It's one thing to count the number of widgets someone has produced; it's another thing to count the number of times someone smiles or cooperates with another person.

The ideal maintenance schedule in most cases seems to be the variable ratio schedule. This schedule will maintain behavior steadily at high rates with very infrequent reinforcement.

> "But if you shape up some new behavior, or increase the rate of some old behavior, with continuous reinforcement and then you switch to a high ratio VR schedule, aren't you going to undo what you've just accomplished?"

An excellent question, Carlotta. And you're right, if you switch *abruptly* from a CRF schedule to a high ratio VR schedule, you're likely to get the same sort of effects you see with extinction: The rate of behavior will drop off, and you may get some emotional behavior, such as aggression or tantrums. These results are referred to as ratio strain:

Ratio strain:
A reduction in the rate of target behavior
and an increase in emotional behavior
resulting from increases in the ratio
of behavior to reinforcement.

To prevent ratio strain, you need to avoid abrupt increases in the ratio. Instead, you *gradually* increase the requirement for reinforcement, a procedure known as stretching the ratio:

Stretching the ratio:
Gradually increasing the number of times
a behavior must be performed to qualify
for reinforcement.

Suppose, for example, that you are a teacher and you have a fifth-grade student named George who rarely does his homework. He always has some excuse: He forgot to take the book home; he forgot the assignment; he didn't know how to do it; he did it, but left it at home; he did it, but his cow ate it. (He's a farm boy, and he doesn't have a dog.)

You collect baseline data, and you find that, on average, George turns in only about 10% of the assignments. Then you begin providing reinforcement for completing homework. Perhaps when George turns in an assignment that is reasonably well done, you congratulate him on his success and give him one of those pogs buttons the kids all like. Or maybe you read George's paper as a model for the rest of the class. Or maybe you post his homework with some others on a bulletin board under the sign, "Good Work!" Every time he turns in an assignment that is complete and well done, you provide some sort of consequence that's likely to be reinforcing. Pretty soon George has become a homework factory. Your records show that, on average, he turns in about 85% of the assignments. Not only that, but he no longer complains about homework; he discovers that it helps him learn better, that it's really not difficult, that sometimes it's fun, and so on.

Once the behavior is occurring at the desired frequency, you can stretch the ratio: You might provide a reinforcer two out of every three times that George turns in homework. If the rate remains steady or increases, you might then reinforce about one out of every two times, then one out of every three times, then one in four, and so on, until you get to a frequency of reinforcement that is not a burden yet continues to maintain the behavior.

> "But isn't the rate of behavior going to fall off? I mean, you're not going to get the same rate of behavior if you're reinforcing an average of one out of every ten homework assignments as you got when you were reinforcing after every assignment, are you?"

Well, Midori, there's a limit to how far you can stretch the ratio, but you would be surprised at how few reinforcers it takes to maintain behavior at high rates.

> "I don't believe it."

Don't believe what, Alfred?

> "I don't believe people are going to work just as hard for a few reinforcers as they did for a lot of reinforcers."

Well, believe it or not, it happens. In fact, you can sometimes get higher rates of behavior on thin (high ratio) schedules than you can on rich (low ratio) schedules. You have to stretch the ratio gradually, or you'll get ratio strain; and there's a limit to how far you can stretch the ratio, but people don't require that every performance be reinforced.

You might think of it like this: Suppose you were asked to shape a target behavior that consisted of hammering five nails into a board. Remember, the target behavior is not pounding one nail into a board; it's pounding *five* nails into a board. How would you shape that behavior, Alfred?

"I guess I'd shape hammering a nail. Then, when I got the person to hammer in one nail, I'd try to shape hammering two nails, then three, then four, then five."

Exactly. And look at what you'd be doing: You'd be stretching the ratio of reinforcement.

"Are you saying that stretching the ratio is a kind of shaping procedure?"

Exactly, Alfred. You shape the number of times the behavior is performed for each reinforcement. Belinda?

"So, if you get homework turned in 85% of the time with continuous reinforcement, you might still get 85% when you reinforce after every fifth assignment or every tenth assignment? The person does more for less?"

That's the idea. You're requiring more for the same amount of reinforcement, so you get more. Of course, as I've said, you have to stretch slowly or the performance will break down.

"So all you have to do to maintain behavior is put the behavior on a maintenance schedule? Is that it?"

Well . . . yes, in most cases. The trouble is that people don't always do that. Often when they've produced the desired changes in behavior, they stop reinforcing the behavior, or they reinforce it so infrequently that the schedule isn't rich enough to maintain the behavior.

Let's say you're a school psychologist. A teacher complains that his students don't work very hard at their assignments; they just sort of go through the motions. The two of you put your heads together and find a way of reinforcing hard work: When the students are working on an assignment of some sort, the teacher is to walk about the room looking at the students' work. He is to ignore students who are doodling or staring out the window, but he's to help those who are struggling and praise them and others who are working hard. The teacher implements the plan, and pretty soon working hard is the rule rather than the exception. You then help the teacher stretch the ratio a bit so that he can ease off on reinforcement yet still maintain the behavior. The teacher thanks you for your help, and you go to the school principal and ask for a big raise. Three weeks later, the teacher comes to you and says, "They're doodling again." He tells you that reinforcement worked great, but the effects didn't last. More than likely what has happened is that the teacher has let the maintenance schedule get thinner and thinner until it was no longer sufficient to maintain the behavior.

> "But why would he do that? I mean, if all he had to do to maintain the behavior was reinforce it once in a while, why wouldn't he continue to do that?"

That's a very good question, Jamal. Does anyone have any good answers? Yes, Brian?

> "I think it might be like going on a diet. People eat too much and get overweight, and then they change their diet. Then as soon as they get their weight down, they go back to their old diet. If they want to keep their weight down, they have to stay on a diet that will maintain that weight, but they don't always do that."

I see the parallel, Brian, but I don't think you've answered the question. Why don't people stay on a diet that will maintain a good weight?

> "I was coming to that. At first when you go on a diet, you lose weight and that probably reinforces staying on the diet. But when you get your weight down to where it's supposed to be, you don't see any further improvement in the mirror or on the bathroom scale. The only positive consequence is that your weight stays the same, and that's probably not very reinforcing."

So as the dieter makes progress, the reinforcement schedule thins out until finally it's too thin to maintain the behavior. That sounds reasonable. Now, can you relate that to the teacher who shapes up hard work in his students and then doesn't provide enough reinforcement to maintain the behavior?

> "I think the same thing is going on. At first, reinforcing hard work produces obvious improvement, and that reinforces the teacher's efforts. But after a while the level of hard work stabilizes, and the teacher doesn't see any additional gains for his trouble. The only positive consequence for the teacher is that things stay the same, and that's probably not very reinforcing."

I think you're on to something, Brian: Providing a maintenance schedule is itself something that needs to be reinforced. What we need to do is to put the teacher's behavior—or that of the parent, trainer, manager, or therapist—on a maintenance schedule. So, if we're serious about maintenance, we have to find some way of reinforcing the act of maintaining the maintenance schedule. That can sometimes be achieved with a contingency contract.

Contingency Contracts

If a maintenance schedule is to stay in force, the effort required in managing such a schedule must itself be reinforced—

"So now we're talking about reinforcing the behavior of the person who's reinforcing someone's behavior?"

That's it, exactly, Maya. One way to do that is to set up a contingency contract:

Contingency contract: An agreement between two or more parties about what each is to do for the other.

A contract between a teacher and his students, for example, would specify what the teacher would do that the students find reinforcing, and what the students would do that the teacher finds reinforcing.[4] What each party is to do is spelled out very clearly, so that everyone understands exactly what is expected. The terms are written down, so that they can be referred to later in the event of a dispute. Now, what should the terms be in the situation we've been discussing? What does each party want? Yes, Midori?

"The teacher may want to sit at his desk, grading papers and filling out forms. He probably doesn't enjoy grading papers and filling out forms for the school board, but he probably prefers doing it at school to doing it at home on his own time."

Okay, so the teacher gets to sit at his desk, rather than walk around the room. What else does the teacher want?

"He wants the students to work hard on their assignments and not send notes, get noisy, or fool around."

Okay. What do you think the students want? Jamal?

"They want help if they run into trouble with the assignment."

Right. So they want to be able to come up to the teacher's desk, or ask the teacher to come to their desk, when they need help. Anything else?

"They want a break from doing schoolwork. Like, if they work hard and they finish the assignment, they don't want the teacher to give them more work to do. And they probably don't want to sit their twiddling their thumbs waiting for everybody else to finish."

How about if, when a student completes the assignment satisfactorily, he gets to spend the rest of the time doing something he likes? Maybe we set aside a part of the room for fun things, like playing computer games or looking at magazines, using coloring books, or playing checkers. Whatever the students like and that they can do quietly.

Okay, so the teacher and the students work out a contractual arrangement. The teacher might propose the contract, but he needs to leave some room for negotiation. After all, if he dictates the terms, it's not really an agreement. So the teacher and the students negotiate and reach an agreement, which someone writes down and then everyone signs. The terms in this situation might say, for example:

1. The teacher will make assignments and set aside a reasonable amount of time for their completion.

2. The students will work diligently on the assignment until they have completed it satisfactorily or the time provided has elapsed.

3. Students who have difficulty with an assignment will raise their hand and wait to be recognized by the teacher. When recognized, they will approach the teacher's desk and he will answer their questions.

4. When a student completes an assignment, she will wait to be recognized and then take the assignment to the teacher for his approval.

5. If the teacher finds that the assignment has been completed satisfactorily, the student will be allowed to go to the play area and play quietly until the assignment period is ended.

The contract specifies what each party has to do and what each will get in return for doing it. From the teacher's point of view, it identifies the student's target behaviors and the consequences he is to provide to maintain them. From the student's view it identifies the teacher's target behaviors and what the students are to do to maintain them. It's a reciprocal relationship.

"It looks to me like this contract might end up in court."

Alfred? What do you mean?

"Well, the kids get to go to the play area, and they're supposed to be quiet, but when they get to playing they're going to start making noise, and that's going to distract the other students."

Quite right. The kids who are working are going to complain, and the teacher's going to complain. So they work something out. Maybe they add a sixth paragraph:

6. Any student who is noisy or unruly in the play area may be required by the teacher to return to his seat for the remainder of the assignment period.

Contract problems such as this are going to arise, because you aren't going to be able to anticipate the effects of the contract perfectly. But when problems arise, you deal with them by renegotiating the contract. The contract creates a situation that makes it likely that the consequences necessary to maintain the target behaviors will continue to be provided. This is so because . . . who can tell me why this is so? Yes, Midori?

"Well, if the teacher doesn't live up to his part of the bargain, the students are going to complain, and they're not going to do their part. It's like a job. You agree to work and your employer agrees to pay you. If the employer stops paying you, you stop working."

That's exactly right. Contingency contracts structure a situation so that the two parties are able to provide reinforcers that will maintain behavior they consider desirable. As long as the teacher likes sitting at her desk while students work hard at their assignments, and as long as the students like having free time, the contract should be effective. Contingency contracts have been used in dozens of studies and have consistently gotten positive results, usually far better than more conventional methods.

An example is provided by Alice Kahle and Mary Kelley.[5] Their study looked at the effects of various procedures on the quantity and quality of homework completed by 40 kids in the second, third, or fourth grades. The researchers assigned each child to one of four groups: In one group, parents encouraged and supported homework activities; in a second group, parents used contingency contracts to set and achieve specific homework goals; in a third group, the researchers merely monitored the homework done; and in the fourth group, the researchers had no contact with the students or their parents. Both the support group and the contingency contract group got better results than the monitoring and no-contact groups. However, only contingency contracts increased the number of homework problems answered correctly each minute.

Not all contingency contracts need to be quite so formal. The parents of a 19-month-old child were concerned because they were soon to take a trip that would involve long hours of driving, and the child had not learned to use a toilet.[6] Long road trips can be stressful, as you know, but when you add the burden of dealing with diapers, not to mention the odor of their contents . . . well, who needs it? The parents attempted to train the child on their own. They'd put the child on a little "training toilet" whenever she asked them to, but somehow she always managed to eliminate in her diapers. Mom, on whose shoulders the training chiefly fell, was beginning to get a bit frustrated, and the little girl was beginning to show signs of unhappiness with the procedure as well.

Finally the parents approached a behaviorist and asked for his help. He proposed a very simple contingency contract: The parents were to put the child on the toilet when she awoke in the morning and after her naps. The parent (again, this was usually Mom) was to read to or otherwise entertain the child while she sat on the toilet, but the child was to leave the toilet when she was ready and there was to be no chastisement for failures on or off the toilet. However, the parents were asked to announce that whenever she managed to make an appropriate deposit into the toilet, she would receive one of her favorite candies.

The second time the child sat on the toilet, she earned a candy. On the fourth day of training, she announced spontaneously that she needed to use the toilet and did so. Progress continued rapidly, and a few weeks later when the family went on their long trip, the girl was ready. The trip included 5 days of driving 8 hours a day and was completed without a single toileting accident.

Contingency contracts are a great way to maintain a target behavior. A variation of the contingency contract is called the token economy.

Token Economy

A token is . . . what, Carlotta?

"Something that can be exchanged for a reinforcer?"

Correct. The reinforcer that you get in exchange for a token is called a *backup reinforcer.* Belinda?

"A backup reinforcer?"

Yes. It's called that because it's what makes the token valuable; it backs it up. One kind of contingency contract that relies heavily on tokens and deserves special consideration is called the token economy. A token economy is a kind of contingency contract that . . . well, I'll put the definition on the board:

> **Token economy:**
> **A form of contingency contract, usually involving a group of people, in which the reinforcers are tokens.**

The name *token economy* implies that there is a sort of micro economy, with tokens used as the currency with which people "purchase" products and services.[7] This is typically the case, but the defining attributes of a token economy are (1) that there is a contractual arrangement involving a group of people, and (2) tokens are used as reinforcers. The tokens are, of course, exchanged at some point for backup reinforcers.

Most token economies have involved students or people in institutions. They can, however, be set up in the home.[8] I'd like to summarize one study that did just that.

As you know, kids in industrialized countries watch a lot of television; by the time most American kids reach the age of 18, they have spent more time in front of a television set than they have spent in classrooms.[9] That's something like 10,000 hours the kids *could* have spent reading books, writing poetry, peering through a microscope, collecting stamps, telling stories, putting on plays—activities that are far more educational than most TV programs are. A lot of parents know this and would like to get their kids to spend less time watching television. The problem is how to do it.

David Wolfe and some of his Canadian colleagues devised a simple but apparently effective way parents can deal with this problem.[10] What they did was this: They found some parents who were concerned that their kids were "addicted" to

TV. There were three 2-parent families, and the kids were between the ages of 8 and 12. The parents had tried to reduce the amount of TV watching, but without success.

"How did they do that?"

Good question, Belinda. They did the usual sort of parent things: They criticized their kids and reminded them they should be doing other things.

"You mean like, 'Why don't you go outside and play?' or 'That's a dumb show; why don't you read a book?' In other words, they nagged."

Yes. As you know, nagging is a form of negative reinforcement that is popular among parents, but it doesn't usually work very well in the long run. It didn't work for these parents, and they were willing to try something new. The behaviorists suggested a plan. First, however, they asked the parents to monitor TV viewing for a minimum of 7 weeks. During this period the parents made no efforts to change TV viewing; they just recorded the amount of time the kids spent on TV each day. Of course, you know that this period of observation is called a . . . what, Jamal?

"Baseline."

Right. The baseline provides a benchmark. Without a baseline, there's no way to tell how much effect the treatment has. The baseline data showed that the kids were watching TV an average of 21 hours a week.

After the parents had a baseline, Wolfe and company asked them to provide each child with 20 tokens. Then the children had to give up one token for each half-hour of TV time. They could not watch TV unless they paid for it in tokens. This meant that the kids could watch no more than 10 hours of TV a week, half their usual "dosage." If the kids abided by the rules for four consecutive weeks, they received a reward, such as a trip to a zoo or an amusement park.

The result of this program was that the time spent watching TV fell immediately to 10 hours a week or less. In fact, for the 3 months that the program continued, only one child ever watched more than 10 hours of TV in a week.

The parents made some interesting observations about their kids. They reported that the kids often saved tokens for special occasions, such as when a friend was to come over to watch a movie. The kids would also reserve tokens for use during special times, such as Saturday morning when the cartoons are on.

"Didn't the kids protest the new rules?"

Apparently not, Carlotta. The parents said that the kids liked the arrangement, and some showed greater interest in family activities.

"What did they do with the extra time?"

A good question. The researchers were interested in that question, too, so they asked the parents to monitor how much time the kids spent on homework and on reading. Two of the children spent a little more time on homework. Really! And all five of the children spent more time reading. I don't want to give the impression that the kids simply replaced TV with books and magazines, but they did read more. In fact, there were weeks when the kids spent as much time reading as they spent watching TV. So if you believe that reading is a better activity for kids than watching TV, then this program was an unqualified success.

You've seen that we can create conditions that will maintain behavior indefinitely. Society can also create conditions to maintain behavior that is beneficial to the society. Let's talk about these social contracts a bit.

Social Contracts

Society attempts to maintain high rates of certain behaviors and low rates of other behaviors by means of contingency contracts. For instance, although most people are disgusted by the high crime rate, the fact is that criminal behavior occurs at a relatively low rate compared to lawful behavior.

No doubt one reason for the relative infrequency of criminal behavior has to do with learning histories. When you look into the backgrounds of people who repeatedly commit criminal acts, you typically find a long history of reinforcement for such behavior.[11] Fortunately, most of us have learning histories that include a good deal of reinforcement for law-abiding behavior and punishment for antisocial behavior.

Another part of the answer has to do with contractual contingencies between society and its members. In other words, we have laws that specify that certain behaviors are not allowed and will result in punishment. This is a form of contingency contract.

One problem with the contingency contracts between society and its members is that they don't take into account what is now known about human behavior. The contracts focus too much on punishment rather than reinforcement; the consequences for behavior are delayed; they are uncertain, and so on. Yet it is possible to set up contingency contracts that will reliably change behavior for the better.

For instance, it is very important for parents to have their children immunized against common diseases, such as diphtheria and pertussis. But as these and other diseases have become less common, parents have gotten lax about immunization. The result is thousands of young people who are vulnerable to disease, a situation that makes epidemics a distinct possibility. Ad campaigns urging parents to take their children in for vaccination are an attempt to prompt the appropriate behavior, but they have not been very successful.

James Yokley and David Glenwich conducted a study to compare various approaches to prompting parents to have their children immunized.[12] The families of more than a thousand preschool children were randomly assigned to six conditions. Some adults were simply advised to immunize their children; others were told what specific immunizations their children needed; those in a third group were told the specific immunizations needed and given improved access to public health clinics; a fourth group was given the specific information and offered money if they obtained the immunizations. There were two control groups: one in which the researchers made contact with the parents but didn't urge them to get immunizations; and one in which the researchers had no contact with the families. Three of the interventions resulted in improved rates of immunization compared to the control groups. The one that did not produce results was the general prompt condition—that was the one in which they simply advised parents that it would be a good idea to have their kids immunized. You probably can guess which group showed the greatest improvement. What do you think, Maya?

"The one that provided a specific prompt and promised money?"

Of course. The specific prompts were effective by themselves. You tell people, "Your children need to be vaccinated to protect them against this and that disease," and a lot of parents are going to get their children vaccinated. You make it easier to get the vaccination by, for example, offering them transportation to a clinic and providing the shots for free, and still more will act. But if you offer a contractual arrangement in which the parents can receive money for having their children vaccinated, the results are even better. A small monetary reward can be very powerful with poor people.

"I don't see why society should pay them to do what is right. I mean, why should my taxes be used to pay somebody to get free immunizations?"

A fair question, Alfred. Does anyone have an answer? Yes, Jamal?

"I have to admit it rubs me the wrong way, too. But I guess if that's what you have to do, then that's what you have to do. It's better than having an epidemic."

You want to add something, Belinda?

"I think you have to think that your taxes are being spent to help those kids, not their parents, because it gets the kids protected against diseases."

A good point. Midori?

"I think the contract has a payoff for taxpayers, too. Some kids who don't get vaccinated are going to get sick, and sometimes the sickness is going to require expensive medical treatment. And that expense is paid for by taxpayers. So if it costs taxpayers $5 to get a parent to bring his kid in for vaccinations, that $5 may save taxpayers thousands of dollars in medical bills."

That's an excellent point. Taxpayers have to pay a lot more to treat poor kids who get sick than it costs to immunize them. So if it costs a few dollars to get parents to bring their kids into the clinic, it's money well spent.

If we get the contingencies right, we can not only reduce suffering but also save money. If we provide tax deductions or other benefits to people who get health insurance, who get prenatal care, who immunize their children, who see to it that their kids get to school, who take care of their children, who work, who obey the law, and so on, we might save the taxpayers a tremendous amount of money.

One lesson that we as a society have not quite learned is the value to society of making reinforcers contingent on socially desirable behavior. I'm not suggesting that behavior analysis has the solutions to all of society's ills. But behavior *isn't* random. The kinds of behavior we get depend in large measure on the consequences we provide for behavior. If we want people to behave differently, then we have to provide different consequences for their behavior.

Well, we've only just scratched the surface on the role of reinforcement schedules in maintaining behavior, but scratching the surface is about all we can do in an introductory course.

I said that there are two basic ways of tackling the maintenance problem. One is to put the behavior on a maintenance schedule. But what if the behavior can't be put on a long-term maintenance schedule? What if no one is willing or able to fulfill the terms of a contract? Maintenance schedules, useful as they are, are not an entirely satisfactory answer to the problem of maintaining behavior because such artificial schedules almost inevitably come to an end. Our students go on to teachers who can't or won't use contingency contracts. Children grow up and go off to live their separate lives, out of the reach of highly reinforcing parents. The mentally retarded man who does well in an institution with a token economy may graduate to a group home in the community, but the group home leaders may not provide tokens for good behavior. Maintenance schedules are powerful tools, and we should make use of them when we can. But in most instances, they are a temporary arrangement. So, what can we do to prevent the benefits of training from deteriorating when our intervention is over? The answer, I think, is maintenance training.

Maintenance Training

By maintenance training, I mean:

> ### Maintenance training:
> Intervention procedures that increase the likelihood that changes in a target behavior will persist when the intervention is ended.

"So what you're talking about is building endurance?"

That's right, Midori. What can we do during the time that we are working with a person to make the behavior changes likely to endure once the person is on his or her own? Let's say you're a fifth-grade teacher and you've got a student, we'll call him Buford, who has no creativity. Zip. Zilch. Zero. Buford never does anything original. A block of wood has more imagination than Buford has. You decide to increase Buford's creative abilities. You attempt to reinforce original ideas by providing praise and other reinforcers.[13] At first, you don't have much to work with, so you reinforce anything that is the least bit original. Gradually, you are able to shape up a tendency to be more creative. By the end of the school year, Buford is a changed boy. When given a problem to solve, he can often see two or three ways of tackling it. During class discussions, he often comes up with points of view that others missed. During art lessons, his productions are always among the most original in class. You've done a wonderful job, but will Buford continue to be creative in the sixth grade? What do you think, Belinda?

"I think that being creative is reinforcing in and of itself, so I think the answer is yes."

What do you think—is Belinda right? Jamal?

"I think Buford might enjoy doing creative things, but the pleasure he gets from being creative might not be enough to keep him creative. If his new teacher doesn't value creativity—"

Stop! What does that mean—"value creativity"?

"What I mean is that if the sixth-grade teacher doesn't provide praise, or recognition, or other reinforcers for creative behavior, Buford's creativity might decline."

I see. Is a thin reinforcement schedule for creativity the only problem Buford may face in the sixth grade? John?

"His new teacher might actually discourage creativity."

You folks sure are using a lot of vague terminology today. What does "discourage" mean?

"He might criticize Buford when he does creative things."

Do you mean creative behavior might be punished?

"Yes."

Now I understand. So the sixth-grade teacher might put creative behavior on extinction and might even punish creative behavior. What else might he do that could reduce Buford's creativity? Yes, Maya?

"The new teacher might reinforce very conventional behavior, behavior that is incompatible with creativity."

You're saying the teacher might differentially reinforce behavior that is incompatible with creative behavior. So, when poor Buford goes on to the sixth grade, the environment there might not maintain the level of creativity you helped him establish in the fifth grade. Your intervention needs to make the desired changes resistant to the influences of a less than ideal future. In a sense, you have to *immunize* Buford against future experiences that might undermine the progress you have helped him make. And how do you do that? What can you do to increase the resistance of behavior to future challenges, such as infrequent reinforcement, punishment, and the reinforcement of incompatible behavior? Let's consider some maintenance training procedures.

1. Continue the intervention well after the target behavior has changed.

The behavior change procedures that you have learned about in this course often produce results with startling speed. A behavior that rarely occurs can be made to occur at a high rate by the judicious use of reinforcement. A behavior that has never occurred can often be shaped up in a matter of minutes. A troublesome behavior that has occurred at a high rate for years can often be reduced dramatically in short order with differential reinforcement. Applied behavior analysis gets results, and it usually gets results quickly.

Unfortunately, once the behavior has changed for the better people often conclude that there's no need to continue the intervention. They are mistaken. The longer an intervention continues, the longer its effects endure.[14] This implies that we should continue the training program even though the behavior problem has been solved and the program produces no obvious additional gains.

Another thing we can do is:

2. Expose the target behavior to its natural reinforcers.

Ultimately, if the changes in behavior produced by an intervention are to endure, the behavior must be maintained by the reinforcers it produces in the natural environment. It is therefore important to expose the target behavior to those consequences. To do this, it may be necessary to prompt the behavior in the natural environment. The hope is that the behavior will come under the influence of those reinforcers, so this procedure is sometimes called *behavior trapping*.[15]

"Could you give us an example of that?"

Certainly, John. Suppose you're a guidance counselor and you've worked with a student (I'll call her Millie) who had a problem with reading. Thanks to you, she's reading much better now, and much more frequently. But you want her to continue reading. You visit the home to talk with the parents, and while there you brag about how well Millie is reading. You ask Millie to demonstrate her skills, and when she reads her parents pay close attention to her and then praise her efforts. You've exposed reading to parental reinforcers, and that may mean that Millie will read more at home. That—

"Wait."

Yes, Alfred?

"I happen to know Millie's parents. They never read if they can avoid it, and they don't care whether Millie reads or not. Now tell us how we're going to use behavior trapping."

Okay, I accept the challenge. The parents do not like to read, so you casually make the observation that Millie might be able to relieve them of the burden of reading by reading aloud to them. She might read *TV Guide* to them when they want to find out what's on the tube; she might read the jokes and humorous stories in *Reader's Digest* to them; she might read a recipe aloud as someone prepares a meal; she might look up numbers and addresses in the phone book; she might read labels on medicine jars; she might read the instructions for setting up a new VCR. You could also propose that Millie read aloud to her aging grandmother, who likes to read but can do so only with the aid of a thick magnifying glass. Even though the parents don't care whether Millie becomes a good reader, reading becomes a way that Millie can do something important in the family, and that's likely to be reinforcing.

"What if the purpose of the intervention is to reduce some unwanted behavior, such as whining?"

Good question, Jamal. One idea would be to establish a more appropriate way of obtaining the reinforcers now obtained by whining, and then expose that new behavior to those reinforcers in the natural environment.

"What if there are no natural reinforcers for the target behavior?"

If the behavior isn't going to pay off in the natural environment, then you should ask yourself why you're trying to establish it.[16] However, sometimes it is possible for the person to increase the availability of natural reinforcers. That brings us to the next strategy:

3. Teach the person to obtain reinforcement for the target behavior.

It's important to remember that people can do things to get others to reinforce their behavior, including target behaviors. One thing they can do is provide reinforcers to people who reinforce their behavior.

Let's say you're a teacher and you've got a student, call him Mycroft, whose attention span has to be measured in seconds. You manage to bring Mycroft's attentive powers up to something close to his classmates' by reinforcing attentiveness. Naturally, you want that improvement to last not only during the current school year, when you're able to reinforce it regularly, but in subsequent years as well. One thing you might do to achieve that goal is to teach Mycroft to do things that make it likely that those around him will reinforce his attentiveness. And if—

"Excuse me, Dr. Cee, but that seems a little far-fetched."

Alfred?

"You're telling us we're supposed to teach Mycroft to say, 'Hey, I've been paying attention. How about giving me a cookie?'"

Well, Alfred, such an abrupt approach might not work, but that's pretty much the idea. Harry Rosenberg and Paul Graubard did something along those lines.[17] They decided to see if troublesome kids could train teachers to be more reinforcing. They selected seven junior high school students between the ages of 12 and 15. All of the kids were considered incorrigible by their teachers.

Each day the students went to a special class where they learned to record their teachers' behavior and to provide reinforcing consequences for desirable teacher behavior. Desirable teacher behavior included offering help, providing praise, and smiling.[18] The students learned that they could reinforce positive teacher behavior by sitting up straight, smiling, making eye contact, chatting, and offering specific praise such as, "That explanation helped a lot." At first, the kids felt really awkward about doing these things, and they actually had to practice the skills in their special class. However, they were able to put their new skills to good use in their regular classes.

The results were impressive. During the baseline, teacher comments toward the students tended to be negative. When the students began reinforcing desirable teacher behavior, positive teacher comments increased, while negative comments declined. When the kids stopped reinforcing positive teacher behavior, the teachers became more negative; when the students resumed reinforcing desirable teacher behavior, teacher behavior improved again.

This research demonstrates that it is possible to teach people how to obtain reinforcement. If people can obtain reinforcement for a target behavior, that behavior is likely to continue.

A fourth thing we can do to maintain behavior is to:

4. Shape tolerance for delayed and uncertain reinforcement.

In increasing the frequency of a target behavior, and especially in shaping new behavior, it's important to make reinforcement immediate and certain. In the natural environment, however, reinforcement is often delayed and uncertain. If, when an intervention ends, there is an abrupt shift from immediate and certain reinforcement to delayed and uncertain reinforcement, the benefits of the intervention are likely to deteriorate. To prevent this, the intervention should include a gradual transition from nearly ideal reinforcement contingencies to those that resemble the contingencies in the natural environment.

You can shape up tolerance for delayed reinforcement by gradually increasing the length of the interval between the target behavior and delivery of reinforcement. You can continue increasing the length of the interval until it is similar to delays in the natural environment. In addition, since the delays are likely to vary in natural settings, with immediate reinforcement on some occasions and long delays on other occasions, the delays in reinforcement should vary randomly in length during the intervention.

You can apply the same procedure to the reinforcement schedule. You can thin the reinforcement schedule gradually until it resembles the schedule likely to be encountered in the natural environment. In addition, since the ratio of reinforcement is likely to vary in natural settings, with the target behavior frequently reinforced on some occasions and seldom reinforced on other occasions, similar variations should be provided during the intervention.

All right, I have one more trick in my maintenance training bag:

5. Fade the intervention program.

Unless the people conducting an intervention will be able to continue the program indefinitely (as in the case of a residential treatment facility), at some point they will have to terminate it. This should be done gradually.

Suppose the victim of a head injury has spent a year or more in a rehabilitation center. There he has learned to perform the kinds of skills he needs to live independently—shopping for groceries, clothes, and other items; using the public transportation system; paying bills; using the phone; doing the laundry; and so on. Once he is able to perform these skills routinely in the rehabilitation center, he may be ready to live in a halfway house. There he may be largely on his own, but he will have supervision and will be among others who have the same sort of problems he has. Next, he may move into his own apartment in an ordinary apartment building, with someone coming around periodically to see how he is getting on. These periodic visits might be weekly at first, then monthly, then quarterly, then annually. Finally, the man might be entirely on his own. Fading the intervention in this way provides a gradual transition from a somewhat artificial environment to a natural one.

"So fading kind of softens the blow of the natural environment?"

That's well put, Belinda. Yes, there are bound to be differences between the intervention environment and the natural environment no matter how hard we try to make them similar, and these differences can affect performance. By fading the intervention, the person is gradually more and more exposed to those differences while still receiving the support of the intervention.

Well, we're running low on time, so we'd better do a quick review of today's topic.

Review

We began today's lesson by saying there are two basic solutions to the maintenance problem. And they are . . . Belinda?

"Putting the behavior on some sort of maintenance schedule and doing maintenance training."

Good. Now, maintenance schedules are really just reinforcement schedules. Can you tell me what a reinforcement schedule is, John?

"Let's see . . . a reinforcement schedule is a rule for delivering reinforcers. How's that?"

That's good. Now, we talked about fixed and variable schedules. What's a fixed schedule, Alfred?

"That's one that ain't broken."

Very funny. And I'm sure that witty remark will provide some reinforcement for those who are paying attention. But, seriously, what is a fixed schedule?

"That's one where the rule for delivering reinforcers is based on a constant number."

A constant number of what?

"Well, that depends. If it's a fixed ratio schedule, it's a constant number of performances of the target behavior. If it's a fixed interval schedule, it's a constant number of seconds or minutes or some other unit of time since the last reinforcement. If it's a fixed duration schedule, it's a fixed duration of the target behavior."

Good. Now, Midori, what is a variable schedule?

"That's a schedule in which the rule for delivering reinforcers is based on an average."

Yes. So, there are fixed and variable ratio schedules, fixed and variable interval schedules, and fixed and variable duration schedules. What does it mean if a behavior is on an FR-40 schedule, Brian?

"It means that the target behavior has to be performed 40 times to be reinforced. Or, to put it another way, reinforcement is contingent on the behavior occurring 40 times."

Right. And if the behavior is on a VR-40 schedule?

"Then the number of times the behavior has to occur varies, but it averages 40."

Exactly. There are other kinds of reinforcement schedules, and schedules can be combined in complicated ways, but the six schedules we discussed are probably the most important ones in applied behavior analysis. And if the goal is to maintain behavior indefinitely, then probably the ratio schedules are the most important, especially the variable ratio schedules.

Suppose you have established a behavior and you want to maintain that behavior at a constant rate indefinitely. What would you do? Brian?

"I'd probably put the behavior on a very rich VR schedule . . ."

A *rich* schedule?

"Yes. That's a schedule with a low ratio of behavior to reinforcers. In other words, the person doesn't have to perform the behavior very many times to receive a reinforcer."

All right. So you'd put the behavior on a rich VR schedule, and then you would . . . ?

"Then, when the behavior was occurring at a steady rate, I'd start to stretch the ratio."

What does that mean, stretch the ratio?

"It means I'd gradually increase the number of times the behavior has to be performed for reinforcement."

So if you put behavior on a ratio schedule, especially a VR schedule, and stretch the ratio, you can maintain a target behavior at a high rate with occasional reinforcement. But there's a problem: What reinforces the behavior of providing reinforcers? Midori?

"The desired changes in behavior may be reinforcing. If a child behaves better when a parent praises desirable behavior, that may reinforce the parent's tendency to praise desirable behavior. If students learn more when a teacher recognizes good work, that may reinforce the teacher's tendency to recognize good work. If—"

Okay, but in fact parents and teachers and other people often stop providing the reinforcers that maintain desirable behavior. Basically, the problem is that the behavior of providing reinforcers is not adequately reinforced. So how do we arrange the situation so that the parent, the teacher, the employer, and so on will continue to provide reinforcers? Yes, Midori?

"You can set up a contingency contract."

And what is that?

"That's an agreement between the parties that specifies what each party will do. It identifies target behaviors and consequences."

Good. So you can set up a contingency contract to maintain behavior indefinitely, but if you're dealing with a group of people—such as a class, or a work force, or the inmates in a prison—providing the agreed-on reinforcers may be difficult. So in that situation you might set up . . . what, Jamal?

"A token economy?"

Right. And what is a token economy?

"It's a kind of maintenance program in which the reinforcers are tokens. The tokens are distributed when appropriate, and are then exchanged later for . . . whatsyacallums."

Yes. Carlotta, what are those whatsyacallums called?

"Backup reinforcers."

Right. The tokens have little value except in so far as they can be exchanged for backup reinforcers. Now, I mentioned that society operates by means of certain contingency contracts, which I referred to as social contracts.

Unfortunately, social contracts almost always involve aversives: Do X, and you have to pay a fine; do Y and you go to jail; do Z and you might be executed. As a society, we aren't very good about setting up contracts that arrange positive reinforcement of desirable behavior. When we do provide positive reinforcement, it's often noncontingent, as in the case of welfare payments, food stamps, and unemployment checks. Your generation needs to do a better job of making use of what we know about positive reinforcement and contingency contracts to create effective social contracts.

We also talked about maintenance training today. Maintenance training means . . . what, John?

"That means doing things during the intervention that make it more likely that the behavior changes will continue after the intervention."

Good. We discussed five things the behaviorist can do to make the changes in behavior more likely to endure. The first had to do with how long an intervention lasts. How long should the intervention last, Maya?

"You should continue the training even after you achieve the desired changes. You shouldn't stop just because the behavior has changed."

Right. The longer the training program is in effect, the more likely the changes are to persist.

Another maintenance training procedure had to do with exposing the target behavior to something. Can you tell me about that, Midori?

"Yes. You're supposed to expose the target behavior to the natural reinforcers for that behavior. The idea is that the behavior may become trapped by the natural consequences."

Yes, okay. Another procedure we discussed had to do with training the person in certain skills other than the principal target behavior. What skills were they, Carlotta?

"You suggested teaching the person to obtain reinforcement for the target behavior."

Can you give me an example?

"Well, you might teach a student who has trouble in school to ask for help from the teacher. And you might teach him to say thanks when a teacher does offer help."

Why is that a good idea?

"Because ultimately he needs to get help and reinforcers from the natural environment, such as the teachers. If he does that, he's changed his environment so that his own target behavior is more likely to be maintained."

Very good. The fourth procedure we discussed was shaping . . . what, Jamal?

"Tolerance for delayed and uncertain reinforcement."

Yes, natural reinforcers are often delayed and unreliable, so the person needs to be prepared for that. The last suggestion for maintenance training had to do with ending the training program. What's the rule there, Brian?

"Fade the intervention. You should gradually phase out the program rather than abruptly end it."

Yes, good. These five procedures are simply stated and, once stated, seem rather commonsensical. Unfortunately, the intervention program that includes them all, or even gives lip service to them all, is rare. Once the target behavior has changed as desired, the tendency is to announce success and move on to another problem. When that happens, the success of the intervention is likely to be short-lived. It's important to put the target behavior on a maintenance schedule and to include procedures in the intervention that will increase the odds that the changed behavior will stay changed.

Well, that's enough for today. Until next time, be sure to maintain your study behavior.

◄ Exercises ►

Feed the Skeleton

I. Reinforcement Schedules
   A. A reinforcement schedule is _____ .
   B. In a ratio schedule, the reinforcer is contingent on _____

   _____ .

   C. In an interval schedule, the reinforcer is contingent on _____

   _____ .

   D. In duration schedules, the target behavior is _____

   _____ .

II. Maintenance Schedules
    A. A maintenance schedule is _____ .
    B. Gradually increasing the requirement for reinforcement is called

    _____ .

    C. Increasing the requirement for reinforcement too rapidly or too far pro-
    duces _____ .

III. Contingency Contracts
    A. A contingency contract is _____ .
    B. An example of a contingency contract is _____

    _____ .

IV. Token Economy
    A. Token economies always involve _____ .
    B. David Wolfe and his colleagues used a token economy to modify

    _____ .

V. Social Contracts
    A. A social contract is _____ .
    B. An example of a social contract is _____ .

VI. Maintenance Training
    A. Maintenance training is _____ .
    B. Five procedures that will enhance maintenance are:
      1. Continue _____ .
      2. Expose the target behavior to _____ .
      3. Teach the person to obtain _____ .
      4. Shape tolerance for _____

      _____ .

      5. Fade the _____ .

Daffy Advice:
Daphne Donchano Answers Your Questions

Dear Daffy:

    I'm a compulsive gambler. I started with slot machines, but I'll gamble on anything: cards, horses, football games, whatever. When I win, I feel terrific, like I'm on a drug high. When I lose, it's like going through withdrawal; I feel sick, and I *have* to win back the money I've lost to feel good again.

    At first I gambled only what I could afford to lose. Then I borrowed money from my friends, my bank, my co-workers, anybody who'd lend it. I lost my job because I stole things to sell for gambling. After that I started shoplifting. Right now I'm in prison serving 5 years for B&E.

I've made a mess of my life, and I've spent a lot of time trying to figure out why. I've always figured there must be some special weakness in me that makes me this way, like a death wish, lack of willpower, or low self-esteem.

Anyway, I read this article that says compulsive gambling has to do with the fact that every once in a while I get lucky and win. The author said this kind of "intermittent" payoff can keep a person gambling forever. Is there anything to this intermittent payoff stuff, or am I just weak?

Gambling Fool #4791006

Dear Mr. Fool:

You're just weak.

Daffy

What do you think? Can occasional reinforcement maintain a losing behavior such as gambling indefinitely? If so, what sort of schedule would it be?

Contracted Boys

Imagine that you are the parent of two argumentative boys. You decide to sit down with them and help them negotiate a contingency contract. What do they come up with?

Durable Crazy Talk

You may recall a study by Henry Rickard and others (1960) involving a 60-year-old man who said things like, "I have a fractured head and a broken nose because of spinal pressure." The behaviorists found that they could reduce the frequency of crazy talk by systematically ignoring it and showing interest whenever the patient said something sensible. Rickard and company then attempted to make normal speech resistant to the thin reinforcement schedule in the patient's natural environment (the hospital) by reducing the frequency of reinforcement for normal speech: For the first 30 treatment sessions, the therapist reinforced sensible speech about 8 times a minute; during the next 5 sessions, he provided reinforcement about once a minute. Unfortunately, what happened during the last five sessions was that there was a very rapid *decline* in normal speech, from about 30 minutes a session to 7.

What accounted for this failure? If you were in charge of a similar case, what would you do differently?

The Crash

Some people who lost their wealth in the stock market crash of 1929 stepped onto window ledges outside their Wall Street offices and jumped to their deaths. These suicides were commonly explained in terms of thoughts and feelings: Those who jumped couldn't bear to be poor, couldn't face starting over, felt humiliated and defeated, etc. By now I hope you have begun to understand why such answers are useless as explanations. The hypothesized states cannot be independently observed; they merely rename the thing to be explained. But then why *did* some people jump, while others picked themselves up and went to work? It has been said that those who jumped were typically people who had been born wealthy, while those who carried on were those who had made their own fortunes. Assuming that this is true, what implications does this have for training people to deal with life's disappointments?

Practice Quiz

1. Maintenance can be thought of as generalization across _____
   _____ .

2. One indication of ratio strain is an increase in _____ .

3. One way to maintain the effects of an intervention is to set up a(n)
   _____ economy.

4. Maintenance training should include shaping tolerance for _____
   _____ and _____ reinforcement.

5. A reinforcement schedule in which reinforcement is contingent on performing the behavior continuously for a certain period of time is called a
   _____ schedule.

6 A reinforcement schedule in which the number of times a behavior must occur varies around an average is called a _____ schedule.

7. It is often possible to reduce the density of reinforcement from, say, VR 2 to VR 50, by using the procedure known as _____ .

8. A(n) _____ is an agreement between people concerning the behaviors each will perform.

9. Behavior _____ means bringing the behavior under the influence of its natural reinforcers by exposing it to those reinforcers.

10. One thing that can cause ratio strain is _____
    _____ .

Reprint: NOVEL MAINTENANCE
by Irving Wallace

Writing, especially fictional writing, has always seemed a mysterious activity. Where do the writer's ideas come from? In ancient times, creative work of any sort was thought to be due to the influence of a muse. A muse was an immortal creature vested with special talents. The muse of poetry would whisper into the ear of the writer, who would then put down the words that had "entered his mind." When the Gods of Mount Olympus fell, the muses were replaced by "inspiration" that arose mysteriously from within the person. Freud gave inspiration a home in the unconscious mind. Instead of listening to the muse, the writer listened to his "inner voice." Many people still cling to these prescientific ideas about creativity. According to them, the writer must wait for inspiration. It turns out, however, that that is not the way professional writers work. To be successful, they must ply their trade on a regular basis, whether they feel inspired or not. But what keeps a writer writing? What consequences maintain the daily grind of turning out words? Wallace discusses how he and other writers have dealt with this problem.

I kept a work chart when I wrote my first book—which remains unpublished—at the age of nineteen. I maintained work charts while writing my first four published books. These charts showed the date I started each chapter, the date I finished it, and the number of pages written in that period. With my fifth book, I started keeping a more detailed chart, which also showed how many pages I had written by the end of every working day. I am not sure why I started keeping such records. I suspect that it was because, as a free-lance writer, entirely on my own, without employer or deadline, I wanted to create disciplines for myself, ones that were guilt-making when ignored. A chart on the wall served as such a discipline, its figures scolding me or encouraging me.

I had never told anyone about these charts, because I always feared that their existence would be considered eccentric or unliterary. But through the years, I have learned that their usage has not been uncommon among well-known novelists of the fairly recent past. Anthony Trollope, author of more than fifty popular novels including *Barchester Towers*, was perhaps the greatest record-keeper known to literature. In his *Autobiography*, published in 1883, Trollope wrote:

"When I have commenced a new book, I have always prepared a diary, divided into weeks, and carried on for the period which I have allowed myself for the completion of the work. In this I have entered, day by day, the number of pages I have written, so that if at any time I have slipped into idleness for a day or two, the record of that idleness has been there, staring me in the face, and demanding of me increased labour, so that the deficiency might be supplied. According to the circumstances of the time—whether my other business might then be heavy or light, or whether the book I was writing was or was not wanted with speed—I have allotted myself so many pages a week. The average number has been about 40. It has been placed as low as 20, and has risen to 112. And as a page is an ambiguous term, my page has been made to contain 250 words; and as words, if not watched, will have a tendency to straggle, I have had every word counted as I went. . . . There has ever been the record before me, and a week passed with an insufficient number of pages has been a blister to my eye and a month so disgraced would have been a sorrow to my heart.

"I have been told that such appliances are beneath the notice of a man of genius. I have never fancied myself to be a man of genius, but had I been so I think I might well have subjected myself to those trammels. Nothing surely is so potent as a law that may not be disobeyed. It has the force of the water-drop that hollows the stone. A small daily task, if it be really daily, will beat the labours of a spasmodic Hercules."

This revelation, as well as other confessions made by Trollope, indicated that "he treated literature as a trade and wrote by the clock," and this offended literary assessors and damaged his reputation for years after. Yet numerous authors have been just as meticulous about their writing output and about recording it, and they have fared better in the eyes of the literati. Arnold Bennett, for one, devotedly charted in his *Journal* his daily progress, by word count, for each new novel. . . .

Ernest Hemingway is an example of a word or page counter in recent times. According to the *Paris Review*:

"He keeps track of his daily progress—'so as not to kid myself'—on a large chart made out of the side of a cardboard packing case and set up against the wall under the nose of a mounted gazelle head. The numbers on the chart showing the daily output of words differ from 450, 575, 462, 1250, back to 512, the higher figures on days Hemingway puts in extra work so he won't feel guilty spending the following day fishing on the Gulf Stream." . . .

As I have said, from the first day I began writing books, I kept private charts of my work progress . . . and I found this acted as a conscience and a goad.

Excerpted from *The Writing of One Novel,* by I. Wallace. Copyright 1968 Simon & Schuster. Reprinted with permission from the Estate of Irving Wallace. I am indebted to J. J. Pear (1977), whose article brought this material to my attention. For further discussion of this topic, see Wallace & Pear (1977).

◄ Recommended Reading ►

1. Alford, J. (1971). The home token economy: A motivational system for the home. *Corrective Psychiatry and Journal of Social Therapy, 17,* 6–13.

2. Carr, E. G., Levin, L., McConnachie, G., Carlson, J. I., Kemp, D. C., & Smith, C. E. (1994). *Communication-based intervention for problem behavior: A user's guide for producing behavior change.* Baltimore: Paul H. Brookes Co.
   This how-to guide devotes an entire chapter to maintenance. The chapter includes an interesting discussion of some of the reasons for maintenance failure.

3. Ferster, C. B., & Skinner, B. F. (1948). *Schedules of reinforcement.* New York: Appleton-Century-Crofts.

This is the classic on schedules. Although the research described involves animals, the nature and kinds of schedules and their various effects are of interest to those concerned with human behavior.

4. Gray, F., Rosenberg, H., & Graubard, P. (March, 1974). Little brother is changing you. *Psychology Today*, pp. 42–46.
This article describes the research of Harry Rosenberg and Paul Graubard in which students learned to modify the behavior of their teachers.

5. Markowitz, H. (1982). *Behavioral enrichment in the zoo*. New York: Van Nostrand Reinhold.
Markowitz has shown that much of the stereotypical and neurotic behavior of captive animals is a function, not of their unnatural environment, but of the lack of reinforcing activities.

6. Skinner, B. F. (1948). *Walden two*. New York: Macmillan.
Skinner wrote this utopian novel (his only novel) in the early days of behavior analysis. Nevertheless, it shows how society's reliance on aversive contingencies can be replaced with schedules of positive reinforcement.

◄ Endnotes ►

1. Not all schedules are reinforcement schedules, of course. There are punishment schedules, and schedules that provide neither reinforcement nor punishment (the extinction schedule). However, reinforcement schedules are most important when the problem is maintaining behavior over time.

2. Fixed interval schedules are often confused with fixed time schedules. The difference is that in the latter the reinforcer is delivered after a fixed period of time, regardless of what the person does; in a fixed interval schedule, however, reinforcement is contingent on the passage of time and the performance of the target behavior.

3. Reinforcement schedules usually involve positive reinforcement. However, in studying for a test, the reinforcer may be avoiding a poor grade (and the consequences thereof), rather than obtaining a good grade. Although grades are often referred to as positive reinforcers (or rewards), they are probably more likely to be negative reinforcers.

4. Contingency contracts can specify punishing as well as reinforcing consequences, but this is not usually recommended. When parties to a contract agree to punish each other for failure to meet criteria, one likely outcome is that a person who is punished will retaliate by punishing in turn, which can lead to further retaliatory punishment, and so on. Another likely outcome is that the contract will be abandoned. The challenge in human relationships is to find ways of reinforcing desirable behavior; punishment is best avoided.

5. Kahle & Kelley (1994).

6. Madsen, C. H. (1965).

7. The backup reinforcers "purchased" with tokens need to be specified in advance. Tokens, unlike money, cannot be exchanged for an unlimited variety of backup reinforcers.

8. See Alvord (1971).

9. Estimates of how much time children spend watching TV vary but range around 20–30 hours a week. In most states, there are no more than 185 school days in a year, and students typically spend 5 hours of each school day in class. Assuming no absences, that works out to 925 hours of class time a year. A child who watches only 20 hours of TV a week for 50 weeks (a conservative estimate) watches TV a total of 1000 hours in a year. Incidentally, Johnson (1969) has estimated that when the average American reaches age 65, he has spent 9 years of his life watching the tube.

10. Wolfe et al. (1984).

11. Blumstein et al. (1986).

12. Yokley & Glenwich (1984).

13. Numerous studies have demonstrated that creative behavior can be increased through reinforcement. See Winston and Baker (1985) for a review; also see Eisenberger and Selbst (1994).

14. Nevin (1988, 1993); Williams (1938).

15. Ayllon & Michael (1959).

16. Carr et al. (1994) note that the availability of natural reinforcers for behavior should be evaluated before attempting to change a target behavior. They argue that there is little point in teaching skills that will not be maintained by the natural environment.

17. Graubard, Rosenberg, & Miller (1971); Graubard & Rosenberg (1974).

18. Some might suggest that much of what the students were learning was simple good manners: Ask politely for help when you need it, smile and say "thank you" when help is provided, and so on. Many kids learn these skills in the home. The point is that these kids were failing and getting in trouble precisely because they had *not* learned these things in the home.

11

Counterconditioning

WELCOME, WELCOME TO MY HUMBLE PEDAGOGICAL ABODE.

So far in this course we have talked about various procedures for increasing or decreasing the rate of behavior. But what *sort* of behavior? . . . Think back to the beginning of the course. We said that there were two kinds of behavior. They're called . . . yes, Brian?

"Operant and respondent."

Right. Operant behavior is defined as . . . Midori?

"That's the kind of behavior that we think of as voluntary or willful."

Yes, but those are rather vague terms. How did we actually define operant behavior?

"Oh . . . as behavior that is modified by its consequences?"

Exactly. Some people like to say that operant behavior is *sensitive* to its consequences. If a behavior can be modified by its consequences, it's operant. And respondent behavior is modified by . . . ?

"Its antecedents?"

Right. Operant behavior, as you suggested, is often called voluntary, while respondent behavior is often called reflexive or involuntary. But for our purposes, the difference between operant and respondent behavior is in the relative effects of consequences and antecedents.[1]

So far we've talked entirely about how to change operant behavior. Today I want to talk about changing respondent behavior with procedures based on Pavlovian conditioning. So, we'd better begin by reviewing Pavlov's work.

Pavlovian Procedures

Conditioning

The great giant in the study of respondent behavior is Ivan Pavlov. No doubt the name rings a bell. What do you think of when you hear the name Pavlov? John?

"Salivating dogs."

Yes. Pavlov was a Russian physiologist whose special interest was digestion. He studied various aspects of the digestive process in dogs. That process begins when food is taken into the mouth. The salivary glands secrete saliva, which helps break down the food. If Pavlov was to understand digestion, he had to understand the action of the salivary glands. Pavlov would give a dog food and record the amount and nature of the saliva produced.

But Pavlov soon ran into a problem. After he had given a dog food a few times and collected saliva, the dog would begin salivating *before* it received any food. The dog would begin salivating when it saw the food, when it saw a person bringing the food, or even when it heard the footsteps of the person who brought food. This was very annoying. You see, Pavlov wanted to study the nature and amount of saliva produced when various kinds of food were put into a dog's mouth, but the dogs were salivating before they got any food! This is the sort of unanticipated problem that researchers in every field face. Most of the time the researcher finds a way of controlling or working around the problem, and goes on with the original line of work. Fortunately for us, Pavlov decided to shift his attention to the problem of why dogs salivated before they got food.[2]

What Pavlov found was that salivating could be induced by any object that had been regularly paired with food. So, for example, if you repeatedly rang a bell and then put food into a dog's mouth, the dog would begin salivating as soon as it heard the bell. Or if you touched the dog with an object before you put food in its mouth, it would salivate when you touched it. Pavlov even found that a dog would learn to salivate at the sight of a geometric form, such as a circle. He called the procedure by which dogs came to salivate at things other than food *conditioning.*[3]

Pavlovian conditioning: Any procedure by which an event comes to elicit a response by being paired with an event that elicits that response.

Today, it's probably safe to say that almost all college graduates have heard of Pavlov and conditioning. But probably very few have any real understanding of what Pavlov accomplished or of the dramatic ways in which Pavlov changed our lives. He is all too often dismissed as having done nothing more than demonstrate that dogs could be taught to salivate at the sound of a bell. Pavlov himself recognized the implications of his work for dealing with behavior problems, and he even wrote about the application of conditioning to the understanding and treatment of behavior disorders. We'll look at some examples of Pavlov's legacy in a moment; for now, let's review what you know about Pavlovian conditioning.

Pavlov began by noting that if you put food into a dog's mouth, the dog salivated. Pavlov called the food an *unconditional stimulus* and the salivating it induced an *unconditional response*. He called a bell that elicits salivating a *conditional stimulus* and salivating at the sound of a bell a *conditional response*. Does anyone know why Pavlov chose these particular terms? Why would he call salivating at the sound of a bell a *conditional* response? Yes, Carlotta?

"Because it depended on certain conditions?"

Outstanding. That's exactly right.[4]

"It was just a guess."

Ah, but it was a very clever guess. The conditional stimulus and the conditional response depended on certain events; they were conditional. The unconditional stimulus and the unconditional response were the products of evolution. The tendency to salivate when food is put into the mouth doesn't depend on having certain experiences; it is unconditional.

Now, if Pavlovian conditioning involved only bells and salivating, Pavlov's work would be of little interest to behaviorists today. But, in fact, all sorts of events can become conditional stimuli, and all sorts of respondent behavior can become conditional responses.

Arthur and Carolyn Staats showed, for example, that Pavlovian conditioning might help explain how prejudices are learned. In one experiment, college students watched as certain ethnic words, such as *German, Italian,* and *French,* appeared briefly on a screen.[5] At the same time, the students repeated words spoken by the experimenter. The researchers paired most of the nationalities with emotionally neutral words such as *chair, with,* and *twelve.* However, the researchers paired *Swedish* and *Dutch* with emotionally charged words. When *Swedish* appeared on the screen, some students would hear negative words such as *bitter, ugly,* and *failure;* when *Dutch* appeared on the screen, they would hear positive words such as *gift, sacred,* and *happy.* Other students heard positive words when *Swedish* appeared, and negative words when *Dutch* appeared. After this conditioning procedure, the students rated each nationality on a scale. The result was that the feelings associated with the words *Swedish* and *Dutch* depended on the emotional value of the words with which they had been paired.

Pavlovian conditioning has helped us understand all emotional reactions, but fear is of special interest to behaviorists because it is the basis of so much human suffering. One example is provided by the eminent British behaviorist, Hans J. Eysenck: A middle-aged man sought help because of impotence.[6] He had been undergoing psychoanalysis for several years. The analyst concluded that the man suffered from an unresolved Oedipus complex, but this revelation did not improve the couple's sex life. The man then sought the help of a therapist who was interested in conditioning procedures. In his interviews with the man, the therapist discovered some interesting facts: He learned that the man was impotent only in his own home; if he and his wife went away on holiday, there was no problem. The therapist also learned that when the client was a young man, he had an affair with a married woman. One day the husband discovered the pair having intercourse. The husband was much stronger than the youngster and gave him a severe beating. The therapist noted that a painful beating might serve as a powerful unconditional stimulus for fear, and anything in the boy's environment during the beating might become a conditional stimulus for fear. What are some things that might have become conditional stimuli for fear during this experience? Yes, John?

"The man who hit him."

Of course. If you ever had a beating, you probably found yourself feeling fearful whenever you saw the person who hurt you. What else might have become a conditional stimulus for fear? Maya?

"What about the wife?"

Yes, a good possibility. Eysenck doesn't tell us whether the love affair continued, but I rather doubt it. The sight of the woman might very well have aroused fear. What else might arouse fear? Yes, Belinda?

"How about the act of intercourse? He was having intercourse immediately before the beating began."

Excellent point. It seems likely that he would have been anxious the first few times he had intercourse after the beating—even if his partner wasn't someone's wife.

These are all likely candidates for conditional stimuli. But none of these can explain his impotence years later. The man who beat him was not present in his home when he had sex with his own wife; nor was the wife of the man who beat him present; and evidently sexual intercourse itself does not arouse fear, since the client is not always impotent. Clearly, you're missing something. I'll give you a hint by reminding you that the client is impotent *only* in his own home; if he goes to a hotel, he's fine. What does that tell you? . . . Yes, Carlotta?

"It tells me that the CS has to be something in the home, probably something in the bedroom."

Keep going. You're on the right track.

"There might be something about the room itself that is similar to the room where he was beaten."

Excellent! How would you discover what that something was?

"I'd ask him to describe the room in which he was beaten—everything about it. Then I'd ask him to describe the bedroom in his home. I'd look for something that was the same in both cases. Something that probably wouldn't be the same in a hotel. Maybe there was a four-poster bed in each case, or maybe there was a big stuffed chair in both rooms, or—"

"Maybe there was a big mirror on the ceiling!"

"Only you would think of something like that, Alfred. Anyway, I'd keep looking for something that was the same in both bedrooms that probably wouldn't be the same in a hotel."

Very impressive, Carlotta. And what your search would turn up, in this case, is not the kind of bed, or a chair, or a mirror on the ceiling. It was the wallpaper! The bedroom where the man was impotent had wallpaper that was very similar to the wallpaper in the bedroom where the beating had occurred. The wallpaper had become a conditional stimulus for fear, which prevented him from performing sexually. He had no problem having intercourse in other places, such as hotel rooms, because the wallpaper was different.

"But how could the wallpaper be a conditional stimulus in the dark?"

Ah! That's a good question, Midori. The answer is that this couple did their love making with the lights on. So the man *could* see the wallpaper.

> "So you're saying this fellow sees the wallpaper in his room, and he thinks, 'Wow! That's just like the wallpaper in the room where I got beat up. I better watch it or I might get beaten again.'"

No, Alfred, I'm *not* saying that. But that's a very common misunderstanding of Pavlovian conditioning. People assume that the environment has to be interpreted, that we have to think about the environment before it can affect our behavior. They assume, for example, that the dog hears the bell and thinks, "Oh, boy! That means food is coming." But we have no reason to think that such thoughts are required for conditioning to occur. In fact, if the Wallpaper Man, as he is called, had thought of the beating when he looked at the wallpaper, he probably would have realized that the wallpaper was causing his problem and he wouldn't have spent all that time and money on psychoanalysis.

Okay. Let's suppose the Wallpaper Man is your client. You've questioned him and discovered that the wallpaper in his bedroom seems to be a CS that elicits fear. It is often difficult to maintain an erection when one is afraid, hence his impotence. At least, that's your theory. But that explanation doesn't, in itself, cure the problem any more than blaming it on Oedipus did. So, what do you do? Yes, Brian?

"Advise him to repaper his bedroom."

Of course! If the wallpaper is the source of the difficulty, then eliminating the wallpaper should eliminate the problem. If it doesn't, then there's something wrong with your theory. The therapist recommended that the man repaper the bedroom, and when he had, the impotence disappeared completely. There was no need for extensive therapy of any sort.

The case of the Wallpaper Man illustrates the way in which conditioning, the same sort of conditioning Pavlov used in his studies of salivating dogs, can contribute to behavior problems. But the case is far from typical. Most of the people who seek help for an unpleasant emotional reaction cannot simply remove the item that arouses fear the way the Wallpaper Man removed the troublesome wallpaper.

A person who is terrified of spiders cannot altogether eliminate spiders from his surroundings. A person who is afraid of heights cannot eliminate tall buildings. Sometimes feared objects can be avoided but only at a great cost. A business executive who is terrified of flying on airplanes must either fly and endure great discomfort or avoid flight and put her job at risk.

Most fears seem to be the products of Pavlovian conditioning. Fortunately, they usually can be eliminated by conditioning. The use of conditioning to undo the undesirable effects of conditioning is called counterconditioning:

> ### Counterconditioning:
> ### The use of Pavlovian conditioning to undo
> ### the adverse effects of earlier conditioning.

The first time conditioning was ever used to eliminate a fear under controlled conditions was when Mary Cover Jones treated a 3-year-old boy named Peter.[7]

Peter was afraid of rabbits. He would become quite upset when a rabbit was placed near him. No one knows just how Peter came by his fear, but presumably rabbits, or something closely resembling rabbits, had been paired with some sort of painful or frightening event. In any case, Jones decided to see if she could use the same sort of conditioning to undo his fear. She began by introducing a rabbit at some distance from Peter while he enjoyed some crackers and milk. The rabbit was far enough away that it did not disturb Peter in the least. In this way, Jones paired the conditional stimulus (a rabbit) with an unconditional stimulus (crackers and milk). In other words, she paired something that elicited negative emotions with something that elicited positive emotions.

The next day, Jones brought the rabbit a little closer, but not so close that it made the child uneasy. On each successive day, Jones brought the rabbit closer, always being careful not to bring it close enough to upset Peter. This continued until Peter showed no fear even when the rabbit was placed in his lap. In the end, Peter would eat with one hand and play with the rabbit with the other.

Counterconditioning *counters* the effects of naturally occurring conditioning, hence its name. It consists of pairing a stimulus that elicits inappropriate respondent behavior with a stimulus that elicits appropriate respondent behavior. There are two main types of counterconditioning: desensitization training and sensitization training.

Desensitization Training

In desensitization training, counterconditioning is used to reduce the strength of a negative emotional response to a particular kind of stimulus or situation:

> ### Desensitization training:
> ### Any form of counterconditioning that reduces
> ### an inappropriate negative response to an event.

This is accomplished by pairing the stimulus that elicits a negative emotional reaction with another stimulus that elicits a positive reaction. This can be done in various ways, but the most commonly used procedure is systematic desensitization.

Systematic Desensitization

Systematic desensitization was devised by Joseph Wolpe, a very prominent behavior therapist. For the sake of simplicity, I will concentrate on its application to the treatment of phobias; however, it can and has been used with other problems, including obsessions, compulsions, and anxiety. Wolpe's procedure consists basically of three steps: constructing a hierarchy; relaxation training; and counterconditioning.

Constructing a hierarchy means identifying the kinds of situations that arouse fear (or other inappropriate emotions) and arranging them in a hierarchy from least to most upsetting. At the top of the hierarchy would be a situation that makes the person profoundly uncomfortable; at the bottom of the hierarchy would be a situation that causes no discomfort whatsoever.

Take the case of Peter and the rabbit. Systematic desensitization hadn't been developed in Peter's day, and Mary Cover Jones did not construct a hierarchy of situations involving rabbits. However, I think you can surmise from her study that she *assumed* a kind of hierarchy. Can anyone describe it to me? Yes, Midori?

> "Well, she started with the rabbit far away from Peter, so I think she was assuming that there was a hierarchy based on nearness of the rabbit. Peter was afraid of the rabbit when it was close by, but not when it was far off."

Yes. There's an implied hierarchy that progresses from having the rabbit far away to having it nearby. Now let's take the person who is afraid of flying in airplanes. At the top of his hierarchy might be sitting on an airplane as it takes off; next might be sitting on an airplane as it prepares for take off. Boarding a plane might also be very frightening, but not as scary as being seated on one. Preparing to board a plane might be next on the hierarchy, followed by sitting in the boarding area of the airport. Entering the airport might be still less nerve-racking, followed by approaching the airport, driving to the airport, leaving the house for the airport, packing a bag, and making a plane reservation. Planning a trip might cause no disturbance at all, so this would be at the bottom of the hierarchy.

Usually there is a sort of logic to the arrangement of items in a hierarchy. However, a hierarchy is not created on the basis of intuition or armchair reasoning. It might be the case, for example, that driving to the airport is more frightening than sitting in the boarding area; or boarding the plane might be scarier than sitting on the plane. The relative fearfulness of situations must be determined by the reactions they evoke in the client, not by what seems logical to the therapist.

The therapist determines the relative fearfulness of situations by asking the client about situations that arouse fear. He may also make use of various other tools, such as the *Fear Survey Schedule,* which Wolpe and a colleague developed.[8] From a scientific point of view, the best way to determine the fearfulness of a situation might be to measure physiological reactions to that situation. For example, the galvanic skin response (or GSR) registers fear by measuring changes in the electrical conductivity of the skin. In actual practice, however, physiological measures are not normally required to construct a good hierarchy.

This last point needs some explaining. Wolpe talks about "subjective units of disturbance," or SUDS. He attempts to measure the degree of disturbance caused by situations in terms of SUDS. The bottom item on the hierarchy should not be disturbing at all, so it has a value of 0 SUDS. The top item on the hierarchy, the most disturbing one, should have a value of 100 SUDS.

"How many items should there be in the hierarchy?"

That's a good question, Maya. There is no prescribed number. However, there should be enough items to meet certain conditions: The lowest item should arouse no discomfort; the highest should be extremely disturbing; and the differences separating the various items should be uniform and small. This implies that there should be at least 10 items in a hierarchy. However, there could be many more than that. A typical hierarchy, if there is such a thing, might have 30 or 40 items.

Once the therapist and client have constructed a hierarchy, the next step is relaxation training. A physician named Edmund Jacobson developed a procedure called *progressive relaxation.*[9] Jacobson realized that some people suffer from a variety of symptoms because they are contracting muscles inappropriately, often without any awareness that they are doing so. They might, for example, grind their teeth; or they might frown or flex their back muscles even when sitting in a chair.

Jacobson knew that a person cannot simultaneously contract and relax a given set of muscles at the same time. The trouble was that a lot of people contracted muscles unnecessarily, without realizing they were doing so. Jacobson discovered that he could teach these people to relax by prompting them to tense and then relax various muscle groups. In this way they would learn to recognize the difference between tense and relaxed muscles. Then, during the day, if they began to tense muscles inappropriately, they might notice it and then deliberately relax them.

Wolpe thought that relaxation could be used in counterconditioning. By systematically pairing a frightening situation with relaxation, the situation will come to elicit relaxation rather than fear. So Wolpe teaches his clients relaxation techniques.

Not everyone who uses systematic desensitization today does relaxation training. Some simply help the client identify a situation that the person finds pleasant, such as a peaceful bucolic scene. Imagining this scene is relaxing, and it is used in counterconditioning.

The third, and usually the longest, step in systematic desensitization is *counterconditioning*. In this step, the therapist systematically pairs situations in the hierarchy with relaxation or with a relaxing scene.

The procedure, as Wolpe developed it, is this: The person is asked to imagine the first item in the hierarchy—a situation that is not distressing. The therapist emphasizes the importance of imagining the scene very clearly, usually with eyes closed. The therapist may aid this process by describing the scene graphically to the client. He may also ask the client to describe what he sees to ensure that he is really visualizing the situation.

If at any time the client begins to feel the least bit anxious, he is to signal this to the therapist, usually by raising the index finger of one hand. When this happens, the therapist instructs him to stop imagining the disturbing scene and to relax. The therapist also looks for subtle indications of distress, such as a furrowed brow, tenseness of the limbs, or faster breathing; if he sees such signs he tells the client to stop imagining the scene, even if the client hasn't signaled that he feels uncomfortable.

After relaxing several seconds, the client is again asked to imagine the disturbing scene. When the client is able to imagine a situation for 10 seconds, the therapist signals him to stop and relax. After doing so for a short while, the therapist asks the client to imagine the situation again. When the client can imagine a situation twice for 10 seconds without feeling anxious, he is ready to advance to the next item in the hierarchy.

By repeatedly pairing the imagined situations in the hierarchy with either relaxation or some relaxing scene, the client is able to work his way up the hierarchy without ever feeling any significant amount of discomfort. In fact, if the client ever feels really afraid, the therapist has made a mistake. With systematic desensitization, the scariest part of treating a phobia is going to the therapist's office in the first place. The treatment itself is almost free of any discomfort.

"How long does this treatment take?"

That varies, John. Some people have gone through an entire hierarchy in one session. Others may need several sessions for each item in the hierarchy. The rate of progress depends on how severe the fear is, how long it has endured, whether the client does the homework assignments, and so on. This is a kind of therapy in which the client is clearly in control. The client decides when it is time to stop imagining a situation, so the client determines how fast he progresses up the hierarchy. With one or two sessions a week, treatment of a severe phobia would probably require somewhere between a few weeks and a few months.

"Did you say something about homework?"

Oh, yes. I should explain, Midori. Some therapists may ask the client to practice visualizing situations at home that they have been able to visualize in the therapy session without discomfort. These outside exercises are sometimes called home-work. Doing homework may affect the rate of progress through the hierarchy.

Now, there's a good deal more to systematic desensitization, but this summary will suffice. Let's take a look at some studies that illustrate its use and effectiveness.

One case involved a woman who became frightened in traffic related situa-tions. Mrs. C, as Wolpe called her, was a woman of 39 years who had been in a traffic accident. The car in which she was a passenger was struck by a truck that had run a red light. Mrs. C was not seriously injured, but she was thrown from the car and spent a week in the hospital because of injuries to her knee and neck. After this experience, Mrs. C became very anxious in certain kinds of traffic situ-ations. She was particularly upset when entering an intersection when other vehi-cles were approaching the intersection.

Wolpe drew a sketch meant to represent two cars, one of them facing north, the other west. The cars were about two blocks apart. Mrs. C was to imagine that she was in the car facing north, while the other car was occupied by a Dr. Garnett, a man she knew and trusted. Wolpe then asked Mrs. C to imagine Dr. Garnett driving his car a half-block toward her as she sat in her own car. Imagining this scene evoked no anxiety, so Wolpe asked Mrs. C to imagine Dr. Garnett driving one block toward her, and then one and a quarter blocks. This last scene caused some anxiety, and Wolpe had her repeat it three times. The scene, however, con-tinued to be upsetting, so Wolpe asked her to imagine Dr. Garnett traveling one block *and two paces* toward her before stopping. This produced a slight reaction, which diminished with repetition. After four exposures, the scene caused no reac-tion. After this, Wolpe was able to increase the distance traveled by Dr. Garnett until finally she was able to imagine him approaching to within two yards of her vehicle without any discomfort.

Wolpe then began working on a new series of scenes in which Dr. Garnett drove in front of Mrs. C's car. The first scene was of Dr. Garnett's car passing at a distance of 30 feet. Each succeeding scene reduced this distance. Finally, Mrs. C was able to imagine Dr. Garnett passing in front of her car at a distance of about three yards. At this point, Wolpe—

"This sounds like more than one hierarchy."

Oh, yes. Good point. Systematic desensitization is usually described as though there were only one hierarchy that the client works through. But, as this case illustrates, it is sometimes more complicated than that. Sometimes there is a series of hierarchies, each of which desensitizes the person to a distinct series of scenes. The first hierarchy includes scenes that are originally less stressful than later hier-archies. I suppose you could say there is a hierarchy of hierarchies.

Wolpe proceeded through these hierarchies, each dealing with a different aspect of traffic. It took 57 treatment sessions, including just under 1500 scene presentations, before Mrs. C was completely at ease in all normal traffic situations.

These presentations took her through 36 different hierarchies. The first three of these hierarchies were ineffective: They aroused too much anxiety and had to be abandoned. These three hierarchies represent miscalculations on Wolpe's part about where to start treatment. I mention this, not as a criticism of Wolpe, but because it illustrates that the apparent simplicity of systematic desensitization is somewhat deceptive. You have a question, Carlotta?

"Are you telling us that this woman overcame her fear just by *imagining* scary situations? Doesn't the therapist have to expose the client to the actual situations?"

Not usually. Of course, the client is encouraged to participate in real situations related to his hierarchy, but only if they don't arouse anxiety.

"And when the person is able to imagine a situation, he's then able to be *in* that situation?"

Hard to believe, isn't it? You're right to be skeptical. What we're talking about is generalization: Changes in behavior in one situation occur in other situations as well. You're surprised that Wolpe got generalization from the therapy sessions to real-life traffic situations because . . . because why? Midori?

"I suppose because *imagining* a situation is very different from *being in* a situation."

Exactly. Generalization occurs when the test situation is similar to the training situation, but the training and testing situations seem very different in this instance. So it is surprising that the results generalize. Yet the results that Wolpe got with Mrs. C are typical; improvements in therapy sessions *do* generalize to real-life situations.

Now, Mrs. C is fairly typical of the people treated with systematic desensitization: She was quite normal in every respect except for a phobic reaction to certain kinds of situations. However, systematic desensitization has been used successfully to treat problems other than phobias.

Wolpe reports the use of systematic desensitization to treat chronic kleptomania in a 36-year-old woman he called Mrs. U.[11] A probation officer referred Mrs. U for treatment after she had been arrested and was facing possible imprisonment.

When Wolpe interviewed Mrs. U, he found that she felt very tense whenever she was in a store and the opportunity to steal something arose. If she were in a department store and no one was around her, so that she could easily take something without being seen, she would feel tense; if she were to try to leave the store without stealing, her tension would increase. Wolpe decided to try desensitizing Mrs. U to these situations.

With Mrs. U's help, Wolpe established a hierarchy of situations in which she might have stolen something but didn't. In one scene, for example, she was outside a supermarket where she might have stolen a can of tuna fish but had not.

After training her in relaxation, Wolpe and Mrs. U worked their way through the hierarchy. The situation in which Mrs. U imagined herself outside a supermarket produced a rating of 30 SUDS on the first presentation, but the rating fell to 0 by the third presentation. As she progressed up the hierarchy, the dollar value of the imagined items she might have taken increased steadily.

The treatment was apparently very successful. Mrs. U reported experiencing a wonderful feeling of freedom in shops because she no longer felt compelled to steal things. Wolpe tells us that there had been apparently no relapses at a 15-month follow-up.

"Dr. Cee?"

Yes, Maya?

"I thought desensitization was for treating respondent behavior."

Yes, that's right.

"Well, isn't stealing operant behavior?"

An excellent question, Maya. And yes, stealing *is* operant behavior. But Wolpe was treating the feeling of tension Mrs. U experienced when she did not steal. This feeling is respondent behavior.

Systematic desensitization is usually used to help people who are functioning pretty well except for a phobia, a compulsion, or other isolated problem. However, it has sometimes been used in people with psychotic disorders. As an illustration, let's take a case reported by Richard Cowden and Leon Ford.[12] The case involves a 27-year-old man with a diagnosis of paranoid schizophrenia. Cowden and Ford don't give him a name, but I will call him Sam. Sam admitted himself to the hospital after he threatened to kill members of his family. In addition to his aggressive impulses, Sam had hallucinations and delusions, including delusions of persecution. While in the hospital, he received insulin coma therapy, tranquilizers, and psychotherapy but showed little improvement.

One of Sam's problems was that he was unable to talk to other people without becoming extremely frightened. Certain topics, such as anger, sex, and his family, were particularly stressful for him. When talking about them he would tremble, chain smoke, and become tearful.

Sam agreed to undergo systematic desensitization. His hierarchy began with easy tasks, such as talking about a movie he had seen or talking with someone about current events, and progressed to more difficult tasks, such as talking about personal difficulties with family members.

One problem that arose in treating Sam was that he was not entirely cooperative. For instance, he refused to raise his hand to indicate when a scene bothered him. The therapist dealt with that particular problem by relying on subtle indications of distress, such as changes in breathing and tensing of the body. The client also refused to follow instructions concerning relaxation exercises outside of therapy sessions. He would lie down rather than sit while practicing relaxation, and then he always fell asleep!

Nevertheless, the treatment was quite successful. After 18 sessions, spread over a period of about 3 months, Sam's ability to talk with others was much improved. He still felt some discomfort when talking in groups if others in the group were very talkative, but otherwise he showed marked improvement. In psychotherapy sessions, he was able to talk freely and at length about things he had not mentioned in over 3 years.

Interestingly, systematic desensitization had some positive side effects. About halfway through the treatment program, the hospital staff began to report not only that Sam was more talkative but that he seemed more relaxed and friendly as well. Sam also was less often troubled by unusual thoughts and dreams, smoked less, and began going home on passes. I am not suggesting that Sam was cured; however, there seems little doubt that systematic desensitization helped him a good deal when nothing else had.

Wolpe's procedure has proved remarkably effective with a wide variety of clients and problems. However, in the 40 years since Wolpe introduced systematic desensitization, several variations of the procedure have been tried. I'll briefly discuss some of these variations.

In Vivo Desensitization

Systematic desensitization uses imagined situations as conditional stimuli. It is possible, however, to use actual situations when doing desensitization. This procedure is called in vivo desensitization.

The words, *in vivo,* mean, literally, "in life." Instead of imagining a disturbing scene, the client actually confronts the scene. Instead of imagining that you are riding in a car, for example, you would actually ride in a car. The therapist still constructs hierarchies, does relaxation training, and provides counterconditioning. It's just that the situations involved are real rather than imagined.[13]

It might seem that in vivo desensitization would be the more "natural" procedure for a behaviorist to use. But you have to remember that when behaviorists speak of behavior, they do not necessarily limit themselves to overt behavior. Imagining is something people do, so it qualifies as behavior.

"But I don't see why everyone doesn't use in vivo desensitization. Why not just use real-life situations?"

A fair question, Alfred. Who would like to answer it? Yes, Belinda?

"If I were a therapist, I don't think I'd want to have snakes in my office."

Yes, that gets at the chief disadvantage of in vivo therapy: It's often inconvenient to provide real situations. If someone is afraid of snakes, and you're going to do in vivo desensitization, then you've got to have a collection of snakes. And if you're going to treat people who are afraid of spiders, then you've got to have a collection of spiders. Then there's dogs, cats, birds, and so on. You end up with a ware-house full of animals. Or you have to take the person to a place where these animals can be found, such as a zoo or an animal shelter. And what do you do if the situations you need to provide can't be fitted into your office? How do you do in vivo desensitization if the problem is a fear of flying? Alfred?

"I guess you'd have to take the person to an airport. You'd have to get them on a real plane."

Right. And if they're afraid of elevators, you have to take them to a building with elevators. If they're afraid of heights, you have to take them up tall buildings. The same thing is true if the problem is something other than a phobia. If a person has a compulsion to sing whenever he's in a public park, then you've got to take him to parks.

So in vivo desensitization is often inconvenient and time consuming for the therapist and the client. Systematic desensitization is much more efficient and, if the research is to be believed, it seems to work about as well as the in vivo variation.

Self-Desensitization

Another variation of Wolpe's procedure is for the client to undergo the procedure without the help of a therapist. This is called self-desensitization.[14] The idea is that people can build hierarchies, teach themselves relaxation, and perform the necessary counterconditioning procedures on their own, provided that they receive some basic instruction.

The critical question about self-desensitization is whether people can do the job as well as a therapist. Some research evidence suggests that many people may do quite well on their own. A study by G. M. Rosen and others found that systematic desensitization was as effective when self-administered as when administered by a therapist.[15]

In a way, this is not terribly surprising, since the procedure doesn't always require years of training and experience. Some caveats are, however, in order: First, while it may be true that many people can successfully treat themselves, there is a question about whether they will do so. People often *intend* to study a subject on their own but never actually hit the books; many people need the structure and support of a class. In the same way, many people might intend to go through systematic desensitization on their own but never get around to it; they need the structure and constraints that come with being in therapy. Second, some problems are more challenging than others. People who attempt to treat themselves may run into problems, and this could discourage them from continuing with treatment.

I suppose the bottom line is that if people study systematic desensitization and feel comfortable with trying it on their own, they might very well do so. But they should be prepared to turn to a professional if they get into trouble or don't make satisfactory progress.

Flooding

The critical difference between systematic desensitization and flooding is that the latter abandons the hierarchy and the gradual pace of therapy.[16] Instead, the client is asked to imagine the most upsetting situation right from the beginning. A person who is afraid of snakes, for example, might be asked to imagine holding a nonpoisonous snake in his hands. A person who is claustrophobic might be asked to imagine being locked in a broom closet or an elevator. The therapist not only asks the client to imagine the frightening scene, he repeatedly describes it for her. This exposure continues until the conditional response, the anxiety, no longer occurs.[17]

Flooding has two main drawbacks. First, the therapy session is *necessarily* anxiety-provoking. The object is to expose the person to a fearful situation until it no longer evokes discomfort. This is markedly different from systematic desensitization, where great effort is taken to avoid provoking severe anxiety. The fact that flooding arouses strong anxiety does not, in itself, condemn it; after all, undergoing surgery arouses anxiety, but the surgery is often helpful. However, most people with phobias have spent years avoiding the situations that frighten them. If a therapy exposes people to the terrifying experiences they have always avoided, they may avoid the therapy.

Second, there is less room for error in flooding than in systematic desensitization. A person exposed to a very disturbing scene may become extremely agitated by it. He may become panicky, start to scream, and hyperventilate. If the therapist then terminates the presentation of the scene, the client has escaped an aversive situation. In other words, the panic, the screaming, and the hyperventilating have all been . . . what, Carlotta?

"Reinforced?"

Yes. And what kind of reinforcement is it?

"Negative reinforcement?"

Right. Panic, screaming, and hyperventilating become ways of escaping from the scary situation. And that means we've made the problem worse, not better. So, flooding requires that the exposure to the upsetting scene continue *until the anxiety passes*. It's only when the person is no longer distressed by a scene that the presentation can be ended.

This means, of course, that flooding is a rather stressful and unpleasant form of therapy. That's the great appeal of Wolpe's systematic desensitization: It's a practically painless way of overcoming phobias, obsessions, and certain other behavior problems.

Controlled studies of systematic desensitization have demonstrated it is highly effective. Self-administered desensitization, in which the client doubles as his or her own therapist, also seems to be effective. There is some debate about whether the *in vivo* variation of the procedure is more or less effective than imagining the relevant stimuli. However, both procedures seem to get good results. The case for flooding is more problematic. The procedure also involves some risk, since if the flooding procedure is interrupted at the wrong time, it may negatively reinforce the target behavior and make the problem worse, rather than better. Flooding is definitely not something for novices like yourselves to be trying.

Desensitization, in its various forms, makes good use of counterconditioning to modify respondent behavior. So does sensitization training.

Sensitization Training

In sensitization training, counterconditioning is used to reduce the strength of a positive emotional response:

> ### Sensitization training:
> ### Any form of counterconditioning that reduces
> ### an inappropriate positive response to an event.

This is accomplished by pairing the stimulus that elicits a positive emotional reaction with another stimulus that elicits a negative reaction. This can—

"What's wrong with having a positive emotional reaction toward something?"

A fair question, Jamal. Notice that I said an *inappropriate* positive reaction. Can anyone think of a situation in which it is inappropriate for a person to have a positive emotional reaction to a stimulus? . . . Yes, John?

"How about people who are seriously overweight. Isn't that a case of liking food too much?"

Yes, that's a good example. Any others? Midori?

"What about alcohol? Some people are overly fond of it, aren't they?"

Indeed they are. What else? Belinda?

"Drugs, such as cocaine and marijuana."

Right. Sensitization training has been used to treat people who consume too much of certain substances, such as food and drugs. Other kinds of stimuli can also elicit positive emotional reactions that society considers inappropriate. Can anyone suggest an example? Carlotta?

"Some people are sexually attracted to children."

Yes. Pedophilia literally means love of children, but the term refers to sexual interest in children. Pedophiles are attracted to children and often will have sexual experiences with them, given the opportunity.

So pedophilia and certain other sexual disorders, excessive use of alcohol or other drugs—these are common examples of problems in which stimuli elicit inappropriate positive reactions. Sensitization training involves reducing these inappropriate positive reactions with counterconditioning. This can be done in various ways, but perhaps the most commonly used procedure is aversion therapy.

Aversion Therapy

As the name implies, aversion therapy involves the use of aversives. You will recall that an aversive stimulus is one that . . . what, Midori?

"A person will escape or avoid, given the opportunity?"

Right. Like desensitization, aversion therapy is a form of counterconditioning. In this case, however, the conditional stimulus is paired with a stimulus that elicits a negative emotional response. The idea is to reduce the attraction the person feels for the conditional stimulus.[18]

One of the earliest cases treated with aversion therapy is the Pram Man, reported by M. J. Raymond in 1956.[19] The Pram Man was a 33-year-old married man who was sexually aroused by perambulators, or prams, now better known as baby carriages. Unfortunately for all concerned, he not only got excited by them, he attacked them. This fellow had a long history of assaults on prams: He would throw oil on them, slash them, or attempt to set them on fire. On one occasion, he rode a motorcycle into a pram that had a baby in it. He also had a thing about handbags, and would damage them whenever he got the chance. He had had these impulses since he was about 10 years old and made attacks an average of 2 or 3 times a week.

By the time he was seen by Raymond, the Pram Man had been in mental hospitals and had received many hours of psychoanalysis. The therapy had led to the hypothesis that certain early experiences with handbags and prams were responsible for the fact that they aroused him. This insight, however, did nothing to stem the arousal or the attacks. He was considered dangerous, and when he was finally seen by Raymond, the medical staff was considering a prefrontal leucotomy, a surgical procedure in which the frontal lobes are deliberately damaged. The fact that drastic treatment was being considered suggests a conviction on the part of the medical staff that desperate measures were indicated.

"Do you mean the doctors were going to carve up this guy's brain, like in that movie, *One Flew Over the Cuckoo's Nest*?"

That's about it, Alfred. Luckily, he escaped this terrible fate thanks to aversion therapy. Raymond treated the man by producing prams and handbags, or pictures of them, just before a nausea-inducing drug took effect. The man would look at the pram or handbag and then get sick to his stomach. The sexually arousing objects were paired with nausea in this way repeatedly. After five days of intensive treatment, he complained that the sight of the objects made him sick. After another week of treatment, he no longer reported having any sexual arousal at seeing prams or handbags and felt no impulse to attack them. He was followed up some months later and apparently had had no recurrence of the problem.

Another problem that has been treated with aversion therapy is transvestism—the wearing of clothes intended for the opposite sex. Usually, transvestites are men who dress in women's clothing. Sometimes the cross-dressing consists merely of wearing a single undergarment, such as women's panties. Other times it involves dressing in an entire set of women's clothes. Many transvestites cross-dress only in the privacy of their own homes; others go out in public and attempt to pass as women.

Psychoanalysts typically attribute transvestism to unconscious sexual-identity conflicts. It might be suggested, for example, that a man cross-dresses because unconsciously he wants to seduce not his mother (as is "normal" in psychoanalytic theory) but his father. Cross-dressing is then supposed to be a disguise to fool the father.

As you must know by now, behaviorists take a different approach; they assume that such behavior is learned and that it can often be unlearned. Cross-dressing usually does little harm to anyone, so behaviorists typically treat it only if the cross-dresser wants help in changing the behavior. Sometimes this happens—as, for example, when a man is afraid his cross-dressing will be discovered and prove embarrassing or detrimental to his marriage or career.

N. I. Lavin and colleagues used aversion therapy to treat a 22-year-old married truck driver who was sexually aroused by dressing in women's clothing and looking at himself in a mirror.[20] I'll call him Howard. Howard's interest in cross-dressing began when he was 8 years old, and he had received sexual pleasure from cross-dressing since the age of 15.

The therapists began by taking a dozen slides of Howard wearing women's clothes. They also made a tape recording of the man describing himself as he put on female clothes. Next they began pairing these stimuli with nausea. He was given a nausea-inducing drug, and as soon as it began to take effect, the therapists projected one of the slides on a screen and played the tape recording. The slides and recording were paired with nausea every 2 hours for 6 days and nights. Over the next 3 months the client and his wife reported no recurrence of cross-dressing. Six months after treatment ended, the client reported that the problem had not returned. No new symptoms or problems appeared.

The aversive stimulus used in aversion therapy is most often either an emetic (nausea-inducing) drug or electric shock. However, all sorts of noxious stimuli have been used with good results. M. Serber, for example, found that being observed was an effective aversive in the treatment of voyeurism.[21] Serber had his client look through a one-way glass (he could see others; they couldn't see him) and observe someone undressing. As he did so, other people in the room with him watched *him* as he did his Peeping Tom act. He found being observed in the act of voyeurism embarrassing, so Serber paired sight of a woman disrobing with an experience that caused embarrassment. As a result, spying on others lost its appeal. Other aversives that have been used in aversion therapy include intense lights, white noise, and unpleasant odors.

Aversion therapy is the best-known sensitization procedure. There are, however, others; one of the more popular is covert sensitization.

Covert Sensitization

Like aversion therapy, covert sensitization consists of pairing an object or situation that arouses positive feelings with one that arouses negative feelings. The difference is that in covert sensitization, the objects or situations are merely imagined.

Covert sensitization was pioneered by Joseph Cautela.[22] Typically, Cautela describes an unpleasant situation in graphic detail and asks the client to visualize it. In one case, the client was a 29-year-old nurse who drank excessively on dates. When she got to drinking, she often did things she later regretted. Cautela asked the woman to imagine that she was on a date. In the imagined scene, she is seated at a table in a restaurant and has just ordered a drink. Just as she reaches for it, she begins to feel sick to her stomach. As she holds the glass, she feels she is about to vomit. Nevertheless, she puts the glass to her lips, but as she does so she vomits all over the table and the floor.

I notice expressions of disgust on some of your faces. It is interesting, isn't it, how merely imagining an unpleasant scene can produce strong, negative reactions, such as disgust and even nausea? Some people can imagine such scenes so well, even to the point of being able to smell the vomit, that they become physically ill.

Anyway, when the nurse could imagine the scene clearly, she raised a finger. At that point Cautela would have her stop and he would describe another scene, such as being at a party, taking a drink, and throwing up all over the hostess's dress. Cautela—

"Wouldn't that treatment cause a problem?"

Brian? How do you mean?

"Well, Cautela is pairing typical dating scenes—a restaurant, a party—with illness and the embarrassment of throwing up on people. I can see that this might help make drinking less attractive, but wouldn't it also make being in restaurants and at parties less attractive, too?"

That's a very astute observation. And you're right, it probably would—except that Cautela also had the nurse imagine being in these scenes *without* taking a drink and *without* getting sick. It's only when the nurse imagines drinking in these situations that she imagines getting sick. The nurse soon went on a date without having a drink, the first time she had done that in five years. During a follow-up 8 months after treatment, she reported no drinking problems.

Although case-study evidence for sensitization training is strong, controlled scientific evidence for its effectiveness is limited. In particular, sensitization training has produced disappointing results in the treatment of addictions, including alcohol and tobacco addictions, despite a great many attempts. For example, Azrin and Powell found that a majority of people in a smoking cessation program involving aversion therapy either did not deliver the self-administered shocks as required or dropped out of the program.[23] Sensitization training is therefore limited to people who are "highly motivated"—that is, those whose problem behavior is more unpleasant to them than the aversives used in treatment.[24]

Not surprisingly, sensitization training brings with it the same sort of problems associated with punishment, including ethical objections. Our society relies a great deal on aversives, so students who have learned a little something about sensitization training are, I suppose, likely to want to try it out. I can only say that if you do, you are playing with matches, and you must expect to get burned. Leave sensitization training to the experts.

Before we leave the topic of counterconditioning, I want to say just a bit about rules therapists follow to improve its effectiveness.

Rules for Counterconditioning

Many experimental studies with counterconditioning have demonstrated that it is an effective way of modifying respondent behavior. However, as with other procedures for changing behavior, good results depend on proper use. In the case of counterconditioning, four rules are especially important. The first, you should be able to guess. What is it, Maya?

"Define the target behavior?"

Right:

1. Define the target behavior.

As always, it is essential to have a clear idea of exactly what behavior is to be changed.

The second rule is to identify the stimuli to be used in the training:

2. Identify the stimuli to be paired.

Counterconditioning is just Pavlovian conditioning used to counter the effects of past learning. In counterconditioning, a stimulus that elicits an inappropriate response is paired with one that elicits a very different reaction.

In desensitization training, for example, we typically pair a stimulus that arouses fear or another negative emotion with a stimulus that has a more positive effect. A person with a fear of spiders might be asked to imagine seeing a spider some distance away. If the imagined scene arouses anxiety, the person would stop thinking of spiders and imagine a relaxing scene. Spiders are systematically paired with feelings of relaxation, and they lose their ability to evoke strong fear.

To do desensitization or sensitization properly, then, it is necessary that appropriate stimuli be identified before the training begins. Once appropriate stimuli have been identified, they must be paired:

3. Pair the appropriate stimuli.

Correctly pairing the appropriate stimuli means presenting them so that the one that elicits the inappropriate response begins slightly *before* the one that elicits an appropriate response. The two events may overlap, but the second must follow the onset of the first without delay. If there is a delay—even one as short as several seconds—between the appearance of the first and second stimuli, the chances of success are greatly reduced.

The last guideline for using counterconditioning is . . . what, Belinda?

"Monitor results. As always."

Yes, as always, it's important to:

4. Monitor results.

In any intervention, it is essential to monitor the results obtained. Counterconditioning procedures usually produce clear changes in behavior almost immediately if they are properly used. Monitoring is especially important in aversion therapy, since noxious stimuli are used. If the desired results are not obtained in short order, the intervention must be evaluated to determine why it is not being effective.

Assuming that these rules are correctly applied, the likelihood of success varies with the form of counterconditioning used and the kind of problem being treated. Now, let's turn to a brief review of today's lesson.

Review

Today's lesson included a review of Pavlovian conditioning. What is Pavlovian conditioning, John?

"That's the pairing of a stimulus that doesn't elicit a response with one that does."

Yes. And usually after several pairings, the one that hadn't had much effect starts to elicit the response; it becomes a conditional stimulus that elicits a conditional response. Why are these events called *conditional* stimuli and *conditional* responses? Jamal?

"Because they depend on certain conditions—especially the pairing of stimuli you were talking about. Innate reflexes don't depend on these experiences, so they're *unconditional*."

What does all this have to do with solving behavior problems? Yes, Belinda?

"Some behavior problems are the result of Pavlovian conditioning."

You mean the ghost of Pavlov is out there making us all neurotic by pairing things?

"Things happen. You might eat spaghetti and then get sick and then after that you might feel ill when you look at spaghetti. The spaghetti becomes a conditional stimulus for nausea because it was paired with something that caused nausea."

Hmm. So some behavior problems are the result of naturally occurring Pavlovian conditioning—is that what you're saying?

"Yes."

Is she right about that, Maya?

"Absolutely!"

You're right, Pavlovian conditioning accounts for some behavior problems—those involving what kind of behavior, Alfred?

"Operant?"

No-o-o-o-o. Try again.

"Respondent?"

That's better. Why else is Pavlovian conditioning important to behaviorists? Midori?

"Because it can be used to solve those problems."

And what do you call procedures that use conditioning to counter the effects of natural conditioning?

"Counterconditioning."

And what are the two basic kinds of counterconditioning?

"Desensitization and sensitization."

Good. When do you use desensitization procedures, Brian?

"When the problem is that a stimulus elicits an inappropriate negative reaction, such as a fear of spiders?"

And when do you use sensitization procedures?

"When the problem is that the stimulus elicits an inappropriate positive reaction, such as sexual arousal in response to children."

Good. So, Carlotta, tell me about one kind of desensitization training.

"Well, there's systematic desensitization. It involves a series of steps. First, you construct a hierarchy of situations that arouse anxiety. Then you train the person to relax. And then you use counterconditioning."

Which in this case means . . . ?

"It means you ask the person to imagine the first item on the hierarchy, the one that elicits very little discomfort. Any time she feels uncomfortable while imagining the scene, she signals the therapist and the therapist has her relax. When the person can visualize a situation repeatedly without feeling any discomfort, it's time to move up to the next item in the hierarchy."

Good. Now you've described systematic desensitization. What other forms of desensitization are there? John?

"There's *in viva.*"

That's in *viv-o*. How is in vivo desensitization different from systematic desensitization?

"Instead of imagining a situation, you actually experience it."

Right. And can you give me an example? One that we haven't talked about already?

"Hmmm. Well, suppose a person is afraid of talking on the telephone."

That's a good example. Some people are as afraid of talking on a telephone as others are of speaking in front of a group. Okay, your hypothetical person doesn't like to talk on the telephone. How do you do in vivo desensitization? Midori?

"The same as you do systematic desensitization, except that instead of having the person imagine looking at a phone or picking up a ringing phone or whatever, you actually have him *do* those things with a telephone."

Exactly right. What other forms of desensitization did we discuss? Maya?

"Well . . . there's the do-it-yourself kind."

Which is called . . . ?

"Uhm . . . self-desensitization?"

Right. And there's one other procedure we discussed.

"Flooding?"

Yes, and that is?

"That's where you start with the situation that really freaks the person out, like talking on the phone or being in an elevator or whatever, and you have the person imagine that situation until it no longer causes discomfort."

Right. That's an approach that might backfire pretty loudly, so you'd best stay away from it until you've had expert training. Now, what can you tell me about sensitization, Brian?

"It's a form of counterconditioning that is used when the reaction to a situation is inappropriately positive."

Can you give us a fresh example, Brian?

"Well . . . there's necrophilia."

Hmm. Not a particularly pleasant example. Perhaps you'd better define necrophilia for us.

"Necrophilia literally means love of the dead. A necrophiliac is someone who is fond of, or maybe sexually aroused by, corpses and other things associated with death. I remember reading about a guy who slept in a coffin, drove a hearse, and when he made love to his wife, he wanted her to lie perfectly still, as if she were dead."

As I said, not a particularly pleasant example. We talked about two forms of sensitization training. What were they, Brian?

"One was aversion therapy; the other was covert sensitization."

Right. So, how would you use aversion therapy to treat necrophilia?

"I would pair the sight of dead bodies and other things associated with death, probably using photographs, with an aversive stimulus, such as an emetic drug. That way things associated with death would come to arouse unpleasant reactions. They would reduce the good feelings, such as sexual arousal."

And how would you use covert sensitization for the same problem, Jamal?

"I'd do the same thing, except I'd have the person imagine the bodies and other stuff and I'd have him imagine getting violently ill."

Exactly. Now, we talked about some rules for using counterconditioning. What's the first one, Alfred?

"Same as always: Define the target behavior."

And the second?

"I think it was to identify the stimuli you're going to pair."

Right. You have to identify appropriate stimuli to use in counterconditioning. Then what?

"You have to pair the stimuli properly."

What does "properly" mean?

"It means that the situation that elicits the inappropriate reaction has to occur first, and the one that elicits the appropriate reaction has to follow it closely."

For example?

"For example, if a person is an alcoholic, alcohol might be paired with nausea. First the person has to taste and smell, or imagine tasting and smelling, alcohol, and then he has to get sick, or imagine feeling sick. The taste of the alcohol has to come first, but the nausea has to come immediately after."

All right. And what's the last rule?

"Same as always: Monitor results."

Right again. Now, counterconditioning works well, if it's done properly, and has relieved a good deal of suffering. But it's not perfect. The benefits of sensitization training are often short-lived, especially when used to treat problems involving substance abuse and sexual abuse.

Counterconditioning procedures, especially sensitization, also tend to arouse all sorts of anxiety about Big Brother. You use aversion therapy to treat a rapist or a child molester, and the next thing you know you're accused of trying to turn everyone into robots. But that's another topic, and we'd best save that for next time. In the meantime, the handouts will help you learn more about counterconditioning. Have fun with them.

◄ Exercises ►

Feed the Skeleton

I. Pavlovian Procedures
   A. In Pavlovian conditioning, an event comes to elicit a response by being paired with _____ .
   B. Pavlovian procedures are used to modify _____ .
   C. There are two basic kinds of counterconditioning procedures: _____ training and _____ training.

II. Desensitization Training
   A. Systematic desensitization involves three steps: constructing a(n) _____ ; _____ training; and
      c._____ .
   B. The chief difference between systematic desensitization and in vivo desensitization is that _____ .
   C. Self-desensitization differs from ordinary systematic desensitization in that _____ .
   D. Flooding is a relatively risky form of desensitization because
      _____ .

III. Sensitization Training
   A. There are two main kinds of sensitization training:
      _____ and _____ .
   B. Sensitization and desensitization procedures differ procedurally in that
      _____ .
   C. The goals of sensitization and desensitization differ in that
      _____ .

IV. The rules for counterconditioning are:
   A. _____ .
   B. Identify the _____ .
   C. Pair _____ .
   D. _____ .

The Security Blanket

The Producers is a very funny movie starring Gene Wilder and Zero Mostel. Gene Wilder plays a terribly self-doubting, highly neurotic accountant who still carries the tattered security blanket of his infant days. Whenever anyone shouts at him, whenever he is in trouble, whenever any problem threatens to overwhelm him—out comes the security blanket, which he rubs against his face.

Imagine that there is to be a sequel to *The Producers* that will revolve about the efforts of the accountant to overcome his dependence on a tattered, 50-year-old rag of a security blanket. In one scene, a behavior therapist uses some form of desensitization to treat the accountant's problem. Your task is to write the dialogue for this scene. The scene might represent one therapy session, or it might represent brief excerpts from several sessions.

The Case of the Dropped Jaw

Feingold (reported in Wolpe 1973) offers an interesting case for your consideration. An 11-year-old girl made a practice of keeping her mouth open. This behavior interfered with certain forms of dental treatment, which required her to close her mouth.

The therapist asked the child's parents to record the number of times they saw the child with her mouth open. Each day she went to the dentist she received a number of shocks, the number being the same as the number of times she had kept her mouth open. This case raises certain questions, of which I would like you to answer two:
   1. What is the name of the procedure used to change the girl's behavior?
   2. Was the procedure properly applied?

Plastic Addiction

Imagine that, until recently, you had a problem with credit cards. You knew you were spending money you didn't have, and you had run up such a debt that you might have had to drop out of college to pay your bills. You knew you had to seek professional help, and your parents agreed to pay for therapy. They suggested that you go to that nice psychoanalyst who has been treating your Uncle Cosmo for the past 37 years, but you insisted on seeing a behavior therapist who specializes in treating credit card addiction with aversion therapy. You underwent treatment and are now free of symptoms after six sessions. Describe the therapy you received.

Colorful Language

Consider the phrases, *people of color* and *colored people*. These phrases are very similar, yet many people react very differently to them. What sort of experiences could account for these different reactions?

Practice Quiz

1. Operant procedures are based largely on the work of B. F. Skinner; respondent procedures are based largely on the work of _____ .

2. _____ is a form of desensitization that involves continuous exposure to situations that cause considerable distress.

3. The goal of counterconditioning is to undo the adverse effects of

_____ .

4. The first step in doing systematic desensitization is to construct a _____ of situations that arouse fear and other negative emotions.

5. Instead of imagining disturbing scenes, as in systematic desensitization, in _____ desensitization the client is exposed to real situations.

6. The Pram Man was treated with a form of counterconditioning called _____ therapy.

7. Carolyn and Arthur Staats showed that Pavlovian conditioning might help explain how _____ are learned.

8. In the case of the Wallpaper Man, the experience that later resulted in impotence was the pairing of a kind of wallpaper with _____ .

9. In creating a hierarchy of fearful situations, Wolpe sometimes made use of a test called the Fear _____ Schedule.

10. In sensitization training, counterconditioning is used to reduce the strength of a _____ emotional response.

Reprint: OLD OBSESSIONS
by John E. Calamari, Samantha D. Faber, Brian L. Hitsman
& Christopher J. Poppe

> *Lots of people worry about things unnecessarily, and lots of us feel com-*
> *pelled to make sure we turned off the iron before we left home. Such obses-*
> *sive-compulsive behavior can be very useful. (I have known few successful*
> *graduate students who were not at least a little obsessive-compulsive.) In*
> *obsessive-compulsive disorder, however, these tendencies interfere with nor-*
> *mal functioning and the enjoyment of life. Various kinds of interventions*
> *have been used to treat this problem, but perhaps none more successfully*
> *than exposure and response prevention. In this form of desensitization, the*
> *client is exposed to the situation that arouses obsessive thinking and is*
> *prevented from performing the "compelled" behavior.*

. . . In this paper, we review the existing treatment literature on OCD in the
elderly and describe the successful treatment of an 80-year-old man. . . .

Presenting Symptoms and Pretreatment Measures

The patient was an 80-year-old man who presented at our clinic, a specialty treatment clinic of OCD and other anxiety disorders. The patient's primary complaints
involved harming obsessions and checking and repeating rituals. The major
obsessional theme focused on harm coming to family or friends through some
fault of the patient. Compulsive behaviors included a broad range of checking
behavior intended to prevent harm, e.g., checking door locks, checking the furnace, etc. Additionally, the patient felt it necessary to repeat many routine behaviors and retrace his steps, also done to prevent harm coming to specific family
members. For example, the patient would have to leave buildings through the
door he entered. Extensive avoidance behavior was present and included not
reading the obituary page or glancing at negative headlines in the paper as such
activities, if inadvertently associated with thoughts of family members, could
cause them harm. The patient was readily able to acknowledge the irrational and
excessive nature of his behavior with a few exceptions. For example, the likelihood of a new furnace being improperly installed and producing carbon monox-
ide poisoning was consistently overestimated. . . .

The YBOCS [Yale-Brown Obsessive Compulsive Scale] was completed during the initial clinical interview. The Obsession score was 10, Compulsion score
10, and the total score 20 indicating a substantial degree of both obsessions and
compulsions. Scores on the YBOCS before and following treatment are shown in
Figure 1.

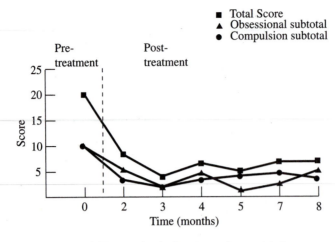

Figure 1. *YBOCS scores (total, obsession, and compulsion) are shown before treatment and over the 8-month follow-up evaluation.*

Patient History

The patient reported that he had been troubled by obsessions at a severe level for approximately 1 year. Close questioning revealed that OCD symptomatology had been present throughout his adult life and had periodically become severe. The OCD symptoms had earlier been misdiagnosed as depression during his sporadic prior contact with mental health professionals. The patient was diagnosed as having OCD by a community psychiatrist and started on medication a few months before beginning treatment at our clinic. He reported no family history of psychiatric disorders with the exception of a twin brother, who seemed to have experienced similar OCD symptoms, but had not sought treatment for his condition.

Treatment Intervention and Outcome

The rationale for the exposure and response prevention intervention was explained to the patient prior to the initiation of treatment. We found it necessary to reiterate this rationale more frequently throughout treatment than has been our experience with other patients. Both the general exposure therapy principles and the specifics of exposure exercises appeared often to be forgotten, necessitating review of these issues at each session. Additionally, education about the nature of anxiety and anxiety symptoms, another initial step in our treatment protocol, proceeded more slowly. Exposure homework assignments proved more difficult for the patient to understand and often had to be repeatedly reviewed and written down. To check his comprehension we found it helpful to have him articulate the specific action being requested and the rationale for this activity at the end of each session. . . .

Exposure and response prevention was carried out in daily sessions conducted 5 days per week for a 3-week period. This intensive intervention format has been recommended for more severe OCD (e.g., Steketee & Foa, 1985; or Riggs & Foa, 1993), although the necessity of the procedure has not been empirically evaluated. A total of 14 sessions were conducted during the intensive treatment phase of the intervention. The patient was then seen for six follow-up sessions with the interval between sessions gradually increased. Contact with clinicians is typically decreased gradually in relation to the significance of the patient's remaining symptoms and patient preference. Exposure therapy activities for this patient were conducted on and off site and included writing the name of loved ones on the obituary page, failing to leave building through the door he had initially entered, and saying people's names while touching tombstones in a local cemetery. The patient periodically experienced difficulty adhering to the ban on ritualizing when exposure activities were related to overvalued ideas. Firm and repeated promptings by the therapists was successful in further motivating the patient.

It was the patient's preference not to involve family members directly in his treatment as a source of support, although such involvement is recommended (e.g., Riggs & Foa, 1993). The patient was comfortable with his family receiving additional information about the nature of OCD and the response prevention paradigm. This was accomplished by having the involved family members read Foa and Wilson (1991), a highly readable review of OCD and its treatment.

The patient was receiving sertraline 50 mg/day at the time exposure and response prevention treatment was initiated. Because the patient had been losing weight while receiving sertraline (he reported a 30-lb weight loss during the course of medication treatment associated with appetite loss and not attributable to any specific medical condition), the treating psychiatrist decreased dosage and discontinued this medication while behavior therapy treatment proceeded. Thus, the patient's sertraline was discontinued by the end of the first week of behavioral treatment, and the patient remained medication free through follow-up. The patient also had a prescription for alprazolam intended for use as a sleep aid, but reported discontinuing his use of this medication prior to initiation of the exposure and response prevention treatment.

The patient experienced rapid and dramatic within- and between-session habituation to anxiety and obsession-precipitating stimuli. For example, within-session exposure therapy exercises, e.g., placing his hand in a large drawer which reminded the patient of a coffin, were continued until the initially experienced anxiety decreased by approximately 50%. This habituation was readily achieved as were between session changes in experienced anxiety, i.e. upon repeated exposure to specific tasks in later sessions, initially anxiety was lower, and habituation proceeded more rapidly. Associated behavioral changes were quickly observed by the patient's family and friends resulting in positive feedback to the patient. For example, the elimination of the patient's repeating rituals resulted in his wife being willing to have him accompany her on shopping trips once again. Pretreatment, post-treatment, and follow-up YBOCS scores are shown in Figure 1. . . . At 8-month follow-up the patient reported minimal obsessing, ritualizing and avoidance behavior, and reported that he was now not taking medication nor had he resumed antidepressant medication at any point during the follow-up period. He indicated that he continued to receive very positive feedback from his family regarding his improved functioning. . . .

Reprinted with permission from *Journal of Behavior Therapy and Experimental Psychiatry,* *Vol. 25.* M. J. E. Calamari, S. D. Faber, B. L. Hitsman, and C. J. Poppe, "Treatment of Obsessive Compulsive Disorder in the Elderly: A Review and Case Example," 1994, Elsevier Science Ltd., Oxford, England.

◄ Recommended Reading ►

1. Jones, M. C. (1924). A laboratory study of fear: The case of Peter. *Pedagogical Seminary, 31,* 308–315.
   This is the classic study of Peter, probably the first controlled demonstration that Pavlovian conditioning could be used to treat a behavior problem.

2. Pavlov, I. P. (1941). *Lectures on conditioned reflexes, Vol. 2: Conditioned reflexes and psychiatry* (W. H. Gantt, Ed. and Trans.). New York: International.
   Pavlov shares his views on how conditioning can be applied to the treatment of human behavior disorders. This book is far less famous than Pavlov's *Conditioned Reflexes,* in which he describes his research with dogs, but it is well worth reading.

3. Rothbaum, B. O., Hodges, L. F., Kooper, R., Opdyke, D., Williford, J. S., & North, M. (1995). Virtual reality graded exposure in the treatment of acrophobia: A case report. *Behavior Therapy, 26,* 547–554.
   These researchers developed a virtual reality version of systematic desensitization for treating a fear of heights. The virtual reality apparatus is extremely expensive, but the procedure may well become commonplace as the technology becomes less costly.

4. Watson, J. B., & Rayner, R. (1920). Conditioned emotional reactions. *Journal of Experimental Psychology, 3,* 1–4.
   This is the famous "Little Albert" paper in which Watson and Rayner describe their theory of the role of conditioning in fears.

5. Wolpe, J. (1973). *The practice of behavior therapy* (2nd ed.). New York: Pergamon Press.
   This book is filled with case studies illustrating the use of counterconditioning, especially systematic desensitization, in the treatment of behavior disorders.

◄ **Endnotes** ►

1. Actually, operant procedures can be used to modify certain respondent behaviors. Fear may be defined in terms of feelings and physiological reactions, but it can also be defined as a tendency to avoid or escape a situation. Running from a spider is operant behavior. So, we might provide reinforcing consequences for approaching (rather than fleeing) a feared object (Leitenberg & Callahan, 1973).

2. Skinner studied Pavlov's conditioning work early in his career and may have learned a valuable lesson from Pavlov's pursuit of what others might have considered a trivial distraction. In describing his own research methods in "A Case History in Scientific Method," Skinner (1956/1961) advises researchers, "when you run onto something interesting, drop everything else and study it" (p. 81).

3. See Pavlov (1927).

4. Most authors use the terms *conditioned* and *unconditioned* rather than *conditional* and *unconditional*. The words *conditional* and *unconditional* are, however, closer to Pavlov's meaning (Gantt, 1966; Thorndike, 1931/1968).

5. Staats, A. W., & Staats, C. K. (1958); see also Staats, C. K., & Staats, A. W. (1957).

6. Eysenck (1965).

7. Jones (1924b); see also Jones (1924a).

8. Wolpe & Lang (1964).

9. Jacobson (1938).

10. Wolpe (1973).

11. Wolpe (1973).

12. Cowden & Ford (1962).

13. Therapists who do systematic desensitization sometimes include some in vivo training. During treatment for acrophobia (fear of heights), for example, a therapist might ask a client to climb to the first step of a small ladder. This would be done only after the client had successfully imagined performing the task, and even then only if the client felt comfortable doing it.

14. A variation of this procedure is for the person to listen to a desensitization audiotape. The voice on the tape serves as a kind of therapist by proxy.

15. Rosen et al. (1977).

16. Stampfl & Levis (1967).

17. It might be argued that the idea behind flooding is not counterconditioning but extinction. A situation that has been paired with unpleasant experiences

in the past is presented in the absence of those unpleasant experiences. The client imagines holding a snake but does not get bitten; the client imagines being locked in a broom closet but does not suffocate. The result is that the situation loses its ability to arouse anxiety. At least, that's the theory.

18. Aversion therapy may be thought of as a method of establishing an *aversion to* something that is currently reinforcing, such as food, alcohol, or pornographic pictures of children. The first report of aversion therapy was probably that of Kantorovich (1930; reported in Wolpe, 1973). Kantorovich paired the sight, smell, and taste of alcohol with electric shock.

19. The "Pram Man" is described in Raymond (1956). The article is reprinted in Eysenck (1960).

20. Lavin et al. (1961); summarized in Ullmann & Krasner (1965).

21. Serber (1970).

22. Cautela (1966; 1967).

23. Azrin & Powell (1968).

24. Compare Bandura (1975), p.16.

12

The Ethics of Behavior Change and the Future of Behavior Analysis

GREETINGS! Once again you have entered my lair, walked into my trap, got caught in my web. Once again you will bask in the radiant sunshine of my brilliant wisdom; be careful of the glare!

"Maybe you should lie down, Dr. Cee."

What, Alfred? Oh no, I feel fine. I just get a bit giddy near the end of a course. I suppose it's the approach of the reinforcer: Like most people, I find completing a task reinforcing. And teaching is a task, however pleasant it may be.

"I feel the same way, but I thought it was just relief that the semester is about over."

Well, that too.

Last time we talked about counterconditioning, a way of treating problems involving a certain kind of behavior. What kind of behavior? Jamal?

"Respondent?"

Right. Most often counterconditioning is used to change the kind of respondent behavior that we call emotions: fear, anger, disgust. We found that there were two basic kinds of counterconditioning procedures. One is used when the problem is an inappropriate negative emotional reaction to a situation. This is called . . . what, Maya?

"Desensitization?"

Right. What's one kind of desensitization procedure?

"Systematic desensitization."

Right again. There's also in vivo desensitization, self-desensitization, and . . . and what, Alfred?

"Flooding?"

Yes. Counterconditioning can also be used when the problem is an inappropriate positive emotional reaction to a situation. In these cases, instead of desensitization behaviorists use . . . what, Belinda?

"Sensitization."

Good. We discussed two kinds of sensitization. What were they, Maya?

"Aversion therapy and . . . something sensitization."

Yes, but what is the something sensitization really called?

"Is it called covert sensitization?"

Indeed it is. Well done.

Now, today's lesson is the penultimate lesson of the course. In fact, since the next class period will be devoted entirely to reviewing for the final exam and will introduce no new material, today's lesson will, in effect, mark the end of the course.

"I'm all broke up."

I knew you would be, Alfred. Well now, today's topic is a dual one: the ethics of behavior change and the future of behavior analysis. The two are closely related because if changing behavior is an unethical activity, then behavior analysis has no future. It will be condemned and banished from civilized society—and rightly so. Let's begin with the ethical question.

Ethics of Changing Behavior

Who Changes Behavior?

Lots of people make a living at changing other people's behavior. Give me an example, Belinda.

"Applied behavior analysts."

An obvious example, but acceptable. Now give me an example that's not so obvious.

"Psychotherapists?"

Of course. Psychotherapists of all stripes are in the business of changing behavior.

"But don't they say they're trying to restructure personality? Isn't that different from changing behavior?"

You tell me, Maya. How will the psychotherapist know when he has restructured a person's personality?

"Hmm. I guess when the person acts differently."

Exactly. A therapist may say he's trying to restructure personality, change attitudes, or produce new insights, but if success will be measured in terms of behavior (and it inevitably is), then the therapist is trying to change behavior. Who else makes a living by changing behavior? Carlotta?

"Teachers?"

Explain what you mean.

"Well, teachers have to deal with disruptive students and with students who don't do their work; teachers try to change the behavior of these students."

True, but a teacher isn't paid just to keep order. What else do teachers do to earn their pay?

> "They teach."

Does that involve changing behavior?

> "Yes. The teacher tries to get students who can't read or write to be able to read and write; she tries to get students who can't solve equations to be able to solve equations; she tries to get students who don't draw well to improve their drawing; so she's attempting to change behavior."[1]

Right. And other educators—principals, supervisors, superintendents—are also in the business of changing behavior. Mostly they try to change the behavior of other educators, especially teachers. So educators are in the behavior-changing business. Who else changes behavior for a living? John?

> "Employers?"

Sure. Employers, company executives, supervisors—anyone in management. A manager's job is to manage the behavior of the workers under her supervision. And managing behavior means changing it. If all workers behaved in the optimum manner, there'd be no need for managers. Managers are important because it's necessary to get workers to behave differently. This may mean getting them to perform a new task, perform a task in a different way, waste less material, show up for work on time, and so on. Managers are paid to change behavior. So are lots of other people: day care workers; health care workers; lawyers; ministers—lots of people are in the business of changing behavior.

Other people spend a good deal of their time attempting to change behavior even though they're not paid to do so. Can you give me an example, Jamal?

> "Parents?"

Yes, parents. Most parents aren't paid to change the behavior of their children, but it's an inevitable part of parenting. Parents want their kids to pick up their toys, put their clothes on hangers, eat their spinach, and do their homework. They also want them to *stop* doing things: picking their noses, shouting, running around the house, teasing the dog. Parents aren't paid to change behavior, but they certainly spend a lot of time trying to do it. Who else spends a good deal of time changing other people's behavior? Midori?

> "Roommates. If you share a room or an apartment with other people, there are always problems because somebody doesn't do the dishes when they're supposed to, or they hang their jacket on the back of a chair, or they tie up the telephone. And their roommates are going to try to change their behavior."

Good example. Who else tries to change behavior? Brian?

"Students. Teachers are trying to change the behavior of students, but students also try to change the behavior of the teacher. They also try to change the behavior of other students."

Can you give us an example of a student trying to change another student's behavior?

"Well, say a fifth-grade boy has a crush on a girl in his class, but she's not interested in him."

She doesn't know he's alive. Yes, I remember the feeling.

"And so he does things to try to win her over, to get her to like him. He's trying to change her behavior."

Okay, good example. Any other examples? Carlotta?

"You said parents try to change the behavior of their kids, but kids also try to change the behavior of their parents. Workers try to change the behavior of their supervisors and employers. Husbands try to change the behavior of their wives, and vice versa."

So you're saying that everybody tries to change somebody's behavior sooner or later?

"Yes. I think it's part of interacting with other people. We all have a stake in the way the people around us behave, and sometimes we try to change that behavior."

That's a very astute observation, Carlotta. So if changing behavior is unethical, it's not just unethical for behavior analysts, it's unethical for everyone: psychotherapists, teachers, lawyers, parents, students, ministers, husbands, wives, roommates—everybody. Which brings us back to the question: Is changing other people's behavior unethical? What do you think, Midori?

"Some people say it is."

What's one reason that people give for saying that changing behavior is unethical?

Arguments Against Changing Behavior

"Some people say that changing a person's behavior dehumanizes people—turns them into automatons."

Yes, Frankenstein's monster. Zombies. Robots.[2] To dehumanize someone means to take his or her humanity away; can you do that by changing the person's behavior?

"I suppose you might be able to in some circumstances. You might get people to behave in a humiliating manner, or you might make a person dependent on others."

Yes, that's true. Now, tell me this: Would you consider a hammer a dangerous weapon?

"A hammer? No, it's a carpenter's tool."

But surely a person could hit someone with a hammer and do great harm. Doesn't that make it a deadly weapon?

"Well, I guess it could be dangerous, but it's just a hammer."

Yes, but it can be used in damaging ways. A blow to the head with a hammer could turn a happy, pleasant, intelligent person into a depressed, surly, idiot. Or into a zombie. The victim would have been dehumanized to some extent. So a hammer can be used to dehumanize people.

"So you're saying any tool can be dangerous if it's not used properly."

Yes. And tools for changing behavior, including behavioral tools, have been misused. Israel Goldiamond reports that on a visit to a psychiatric hospital, he found patients sleeping on the floor because they had not earned enough tokens for the use of a bed.[3] At another hospital, the treatment of a drug addict included attempts to use shaping to remove her southern accent. Most of us would probably consider such practices unethical, but the therapists involved (who, by the way, were *not* trained behavior analysts) evidently thought they were applying behavioral procedures in an ethical manner. Any powerful tool can be misused.

We should keep in mind, however, that people who spend a lot of time trying to change behavior (behavior analysts, psychotherapists, teachers, parents, etc.) are more likely to be humanizing people than dehumanizing them.

"People are born human. You can't humanize them."

Are you sure, Alfred? Every once in a while there is an item in the newspaper about someone who kept a child in a closet for several years. The parent feeds the child enough to keep him or her alive, but provides none of the experiences that children ordinarily receive as they are growing up. I know some of you have read or heard about these cases. What are these kids like? Carlotta?

"They don't speak. They don't know how to interact with other people. They seem to be retarded. They act more like animals than people."

More like animals than people. Yes, exactly. Being human is not entirely a matter of genetics. We inherit the biological equipment for becoming human beings, but the skills that constitute being human are largely learned. Mostly they're learned from other people. So parents literally humanize their children. Siblings, teachers, neighbors, and other people also play a part in that process.

For some children, these ordinary experiences are not sufficient to achieve humanization—or, as it is usually called, socialization. These children (usually with labels such as autistic or retarded) need more than usual parenting experiences. The behaviorist can either provide these humanizing experiences or show the parent how to provide them.

Adults also sometimes need help in regaining their humanity. There is no medical cure for schizophrenia, but it is often possible to improve the patient's condition by changing key behaviors. We may, for example, be able to reduce the frequency of hallucinations, delusions, nonsensical speech, strange mannerisms, and other forms of bizarre behavior. We can also add positive behavior to the person's repertoire.

So, efforts to change behavior can dehumanize, or they can humanize. I don't think you can say that changing behavior is unethical because it dehumanizes people, because that is not the inevitable, or even the customary, result. Nevertheless, it is possible to dehumanize people by changing their behavior in undesirable ways, and that is certainly unethical.

Why else is changing behavior said to be unethical? Yes, John?

"Some people say it's cruel to use aversives to change behavior."

Can you give me an example of the use of aversives that would be unethical?[4]

"Sometimes parents shake a child, or even an infant, when the child cries or does something else that's annoying."

And why is that unethical?

"Because it can result in serious injury, such as permanent brain damage or a broken neck, especially in the case of an infant."

Is there any other reason it's unethical?

"Because it's unnecessary. There are usually better ways of changing behavior than using aversives."

You're right, John. I have, as you know, stressed that aversives should be used only as a last resort, and then only when the target behavior poses more of a risk than the aversive used in treatment. But is it *always* unethical to change behavior with aversives? Let me give you an example.

Goldiamond describes a film in which a little girl wears a football helmet.[5] She's a head banger, and the helmet is intended to reduce the damage she can do by hitting her head. Her hands are tied to the crib in which she is kept to prevent her from removing the helmet. She doesn't have much hair because she pulls it out whenever her hands are free. Her face is bruised from self-inflicted injuries. She does not speak. Her neck muscles are inordinantly large because of the exercise they get from tossing her helmeted head about.

At first, the therapists try to reinforce appropriate behavior in a variety of ways, but these efforts are unsuccessful. Finally the treatment team turns to punishment. They yell, "Don't!" and slap the girl each time she tosses her head. After fewer than a dozen slaps, the word *don't* has become an effective punisher by itself, and slapping is no longer necessary. Progress is rapid, and soon the helmet comes off and the girl begins eating at a table and sleeping in a regular bed. Her hair starts to grow out, and within a year she has become a very pretty little girl with delicate features who often smiles.

The use of aversives is controversial, even among behaviorists, and it should be. But this case illustrates the good that can come from the proper use of aversives when all else fails. The girl was slapped and yelled at several times, but the result was that she no longer had to wear a helmet, no longer pulled out her hair, no longer had a bruised face, no longer slept in a baby's crib; instead, she began to look and act like a normal little girl. She—

"I don't see what's so controversial about this. Where's the ethical problem?"

Brian?

"What I mean is, if I have a toothache, I go to the dentist. Maybe the dentist fills a cavity, or maybe she has to pull the tooth, or maybe she has to do a root canal. All of these things hurt, but I know they're in my best interests. If I had a child who had a toothache, I'd take him to the dentist. He might not want to go, but I know that the treatment is in his best interest, so I would insist even though the treatment will cause pain. But nobody would accuse me or the dentist of being cruel."

That's a good point: Health care procedures are not considered cruel merely because they cause discomfort. The parent who cleans a child's cut is not being cruel, even though the procedure hurts. If we do something that causes discomfort unnecessarily, that's cruel; but if the procedure is necessary to help the person, it's not cruel. Perhaps we should take a similar view with regard to aversives. Using aversives to change behavior is not cruel if the procedure is necessary to help the person.

Okay. Are there any other reasons changing behavior might be considered unethical? Yes, Belinda?

"Some people say it's manipulative."

How do you mean, manipulative?

"You know, manipulating; getting a person to do something he doesn't really want to do."

And that's unethical?

"Yes."

Give me an example of manipulation.

"Well, an encyclopedia salesman went to my grandmother's house. She let him in and they talked for a while and the next thing my grandmother knew, the salesman was leaving with a check for $1300. My grandmother didn't want that encyclopedia; she had cataracts so she couldn't even read it."

And so you're saying the salesman manipulated her into doing something she didn't really want to do, buying an encyclopedia, and that was wrong?

"Right."

Well, what about this example: An employer talks to one of his workers, a high school dropout who works on the assembly line. He persuades the worker to go back to school and earn a high school equivalency certificate. When he does, he receives a promotion. Has the employer acted unethically?

"No, not at all."

But the employee didn't want to go back to school. He had quit school because he didn't like it. The employer got him to do something he didn't want to do. The employer manipulated him. Isn't that wrong?

"Well, not in that case."

What's the difference between the manipulativeness of the employer and the manipulativeness of the salesman?

"The salesman benefits."

So does the employer. He has a smarter, more effective employee. Is there any other difference between the salesman and the employer?

"Hmmm. Yes! The employee benefited when the employer changed his behavior, but my grandmother didn't. She couldn't even read the encyclopedia because she had cataracts."

So, changing behavior is unethical if the change is harmful to the person whose behavior is affected. The salesman's behavior was unethical because he got your grandmother to do something that was not in her own best interests. The employer's behavior was ethical because he got the employee to do something that was in the *employee's* best interest. Perhaps what is unethical is not changing a person's behavior, but changing it in a way that is harmful to the person.

We have discussed three reasons some people give for saying that changing behavior is unethical. What was the first one, Jamal?

"Oh, uhm, hmm . . . some people say that changing a person's behavior dehumanizes them."

Right. And the second reason, Midori?

"Some people say that changing behavior is cruel. They have in mind the use of aversives."

Good. And the third argument, Maya?

"That was the idea that changing behavior is manipulative."

Yes. Those are the main reasons given for saying that changing behavior is unethical, and there is some truth to each of them: It is possible to change behavior in dehumanizing ways; it is possible to use aversives in a way that is cruel; and it is possible to get people to do things that are not in their best interests. There is, then, a potential for abuse in changing behavior.

Please note that these abuses can arise whether the person who is attempting to change behavior is a Freudian, a Rogerian, a Skinnerian—or any other sort of "-ian." The potential for unethical behavior arises out of the effort to change behavior, not out of the theoretical orientation of the person involved. That doesn't mean—

"Excuse me, Dr. Cee, but I have a question about that."

Go ahead, Maya.

"Aren't these criticisms aimed more at behavior analysis than at other procedures? I mean, I've read articles about behavior analysis, or about behaviorism, that said it was dehumanizing, cruel, and manipulative. I don't remember anybody saying those things about psychoanalysis, humanistic psychology, Jungian analysis, cognitive psychology, or other approaches to behavior. Isn't behavior analysis more likely to involve ethical problems?"

Why Do Critics Focus on Behavior Analysis?

That's an excellent question, Maya. Actually, other approaches have come in for some criticism, but it does seem that people are more critical of behavior analysis than they are of other approaches.[6] Why do you suppose that is? . . . No ideas? I'll give you a hint: Suppose your hobby is wood carving. You create statuettes of birds and old farmers that people buy and put on their knickknack shelf to give the dust a place to settle. Now, if you're going to carve something out of wood, you want a sharp knife. A dull knife just won't do the job, or it will take you forever. A sharp knife will enable you to shape the wood. But a sharp knife also brings with it some hazards. You can cut yourself. You can make a mistake that will damage the wood.

"Dr. Cee, I honestly think you're losing it. I haven't the slightest idea what wood carving has got to do with the dangers of behavior analysis."

I'm sorry, Alfred. Does anybody see what I'm driving at? Yes, Brian?

"It's an analogy. The wood carver has a problem: He has a block of wood that he wants to make look like a duck. He's got a choice of tools; some of them work well and some of them don't—sharp knives and dull knives. In dealing with behavior problems, we've got a choice of tools. Some of them work well and some of them don't—sharp knives and dull knives.

"Tools that work well have some risks, and behavior analysis is a set of sharp tools, so it's potentially more dangerous than, say, nondirective counseling."

That's it, Brian. The more effective you are at changing behavior, the greater the potential for abusing that power. The tools that behavior analysis provides are very powerful.

"Dr. Cee?"

Yes, Midori?

"I am not a happy camper, Dr. Cee. You seem to be saying that we can't use behavior analysis because something could go wrong—the knives are sharp and we might cut ourselves or someone else. Did I waste the whole semester studying this stuff?"

What do *you* think?

"If these tools are so dangerous that we can't use them, then I guess so."

And what happens to the kids who need toilet training, who have tantrums, who bang their heads against a wall? What happens to the students who are not learning to read? What happens to the business that is in danger of going under because the workers aren't productive enough? What happens to teen pregnancy, crime, and other social problems? Are those problems still there?

"Yes."

Yes. Behavior problems don't go away just because we elect not to deal with them effectively.

"But you've been saying that we *can't* deal with them effectively."

No, I haven't. I've been saying that there are some risks in attempting to change behavior, and these risks may be greater if you have powerful tools for changing behavior. But there are things we can do to prevent these tools from being used inappropriately.

One thing that we can do is support laws that ensure competence in the use of a particular set of tools. For example, in some states, it is possible for a person to do behavior therapy without having had any training in behavior therapy. We can also support the establishment of review boards to oversee efforts to change behavior. Most universities and hospitals already have boards that review research and treatment projects, but such boards are not generally in use in schools and corporations. And we can support educational efforts so that people understand the tools for changing behavior and how they work.

Another thing we can do to prevent abuses is to follow, and demand that others follow, guidelines for the ethical use of procedures for changing behavior. The American Psychological Association and the Association for Advancement of Behavior Therapy have both published codes of ethics that include guidelines concerning the use of behavior change procedures.[7] These cover all sorts of issues, such as competence and the relationship with the client, but they are oriented mainly toward therapists. Most of you are not going to be therapists, but you are going to be changing other people's behavior. I have therefore come up with four simple rules to help keep you ethically pure in your efforts to solve everyday behavior problems.

Rules for Changing Behavior Ethically

Rule number one is:

> ## 1. Encourage the person whose behavior is to be changed to participate in the design of the intervention.

Behavior change procedures should not be something you do *to* someone but something you do *with* someone.[8] The person who is the focus of study should participate, whenever possible, in the design of the intervention program.

Suppose you're a teacher, for example, and you've got a student who's falling behind because he's not doing his homework. You can go off on your own and design some sort of intervention program, but you're more likely to be successful, and less likely to do harm, if you involve the student in this process. You might say something like, "Johnny, you're not doing your homework, and that means you're not learning as much as you should. Let's talk about this problem and see if we can come up with a solution. . . ."

One advantage of this approach is that sometimes you will acquire some very useful information. For example, you may learn that Johnny doesn't do his homework because there's no quiet place to do it; in some families, there is a constant cacophony of background noise. Without this information, you might have tried to set up a reinforcement contingency, and the results might not have been very good. With this information, you might try to find a quiet place for Johnny to work, and this alone might solve the problem. Involving the person whose behavior you're trying to change is likely to lead to a better solution and avoid accusations of manipulativeness.

> "You can't always do that—involve the person. You told us about an infant who regurgitated her food. You can't sit down with an infant and say, 'Let's talk about this problem.'"

You're right, Belinda.

> "And if a person is psychotic, he may not be able to participate in his treatment."

True, true. So if the person you're trying to help can't participate effectively, who else could you call on?

> "Oh, you mean like a representative? Someone to act on behalf of the client?"

Exactly. A relative maybe, or an officer of the court, or a professional ombudsman. It's usually possible to find someone to stand in for a person and represent his or her best interests.

"But what if the client or the ombudsman doesn't agree to a program that you know will be effective?"

It's an imperfect world, Brian. Earlier I mentioned a film that showed a little girl whose self-injurious behavior was stopped with mild aversives. Once they had stopped the self-injurious behavior, she began to make all sorts of progress. What I didn't tell you is that the parents found out about the aversives. They disapproved and withdrew her from the program.

Lots of parents in that situation would do the same thing: "You're hitting my little girl?! And you call yourselves therapists! You're not therapists, you're monsters. You can't hit a child who does something because she's sick!" I wouldn't be surprised if something of that sort was said. The end of the film shows the little girl some time after her removal from the program. She is strapped into a crib, her hands tied to one side, and she's wearing a football helmet. She has torn out a lot of her hair; her face is badly bruised. She has returned to the same sad state she was in before the intervention.

"But their daughter was helped by the treatment! She did a lot more injury to herself than the therapists did with a few slaps."

You're right, Brian, you're right. It's like the dentist who causes some pain in order to correct a dental problem.

"Well, the parents were stupid to pull her out of that program."

What the parents did may have been a mistake, but you must remember that calling someone stupid doesn't explain their behavior; it just names it.

"But doesn't that case argue against involving people in the intervention?"

On the contrary, I think it shows how important such involvement is. Goldiamond doesn't provide many details, but I can't help wondering if those parents wouldn't have behaved differently if the therapists had involved them at the beginning. If they had said, "Look, your little girl is hurting herself physically every chance she gets. Preventing her from doing this by having her wear a football helmet and tying her hands to a crib isn't solving the problem, and it's preventing her from developing normally. Some research shows that it's possible to reduce this kind of behavior with physical punishment, such as a slap. We'd like to try this with your little girl. The slaps will do less harm than she's doing to herself now, and the research suggests that if the procedure works, we'll see progress right away. If we can get her to stop hurting herself, she may be able to learn all sorts of other things." If the therapists had sought out the cooperation of the parents in this way, the story might have had a happier ending.

"And if the parents had refused?"

As I said, Carlotta, it's an imperfect world. In rare instances, a court may order parents to permit treatment, essentially arguing that denying effective treatment is a form of abuse. But circumventing the wishes of the client, or the client's representative, can also be a form of abuse. If we're going to help people, we have to try to work *with* them, not *on* them. If, because of age or disability, the person is unable to participate effectively in decisions about an intervention, then we have to work with a parent or other person representing the client's interests. A question, Jamal?

"Is that why therapists have the client sign an informed consent form?"

It is common practice in therapeutic settings, such as clinics and hospitals, to obtain an informed consent form, particularly when aversives are involved. A properly executed informed consent form is not, however, equivalent to client involvement in intervention design. At best, the informed consent form means that the client understands what the therapist is going to do and gives permission to do it. It doesn't mean that the client actively participated in the decision about what will be done.[9]

The second ethics rule concerns aversives:

2. Avoid aversives whenever possible.

This is important because the use of aversives always borders on abuse. Please understand that I am *not* saying that anyone who uses aversives is guilty of abuse, merely that the use of aversives carries with it the risk of abuse.[10] Because of this danger, and because of the other problems with aversives that we've discussed, they should always be used as a last resort.

The case of the little girl in the football helmet illustrates this principle: The researchers turned to physical punishment only after other procedures proved ineffective. This girl was treated many years ago, and there's been a great deal of progress since then; today behaviorists have many ways of dealing with problems that used to be treated with aversives. I haven't seen figures on this, but I'm sure behaviorists use aversives much less often today than they did 20 years ago. The aversives used today are also likely to be much milder than in the past. There may be times when punishment, negative reinforcement, or aversion therapy is the only procedure that is likely to produce positive results. But the behavior analyst should always make sure that these procedures are used only when more positive approaches have failed or are extremely likely to fail.

That brings us to the third ethical principle:

3. Consider the alternatives to the planned intervention.

Before implementing an intervention, it's always a good idea to ask, "What other options are available?" Suppose you have a student who acts out in class, disrupting the lesson and interfering with the learning process. You may be able to change this behavior by putting it on extinction and providing reinforcement for more appropriate behavior. Some people find such efforts objectionable. You are, they claim, interfering with the child's natural exuberance; you are treading on the child's right to self-expression; you are taking away the child's freedom, and so on. Well, what you need to ask yourself and your critic is, "What is the alternative?"

One benefit of asking this question is that sometimes a more attractive alternative does present itself. Often, however, the alternative is some procedure that is unlikely to be effective. In the case of a disruptive student, for example, one alternative might be to "reason" with the child. Sometimes the suggestion is to tolerate the behavior in the hope that the child will "outgrow it." But these alternatives mean that the disruptions will probably continue, and the student and his classmates will learn less than they could.

It is also important to consider alternatives in the workplace. If a behavior problem (such as low productivity, high accident rates, absenteeism, wasted raw materials, theft of supplies, etc.) isn't solved, what will happen? Will the company have to reduce the number of employees? Will it have to relocate where labor is cheaper? What will happen to the company and its employees if an effective intervention isn't found? When you compare what is likely to be an effective plan for changing behavior against the alternatives, the ethics of proceeding often become clear.

The Pram Man—the fellow who attacked baby carriages and women's handbags—provides a convenient example. When the Pram Man was referred for treatment, he was under consideration for a leucotomy, a procedure that would have destroyed a good deal of brain tissue. I can't say whether the surgery would have prevented him from attacking baby carriages, but it's certain that it would have had drastic and undesirable side effects.

The aversion therapy that the Pram Man received would be considered an unethical procedure by some people. But in evaluating the ethics of a procedure, we have to consider the alternatives. If the behaviorists who treated this man had said, "We're uncomfortable using aversives so we refuse to treat him," the patient might well have found himself under the care of neurosurgeons. The consequences for him would have been far worse than the brief exposure to aversives he endured.

Or, consider again the little girl Goldiamond told us about. What was the alternative to a few slaps and loud reprimands? All sorts of reinforcement procedures had apparently been tried without success, so the alternative to punishment was to prevent her from injuring herself by making her wear a football helmet and tying her hands to the side of a crib. People who find a procedure objectionable should always be asked to consider how objectionable the alternatives are. The use of aversives with this little girl is objectionable; the question is, is it more objectionable than a lifetime in restraints? Consider the alternatives.

My fourth rule for ethical practice is:

4. Monitor the results of an intervention.

Over and over again I have mentioned the importance of monitoring the effects of a procedure. This means collecting data on the frequency of the target behavior. Such data provide the only reliable means of evaluating the effects of an intervention. However, it also means looking for the appearance of new problems that may arise during the intervention. When new problems arise, it is necessary to collect data on them as well.

Although the importance of monitoring results may seem obvious, it is often neglected. Educators, for example, quite frequently experiment with interventions without adequately monitoring their effects. Right now, thousands of schools are implementing some sort of program for raising students' self-esteem. The interventions are *assumed* to improve self-esteem and reduce behavior problems, but typically no objective data are collected to verify those effects.[11]

> "So, are you saying that it is *unethical* to implement a program if you don't monitor its effects?"

Yes, Brian, I am. I think it is unethical to implement a program that is having negative effects, and there's no way you can rule out that possibility except by monitoring results. This doesn't mean that a teacher, for example, has to spend hours and hours monitoring a program. Once you have good objective evidence that a program is having the desired effects, you can monitor results intermittently. But I do believe it is irresponsible to implement a program and simply *assume* that it is accomplishing what it is intended to accomplish.

Now, I have described four principles, four rules of thumb, that will help keep you out of ethical jams. Let's see, rule number 1 was . . . Maya?

> "Hmm. Was that the idea that you should encourage the participation of the person whose behavior you're trying to change?"

What do you think?

> "I think it was."

You think right. What was the second ethics rule, Belinda?

> "Avoid aversives."

Yes. Avoid aversives whenever possible. And rule number 3, Jamal?

> "Consider the alternatives to the intervention you're proposing."

Right. And rule number 4, John?

"Monitor the results you get from your intervention."

Excellent.[12] But such rules are helpful only to the extent that people follow them. The real problem is, Will people follow the rules? What do you think? Will therapists and teachers and managers and parents obey these rules when they attempt to change the behavior of others? . . . Nobody knows? Well, let me give you a hint: Ethical behavior is *behavior*; unethical behavior is *behavior*. And behavior is a function of . . . ? Everybody: Behavior is a function of its . . .

"CONSEQUENCES!"

Exactly. Ethical behavior is a function of its consequences. Unethical behavior is a function of its consequences. So what does that tell you about whether people will behave ethically? Yes, Belinda?

"It tells me that it depends on what the consequences are for behaving ethically and unethically."

Exactly! If behaving ethically has reinforcing consequences, people will do it. If behaving unethically pays off, people will do that. So having a set of rules about ethical behavior isn't enough. The rules identify the kinds of behavior that *should* be performed or avoided, but if rule following doesn't have reinforcing consequences, then you aren't going to see rules followed. So, what do we need to do if we want to see people behaving ethically? Jamal?

"See to it that following ethical guidelines is reinforced?"

Of course. So then the problem is, how do you arrange these consequences? Unfortunately, I don't think we have a very good answer to that question. Hospitals, clinics, residential treatment facilities, and universities often have review boards that decide whether a proposed research project or intervention program meets ethical standards. And professional organizations such as APA, AABT, and ABA have procedures whereby members who are guilty of ethics violations can be punished in some way. State laws also provide penalties for certain forms of unethical behavior.

But these efforts focus on punishing unethical behavior; little or nothing is done to reinforce ethical behavior in a systematic way. Moreover, these contingencies do not readily reach teachers in the classroom, managers in the workplace, and parents in the home who may be attempting to change behavior in entirely inappropriate and unethical ways.

Nevertheless, I think we have established that changing behavior can be an ethical activity. That's a good thing because most of us are trying to change other people's behavior a good deal of the time. And I hope you will agree that using powerful tools, such as those provided by behavior analysis, to change behavior is ethical if they are used correctly and in accordance with ethical principles.

If changing behavior is ethical, then behavior analysis may have a future. But what sort of future is it likely to have? Is the world ready to embrace the idea of applying scientific method to behavior problems?

Future of Behavior Analysis

Behavior analysis is a very young field. Although it has its roots in the work of E. L. Thorndike at the turn of the 20th century, it did not become a formal discipline until Skinner's 1938 publication *The Behavior of Organisms*. Applied behavior analysis is even younger; for the most part, there was no such thing as applied behavior analysis until the late forties.

Despite the youth of behavior analysis, one hears a great deal about its death, or the death of behaviorism.[13] Behaviorism (or behavior theory) is the set of assumptions on which behavior analysis rests, so if behaviorism is dead, as is so often claimed, then behavior analysis must, at the very least, be *in extremis*. Is behavior analysis dying?

Is Behavior Analysis Dying?

One way of measuring the vitality of a discipline is by counting how often articles by its key representatives are cited by other people. It turns out that articles and books by B. F. Skinner are among the most frequently cited of all articles and books written by psychologists.[14]

Another way of evaluating the life signs of a field is by asking people to judge the contributions of its most prominent figures. One study asked historians to rank psychologists according to their importance to the field; another asked the heads of psychology departments to do the same. In both cases, the judges ranked Skinner the most important figure in psychology.[15]

In another study, prominent psychologists listed the books that they considered important. Those psychologists who had earned their Ph.D. between 1927 and 1950—

"Really old psychologists."

Well, Alfred, let us say "mature psychologists." Anyway, psychologists who had earned their degree between 1927 and 1950 listed works by Freud most often; works by Skinner did not even appear in the top 10.[16] Those psychologists who had earned their degree between 1951 and 1967 listed works by Skinner most often. This does not support the popular notion that behavior analysis has declined in popularity.

Yet another way of measuring the vitality of a field is to look at publications on the subject. If a field is dying, the number of related books and journals published each year should fall. A 1986 study found that nearly 900 books on behavior analysis had been published by 1985, and over half of those books had been published since 1976. This suggests an increase, rather than a decrease, of interest in behavior analysis.

As to journals: The first behavioral journal, the *Journal of the Experimental Analysis of Behavior,* did not appear until 1958.[17] Since then, new behavioral journals have appeared steadily. By 1985, there were at least 25 behavioral journals.[18] I just happen to have a graph on a transparency. . . . You can see the growth of behavioral journals has been pretty dramatic:

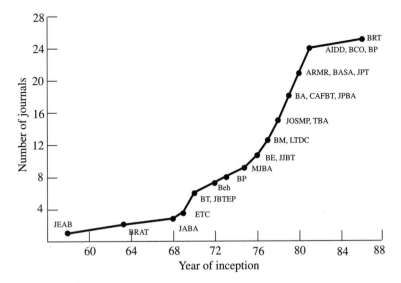

Figure 12-1. *Cumulative number of behavioral journals published per year. From "Behaviorism: Are Reports of Its Death Exaggerated?" by W. J. Wyatt, R. P. Hawkins, and P. Davis. In* Behavior Analyst, *Vol. 9, copyright 1986 Association for Behavior Analysis. Reprinted with permission.*

The formation and survival of behavioral organizations also suggests that there is a lively interest in behavior analysis. The Association for Behavior Analysis was not formed until 1974, and it currently has about 2500 members.

Although ABA is an international organization, in fact the vast majority of its members are Americans. There are, however, behavioral organizations in other countries: the Italian Association for the Analysis and Modification of Behavior; the European Association for Behavior Analysis; the Mexican Association for Behavior Analysis; and Behavior Analysis in Ireland, to mention a few. Most of these organizations were formed after 1975.

Finally, the health of a field may be judged by its influence on society as a whole. The influence of behavior analysis can be seen in the terms that have filtered into the language: *positive reinforcement* is a term that seems to have become part of the educated person's vocabulary. Other terms that seem to be filtering into the culture are *extinction, time out, token economy, shaping, intermittent reinforcement,* and *generalization.* Businesses are making increasing use of contingency analysis in their management strategies. Health professionals now turn to behaviorists for help in dealing with behavioral problems. Even education, which has been slow to adopt behavioral procedures, has acknowledged their effectiveness in special education and in classroom management.

It would appear, then, that behaviorists are in no danger of imminent extinction, despite the frequent prognostications to the contrary. That, in my view, is very good news. We need people who are able to apply scientific method to behavior problems.

We are not making much use of what we know about the way behavior is affected by experience. Take education, for example: We know how to teach far better than we do, yet despite all the talk about educational reform, we continue to teach in ineffective ways. We know, for example, that students learn at different rates; yet most instruction is group paced. We know that how well a student learns new skills depends on how well he has mastered prerequisite skills, yet we routinely teach new skills to students who have not mastered the prerequisites. We know that positive reinforcement is much to be preferred over negative reinforcement and punishment, yet negative teacher comments typically outnumber positive ones.[19] And so on. The result is that students could learn far more than they do, and enjoy learning more, if only we applied what we know about learning.[20]

We have a set of tools for dealing with behavior problems. We know how to analyze a problem, devise and test an intervention, and evaluate the results. But if we do not use those tools, then they may as well not exist. We must think about behavior problems differently. We must—

"Excuse me, Dr. Cee. I apologize for interrupting your sermon—uhm, lecture—but as your chief foil in this novel, it is my duty to interrupt."

Yes, I'm ready for you, Alfred.

"If behavior analysis is so great, if it can help us teach better, and parent better, and rehabilitate people better, and do all that wonderful stuff, then why isn't everybody a behaviorist? How come there are tens of thousands of traditional psychologists, and only a few thousand behavior analysts? And why hasn't the behavioral approach caught on with the general public?"

Those are excellent questions, Alfred. I can't give you definitive answers, but I can offer some reasonable speculations.

Why Isn't the Behavioral Approach More Popular?
First, behaviorists don't do a very good job of telling people about the good work they do.[21] Skinner wrote a few popular books, the best known of which were *Walden Two, Science and Human Behavior,* and *Beyond Freedom and Dignity.* But

these were mainly theoretical analyses; in them, Skinner talked about behavior analysis and how it *could* be applied to social problems. They don't tell the reader much about how behavior analysis has actually been used to help people. And not many other behaviorists have done much to spread the good word, either.[22] There is a huge technical literature about the uses of behavior analysis, but very few people know about it. That is partly because behaviorists have generally failed to share that information with the public.

Second, the theories and work of behaviorists are often misrepresented. Criticism is important to the growth of any field, but much of the criticism of behavior analysis misrepresents it. Critics have claimed that behaviorists deny that people think; assert that people are no different from rats and pigeons; deny that heredity plays any part in behavior; and emphasize aversives. None of this is true, but since behaviorists don't do a good job of publicizing what is true, the misrepresentations prevail. It's hard to win people over to a point of view when it is routinely misrepresented in negative ways.

Third, behavior analysis hasn't been around very long. The idea of looking for functional relations between behavior and its antecedents and consequences really began in 1938, with the publication of Skinner's book *The Behavior of Organisms*. The idea of applying the methods of behavior analysis to practical problems didn't get going until the late forties. The first issue of the *Journal of Applied Behavior Analysis* didn't appear until 1968. That may seem like the distant past to some of you, but when you consider how long the traditional approach has been around, behavior analysis is definitely the new kid on the block. New ideas, even good ones, often take a long time to be accepted, especially when they conflict with ideas that have been around for centuries.

Fourth, I think behavior analysis hasn't been widely accepted because the need for it hasn't been great. Look at the areas where applied behavior analysis prevails: The education of kids with severe learning or conduct problems; the rehabilitation of people who have suffered strokes and head injuries; the treatment of people diagnosed autistic, retarded, or schizophrenic. These are problems with which the conventional approach fails miserably. With these kinds of problems, you have to be systematic, you have to define your goals in terms of specific target behaviors, you have to provide clear antecedents and consequences, you have to monitor your results. Behavior analysis has proved itself by dealing with these kinds of difficult behavior problems that no one else could handle. So, as a society, we *have* embraced behavior analysis when we've had to. But we can get by with the traditional methods if we're dealing with less severe problems, such as teaching ordinary kids how to read or getting a child to carry out the garbage. The traditional approach may not be optimal, but it usually gets the job done—more or less.

"You seem to be saying behavior analysis doesn't have much of a future."

Not at all, Carlotta. As problems become more severe, and as we repeatedly fail to solve them with traditional approaches, I believe we will turn to more scientific approaches, including behavior analysis. For example, as unskilled labor is increasingly done by machines and jobs require more sophisticated skills from workers, the education of ordinary students becomes increasingly important. Students who might have gotten good jobs a generation ago despite being barely able to read and write must now be able to read operating manuals, interpret graphical data, and complete production reports. As the standard for literacy rises, traditional methods of teaching become less acceptable. At some point, parents will demand that the schools adopt methods that can produce the level of skill the workplace requires. Behavior analysts have already devised and tested those methods.[23]

Other problems—worker productivity, welfare, teen pregnancy, crime, child abuse, etc.—are becoming more onerous to our society. As the monetary and human costs of these problems rise, there will be increasing pressure to turn to more effective methods. If—

"I'm sorry, Dr. Cee, but this doesn't sound very reassuring."

What do you mean, Brian?

"Well, basically you're saying 'Behaviorists have a better idea, so people will accept it.'"

Yes. So?

"So Ignaz Semmelweis had a better idea. He discovered that doctors could prevent deaths from childbed fever simply by washing their hands before they examined women who had given birth. He had scientific evidence, too, but it didn't make any difference; the other doctors just laughed at him. Thousands of people died because doctors refused to wash their hands. Behavior analysts may have a better idea, but that doesn't mean it has a bright future."

Hmm. As usual, Brian, your point is well taken. People are often slow to accept scientific discoveries, even when the need for them is great. They are apt to be even slower to accept new sciences. And behavior analysis is not only a new science, it's a science that affects us in very personal ways because it deals with behavior.

Will people accept the idea that behavior is lawfully related to environmental events? Will they embrace a technology that allows us to deal much more effectively with behavior problems than we have ever done in the past?

No one can say for sure, but I believe that the law of effect will hold. Those who adopt an approach that makes them more effective are better off than those who do not. Semmelweis eventually won out: No doctor worthy of the name would dream of examining a postpartum patient today without first scrubbing up and putting on surgical gloves. Washing one's hands makes the doctor more effective, so eventually the procedure was adopted. Behavior analysis makes people more effective in dealing with behavior problems, so I believe that it, too, will win out.

But Brian is right. History offers many examples of ideas that made people more effective but were not generally accepted for many decades. If you embrace behavior analysis, if you replace the traditional approach to behavior with scientific method, you will be joining a small number of people in the advance guard. You will be like the early followers of Semmelweis. You will be a kind of pioneer.

Review

Well, that concludes my final effort to win you over to the natural science approach to behavior known as behavior analysis. Now let's review today's lesson. Mostly we've talked about the ethics of changing behavior. We pointed out that lots of people, not just behavior analysts, are interested in changing behavior. Some examples were . . . yes, Carlotta?

"Teachers, students, psychotherapists, employers, supervisors, parents—"

Yes, and lots of others. You could say that everybody is, to some extent, in the behavior modification business. Despite this, a lot of people are very suspicious of people who admit outright that they are trying to change behavior. What was one criticism we discussed? Midori?

"Some people say that changing a person's behavior dehumanizes them, robs them of their freedom and dignity."

And how do behaviorists defend themselves against that criticism?

"They argue that they're trying to help the person, to make him or her a more effective human being."

Shouldn't we outlaw procedures that *can* be used to dehumanize people, even if they aren't usually used for that purpose?

"No, I don't think so. If you're going to do that, then you'd have to outlaw anything that could detract from a person's humanity. You'd have to outlaw medications because some people abuse them. You'd have to outlaw computers because somebody might get so involved with computers that he wouldn't develop relationships with people. You'd have to—"

Okay, okay. You've convinced me. What other ethical charges have been brought against behaviorists? Yes, Jamal?

"Some people say it's cruel when aversives are used."

So how do you justify the use of aversives to change behavior?

"You don't, unless nothing else works and it's really, really necessary."

What would make the use of aversives really, really necessary?

"Well, like that film that Goldsomething—"

Goldiamond. A very famous behaviorist.

"Right. That Goldiamond saw. The girl was banging her head and pulling her hair and all that. Sometimes an effective treatment hurts, like when you see a dentist."

But the dentist doesn't slap people.

"The dentist does what it takes to fix your tooth. She doesn't do something because it hurts, she does it because it's necessary to solve the problem. Sometimes aversives might be needed to solve a behavior problem."

Why not just let the undesirable behavior persist?

"Because the behavior can cause injury. Aversives are used to decrease behavior that is harmful to someone, usually the person who's engaging in the behavior. That girl in the film was hurting herself by hitting her head and pulling her hair; the aversives got her to stop hurting herself."

All right. We discussed one more charge that is brought against those who change behavior; what was it, Belinda?

"Manipulativeness."

Which means?

"Which means getting people to do things they wouldn't ordinarily do."

And that's unethical?

"Not necessarily. You pointed out that lots of times it's good to get people to do things they're reluctant to do. It's really only unethical if we get someone to do something that isn't in their own best interests."

Such as . . . ?

"Such as getting employees to work under unsafe conditions."

Okay, so people say that changing behavior is unethical because it's dehumanizing, cruel, or manipulative. Tell me again: Who needs to be concerned about these possible ethical problems? John?

"Anybody who tries to change behavior."

Not just behavior analysts?

"No."

So why do so many people seem to think that these ethical concerns apply only to behavior analysis? Alfred?

"Because they've got the sharp knife."

Meaning?

"Behavior analysis makes people more effective at changing behavior, so people worry that they might abuse that power."

Effective tools have always been misused by a few people. Behavioral tools are no different. So why don't we just outlaw behavior analysis? Make it a felony to deliberately change a person's behavior? Maya?

"Because there's lots of behavior problems that people need help with. They're not going to go away. We have to use the most effective tools we have."

Are there things we can do to avoid using behavior analysis unethically?

"You told us four rules we could follow to prevent unethical behavior."

Yes, I did, didn't I? What was rule number 1, Midori?

"Encourage the person you're working with, the one whose behavior you're trying to change, to be involved in designing the intervention."

And rule number 2? Yes, John?

"Avoid aversives whenever possible."

Precisely right. Don't use any form of aversive if you can solve the problem in another way. Rule number 3, Belinda?

"Consider the alternatives."

And that means . . . ?

"It means that before you try an intervention, you should ask yourself what other options you have. Maybe there's another kind of intervention that would be better."

Excellent. This step is especially important if you're thinking of using aversives. Now, what was the last rule of ethical practice? Carlotta?

"Monitor the results of your intervention."

Good. Why is that important?

"Because it's unethical to do something that's not working, or doing harm, and the only way you can tell if that's happening is if you monitor the results you get."

Right. Teachers, managers, psychotherapists, physicians, ministers, parents do all sorts of things to change behavior without monitoring the results of their efforts. They decide whether something worked on the basis of their impression or what someone said. That's not good enough. We need to get objective measures of the effects of our interventions—whatever they are.

Now, what about the future? Does all the criticism of behaviorists mean they are in danger of imminent extinction? Brian?

"No. You cited all kinds of evidence that behaviorists are very influential."

What evidence?

> "Well, like the fact that works by B. F. Skinner get cited a lot; that there's a steady stream of books on behavior analysis; that lots of new journals on behavior analysis have come out; that there's lots of behavioral organizations; and . . . there were some other points, but I can't remember them."

Yes, well, let the readers look them up for themselves; you got most of the evidence. The point is that behavior analysis will be around for a while. But if behavior analysis is so important, why do so few people accept this approach to behavior problems? John?

> "You gave us four reasons. One was, you said that behaviorists weren't good about publicizing what they do."

What else has discouraged the acceptance of the behavioral approach? Maya?

> "Misrepresentation. A lot of people who criticize behaviorists set up a kind of straw man to attack. They claim that behaviorists believe people are just big rats; that behaviorists don't believe people think; that behaviorists go around shocking people—"

What else has held back the acceptance of behavior analysis? Jamal?

> "Time?"

How do you mean?

> "You said that it takes time for new ideas to be accepted, and behavior analysis hasn't been around long."

That's right. Darwin's ideas about the origin of species have been around for 150 years, and they still aren't accepted by everyone. Skinner's ideas about the origins of behavior are just as untraditional as Darwin's, and they've been around for only a few decades.[24] It will take time for behavior analysis to be accepted. What else has held behavior analysis back? Yes, Carlotta?

> "You said there hasn't been much need for it."

Did I? What did I mean by that?

> "Behavior analysis has been adopted where traditional methods just don't work—in the treatment of people with schizophrenia, retardation, autism, and other really tough problems. I guess people turned to it as a last resort. But ordinary methods work well enough with ordinary behavior problems. Most kids learn to read eventually even if they aren't taught in a very effective way. As long as you can accept a high failure rate, you don't need to use a scientific approach."

So, does that mean the future is bleak for behavior analysts?

> "No. Applied behavior analysts will continue to be in demand because they have proved their worth in dealing with difficult problems. But the idea

of applying the same scientific approach to everyday behavior in ordinary people hasn't caught on yet."

Yes. That is the really big challenge facing us. Only the pioneers among you will dare to do it. Do we have any pioneers in this class?

Or among the readers of this book?

I wonder.

◄ Exercises ►

Feed the Skeleton

I. Ethics of Changing Behavior
    A. Examples
        1. Behavior analysts are professional behavior changers. Two other examples of people whose job is changing behavior are

        _____

        _____ .

        2. The last time I tried to change another person's behavior was when I _____ .

    B. Three arguments are commonly made against changing other people's behavior. These are

        1. _____ .
        2. _____ .
        3. _____ .

    C. Those who oppose efforts to change behavior tend to focus criticism on behavior analysis. This is because _____

    _____ .

    D. Ethical problems are less likely if we follow certain rules. These are:
        1. Encourage _____ .
        2. Avoid _____ .
        3. Consider _____ .
        4. M _____ .

II. Future of Behavior Analysis
    A. Behavior analysis is very much alive. This is indicated by evidence showing that _____ .
    B. Despite its effectiveness, the behavioral approach is not very popular. This may be because of:
        1. A lack of _____ .
        2. Mis _____ .
        3. Time: _____ .
        4. A lack of _____ .

Critic's Corner

You run into your former philosophy professor in the student center's coffee shop, and you get into a discussion about behavior analysis.

"I like it," you say, "because it's so practical. Other approaches to behavior are interesting, but they don't translate into workable solutions to problems. Today we learned about shaping."

"I've heard about shaping," the good professor interrupts. "Shaping is the perfect illustration of the manipulative and controlling nature of behavior analysis. What you behaviorists don't understand is that we shouldn't be shaping people as though they were lumps of clay; we should be freeing them from constraints so that they can be true to their innermost selves."

Continue this exchange. Write an effective rebuttal to the philosopher's remark. (The reply must be verbal; hitting the professor is not allowed.)

Weiss's Walk

You are working in a psychiatric hospital. One of the patients on your ward, Mr. Weiss, is a middle-aged man with a diagnosis of chronic, undifferentiated schizophrenia who spends an inordinate amount of time pacing up and down the ward. You ask him why he does so, but he is unresponsive. You gather baseline data and determine that Mr. Weiss spends 70% of his free time (the time he doesn't have to be somewhere else, such as the dining hall or group therapy) walking up and down the ward.

As Mr. Weiss travels the ward, he periodically encounters nurses, doctors, and aides, some of whom make eye contact, smile, or say "hello" as they pass. You suspect that these social encounters are reinforcing pacing. With the cooperation of the staff, you put pacing on extinction and reinforce other activities. Data graphing reveals that in a matter of weeks, there is a marked change in Mr. Weiss's behavior. He now spends only about 10% of his free time walking the corridor. The amount of time spent in other ward activities increases correspondingly.

You have been successful. The question is, have you been ethical?

The Walk Continues

The staff asked you to do something about Mr. Weiss's pacing (see above item) because he was constantly getting in the way. He'd walk in people's paths so they'd have to stop or go around him. He never hurt anyone, but he was a major nuisance and irritated the staff. Does this information change your judgment about the ethics of the intervention?

The Walk Goes On

Mr. Weiss's pacing (see above item) interfered with the staff's efforts to serve the patients in their care. He distracted the staff members from their duties, slowed them down, and took time that might be better used in other ways. The irritation of the staff members showed itself in their rudeness to other patients. Does this information change your judgment about the ethics of the procedure?

More on Weiss's Walk

Mr. Weiss's pacing (see above item) had led some of the staff to ask the ward psychiatrist to prescribe heavy doses of a tranquilizer to reduce Mr. Weiss's mobility. Others wanted him strapped to a chair for much of the day. The psychiatrist told you that one of these procedures would be adopted if you were unable to solve the problem. Does this information change your judgment about the ethics of the intervention?

End of the Walk

What have you learned from the exercises on Weiss's Walk?

Practice Quiz

1. When attempting to solve behavior problems, it's a good idea to encourage the person concerned to participate in the design of the _____ _____ .

2. One reason that behavior analysis is not more popular is _____ _____ .

3. Before implementing an intervention, you should always consider the _____ .

4. One way in which behavior analysis is frequently misrepresented is _____ _____ .

5. Some critics say that applied behavior analysis is _____ _____ . Behaviorists reply that their work is more likely to make the person more human.

6. Some people say that behavior analysis is cruel because solving behavior problems sometimes causes discomfort. Behaviorists reply by pointing to _____ , who sometimes cause discomfort while solving problems.

7. A survey of journals related to behavior analysis suggests that interest in the field has _____ .

8. In solving behavior problems, _____ should be avoided whenever possible.

9. It is unethical to implement an intervention that may be making matters worse; therefore it is important to _____ the results of the intervention.

10. Applied behavior analysts are specialists in changing behavior. Another group of people whose work involves changing behavior is _____ _____ .

Reprint: THE RIGHT TO EFFECTIVE TREATMENT
by Ron Van Houten, Chair and the Task Force
on the Right to Effective Treatment

Effective treatment for behavior problems is almost by definition controversial. If a therapist provides hard evidence that particular procedures, rather than mysterious forces within the client, are producing changes in that client's behavior, concerns about Big Brother and individual rights are bound to follow. But what about the rights of that client to receive treatment that will help him live a fuller, happier life? The Association for Behavior Analysis assigned a task force, headed by Ron Van Houten, to formulate a statement concerning the right to effective treatment. What follows is the report of that task force.

Over the last several decades, a number of clinical procedures derived from experimental and applied behavior analysis have been developed, evaluated, and refined. These procedures have the demonstrated ability to teach new behavior and alleviate a variety of behavioral disorders. Unfortunately, many who would benefit from behavioral treatment are not receiving it. Behavior analysts have a professional obligation to make available the most effective treatment that the discipline can provide. Toward this end, the following statement of clients' rights is offered to direct both the ethical and appropriate application of behavioral treatment.

1. An Individual Has a Right to a Therapeutic Environment. A physical and social environment that is safe, humane, and responsive to individual needs is a necessary prerequisite for effective treatment. Such an environment provides not only training, but also an acceptable living standard. The dimensions of an adequate living environment are complex and varied; nevertheless, several elements appear essential. Individuals should have access to therapeutic services, leisure activities, and materials that are enjoyable as well as instructive. Thus, client preference, in addition to factors such as age-appropriateness and educative value, is relevant in the selection of activities and materials. An adequate environment also includes parents, teachers, and staff who are competent, responsive, and caring. Such qualities may be characterized in terms of frequent positive interactions that are directed toward enjoyment, learning, and independence. Finally, a therapeutic environment imposes the fewest restrictions necessary, while insuring individual safety and development. Freedom of individual movement and access to preferred activities, rather than type of location of placement, are the defining characteristics of a least restrictive environment.

2. An Individual Has a Right to Services Whose Overriding Goal Is Personal Welfare. The primary purpose of behavioral treatment is to assist individuals in acquiring functional skills that promote independence. Both the immediate and long-term welfare of an individual are taken into account through active participation by the client or an authorized proxy in making treatment-related decisions. In cases where withholding or implementing treatment involves potential risk, Peer Review Committees and Human Rights Committees play distinctive roles in protecting client welfare. Peer Review Committees, comprised of experts in behavior analysis, impose professional standards in determining the clinical propriety of treatment programs. Human Rights Committees, comprised of consumers, advocates, and other interested citizens, impose community standards in determining the acceptability of programs and the extent to which a program compromises an individual's basic rights to dignity, privacy, and humane care; appropriate education and training; prompt medical treatment; access to personal possessions, social interaction, and physical exercise; humane discipline; and physical examination prior to the initiation of a program that may affect or be affected by an individual's health status. Professional competence aided by peer and human rights review will ensure that behavioral treatment is delivered within a context of concern for client welfare.

3. An Individual Has a Right to Treatment by a Competent Behavior Analyst. Professionals responsible for delivering, directing or evaluating the effects of behavioral treatment possess appropriate education and experience. The behavior analyst's academic training reflects thorough knowledge of behavioral principles, methods of assessment and treatment, research methodology, and professional ethics. Clinical competence also requires adequate practicum training and supervision, including experience with the relevant client population.

In cases where a problem or treatment is complex or may pose risk, individuals have a right to direct involvement by a doctoral-level behavior analyst who has the expertise to detect, analyze, and manage subtle aspects of the assessment and treatment process that often determine the success or failure of intervention. A doctoral-level behavior analyst also has the ability, as well as the responsibility to ensure that all individuals who participate in the delivery of treatment or who provide support services are trained in the methods of intervention, to assess the competence of individuals who assume subsequent responsibility for treatment, and to provide consultation and follow-up services as needed.

4. An Individual Has a Right to Programs That Teach Functional Skills. The ultimate goal of all services is to increase the ability of individuals to function effectively in both their immediate environment and the larger society. Improvement of functioning may take several forms. First, it often will require the acquisition, maintenance, or generalization of behaviors that allow the individual to gain wider access to preferred materials, activities, or social interaction. Second, it may require the acquisition of behaviors that allow the individual to terminate or reduce sources of unpleasant stimulation. Third, improved functioning may require the reduction or elimination of certain behaviors that are dangerous or that in some way serve as barriers to further independence or social acceptability. Finally, as a member of society at large, an individual has a right to services that will assist in the development of behavior beneficial to that society.

Decisions regarding the selection of service goals are not based on a priori assumptions of an individual's behavioral potential or limitations. It is conceivable that some goals might be achieved very slowly, that others may be only approximated, and that, in the process of achieving still other goals, it may be necessary to expose the individual to either immediate temporary discomfort (e.g., as in teaching physical exercise as a means of promoting health) or future risk (e.g., as in teaching an individual to cross streets or to drive an automobile). Still, unless evidence clearly exists to the contrary, an individual is assumed capable of full participation in all aspects of community life and to have a right to such participation.

5. An Individual Has a Right to Behavioral Assessment and Ongoing Evaluation. Prior to the onset of treatment, individuals are entitled to a compete diagnostic evaluation to identify factors that contribute to the presence of a skill deficit or a behavior disorder. A complete and functional analysis emphasizes the importance of events that are antecedent, as well as consequent, to the behavior of interest. For example, identification of preexisting physiological or environmental determinants may lead to the development of a treatment program that does not require extensive use of behavioral contingencies.

The initial behavioral analysis is performed in three stages. First, answers to the following types of questions are obtained through interview. Is there any circumstance in which behavior *always* occurs? Is there any circumstance in which the behavior *never* occurs? Does the behavior typically occur at certain times of the day? Could the behavior be associated with any form of discomfort or deprivation? Could events following the behavior serve as either positive reinforcement (e.g., attention) or negative reinforcement (e.g., escape from demands)? The second stage of analysis, direct observation of the individual's behavior under varied and relevant circumstances, confirms suspected relationships identified during the interview. Finally, the assessment findings are incorporated into a systematic treatment plan.

Successful intervention requires ongoing evaluation in the form of objective data to determine the effects of treatment, to quickly identify unanticipated problems, and, if necessary, to modify the treatment plan. The behavior analyst maintains accountability and solicits timely input into the decision-making process by sharing these data regularly with all concerned parties.

6. An Individual Has a Right to the Most Effective Treatment Procedures Available. An individual is entitled to effective and scientifically validated treatment. In turn, behavior analysts have an obligation to use only those techniques that have been demonstrated by researchers to be effective, to acquaint consumers and the public with the advantages and disadvantages of these techniques, and to search continuously for the most optimal means of changing behavior.

Consistent with the philosophy of least restrictive yet effective treatment, exposure of an individual to restrictive procedures is unacceptable unless it can be shown that such procedures are necessary to produce safe and clinically significant behavior change. It is equally unacceptable to expose an individual to a nonrestrictive intervention (or a series of such interventions) if assessment results or available research indicate that other procedures would be more effective. Indeed, a slow-acting but nonrestrictive procedures could be highly restrictive if prolonged treatment increases risk, significantly inhibits or prevents participation in needed training programs, delays entry into a more optimal social or living environment, or leads to adaptation and the eventual use of a more restrictive procedure. Thus, in some cases, a client's right to effective treatment may dictate the immediate use of quicker-acting, but temporarily more restrictive procedures.

A procedure's overall level of restrictiveness is a combined function of its absolute level of restrictiveness, the amount of time required to produce a clinically acceptable outcome, and the consequences associated with delayed intervention. Furthermore, selection of a specific treatment technique is not based on personal conviction. Techniques are not considered as either "good" or "bad" according to whether they involve the use of antecedent rather than consequent stimuli or reinforcement rather than punishment. For example, positive reinforcement, as well as punishment, can produce a number of indirect effects, some of which are undesirable.

In summary, decisions related to treatment selection are based on information obtained during assessment about the behavior, the risk it poses, and its controlling variables; on a careful consideration of the available treatment options, including their relative effectiveness, risks, restrictiveness, and potential side effects; and on examination of the overall context in which treatment will be applied.

Conclusion

Behavior analysts have a responsibility to insure that their clients' rights are protected, that their specialized services are based on the most recent scientific and technological findings, that treatment is provided in a manner consistent with the highest standards of excellence, and that individuals who are in need of service will not be denied access to the most effective treatment available. In promulgating the rights described in this document, the field of behavior analysis acknowledges its responsibilities by reaffirming its concern for individual welfare and by prescribing the means by which behavioral treatment can be delivered in the most beneficial manner.

From "Report of the Task Force on the Right to Effective Treatment," by Ron Van Houten, Chair. In *Behavior Analyst, Vol. 11,*1988.

◄ Recommended Reading ►

1. American Psychological Association. (1992). Ethical principles of psychologists and code of conduct. *American Psychologist, 47,* 1597–1611.
   The APA code is widely recognized as the standard for ethical conduct in the helping professions.

2. Bandura, A. (1975). The ethical and social purposes of behavior modification. In C. M. Franks & G. T. Wilson (Eds.), *Annual review of behavior therapy theory and practice: 1975* (pp. 13–20). New York: Brunner/Mazel.
   Bandura discusses ethical problems involved in changing behavior.

3. Franks, C. M., & Wilson, G. T. (1975). Ethical and related issues in behavior therapy. In C. M. Franks & G. T. Wilson (Eds.), *Annual review of behavior therapy theory and practice: 1975* (pp. 1–11). New York: Brunner/Mazel.
   Franks and Wilson discuss ethical issues as they apply specifically to behavior therapy.

4. Wyatt, W. J., Hawkins, R. P., & Davis, P. (1986). Behaviorism: Are reports of its death exaggerated? *The Behavior Analyst, 9,* 101–105.
   Wyatt et al. studied the "corpse" and found it very much alive.

◄ Endnotes ►

1. A lot of people preparing to be teachers take a course in classroom management when they're in college. These courses usually tell the prospective teachers how to deal with disruptive behavior. Usually, they emphasize the same tools you have learned about in this course: reinforcement, extinction, and so on. It is important to remember, however, that disruptive behavior is also affected by how students are taught; see, for example, Armendariz (1996).

2. See, for example, Krutch (1953) and Koestler (1968).

3. Goldiamond (1974).

4. The aversives used by behavior analysts for therapeutic purposes are typically *less* severe than those commonly used in our society. Some parents, for example, hit their children repeatedly in the name of discipline, and educators sometimes expel students for rule infractions, including (ironically) truancy.

5. Goldiamond (1974). Goldiamond describes the film and discusses various ethical issues.

6. In the 1970s, behavioral procedures came under especially sharp criticism. A U.S. Senate committee chaired by Senator Sam Ervin was wary of behavior change procedures (Ervin, 1973). On February 14, 1974, the Law Enforcement Assistance Act banned the use of federal funds for behavior modification programs for prisoners, juvenile offenders, and alcoholics (Goldiamond, 1974, note 1). Stolz (1978) notes that this ban apparently applies only to the use of aversive procedures.

7. APA (1992); AABT (1977). The APA ethics code covers a wide variety of topics: competence, integrity, sexual harassment, exploitation, informed consent, etc. Unfortunately, much of the code is in the form of noble but vague generalizations such as, "Psychologists accord appropriate respect to the fundamental rights, dignity, and worth of all people" (APA, 1992, p. 1599).

8. Bandura (1975) writes that "behavioral approaches achieve their successes by the joint efforts of participants, not through unilateral control" (p. 15). People *can* change another person's behavior without the person's knowledge or consent, but doing so is often on shaky grounds ethically.

9. According to APA (1992), informed consent implies that the person (a) has the capacity to consent to an intervention, (b) has been informed about the nature of the procedure, (c) has freely agreed to the intervention, and (d) the consent has been documented (i.e., there is a witnessed signature on a consent form). A special problem arises when the person involved engages in behavior that society condemns but that the "client" does not. The pedophile, rapist, serial murderer, and career thief may have no interest in changing his behavior. If an effective intervention program were available for treating such problems, would it be ethical to use it against the person's wishes? The point is debatable. It is ironic, however, that some people who object strenuously to programs aimed at modifying such behavior do not object at all to life imprisonment and execution.

10. For more on this, see Sidman (1989).

11. Other examples of popular (but unproven) educational interventions that are typically implemented without efforts to monitor their effects include "whole language" reading instruction, "whole brain" teaching, and teaching for "multiple intelligences."

12. Keep in mind that these rules for ethical practice apply to anyone attempting to change another person's behavior, not just to those using applied behavior analysis.

13. Those who write the obituaries of behaviorism often suggest that behavior theory once had a hegemony in psychology. So far as I can tell, however, there has never been a time when most or even a plurality of psychologists described themselves as behaviorists or identified their field of study as behavior analysis or even "behavioral psychology." The fact that behavior theory has seemed to dominate psychology probably reflects the power of the theory. For more on the ostensible death of behaviorism and behavior analysis, see Wyatt et al. (1986b).

14. Garfield (1978).

15. Korn et al. (1991). This finding is particularly impressive when you consider that few of the department heads and even fewer of the historians are likely to consider themselves "Skinnerians."

16. Heyduk & Fenigstein (1984).

17. JABA (the *Journal of Applied Behavior Analysis*) appeared ten years later, in 1968.

18. Wyatt et al. (1986a). The list of 25 journals does not include newsletters or journals that have ceased publication.

19. Thomas et al. (1978); White (1975).

20. Hopkins & Conard (1975); Johnson & Layng (1992).

21. Franks and Wilson (1975) discussed this problem, observing that, "Clearly, behavior modifiers are not very good at public relations . . ." (p. 6).

22. A notable exception is *Toilet Training in Less Than a Day* by Nathan Azrin and Richard Foxx (1974). The book tells parents how they can use simple behavioral procedures to deal with what is, for many parents, a very difficult assignment. Originally published in 1974, the book has sold over a million copies and is still in print.

23. See, for example, Hopkins & Conard (1975); Johnson & Layng (1992).

24. Effective procedures may gain acceptance even though the theory from which the procedures are derived does not. In Semmelweis's day, a doctor might have adopted the practice of washing his hands before an operation while rejecting the germ theory of disease. Today, a person may use reinforcement to change behavior, yet cling to old ideas about the origins of behavior.

13

Review and Sham Exam

Hello, hello, hello! This is the last of our meetings on applied behavior analysis. I like to reserve the last day of class for review, so today we won't be covering any new material.

We're going to review the course topics in more or less the same order in which they were covered. Of course, we can't cover every point that was covered in the course, but this review should give you a pretty good idea of which topics you need to study most. After the review, I will have you take a practice final exam; that will also help you assess your level of mastery. More on that later. All right, let's begin the review.

ABC's

Let's start with a definition of behavior analysis. Jamal?

"The science of behavior change."

Ah, yes. That's the definition I'm trying to get the behavioral community to adopt. Unfortunately, it hasn't been widely accepted as yet. What's a more traditional definition?

"The study of the functional relations between behavior and environmental events."

Good. And what is a functional relation, Midori?

"The tendency for two or more events to vary together in some way."

Okay. So we're looking for functional relations among the ABC's of behavior analysis. What are the ABC's of behavior analysis, John?

"Antecedents, behavior, and consequences."

Right. What's an antecedent, Alfred?

"That's any event that occurs before the behavior we're interested in."

And what's a consequence?

"That's an event that occurs after the behavior."

Good. And what's behavior, Maya?

"Anything a person does that can be observed?"

Right. And how many categories of behavior did we discuss?

"Four."

What are they?

"There's overt operant behavior, covert operant behavior, overt respondent behavior, and covert respondent behavior."

Right. What is covert behavior, . . . John?

"Behavior that can be observed only by the person who performs it."

Excellent. What's the difference between operant and respondent behavior, Belinda?

"Respondent behavior is an automatic response to an event, like a reflex. It isn't modified by its consequences very well; it's affected more by its antecedents. Operant behavior isn't so automatic, but it can be modified by its consequences."

Good. Now, behavior theory says that behavior is the product of biological and environmental events, but behavior analysts are interested mainly in the effects of the environment on behavior. The events that change our behavior over time are called our learning . . . what, Brian?

"Learning history."

Right. Our learning history results in our tendency to perform certain behaviors and not others. If we made a list of all the things we are inclined to do, what would that list be called, Carlotta?

"A behavioral repertoire."

Yes, a behavioral repertoire. Now, our emphasis in this course was on applied behavior analysis. And the definition of applied behavior analysis is . . . Jamal?

"It's the attempt to solve behavior problems by providing antecedents and consequences that change behavior."

Excellent. You mentioned behavior problems. You learned that, as far as behaviorists are concerned, most behavior problems fall into one of two types. What are they, Midori?

"One is when a behavior occurs too frequently; the other is when it doesn't occur frequently enough."

Good. So solving behavior problems usually means . . .

"Increasing or decreasing the rate of behavior."

Yes. But psychodynamic psychologists believe that the frequency of a problem behavior is merely a symptom of something. What is it supposed to be a symptom of, Midori?

"An underlying psychological disorder, such as an unconscious Oedipal conflict."

Right. And that view is called . . . ?

"The medical model."

Right again. And according to the medical model, if you solve a behavior problem without correcting the underlying disorder, the result will be . . . what, Belinda?

"Symptom substitution."

What does that mean?

"It means that when you get rid of one problem, another one will take its place."

Can you give me an example?

"Well, if a person is hallucinating, and you reduce the frequency of the hallucinations, symptom substitution predicts that the person might become aggressive, or start having delusions, or adopt weird mannerisms, or—"

Okay, yes. Some other problem will take the place of the problem you've solved. Is symptom substitution an important issue for behaviorists?

"Yes, because if it were true, it would make behavior analysis a lot less useful. There wouldn't be much point in reducing hallucinations if the person was just going to develop a new problem."

You say, "if it were true." Does symptom substitution occur?

"There's no good evidence that it's a problem. Even the American Psychiatric Association said that after reviewing the evidence."

Well done. We haven't talked a lot about behavior theory in this course, but there was a handout on the relationship between behaviorism and behavior analysis. You should study that. There was also a handout on feelings written by Skinner. What does Skinner think of feelings? Brian?

"They're behavior. When you feel angry, for example, what you're feeling is things going on in your body, and maybe an inclination to hit someone."

So Skinner doesn't deny that people have feelings? He doesn't say feelings don't matter?

"No. He doesn't believe they *cause* behavior, but he believes they're important *as* behavior."

Yes. Skinner's views on thoughts and feelings are very different from those of most people. They might be a good topic for an essay exam, don't you think? Now, let's talk about research methods.

Methods

We started our discussion of methods with behavioral assessment. What are the similarities and differences between behavioral and psychological assessment? Brian?

"They're similar because both attempt to find the cause of troublesome behavior. The difference is in where they look. When people do psychological assessments, they attempt to look for the causes of behavior problems inside the person's mind. When people do behavioral assessment, they look in the environment—at the antecedents and consequences of behavior."

Right. Behavioral assessment attempts to do three things. What are they, Carlotta?

"Define the target behavior; identify the functional relations between the target behavior and its antecedents and consequences; and propose an intervention."

Excellent. What's a target behavior, Belinda?

"That's the behavior that needs to be changed."

Good. And what's a functional analysis, Jamal?

"That means looking for functional relations between the target behavior and other events."

What sort of other events?

"Things that happen before or after the behavior—antecedents and consequences."

Right! Now, recording behavior rates is very important in applied behavior analysis. What are the two main ways of recording rate data? Midori?

"Continuous recording and interval recording."

Good. You should be able to define both kinds of recording. You should also be able to calculate the reliability of rate records. That's called . . . John?

"Inter-observer reliability?"

Right. As you obtain rate data, it's customary to plot it on a graph. What are the two kinds of graphs we talked about? Maya?

"Simple frequency graphs and cumulative frequency graphs."

Correct. And what's the difference between them?

"A simple frequency graph plots the number of times the behavior occurred in each observation period. A cumulative frequency graph plots the total number of times the behavior has occurred as of a particular point."

You should be able to interpret data on either kind of graph. There are several kinds of research designs that are commonly used in applied behavior analysis. What would you say is the main difference between these designs and those used in, say, social or cognitive psychology? Brian?

"Behaviorists usually use single case designs, whereas most psychologists use group designs."

Isn't single case design just another name for case study?

"No! In a single case study, you manipulate an independent variable, such as therapy, and carefully record behavior rates. You don't do that in a case study."

Well, then, what's the main difference between a single case study and a group study?

"In the single case design, the person whose behavior is being studied acts as his own control. In other words, you compare the behavior of one person under different conditions. In the group design, you're comparing different people in different conditions."

So, in a group design, the results could be due either to the independent variable, or to . . .

"Differences between the people in the experimental and control groups."

All right. So behaviorists like single case designs. What's one kind of single case design? Midori?

"ABAB reversal."

What's that?

"That's a design with a baseline, followed by an intervention, followed by a return to the baseline condition, followed by a return to the intervention. A-B-A-B. It's like turning a light switch on and off."

Good. Now, what's a multiple baseline design? Yes, Brian?

"A multiple baseline design is an alternative to the ABAB reversal design. You collect more than one baseline, and test the intervention after each baseline. You can have a design that's a multiple baseline across situations, across different behaviors, or across different people. If you get similar results in different situations, with different behaviors, or with different people, you've got a pretty good case for saying the intervention produced the changes."

What if you wanted to test the effects of different interventions? How would you do that, Carlotta?

"I'd use an alternating treatments design. That's where you get a baseline and then alternate interventions."

Good. Okay, one of the handouts I gave you when we discussed methods was about a psychiatric patient who spent a lot of time holding onto a broom. What did the researchers hope to prove with that study? . . . No one knows? Well, you should. But maybe I'll save that question for the final exam. Now let's talk about reinforcement.

Reinforcement

Reinforcement is based on a law. What law, Jamal?

"The law of effect?"

Right. And the law of effect says?

"Behavior is a function of its consequences. The likelihood of a behavior occurring in a particular situation depends on the consequences the behavior has had in that situation in the past."

Excellent. Now, what is reinforcement? Belinda?

"That's the procedure of providing consequences for a behavior that increase or maintain the frequency of that behavior."

Good. And what is a reinforcer?

"That's an event that, when it is made contingent on a behavior, increases or maintains the frequency of that behavior."

Excellent. What's the difference between positive and negative reinforcers, Alfred?

"A positive reinforcer is something that's added following a behavior; a negative reinforcer is something that's taken away."

Exactly right. Remember that a reinforcer increases the frequency of a behavior, whether it's positive or negative. What other kinds of reinforcers are there? John?

"Primary. Those are the ones that are unlearned, like food and water."

Yes, and reinforcers that aren't primary are . . .

"Secondary. They're the ones that depend on past learning. Like praise and money."

Good. What are contrived reinforcers, Maya?

"They're reinforcers that have been provided by someone to change behavior. They're part of an intervention program."

That's right. And reinforcers that haven't been programmed in that way, that are just the ordinary consequences of the behavior, are called . . .

"Natural reinforcers."

Very good. Now, to use reinforcement effectively, you have to follow certain rules. I'm not going to review those, but you should go back to your notes to make sure you know them.

Reinforcement is a powerful procedure, but there are some problems with it. What's one problem, Maya?

"It can be misused. You can make a problem worse if you reinforce the wrong behavior or reinforce in the wrong way."

Good. What's another problem with reinforcement? Alfred?

"Some people object to it on moral grounds. They say it spoils people, that it's bribery."

Yes. There was one more argument against reinforcement. What was that, Belinda?

"Negative side effects?"

Yes. For example, some people say that reinforcing an activity makes people less interested in the activity. According to this idea, if people cheer for you when you play basketball and tell you afterward what a great job you did, you won't want to play basketball. What about that? Is that a legitimate argument? Carlotta?

"No. I read this really great article by Paul Chance—it was mentioned in one of the handouts—and it summarized the research on this. The article showed that, basically, reinforcement only reduces interest under very special circumstances—like if you hold out a reward of some sort to get someone to do something they already do a lot."

Yes, that's true. There are more recent and more scholarly articles on this problem, but the conclusions are essentially the same. Reinforcement is a very safe procedure, provided that the intended behavior gets reinforced. Negative side effects of reinforcement—properly used reinforcement—are rare.

I meant to review the handout on finding reinforcers—remember that one?—but our time is limited, so we'll have to move on to prompting and fading.

Prompting and Fading

What is a prompt, Jamal?

"A prompt is an antecedent that induces a person to perform a behavior that otherwise would not occur."

All right. There are five kinds of prompts. Can you name them?

"Let's see. There's verbal prompts, gestural, physical, . . . modeling, . . . and one more that I can't think of."

Can you think of it, John?

"Is it environmental?"

Yes, it is.

You should be able to define each of these kinds of prompts and provide examples, and if I give you an example of a prompt, you should be able to tell me what kind it is. For example, if you're called on in class and you're drifting off into dreamland, a nearby student might give you a little jab with his elbow. What sort of prompt would that be, Midori?

"That would be a physical prompt."

That would be right. And if I say to you, "Riding a bike is easy. Watch," and then I ride a bike around, what sort of prompt am I providing, Carlotta?

"Well, when you say 'Watch,' you could be providing a verbal prompt for looking at you as you ride the bike. And when you ride the bike, you're modeling the behavior, so that could be a modeling prompt."

What do you mean, "could be"?

"I can't tell whether they're prompts until I see their effects on behavior."

Why should that matter, Belinda?

"Well, because prompting means doing something that evokes a behavior. If the person doesn't watch you when you say, 'Watch,' then 'Watch' isn't a prompt. And if he doesn't imitate you by riding the bike, then riding the bike isn't a prompt."

Both of you are very clever today. I hope you do as well on the exam. What sort of prompt was used to get Dicky to imitate speech? Dicky was the little autistic boy who didn't speak normally. Instead of responding to a question in the usual way, he would just repeat the question, like an echo. What sort of prompt did the therapists use to get him to speak more normally? Midori?

"Didn't they show him some photographs? They'd show him a picture of a cat and say, 'What's this? Say *Cat*.' And when he imitated by saying 'cat,' they'd reinforce that. So they used verbal prompts."

Right. Now, one of the handouts I gave you was something by Skinner on rules. Do you remember that? What did he say about rules, Carlotta?

"He said that one of the things we learn to do is to follow instructions and rules, and that helps us do things we've never done before. Like, the instruction booklet for your computer might say, 'Quit all programs before shutting down the computer.' By following those instructions, you can avoid damaging your software. So the rule, 'Quit programs before shutting down,' prompts the behavior—if you've learned to follow rules."

Excellent. And Skinner gave that kind of behavior, behavior that is prompted by a rule or instructions, a name. What was it?

"He called it rule-governed behavior."

Yes, that's right. And what did Skinner call behavior that isn't rule-governed, Brian?

"Contingency-shaped?"

Yes. Okay. Now, what is the reason for prompting a behavior? Alfred?

"So that the behavior will occur?"

But *why* do you want the behavior to occur?

"Oh, yeah, so that you can reinforce it."

Right. You prompt behavior because, although it's in the person's repertoire, it doesn't occur often enough. So you prompt it in order to reinforce it.

Now, prompting and reinforcing behavior are fine as far as they go, but they don't go far enough. If all you do is prompt and reinforce, the behavior is certain to occur when you provide the prompt, but we typically want the behavior to occur without the prompt. So, how do you accomplish that? Carlotta?

"By fading the prompts. You gradually reduce the strength of the prompt."

Right. And that's why we speak of prompting and fading. Prompting and fading is a good tool when the target behavior is in the person's repertoire, but what if it isn't? What do you do then, Brian?

"That's when you have to turn to shaping and chaining."

Shaping and Chaining

Let's start with shaping. What is shaping, John?

"The reinforcement of successive approximations of a desired behavior."

What are successive approximations?

"Well, an approximation is a behavior that resembles the target behavior in some way. And successive approximations are behaviors that resemble the target behavior more and more."

Where do these successive approximations come from, Jamal?

"They're just the natural variations in behavior. Nobody does *exactly* the same thing twice. The slight variations mean that something a person does will be more like the target behavior than other things he does."

Good answer, Jamal. We talked about some studies in which therapists used shaping to deal with problems—stuttering, mutism, and wearing unnecessary articles of clothing. We don't have time to review those studies, but you should be familiar with how shaping helped. You should also be able to describe how shaping could be used to deal with a new, hypothetical problem, if I were to give you one.

Okay, onward and upward: What's chaining? Midori?

"Chaining is the procedure of reinforcing successive elements of a behavior chain."

And what, pray tell, is a behavior chain?

"That's a series of related actions, the last of which produces reinforcement."

Okay. So, how do you do chaining?

"First, you define the target behavior, the chain. You might have to do a task analysis to do that. Then you reinforce the performance of each link in the chain."

Does it matter which element you train first, Alfred?

"Yes. You should start at the beginning and work toward the end—that's called forward chaining—or you should start at the end and work toward the beginning—that's called backward chaining."

Very good, Alfred. Well, it sounds like shaping and chaining are very similar. Are there any differences, Carlotta?

"Shaping always moves toward the target behavior, but chaining can work forward or backward. Also, in shaping you provide reinforcers right from the beginning, but in chaining the main reinforcer comes after doing the last element in the chain."

Okay, good. Now let's talk about ways of reducing the frequency of behavior. The first two procedures for reducing behavior rates were . . . Jamal?

"Extinction and differential reinforcement, I think."

You think right.

Extinction and Differential Reinforcement

What is extinction?

"Withholding the reinforcers that maintain a behavior."

Right. It's a procedure, like reinforcement, only in the case of extinction you're preventing reinforcement. What happens when you put a person on extinction? Carlotta?

"You don't put a *person* on extinction. You put a *behavior* on extinction."

Oh, my. Did I say "put a person on extinction"? Shame on me. Well, what happens when you put a behavior on extinction?

"A number of things can happen. Eventually, the rate of the behavior is going to decline. But other things can happen. At first the behavior is likely to increase in frequency."

What's that called, Jamal?

"An extinction burst?"

Right. What else can happen during extinction, Carlotta?

"Emotional behavior, such as aggression or crying."

Any other effects of extinction?

"Sometimes another behavior that used to produce reinforcement will reappear during extinction."

What's that called, Belinda?

"Resurging?"

Resurgence. Are there any other effects of extinction, Belinda?

"Sometimes after the target behavior has fallen off, it will suddenly reappear again."

What's that called, Midori?

"Spontaneous recovery."

Right. The rate of the behavior falls off and stabilizes at a low rate, probably close to its baseline rate. Then suddenly the rate shoots up again, even though it hasn't been reinforced. What's the difference between these two side effects, resurgence and spontaneous recovery. Carlotta?

"Spontaneous recovery involves the target behavior, the behavior that's on extinction; resurgence involves some other behavior, a behavior that used to be effective."

Right. Sometimes behavior that was extinguished years before resurges during an extinction, so resurgence is similar to Freud's notion of . . . of what, Maya?

"Regression?"

Right. But the work on resurgence shows that resurgence occurs as the result of certain experiences, not because of mysterious unconscious forces.

All right. We discussed four rules to follow in using extinction. I won't go over those—I'm sure you have them in your notes—but I want to talk about one of them: Identify reinforcers that maintain the target behavior. Why is that rule important? John?

"You need to identify the reinforcers that maintain the behavior because you need to know what consequences to prevent."

What if you don't have any control over the reinforcers that maintain the target behavior?

"Then you can't use extinction."

Exactly right. That's really important because if you can't prevent the behavior from being reinforced, then you may just make matters worse. That brings up one of the problems with extinction, the fact that sometimes the behavior is reinforced despite your best efforts. What is the name for such reinforcement? Alfred?

"Bootleg reinforcement."

Yes, that's it. Do you remember any other problems with extinction, Alfred?

"It can take a long time."

Why is that a problem?

"Because if it takes a long time, people might start reinforcing the behavior again."

Anything else?

"If the behavior is dangerous, then someone could be hurt before extinction works."

Exactly right. Another way of reducing a rate of behavior is called differential reinforcement. What is differential reinforcement? Brian?

"It's a procedure that combines extinction and reinforcement to change the frequency of some behavior."

Very good. Now, do you remember Helen? She was the woman who talked so incessantly and nonsensically that the other patients hit her. The behaviorists who took on her case asked the nurses to pay attention to Helen whenever she talked sensibly, and to ignore her whenever she talked nonsense. What procedure is that, Jamal?

"DRI."

Right. Can you explain why it's DRI?

"The two kinds of behavior, talking sense and talking nonsense, are incompatible. If you reinforce one, the other decreases."

Excellent. Another option would be to use DRA. What's that?

"That's differential reinforcement of alternative behavior. It means providing the person with another way of obtaining reinforcers."

Could you use DRL with a problem like Helen's?

"I think so. You reinforce talking nonsense, but only when it occurs at a low rate. Then you'd keep lowering the rate required for reinforcement."

That sounds good. Now, when you use differential reinforcement, one of the rules is to define the target behaviors. Why is there more than one target behavior with differential reinforcement? Carlotta?

"Because you use differential reinforcement together with extinction. You have the behavior on extinction and the behavior being reinforced."

Right. Well, what if extinction and differential reinforcement don't work or can't be used for some reason? What else can you do? Yes, Alfred?

"Use punishment."

Punishment

Yes. What exactly is punishment, Alfred?

"It's the procedure of providing consequences for a behavior that reduce the frequency of the behavior."

So, Alfred, if I smack somebody for giving a wrong answer, is that punishment?

"It is if the person is less likely to give that answer again."

Good for you. Punishment is not just a matter of providing aversive consequences for behavior; the behavior then has to be less likely to occur. Otherwise it's just . . . what, Jamal?

"Abuse."

Exactly. Now, we talked about various forms of punishment—reprimanding, response cost, time out, overcorrection, and physical punishment. I assume you can define each of these terms, give examples of them, and identify them when you are given examples of them. If you can't, you should review your notes.

Does punishment, like reinforcement, depend on the law of effect? John?

"Yes. Punishment is more or less the opposite of reinforcement."

Does that mean the rules for using punishment are the same as those for using reinforcement?

"Not exactly. When you use punishment, you also should use extinction and differential reinforcement."

Excellent. That's a really important point to remember: You don't just punish unwanted behavior; you also make sure the behavior is not reinforced, and you provide other ways of obtaining reinforcers.

Now, you have to be particularly careful about using punishment. What are the three kinds of problems we said were associated with punishment? Midori?

"It's likely to be used inappropriately and make matters worse . . . and . . . some people object to punishment on moral grounds; they don't feel anyone has the right to punish another person. . . ."

What's the third one, Jamal?

"There are some negative side effects."

Yes. Which kind of punishment is most likely to produce negative side effects?

"Physical punishment."

Right. So we have to be particularly careful about using physical punishment; we have to be discriminating about its use. How's that for a transition to discrimination training?

Discrimination Training

What is discrimination training? Carlotta?

"It's a procedure that results in a target behavior having different probabilities in different situations."

So the situations have to be different in some way. How do behaviorists talk about those differences?

"They refer to the differences as discriminative stimuli. Like, a student should say 'b' when shown a *b*, but not when shown a *d*. The two letters are discriminative stimuli."

So then there are two kinds of discriminative stimuli? What are they?

"They're called S^Ds and S^Δs."

What is an S^D? Midori?

"That's something in the presence of which the target behavior is likely to be reinforced."

And what's an S^Δ?

"That's an event in the presence of which the target behavior is unlikely to be reinforced."

All right, fine. Describe one kind of discrimination training, Alfred.

"Okay. In one, you present the S^D and the S^Δ at the same time, so the person has a choice."

What's that discrimination procedure called?

"Simultaneous training."

Good. What's another procedure?

"There's one where you alternate between the S^D and the S^Δ. You present one, then you present the other in random order."

And what's that procedure called?

"Successive training."

Right. Are there any other kinds of discrimination training? Yes, Brian?

"There's errorless discrimination training."

Tell me about that.

"You present the S^D in very weak form so that it doesn't evoke a response, and then gradually increase its strength."

Good. What does discrimination training get you? What do you end up with when the person has completed discrimination training? Maya?

"Do you mean stimulus control?"

Yes, I do. What is stimulus control?

"That's the tendency for the target behavior to occur in the presence of the S^D but not in the presence of the S^Δ."

That sounds rather Orwellian. It conjures up an image of human robots. Is it a bad thing for people to be under stimulus control?

"No, not if the behavior is useful."

What do you mean by "useful?"

"Well, if you run to a doctor every time you get a little ache or pain, that might not be helpful. But if you never went to a doctor no matter how sick you felt, that could be dangerous to your health."

So you're saying that it's desirable to discriminate between situations that require a doctor's help from those that don't?

"Right. And that's a good form of stimulus control."

So being under stimulus control doesn't necessarily mean turning into an automaton? Brian?

"It's a matter of being effective. If the discrimination training makes you more effective, then stimulus control is a good thing. If the training makes you less effective, then stimulus control is a bad thing."

I see. Well, that's a good generalization. Speaking of generalization, that's our next topic.

Generalization Training

What is generalization, Midori?

"It's the tendency for the effects of training to spread."

Exactly right. And what are the two kinds of generalization?

"Stimulus generalization and response generalization."

Right again. Can you define stimulus generalization for me, Belinda?

"That's the tendency for the effects of training to spread across situations."

All right. So stimulus generalization is the tendency for the effects of training to spread from . . .

"From the training situation to other situations."

And response generalization is . . . Carlotta?

"That's the tendency for the effects of training one behavior to spread to other behaviors."

Good. What do you have to do to be sure of getting generalization, Jamal?

"You do generalization training."

What is that?

"It means you do the training in a way that will increase generalization."

How do you do that?

"Basically, you make the training situations resemble natural situations."

That seems pretty simple. Is that really all there is to it? Brian?

"It's more complicated than it sounds. Natural situations take lots of different forms, so that means the training situation has to take lots of different forms. And different forms of the target behavior may be required, so you have to train lots of different forms of the target behavior. You're making the training situation resemble natural situations, but that means doing a lot."

Okay. So does the training in a course like this generalize? Does the training you've had enable you to solve behavior problems? Carlotta?

"It should enable us to do a better job in dealing with some problems. For example, if I have children some day, I think I'll use punishment a lot less in rearing them than I would have if I hadn't had this course. And I think I'll do a better job of using reinforcers when I interact with other people. But I don't think I'm ready to do behavior therapy."

Why not?

"Because my training has been in talking about the use of applied behavior analysis, not in *doing* it. I'd need to have some practical experience under the supervision of an experienced behavior analyst before I'd feel comfortable treating schizophrenics, or even working with juvenile delinquents."

I'm glad to hear you say that, Carlotta. There is a difference between "book learning" and on the job training. However, let's not knock book learning too much: What you've learned in this course should be useful.

Okay. Now let's consider maintenance.

Maintenance

To what does the term *maintenance* refer, John?

"Keeping the behavior going at the desired rate?"

All right. Once you've established the desired rate of a target behavior, your task is to see to it that it continues at that rate. How do you do that?

"There are two ways to do it. One is to put the behavior on a maintenance schedule."

What's a maintenance schedule?

"That's a reinforcement schedule—"

Hold it. What's a reinforcement schedule?

"That's a plan or a rule for providing reinforcers."

What kinds of reinforcement schedules are there?

"We discussed ratio schedules, interval schedules, and duration schedules. Each of them can be fixed or variable. So you have fixed ratio and variable ratio, fixed interval, and—"

Okay, good. You should be familiar with all the schedules we discussed. You should be able, for example, to say what it means for a behavior to be on a VR-50 schedule or an FR-5 schedule. And if I describe a reinforcement schedule, you should be able to tell me what the schedule is.

Now, back to maintenance schedules: You're telling me that one way to maintain a behavior is to put it on a reinforcement schedule indefinitely. One way of doing that is to work out an agreement between the people involved about the target behaviors to be performed and the consequences provided. What is that called, Midori?

"A contingency contract."

Yes. What's another way of putting behavior on a maintenance schedule?

"Setting up a token economy?"

Right. I suggested that societies do the same sort of thing with their citizens; I called these arrangements social contracts. What's the main difference between the typical social contract and the contingency contracts and token economies that behaviorists use to solve behavior problems? Brian?

"Society emphasizes punishment contingencies. You break the rules and you go to jail, you pay a fine, or you lose your license. Token economies and contingency contracts emphasize positive consequences."

Yes, we as a society haven't really learned to make good use of positive reinforcement in dealing with behavior problems. I won't get back on that soap box again, but that's something you should think about. Parents have to make a choice in child rearing: Do they emphasize positive consequences for good behavior, or negative consequences for bad behavior? Society as a whole has the same choice. Right now, society emphasizes negative consequences for bad behavior. You *are* society, so you can change that.

A while ago, John said that there were two ways of maintaining behavior. One is to put the behavior on a maintenance schedule; what's the other? Maya?

"You can do maintenance training."

What's that?

"That means doing things during the intervention that make it likely that the target behavior will persist after the intervention is over."

Doing things? What kinds of things?

"Well, you're not supposed to discontinue the intervention the instant you get the behavior change you want; you're supposed to continue the intervention."

All right. What else can you do, Belinda?

"You can do behavior trapping. That's where you expose the behavior to its natural reinforcers."

What's another maintenance training trick, Alfred?

"You might be able to teach the person how to obtain reinforcers for the target behavior. Like, some guys trained students to reinforce teachers for reinforcing *their* behavior. That was neat."

Yes, that was very clever. Are there any other maintenance training ideas, Brian?

"During training, you're supposed to make reinforcement immediate and certain. But to get maintenance, you need to shift that gradually so that you shape up tolerance for delayed and uncertain reinforcement. It seems to me there's another idea we discussed, but I can't think of it now."

Well, I suppose it has faded from your memory. Maybe it'll fade back in during the exam. Now, let's turn to counterconditioning.

Counterconditioning

What is counterconditioning, Carlotta?

"That's the use of procedures based on Pavlovian conditioning to undo the undesirable effects of past conditioning."

Okay. Conditioning involves pairing events in the environment. What kind of events, Belinda?

"A stimulus that doesn't have a particular effect on the person's behavior is paired with one that does."

Right. Why is Pavlovian conditioning important to behaviorists?

"Because it accounts for some behavior problems, such as phobias and compulsions, and because it's useful in treating those problems."

Good. We discussed two basic kinds of treatment based on Pavlovian procedures. In one, the person learns to be less fearful or anxious. That procedure is called . . . what, Brian?

"Desensitization training?"

Right. We discussed four kinds of desensitization training. What's the one that is associated with Joseph Wolpe? Maya?

"Systematic desensitization?"

Right. There's a variation of this procedure in which the client is exposed to the disturbing situation, rather than merely imagining it. What's that procedure called?

"That's in vivo desensitization."

Good. And if you do systematic desensitization on your own, what's that called?

"Self-desensitization."

Right. And there's a somewhat controversial desensitization procedure in which the therapist exposes the client to the troubling situation at full strength until it no longer causes trouble. What's that procedure called, John?

"Is it called flooding?"

Yes, it is. Now, the various forms of desensitization are used when the problem is that a situation arouses an inappropriate negative emotion, usually fear. What do we call the use of conditioning to deal with problems in which a situation arouses an inappropriate positive emotion? Yes, Maya?

"Sensitization training."

Yes. Under the heading of sensitization training, we considered aversion therapy and . . . what was the other one, Jamal?

"Covert sensitization."

Yes, that was it. Can you give us an example of a case in which sensitization training might be appropriate?

"A person who has a shoe fetish."

What's a shoe fetish?

"That's when a person is turned on by shoes."

What's wrong with that? To each his own.

> "Yeah, but if a person is so attracted to shoes that he steals them or spends the kid's college money buying women's shoes, then it's a problem."

I guess you have a point there. So if the client wanted to be less aroused by shoes, you'd do sensitization training? How would you do that? John?

> "With aversion therapy; the therapist would pair the attractive stimulus, such as shoes, with an aversive stimulus, such as a nausea-inducing drug."

How does covert sensitization therapy differ from that?

> "Instead of exposing the client to the shoes and the nausea-inducing drug, the therapist would have him imagine them. Like, the client might have to imagine throwing up while holding a shoe."

Good. All right, so much for counterconditioning. Let's see, that leaves us with the topics that we covered at our last meeting: ethics and the future of behavior analysis.

Ethics and the Future of Behavior Analysis

Is it ethical to change other people's behavior? Brian?

> "There are people who say no, but I think the answer is yes."

Why?

> "Because I think that helping people with behavior problems means changing their behavior."

What if they're happy the way they are? What if they don't want to change?

> "That might be okay in some circumstances, but in others it's just not a good answer. Somebody might like being a rapist or a pedophile. We can't say, 'That's cool. As long as it makes you happy' because that behavior hurts other people."

Well, all right. But what if their behavior doesn't hurt anyone else. Let's take that woman, Helen, who wore all those extra clothes. That didn't hurt anyone else, yet the therapists changed her behavior. Was that ethical?

> "That's not as easy a case to argue, but I think it was. That behavior had to interfere with the quality of her life. Her family apparently didn't want to take her out of the hospital, for example, when she was dressing weirdly. So she *was* hurting someone—she was hurting herself. She might also have been hurting other people. It must be painful to have a friend or relative confined to a psychiatric hospital because that person behaves oddly."

Well, I have to say I agree with you, but I think there are a lot of people who wouldn't. Maybe that's not such a bad thing. We need people who are suspicious about people who make a living changing behavior, because if somebody doesn't watch them pretty carefully, they might abuse their powers. But we also have to guard against preventing the use of effective tools. Otherwise, we end up merely warehousing people, and that itself is a kind of abuse. The ABA published a task force statement on this called . . . what was it called, Midori?

"'The Right to Effective Treatment,' I think."

Yes, that's the one. Now, one way of preventing abuse is to follow the four rules I gave you for ethical behavior change. What was rule number 1, Belinda?

"Encourage the active participation of the person whose behavior you're trying to change."

Right. The second rule, about aversives, was . . . what, Alfred?

"Avoid them—whenever possible."

Yes. People are much more likely to object to an intervention involving aversives than to one involving positive reinforcers, and rightly so. What was the third rule, Maya?

"Was that the one about alternatives?"

Yes, go on.

"You should consider the alternatives to the proposed intervention. If there's a safer, more effective intervention, you should use that."

Good. And the last rule?

"Monitor results. We always have to monitor results because it's unethical to do something that's making a problem worse, and there's no way of knowing for sure whether you're making a problem worse except to monitor the results you get."

Good. Well, I think that's all we can do today to review for the final exam. I want to say a few words about today's handout.

Today's handout is a practice exam. I call it a sham exam. The idea is to give you an opportunity to take a comprehensive exam that could be very similar to the final exam you will be taking for this course. Most of the questions won't be the same, of course, but the sham exam will give you a good idea of the kind of questions you should be able to answer.

Students tell me that taking the sham exam is a big help. They say it reduces their anxiety about the final exam and provides them with one more way of studying for it.

I strongly urge you to take the sham exam just as you would a real final exam: If possible, take it in a classroom, or at least a quiet place free of interruptions; follow the instructions exactly; write your answers to the essay questions (don't just think about how you would answer them); and don't use your notes or discuss questions with anyone else while you work on the exam.

After you have completed the sham exam, score it by referring to your notes and by comparing your answers with at least one other student. Discuss any discrepancies you and your classmates have, and resolve them by talking with other students or referring to textbooks or journals. The sham exam can be a great help to you if you make proper use of it.

Well, this is the end of your first course in applied behavior analysis. I hope you have been won over to the idea of applying scientific method to behavior problems. If not, I hope you have at least divested yourself of some of the common misconceptions about behaviorists and what they do.

You've been a good class, and I hope some of you will find your way into another textbook some day. As for me, I have to return to the world of reality. Good-bye!

Sham Exam

This practice exam is intended to help you prepare for the final examination you will be taking for this course. Answer the questions as though you were actually taking the final exam. Then, check your answers against your notes. Compare your answers with your classmates' and resolve any discrepancies.

Short Answer (2 points each)

Answer each question in 25 words or less. (Some questions may be answered satisfactorily in a word or two.) Use the space provided after each question.

1. What is a negative reinforcer?
2. What is the law of effect?
3. What is faded in the prompting and fading procedure?
4. What is the goal of maintenance training?
5. There are two procedures for doing DRL. What are they?

Fill in the Blank (2 points each)

Write a word or phrase that accurately completes the sentence.

1. There are three undesirable side effects of punishment; one of them is

   _____ .

2. Differential reinforcement combines reinforcement and _____ .

3. One step in maintenance training is to expose the behavior to its natural reinforcers. This is called behavior _____ .

4. Desensitization and sensitization are based on the laboratory research of

   _____ .

5. A(n) _____ schedule makes reinforcement contingent on the length of time a behavior persists.

True or False (2 points each)

If the statement is true, write the word *True* in the blank. Otherwise, write *False*.

_____ 1. Inter-observer reliability is calculated the same way for continuous and interval data.

_____ 2. One way of finding reinforcers is to create them.

_____ 3. DRH stands for differential reinforcement of high rate.

_____ 4. Some animals use procedures with their young that resemble shaping.

_____ 5. Stretching a reinforcement ratio too quickly can produce ratio strain.

Multiple Choice (2 points each)

Write the *letter* of the alternative that best completes the sentence.

1. Natural reinforcement that undermines an intervention is called _____ reinforcement.

   a. ordant

   b. resurgent

   c. spontaneous

   d. bootleg

2. _____ has demonstrated that abnormal and normal behavior are often functionally equivalent; that is, they produce similar consequences.

   a. J. B. Watson

   b. B. F. Skinner

   c. E. G. Carr

   d. E. L. Thorndike

3. In generalization training, the goal is for the behavior to occur in the _____ situation.

   a. resident

   b. stimulus

   c. target

   d. terminal

4. Stretching the ratio is most like _____ .

   a. discrimination training

   b. stimulus generalization

   c. shaping

   d. contingency contracting

5. A golf pro who demonstrates how to hit a shot is using a _____ prompt.

   a. verbal

   b. gestural

   c. physical

   d. modeling

Short Essay (4 points each)

Answer any *five* of the following seven questions. Answer each question in 250 words or *less*:

1. Why is evidence from ABAB research designs better than case study evidence?

2. Some people who are capable of working collect unemployment or welfare benefits instead. Their behavior is often attributed to laziness and weak moral character. What is the fundamental weakness of this explanation? How might the behavior be explained in terms of reinforcement schedules and learning history?

3. There are three rules for selecting reinforcers: think positive, secondaries first, and go natural. Explain what these rules mean.

4. What three questions should you ask before using punishment to change behavior?

5. The president of your college has asked you and other student leaders to suggest ways of reducing energy costs in the dorms. How could you incorporate prompting and fading into your plan?

6. The state ornithological association uses volunteers to conduct a bird survey every winter, but it is not known how accurately these volunteers identify birds. One proposal for dealing with this problem is to have volunteers undergo a training program that brings everyone up to a certain minimum standard. The ornithological association comes to you for help in designing a short, effective, and fun training program for its volunteers. What do you propose?

7. You are a family therapist working with a couple and the couple's two boys, ages 11 and 13. The parents relied almost exclusively on negative reinforcement, chiefly in the form of nagging, to modify the children's behavior. Thanks to you, the parents now use positive reinforcement a lot and almost never nag. The family is about to move to another town, but you will have three more sessions with the boys alone. How do you spend the time in these last sessions with the boys?

Glossary

ABAB reversal design: A single case design in which baseline and intervention conditions are repeated with the same person.

Alternating treatments design: A single case design in which two or more interventions alternate systematically.

Antecedents: Environmental events that occur *before* a behavior.

Applied behavior analysis: The attempt to solve behavior problems by providing antecedents and/or consequences that change behavior.

Aversion therapy: A form of sensitization training in which a stimulus that arouses an inappropriate positive response is paired with an aversive stimulus. Used especially in the treatment of drug abuse and criminal sexual behavior such as pedophilia.

Backward chaining: A chaining procedure that begins with the last element in the chain and progresses to the first element.

Backup reinforcer: A reinforcer that may be received in exchange for a token. (See token economy.)

Baseline: A period during which the target behavior is recorded, but no attempt is made to modify it.

Behavior: Anything a person does that can be observed.

Behavior analysis: The science of behavior change; the study of the functional relations between behavior and environmental events.

Behavior chain: A sequence of related behaviors, each of which provides the cue for the next, and the last of which produces a reinforcer.

Behavior trapping: The procedure of bringing a target behavior under the influence of its natural reinforcers by exposing it to those reinforcers.

Behavioral assessment: The attempt to (1) define the target behavior; (2) identify functional relations between the target behavior and its antecedents and consequences; and (3) identify an effective intervention for changing the target behavior.

Behavioral contrast: The tendency for changes in behavior *outside* the training environment to be the opposite of the changes produced *in* the training environment. (Compare stimulus generalization.)

Behavioral repertoire: All the things an individual is capable of doing at any given moment.

Bootleg reinforcement: Reinforcement that is not part of, and tends to undermine, an intervention.

Chain: See behavior chain.

Chaining: The reinforcement of successive elements of a behavior chain.

Conditioned reinforcers: See secondary reinforcers.

Conditioning: See Pavlovian conditioning.

Consequences: Environmental events that occur *after* a behavior. (Consequences that are not produced by the behavior are called adventitious.)

Contingency contract: An agreement between two or more parties about what each is to do for the other.

Continuous recording: Recording each and every occurrence of a behavior during a prescribed period.

Contrived reinforcers: Reinforcers that have been arranged by someone for the purpose of modifying behavior.

Counterconditioning: The use of Pavlovian conditioning to undo the adverse effects of earlier conditioning.

Covert behavior: Behavior that can be observed only by the person performing it.

Covert sensitization: A variation of aversion therapy in which the paired events are imagined.

Cumulative frequency graph: A graph in which each data point indicates the total number of times the behavior has occurred up to that point.

Daniels' dictum: The principle that solving behavior problems with behavior analysis is more difficult than it appears. Daniels is known for telling people, "If you think this stuff is easy, you're doing it wrong."

Desensitization training: Any form of counterconditioning that reduces an inappropriate negative response to an event. (Compare sensitization training.)

Differential reinforcement: Any procedure that combines extinction and reinforcement to change the frequency of a target behavior.

Discrimination training: Any procedure that results in a target behavior having different frequencies in different situations.

Discriminative stimulus: Any event in the presence of which a target behavior is likely to have consequences that affect its frequency. Discriminative stimuli include S^Ds ("ess-dees") and S^Δs ("ess-deltas").

DRA (differential reinforcement of alternative behavior): The procedure of reducing the frequency of a target behavior by reinforcing an alternative behavior. The idea is to give the person an *alternative* way of obtaining reinforcers.

DRI (differential reinforcement of incompatible behavior): The procedure of reducing the frequency of a target behavior by reinforcing a behavior that is incompatible with the target behavior.

DRL (differential reinforcement of low rate): The procedure of reducing the frequency of a target behavior by reinforcing it only when it occurs at a low rate.

Environmental event: Any event in a person's environment that can be observed.

Escape-avoidance learning: A learning situation in which the target behavior results in escape from, or avoidance of, an aversive event.

Extinction: Withholding the reinforcers that maintain a target behavior.

Extinction burst: A sharp increase in the frequency of a behavior that is on extinction. Extinction bursts usually occur soon after a behavior is placed on extinction.

Fading: Gradually reducing the strength of a prompt.

Fixed duration schedule: A reinforcement schedule in which a reinforcer is provided after the target behavior has been performed continuously for a period of *n* length.

Fixed interval schedule: A reinforcement schedule in which a reinforcer is provided the first time the target behavior occurs after an interval of *n* length since the last reinforcement.

Fixed ratio schedule: A reinforcement schedule in which a reinforcer is provided after the target behavior has occurred *n* number of times.

Flooding: A form of desensitization training in which the client is exposed to real or imagined situations that are very disturbing until they no longer arouse anxiety. The procedure typically causes great discomfort initially and is of uncertain effectiveness.

Forward chaining: A chaining procedure that begins with the first element in a behavior chain and progresses to the last element.

Functional analysis: The process of testing hypotheses about the functional relations among antecedents, target behavior, and consequences.

Functional relation: The tendency of one event to vary in a regular way with one or more other events.

Generalization: The tendency for the effects of training to spread.

Inter-observer reliability: A measure of the degree of agreement in data tallies made by two or more observers.

Interval recording: Recording whether a behavior occurs during each of a series of short intervals within an observation period.

In vivo desensitization: A variation of systematic desensitization in which the anxiety-arousing situations to which the person is exposed are real, rather than imagined.

Law of effect: The principle that, in any given situation, the probability of a behavior occurring is a function of the consequences that behavior has had in that situation in the past. An abbreviated form says that behavior is a function of its consequences.

Learning history: All the environmental events (antecedents and consequences) that have affected a person's behavior up to the present.

Maintenance schedule: A reinforcement schedule that maintains a target behavior at a desired rate.

Maintenance training: Intervention procedures that increase the likelihood that changes in a target behavior will persist when the intervention is ended.

Medical model: The view that behavior problems are merely symptoms of an underlying psychological disorder.

Multiple baseline design: A single case design in which the effects of an intervention are recorded across situations, behaviors, or individuals.

Natural reinforcers: Reinforcers that have *not* been arranged by someone for the purpose of modifying behavior; also called spontaneous or unplanned reinforcers.

Negative reinforcer: A reinforcing event in which something is removed following a behavior.

Operant behavior: Behavior that is readily influenced by events that follow it.

Overcorrection: The procedure of reducing the frequency of a target behavior by making restitution for damage done and practice of appropriate behavior contingent on the target behavior.

Overt behavior: Behavior that can be observed by someone other than the person performing it.

Partial Reinforcement Effect (PRE): The principle that resistance to extinction is greater following intermittent reinforcement than it is following continuous reinforcement.

Pavlovian conditioning: Any procedure by which an event comes to elicit a response by being paired with an event that elicits that response.

Physical punishment: The procedure of reducing the frequency of a target behavior by making brief and noninjurious contact with the skin contingent on the target behavior.

Positive reinforcer: A reinforcing event in which something is added following a behavior.

Primary reinforcers: Reinforcers that are *not* dependent on their association with other reinforcers. (Compare secondary reinforcers.)

Prompt: An antecedent that induces a person to perform a behavior that otherwise does not occur.

Prompting: The procedure of providing antecedents that evoke a target behavior.

Punisher: An event that, when made contingent on a behavior, decreases the frequency of that behavior.

Punishment: The procedure of providing consequences for a behavior that decrease the frequency of that behavior.

Ratio strain: A reduction in the rate of a target behavior and an increase in emotional behavior resulting from an increase in the ratio of behavior to reinforcement. (See stretching the ratio.)

Reinforcement: The procedure of providing consequences for a behavior that increase or maintain the frequency of that behavior.

Reinforcement schedule: See schedule of reinforcement.

Reinforcer: An event that, when made contingent on a behavior, increases or maintains the frequency of that behavior.

Reprimand: To reduce the frequency of a target behavior by making disapproval contingent on the target behavior.

Respondent behavior: Behavior that is most readily influenced by events that precede it; reflexive behavior.

Response cost: The procedure of reducing the frequency of a target behavior by making removal of a reinforcer contingent on the target behavior.

Response generalization: The tendency for the effects of training one behavior to spread to other behaviors.

Resurgence: The reappearance, during extinction, of previously effective behavior.

S^D: An event in the presence of which a target behavior is reinforced. (Pronounced "ess-dee.") See discriminative stimulus.

S^Δ: An event in the presence of which a target behavior is not reinforced. (Pronounced "ess-delta.") See discriminative stimulus.

Schedule of reinforcement: A rule governing the delivery of reinforcers. (See, for example, fixed ratio schedule.)

Secondary reinforcers: Reinforcers that are dependent on their association with other reinforcers. Also called conditioned reinforcers. (compare primary reinforcers.)

Self-desensitization: A variation of systematic desensitization in which the client conducts the treatment without the aid of a therapist.

Sensitization training: Any form of counterconditioning that reduces an inappropriate positive response to an event. (Compare desensitization training.)

Shaping: The reinforcement of successive approximations of a target behavior.

Simple frequency graph: A graph in which each data point indicates the number of times a behavior occurred at a particular time.

Single case experimental design: A research design in which the behavior of an individual is compared under experimental and control conditions.

Spontaneous recovery: The reappearance of a target behavior following its extinction.

Stimulus control: The tendency for the target behavior to occur in the presence of the S^D but not in the presence of the S^Δ.

Stimulus discrimination: The tendency for behavior to have different frequencies in different situations.

Stimulus generalization: The tendency for the effects of training in one situation to spread to other situations.

Stretching the ratio: Gradually increasing the number of times a behavior must be performed to qualify for reinforcement. May produce ratio strain if done incorrectly.

Symptom substitution: The idea that if a behavior problem is solved without resolving the psychological conflicts that are presumed to have produced it, another behavior problem will take its place.

Systematic desensitization: A form of desensitization training in which the client repeatedly imagines anxiety-arousing situations while relaxed. The client progresses systematically through a hierarchy of more and more disturbing situations, typically without ever experiencing great anxiety.

Target behavior: The behavior to be changed by an intervention. Usually the goal of an intervention is to change the frequency of a target behavior.

Time out: The procedure of reducing the frequency of a target behavior by making removal of a person from a reinforcing situation contingent on the target behavior.

Token economy: A form of contingency contract, usually involving a group of people, in which the reinforcers are tokens that may be exchanged for other (backup) reinforcers in the future.

Variable duration schedule: A reinforcement schedule in which a reinforcer is provided after a target behavior has been performed continuously for a period, with the period varying around an average of n length.

Variable interval schedule: A reinforcement schedule in which a reinforcer is provided the first time the target behavior occurs after an interval, with the interval varying around an average of n seconds or minutes.

Variable ratio schedule: A reinforcement schedule in which a reinforcer is provided after a target behavior has occurred a number of times, with the number varying around an average of n.

References

Aldis, O. (1961, July/August). Of pigeons and men. *Harvard Business Review, 59–63.*

Allen, K. D., & Miltenberger, R. G. (1991). Burying the dead man test: A reply to Mallott. *TBA Newsletter, 14* (4), 11.

Allen, K. E., Hart, B. M., Buell, J. S., Harris, F. R., & Wolf, M. M. (1964). The effects of social reinforcement on isolate behavior of a nursery school child. *Child Development, 35,* 511–518.

Alvord, J. (1971). The home token economy: A motivational system for the home. *Corrective Psychiatry and Journal of Social Therapy, 17,* 6–13.

American Psychiatric Association. (1973). *Behavior therapy in psychiatry.* New York: Aronson.

American Psychological Association. (1992). Ethical principles of psychologists and code of conduct. *American Psychologist, 47,* 1597–1611.

Association for Advancement of Behavior Therapy. (1977). Ethical issues for human services. *Behavior Therapist, 8,* v–vi.

Ayllon, T. (1963). Intensive treatment of psychotic behavior by stimulus satiation and food reinforcement. *Behavior Research and Therapy, 1,* 53–61.

Ayllon, T., & Haughton, E. (1962). Control of the behavior of schizophrenic patients by food. *Journal of the Experimental Analysis of Behavior, 5,* 343–352.

Ayllon, T., & Michael, J. (1959). The psychiatric nurse as a behavioral engineer. *Journal of the Experimental Analysis of Behavior, 2,* 323–334.

Azrin, N. H., & Foxx, R. M. (1974). *Toilet training in less than a day.* New York: Pocket Books.

Azrin, N. H., & Powell, J. (1968). Behavioral engineering: The reduction of smoking behavior by a conditioning apparatus and procedure. *Journal of Applied Behavior Analysis, 1,* 193–200.

Azrin, R. D., & Hayes, S. C. (1984). The discrimination of interest within a heterosexual interaction: Training, generalization, and effects on social skills. *Behavior Therapy, 15,* 173–184.

Baer, D. M., Peterson, R. F., & Sherman, J. A. (1967). The development of imitation by reinforcing behavioral similarity to a model. *Journal of the Experimental Analysis of Behavior, 10,* 405–416.

Baer, D. M., Wolf, M. M., & Risley, T. R. (1968). Some current dimensions of applied behavior analysis. *Journal of Applied Behavior Analysis, 1,* 91–97.

Baer, D. M., Wolf, M. M., & Risley, T. R. (1987). Some still-current dimensions of applied behavior analysis. *Journal of Applied Behavior Analysis, 20,* 313–328.

Baldwin, J. D., & Baldwin, J. I. (1986). *Behavior principles in daily life (2nd ed.).* Englewood Cliffs, NJ: Prentice-Hall.

Ball, R. S. (1952). Reinforcement of conditioning of verbal behavior by verbal and non-verbal stimuli in a situation resembling a clinical interview. Unpublished doctoral dissertation, University of Indiana.

Bandura, A. (1975). The ethics and social purposes of behavior modification. In C. M. Franks & G. T. Wilson (Eds.), *Annual review of behavior therapy: Theory and practice* (pp. 13–20). New York: Bruner/Mazel.

Bandura, A., & Walters, R. H. (1959). *Adolescent aggression.* New York: Ronald Press.

Bell, S. M., & Ainsworth, M. D. S. (1972). Infant crying and maternal responsiveness. *Child Development, 43,* 1171–1190.

Blumstein, J. C., Roth, J. A., & Visher, C. A. (1986). Criminal careers and "career criminals" (Vol. 1). Washington, DC: National Academy Press.

Brownlee, J. R., & Bakeman, R. (1981). Hitting in toddler-peer interaction. *Child Development, 52,* 1076–1079.

Bruner, J. S. (1983). *In search of mind.* New York: Harper & Row.

Bueler, R. E., Patterson, G. R., & Furniss, J. M. (1966). The reinforcement of behavior in institutional settings. *Behavior Research and Therapy, 4,* 157–167.

Burrell, C. (1995, January 19). Action urged on sleepy truckers. *The (Wilmington) News Journal,* p. A2.

Cameron, J., & Pierce, W. D. (1994). Reinforcement, reward, and intrinsic motivation: A meta-analysis. *Review of Educational Research, 64,* 363–423.

Camp, D. S., Raymond, G. A., & Church, R. M. (1967). Temporal relationship between response and punishment. *Journal of Experimental Psychology, 74,* 114–123.

Carr, E. G. (1977). The motivation of self-injurious behavior: A review of some hypotheses. *Psychological Bulletin, 84,* 800–816.

Carr, E. G. (1985). Behavioral approaches to language and communication. In E. Schopler, & G. Mesibov (Eds.), *Communication problems in autism* (pp. 37–57). New York: Plenum.

Carr, E. G. (1993). Behavior analysis is not ultimately about behavior. *The Behavior Analyst, 16,* 47–49.

Carr, E. G., & Durand, V. M. (1985). Reducing behavior problems through functional communication training. *Journal of Applied Behavior Analysis, 18,* 111–126.

Carr, E. G., Levin, L., McConnachie, G., Carlson, J. I., Kemp, D. C., & Smith, C. E. (1994). *Communication-based intervention for problem behavior: A user's guide for producing positive change.* Baltimore: Paul Brookes.

Carr, E. G., & Lovaas, O. I. (1983). Contingent electric shock as a treatment for severe behavior problems. In S. Axelrod & J. Apsche (Eds.), *The effects of punishment on human behavior.* (pp. 221–245). New York: Academic Press.

Carr, J. E., & Bailey, J. S. (1996). A brief behavior therapy protocol for Tourette syndrome. *Journal of Behavior Therapy and Experimental Psychiatry, 27* (1), 33–40.

Catania, A. C. (1998). *Learning* (4th ed.). Upper Saddle River, NJ: Prentice-Hall.

Cautela, J. R. (1966). Treatment of compulsive behavior by covert sensitization. *Psychological Record, 16,* 33–41.

Cautela, J. R. (1967). Covert sensitization. *Psychological Reports, 20,* 459–468.

Chance, P. (1992, November). The rewards of learning. *Phi Delta Kappan,* pp. 200–207.

Cowden, R. C., & Ford, L. I. (1962). Systematic desensitization with phobic schizophrenics. *American Journal of Psychiatry, 119,* 241–245.

DeBell, C. S., & Harless, D. K. (1992). B. F. Skinner: Myth and misperception. *Teaching of Psychology, 19,* 68–73.

Deci, E., & Ryan, R. (1985). *Intrinsic motivation and self-determination in human behavior.* New York: Plenum.

Dickinson, A. M. (1989). The detrimental effects of extrinsic reinforcement on "intrinsic motivation." *The Behavior Analyst, 12,* 1–16.

Dickinson, D. (1974). But what happens when you take that reinforcement away? *Psychology in the Schools, 11,* 158–160.

Donnellan, A. M., LaVigna, G. W., Negri-Shoultz, N., & Fassbender, L. L. (1988). *Progress without punishment: Effective approaches for learners with behavior problems.* New York: Teachers College Press.

Dorsey, M. F., Iwata, B. A., Ong, P., & McSween, T. E. (1980). Treatment of self-injurious behavior using a water mist: Initial response suppression and generalization. *Journal of Applied Behavior Analysis, 13,* 343–353.

Drabman, R., & Spitalnik, R. (1973). Social isolation as a punishment procedure: A controlled study. *Journal of Experimental Child Psychology, 16,* 236–249.

Dworkin, B. R., & Miller, N. E. (1986). Failure to replicate visceral learning in the acute curarized rat in preparation. *Behavioral Neuroscience, 100,* 299–314.

Eisenberger, R., & Cameron, J. (1996). Detrimental effects of reward: Reality or myth? *American Psychologist, 51,* 1153–1166.

Eisenberger, R., & Selbst, M. (1994). Does reward increase or decrease creativity? *Journal of Personality and Social Psychology, 66,* 1116–1127.

Engelmann, S., & Carnine, D. (1982). *Theory of instruction: Principles and applications.* New York: Irvington.

Epstein, R. (1983). Resurgence of previously reinforced behavior during extinction. *The Behavior Analyst, 3,* 391–397.

Epstein, R. (1985a). Extinction-induced resurgence: Preliminary investigation and possible application. *Psychological Record, 35,* 143–153.

Epstein, R. (1985b). The positive side effects of reinforcement: A commentary on Balsam and Bondy (1983). *Journal of Applied Behavior Analysis, 18,* 73–78.

Ervin, S. J., Jr. (1973). Quality of health care—human experimentation. Statement before the subcommittee on health, committee on labor and public welfare, U. S. Senate, ninety-third congress, first session. Washington, DC: Government Printing Office.

Eysenck, H. J. (1959). Learning theory and behavior therapy. *Journal of Mental Science, 105,* 61–75.

Eysenck, H. J. (Ed.). (1960). *Behavior therapy and the neuroses.* New York: Pergamon.

Eysenck, H. J. (1965). *Fact and fiction in psychology.* Baltimore: Penguin.

Fleece, L., Gross, A., O'Brien, T., Kistner, J., Rothblum, E., and Drabman, R. (1981). Elevation of voice volume in young developmentally delayed children via an operant shaping procedure. *Journal of Applied Behavior Analysis, 14,* 351–355.

Foxx, R. M., & Azrin, N. H. (1973). The elimination of autistic self-stimulatory behavior by overcorrection. *Journal of Applied Behavior Analysis, 6,* 1–14.

Foxx, R. M., & Bechtel, D. R. (1983). Overcorrection: A review and analysis. In S. Axelrod & J. Apsche (Eds.), *The Effects of punishment on human behavior* (pp. 133–220). New York: Academic Press.

Franks, C. M., & Wilson, G. T. (1975). Ethical and related issues in behavior therapy: Commentary. In C. M. Franks & G. T. Wilson (Eds.), *Annual review of behavior therapy: Theory and practice* (pp. 1–11). New York: Bruner/Mazel.

Gantt, W. H. (1966). Conditional or conditioned, reflex or response. *Conditioned Reflex, 1,* 69–74.

Garfield, E. (1978). The 100 most-cited SSCI authors, 1969–1977. *Current Contents, 10,* 5–11.

Goldiamond, I. (1972). Justified and unjustified alarm over behavioral control. In R. E. Ulrich & P. T. Mountjoy (Eds.), *The experimental analysis of social behavior.* (pp. 487–510). New York: ACC. (Paper originally presented at the American Psychological Association convention, Philadelphia, PA, August, 1963)

Goldiamond, I. (1974). Toward a constructional approach to social problems: Ethical and constitutional issues raised by applied behavior analysis. *Behaviorism, 2,* 1–84. Reprinted in C. M. Franks & G. T. Wilson (Eds.), *Annual review of behavior therapy: Theory and practice.* (pp. 21–63). New York: Bruner/Mazel.

Graf, S. A. (1994). *Monitoring behavior: An introduction to psychology (2nd ed.).* Poland, OH: Graf Implements.

Grant, L., & Evans, A. (1994). *Principles of behavior analysis.* New York: Harper Collins.

Graubard, P. S., & Rosenberg, H. (1974). *Classrooms that work: Prescription for change.* New York: Dutton.

Graubard, P. S., Rosenberg, H., & Miller, M. B. (1971). A new direction for education: Behavior analysis. In E. A. Ramp & B. L. Hopkins (Eds.), *Behavior analysis in education* (Vol. 1). Lawrence, KS: University of Kansas.

Greene, D., & Lepper, M. R. (1974, September). Intrinsic motivation: How to turn play into work. *Psychology Today,* pp. 49–54.

Greenspoon, J. (1955). The reinforcing effect of two spoken sounds on the frequency of two responses. *American Journal of Psychology, 68,* 409–416.

Gruber, B., Reeser, R., & Reid, D. H. (1979). Providing a less restrictive environment for profoundly retarded persons by teaching independent walking skills. *Journal of Applied Behavior Analysis, 12,* 285–297.

Gursky, D. (1992, March). The writing life. *Teacher Magazine,* pp. 10–11.

Guttman, N. (1963). Laws of behavior and facts of perception. In S. Koch (Eds.), *Psychology: A study of a science* (Vol. 5). New York: McGraw-Hill.

Guttman, N., & Kalish, H. I. (1956). Discriminability and stimulus generalization. *Journal of Experimental Psychology, 51,* 79–88.

Hall, R. V., & Hall, M. C. (1980). *How to use planned ignoring.* Austin, TX: Pro-Ed.

Hart, B., & Risley, T. R. (1995). *Meaningful differences in the everyday experience of young American children.* Baltimore: Paul Brookes.

Hart, B. M., Allen, K. E., Buell, J. S., Harris, F. R., & Wolf, M. M. (1964). Effects of social reinforcement on operant crying. *Journal of Experimental Child Psychology, 1,* 145–153.

Herrnstein, R. J. (1966). Superstition: A corollary of the principle of operant conditioning. In W. K. Honig (Ed.), *Operant behavior: Areas of research and application* (pp. 33–51). New York: Appleton-Century-Crofts.

Herrnstein, R. J. (1993). Comments made at the Cambridge Forum on Executive Leadership sponsored by the Cambridge Center for Behavioral Studies, Cambridge, MA, June 21–22.

Heyduk, R. G., & Fenigstein, A. (1984). Influential works and authors in psychology: A survey of eminent psychologists. *American Psychologist, 37,* 556–559.

Higgins, S. T., & Morris, E. K. (1985). A comment on contemporary definitions of reinforcement as a behavioral process. *The Psychological Record, 35,* 81–88.

Hopkins, B. L., & Conard, R. J. (1975). Putting it all together: Superschool. In N. G. Haring & R. L. Schiefelbusch (Eds.), *Teaching special children* (pp. 342–385). New York: McGraw-Hill.

Horner, R. H., Eberhard, J. M., & Sheehan, M. R. (1986). Teaching generalized table bussing. *Behavior Modification, 10,* 457–471.

Isaacs, W., Thomas, J., & Goldiamond, I. (1960). Application of operant conditioning to reinstate verbal behavior in psychotics. *Journal of Speech and Hearing Disorders, 25,* 8–12.

Iwata, B. A., Pace, G. M., Dorsey, M. F., Zarcone, J. R., et al. (1994). The functions of self-injurious behavior: An experimental-epidemiological analysis. *Journal of Applied Behavior Analysis, 27* (2), 215–240.

Jackson, G. M., Johnson, C. R. Ackron, G. S., & Crowley, R. (1975). Food satiation as a procedure to decelerate vomiting. *American Journal of Mental Deficiency, 80,* 223–227.

Jacobson, E. (1938). *Progressive relaxation.* Chicago: University of Chicago Press.

Jewett, J., & Clark, H. B. (1979). Teaching pre-schoolers to use appropriate dinner time conversation: An analysis of generalization from school to home. *Behavior Therapy, 10,* 589–605.

Johnson, K. R., & Layng, T. V. J. (1992). Breaking the structuralist barrier: Literacy and numeracy with fluency. *American Psychologist, 47,* 1475–1490.

Johnson, N. (1969, February). Through the video-screen darkly. *Christian Science Monitor,* p. 12.

Jonas, G. (1973). *Visceral learning.* New York: Viking Press.

Jones, M. C. (1924a). The elimination of children's fears. *Journal of Experimental Psychology, 7,* 382–390.

Jones, M. C. (1924b). A laboratory study of fear: The case of Peter. *Pedagogical Seminary, 31,* 308–315.

Kahle, A. L., & Kelley, M. L. (1994). Children's homework problems: A comparison of goal setting and parent training. *Behavior Therapy, 25,* 275–290.

Kantorovich, N. V. (1930). An attempt at associative reflex therapy in alcoholics. *Psychological Abstracts* (No. 4282).

Kazdin, A. E. (1994). *Behavior modification in applied settings* (5th ed.). Pacific Grove, CA: Brooks/Cole.

Kelly, J. A., & Drabman, R. S. (1977). Generalizing response suppression of self-injurious behavior through an overcorrection punishment procedure: A case study. *Behavior Therapy, 8,* 468–472.

Kemp, D. C., & Carr, E. G. (1995). Reduction of severe problem behavior in community employment using an hypothesis-driven multicomponent intervention approach. *Journal of the Association for Persons with Severe Handicaps, 20,* 229–247.

Koestler, A. (1968). *The ghost in the machine.* New York: Macmillan.

Korn, J. H., Davis, R., & Davis, S. F. (1991). Historian's and chairpersons' judgments of eminence among psychologists. *American Psychologist, 46,* 789–792.

Krutch, J. W. (1953). *The measure of man.* Indianapolis: Bobbs-Merrill.

Kushner, M. (1965). The reduction of a long-standing fetish by means of aversive conditioning. In L. P. Ullmann & L. Krasner (Eds.), *Case studies in behavior modification* (pp. 239–245). New York: Holt, Rinehart & Winston.

Latham, G. (1996). *Lessons learned by the therapist from the client: Something for the good of the order.* Paper presented at the annual meeting of The International Behaviorology Association, Logan, Utah.

Lattal, K. A. (1989). Contingencies of response rate and resistance to change. *Learning and Motivation, 20,* 191–203.

Lattal, K. A. (1995). Contingency and behavior analysis. *The Behavior Analyst, 18,* 209–224.

Lavin, N. I., Thorpe, J. G., Barker, J. C., Blakemore, C. B., & Conway, C. G. (1961). Behavior therapy in a case of transvestism. *Journal of Nervous and Mental Diseases, 133,* 346–353.

Lee, V. L. (1996). Why operant research is not about the behavior of organisms. *Journal of Behavior Analysis and Therapy, 1,* 52–58.

Leitenberg, H., & Callahan, E. J. (1973). Reinforced practice and reduction of different kinds of fears in adults and children. *Behavioral Research and Therapy, 11,* 19–30.

Lennox, D. B., Miltenberger, R. G., & Donnelly, D. R. (1987). Response interruption and DRL for the reduction of rapid eating. *Journal of Applied Behavior Analysis, 20,* 279–284.

Lepper, M. R., & Greene, D. (Eds.) (1978). *The hidden costs of reward: New perspectives on the psychology of human motivation.* Hillsdale, NJ: Erlbaum.

Lewis, D. J. (1960). Partial reinforcement: A selective review of the literature since 1950. *Psychological Bulletin, 57,* 1–28.

Lichstein, K. L., & Schreibman, L. (1976). Employing electric shock with autistic children: A review of the side effects. *Journal of Autism and Childhood Schizophrenia, 6,* 163–173.

Lindsley, O. R. (1968). A reliable wrist counter for recording behavior rates. *Journal of Applied Behavior Analysis, 1,* 77–78.

Linscheid, T. R., Iwata, B. A., Ricketts, R. W., Williams, D. E., & Griff, J. C. (1990). Clinical evaluation of the self-injurious inhibiting system (SIBIS). *Journal of Applied Behavior Analysis, 23,* 53–78.

Lovaas, O. I. (1987). Behavioral treatment and normal educational and intellectual functioning in young autistic children. *Journal of Consulting and Clinical Psychology, 55,* 3–9.

Lovaas, O. I., Berberich, J. P., Perloff, B. F., & Schaeffer, B. (1966). Acquisition of imitative speech by schizophrenic children. *Science, 151,* 705–707.

MacKenzie-Keating, S. E., & McDonald, L. (1990). Overcorrection: Reviewed, revisited and revised. *The Behavior Analyst, 13,* 39–48.

Madsen, C. H. (1965). Positive reinforcement in the toilet training of a normal child: A case report. In L. P. Ullmann, and Leonard Krasner (Eds.), *Case studies in behavior modification* (pp. 305–307). New York: Holt, Rinehart, & Winston.

Madsen, C. H., Becker, W. C., Thomas, D. R., Koser, L., & Plager, E. (1970a). An analysis of the reinforcing effects of "sit down" commands. In R. K. Parker (Ed.), *Readings in educational psychology.* (pp. 265–278). Boston: Allyn & Bacon.

Madsen, C. H., Madsen, C. K., Saudargas, R. A., Hammond, W. R., & Edgar, D. E. (1970b). Classroom RAID (Rules, Approval, Ignore, Disapproval): A cooperative approach for professionals and volunteers. *Journal of School Psychology, 8,* 180.

Malott, R. W., Whaley, D. L., & Malott, M. E. (1993). *Elementary principles of behavior.* Englewood Cliffs, NJ: Prentice-Hall.

Martin, G. L. (1972). Teaching operant technology to psychiatric nurses, aides, and attendants. In F. W. Clark, D. R. Evans, & L. A. Haneslynch (Eds.), *Implementing behavior programs for schools and clinics* (pp. 63–87). Champaign, IL: Research Press.

Matson, J. L., & DiLorenzo, T. M. (1984). *Punishment and its alternatives.* New York: Springer.

Matson, J. L., Horne, A. M., Ollendick, D. G., Ollendick, T. H. (1979). Overcorrection: A further evaluation of restitution and positive practice. *Journal of Behavior Therapy and Experimental Psychiatry, 10,* 295–298.

Matson, J. L., & Stephens, R. M. (1977). Overcorrection of aggressive behavior in a chronic psychiatric patient. *Behavior Modification, 1,* 559–564.

Matson, J. L., Stephens, R. M., & Smith, C. (1978). Treatment of self-injurious behavior with overcorrection. *Journal of Mental Deficiency Research, 22,* 175–178.

Maurice, C. (1993). *Let me hear your voice: A family's triumph over autism.* New York: Fawcett Columbine.

Mawhinney, T. C. (1990). Decreasing intrinsic "motivation" with extrinsic rewards: Easier said than done. *Journal of Organizational Management, 11,* 175–191.

McEachin, J. J., Smith, T., & Lovaas, O. I. (1993). Long-term outcome for children with autism who received early intensive behavioral treatment. *American Journal of Mental Retardation, 97,* 359–372.

Meichenbaum, D. H., Bowers, K. S., & Ross, R. R. (1969). A behavioral analysis of teacher expectancy effect. *Journal of Personality and Social Psychology, 13,* 306–316.

Michael, J. (1975). Positive and negative reinforcement, a distinction that is no longer necessary: Or, a better way to talk about bad things. *Behaviorism, 3,* 33–44.

Michael, J. (1984). Verbal behavior. *Journal of the Experimental Analysis of Behavior, 42,* 363–376.

Miller, N. E. (1978). Biofeedback and visceral learning. *Annual Review of Psychology, 29,* 373–404.

Miller, N. E., & DiCara, L. (1967). Instrumental learning of heart rate changes in curarized rats: Shaping and specificity to discriminative stimuli. *Journal of Comparative and Physiological Psychology, 63,* 12–19.

Myers, L. L., & Thyer, B. A. (1994). Behavioral therapy: Popular misconceptions. *Scandinavian Journal of Behavior Therapy, 23,* 97–107.

Nation, J. R., & Woods, D. J. (1980). Persistence: The role of partial reinforcement in psychotherapy. *Journal of Experimental Psychology: General, 109,* 175–207.

Nevin, J. A. (1974). Response strength in multiple schedules of reinforcement. *Journal of the Experimental Analysis of Behavior, 21,* 389–408.

Nevin, J. A. (1987). Does contingent reinforcement strengthen operant behavior? *Journal of the Experimental Analysis of Behavior, 48,* 17–33.

Nevin, J. A. (1988). Behavioral momentum and the partial reinforcement effect. *Psychological Bulletin, 103,* 44–56.

Nevin, J. A. (1993). Behavioral momentum: Implications for clinical practice. *Behavior Change, 10,* 162–168.

O'Brien, R. M., & Dickinson, A. M. (1982). Introduction to industrial behavior modification. In R. M. O'Brien, A. M. Dickinson, & M. P. Rosow (Eds.), *Industrial behavior modification* (pp. 7–34). New York: Pergamon Press.

O'Brien, S., & Repp, A. C. (1990). Reinforcement-based reductive procedures: A review of 20 years of their use with persons with severe or profound retardation. *Journal of the Association for Persons with Severe Handicaps, 15,* 148–159.

O'Leary, K. D., Kaufman, K. F., Kass, R. E., & Drabman, R. S. (1970). The effects of loud and soft reprimands on the behavior of disruptive students. *Exceptional Children, 37,* 145–155.

Patterson, G. R. (1965). An application of conditioning techniques to the control of a hyperactive child. In L. P. Ullmann & L. Krasner (Eds.), *Case studies in behavior modification* (pp. 370–375). New York: Holt, Rinehart & Winston.

Pavlov, I. (1927). *Conditioned reflexes* (G. V. Anrep, Ed. and Trans.). London: Oxford University Press.

Peterson, A. L., & Azrin, N. H. (1993). Behavioral and pharmacological treatments for Tourette syndrome: A review. *Applied and Preventive Psychology, 2,* 231–242.

Pfaus, J. G., Blackburn, J. R., Harpur, T. J., MacDonald, M. A., Mana, M. J., & Jacobs, W. J. (1988). Has psychology ever been a science of behavior? A comment on Skinner. *American Psychologist, 43,* 821–822.

Pryor, K. (1996). Clicker training aids shelter adoption rates. *Don't Shoot the Dog! News,* 1, (2), 2.

Quay, H. C. (1959). The effect of verbal reinforcement on the recall of early memories. *Journal of Abnormal and Social Psychology, 59,* 254–257.

Raymond, M. J. (1956). Case of fetishism treated by aversion therapy. *British Medical Journal, 2,* 854–857.

Raymond, M. J. (1964). The treatment of addiction by aversion conditioning with apomorphine. *Behavior Research and Therapy, 1,* 287–291.

Renner, K. E. (1964). Delay of reinforcement: A historical review. *Psychological Bulletin, 61,* 341–361.

Rickard, H. C., Dignam, P. J., & Horner, R. F. (1960). Verbal manipulation in a psychotherapeutic relationship. *Journal of Clinical Psychology, 16,* 364–367.

Rickard, H. C., & Mundy, M. B. (1965). Direct manipulation of stuttering behavior: An experimental-clinical approach. In L. P. Ullmann & L. Krasner (Eds.), *Case studies in behavior modification* (pp. 268–274). New York: Holt, Rinehart & Winston.

Risley, T., & Hart, B. (1968). Developing correspondence between the nonverbal and verbal behavior of preschool children. *Journal of Applied Behavior Analysis, 1,* 267–281.

Rokeach, M. (1964). *The three Christs of Ypsilanti.* New York: Knopf.

Rosen, G. M., Glasgow, R. E., & Barrera, M., Jr. (1977). A two-year follow-up on systematic desensitization with data pertaining to the external validity of laboratory fear assessment. *Journal of Consulting and Clinical Psychology, 45,* 1188–1189.

Rosenthal, R. (1973, September). The Pygmalion effect lives. *Psychology Today,* 56–63.

Rosenthal, R., & Jacobson, L. (1968). *Pygmalion in the classroom.* New York: Holt.

Rothbaum, B. O., Hodges, L. F., Kooper, R., Opdyke, D., Williford, J. S., & North, M. (1995). Virtual reality graded exposure in the treatment of acrophobia: A case report. *Behavior Therapy, 26,* 547–554.

Ryback, D., & Staats, A. W. (1970). Parents as behavior therapy technicians in treating reading deficits (dyslexia). *Journal of Behavior Therapy and Experimental Psychiatry, 1,* 109–111.

Sajwaj, T., Libet, J., & Agras, S. (1974). Lemon-juice therapy: The control of life-threatening rumination in a six-month-old infant. *Journal of Applied Behavior Analysis, 7,* 557–563.

Schlinger, H. D., Jr. (n.d.). Of planets and cognitions: The use of deductive inference in the natural sciences and psychology. Unpublished manuscript.

Schneider, S. M. (1990). The role of contiguity in free-operant unsignaled delay of positive reinforcement: A brief review. *Psychological Record, 40,* 239–257.

Sears, R. R., Maccoby, E. E., & Levin, H. (1957). *Patterns of child rearing.* Evanston, IL: Row, Peterson.

Serber, M. (1970). Shame aversion therapy. *Journal of Behavior Therapy and Experimental Psychiatry, 1,* 213.

Sidman, M. (1989). *Coercion and its fallout.* Boston: Authors Cooperative, Inc.

Skaggs, K. J., Dickinson, A. M., & O'Connor, K. A. (1992). The use of concurrent schedules to evaluate the effects of extrinsic rewards on "intrinsic motivation": A replication. *Journal of Organizational Behavior Magagement, 12,* 45–74.

Skinner, B. F. (1938). *The behavior of organisms: An experimental analysis.* New York: Appleton-Century-Crofts.

Skinner, B. F. (1945, October). Baby in a box. *Ladies Home Journal*, pp. 30–31, 135–136, 138. Reprinted in B. F. Skinner (Ed.), *Cumulative Record: Enlarged Edition* (pp. 419–426). New York: Appleton-Century-Crofts.

Skinner, B. F. (1953). *Science and human behavior.* New York: Free Press.

Skinner, B. F. (1961). A case history in scientific method. In Skinner, B. F., *Cumulative record: Enlarged edition* (pp. 76–100). New York: Appleton-Century-Crofts. (Originally published in 1956)

Skinner, B.F. (1969). *Contingencies of reinforcement: A theoretical analysis.* New York: Appleton-Century-Crofts.

Skinner, B. F. (1975). The shaping of phylogenic behavior. *Journal of the Experimental Analysis of Behavior, 24,* 117–120.

Skinner, B.F. (1981). Selection by consequences. *Science, 213* (4507), 501–504.

Skinner, B.F. (1984). The evolution of behavior. *Journal of the Experimental Analysis of Behavior, 41,* 217–221.

Skinner, B. F. (1987). Whatever happened to psychology as the science of behavior? *American Psychologist, 42,* 780–786.

Skinner, B. F. (1989). The origins of cognitive thought. *American Psychologist, 44,* 13–18.

Socolar, R. R., & Stein, R. E. (1995). Spanking infants and toddlers: Maternal beliefs and practice. *Pediatrics, 95,* 105–111.

Staats, A. W., & Staats, C. K. (1958). Attitudes established by classical conditioning. *Journal of Abnormal and Social Psychology, 57,* 37–40.

Staats, C. K., & Staats, A. W. (1957). Meaning established by classical conditioning. *Journal of Experimental Psychology, 54,* 74–80.

Stampfl, T. G., & Levis, D. J. (1967). Essential of implosive therapy: A learning-theory based psychodynamic behavioral therapy. *Journal of Abnormal and Social Psychology, 72,* 157–163.

Stokes, T. F., & Baer, D.M. (1977). An implicit technology of generalization. *Journal of Applied Behavior Analysis, 10,* 349–367.

Stokes, T. F., & Osnes, P. G. (1989). An operant pursuit of generalization. *Behavior Therapy, 20,* 337–355.

Stolz, S. B., & Associates. (1978). *Ethical issues in behavior modification.* New York: Jossey-Bass.

Sutherland, S. (1993, 26 August). Impoverished minds. *Nature, 364,* 767.

Tannen, D. (1986). *That's not what I meant: How conversational style makes or breaks your relations with others.* New York: Morrow.

Teale, E. W. (1946). *The lost woods.* New York: Dodd, Mead.

Thomas, J. D., Presland, I. E., Grant, M. D., & Glynn, T. L. (1978). Natural rates of teacher approval and disapproval in grade-seven classrooms. *Journal of Applied Behavior Analysis, 11,* 91–94.

Thorndike, E. L. (1898). Animal intelligence. *Psychological Review Monographs, 2*(8).

Thorndike, E. L. (1911). *Animal intelligence: Experimental studies.* New York: Hafner.

Thorndike, E. L. (1968). *Human learning.* Cambridge, MA: MIT Press. (Originally published in 1931)

Todd, D. E., Besko, G. T., & Pear, J. J. (1995). Human shaping parameters: A 3-dimensional investigation. A poster presented at the meeting of the Association for Behavior Analysis.

Todd, J. T., & Morris, E. K. (1992). Case histories in the great power of steady misrepresentation. *American Psychologist, 47,* 1441–1453.

Trotter, R. S., & Warren, J. (1974). Behavior modification under fire. *APA Monitor, 5* (1), 4.

Ullmann, L. P., & Krasner, L. (1965). *Case studies in behavior modification.* New York: Holt, Rinehart & Winston.

Ulrich, R. E. (1967). Behavior control and public concern. *Psychological Record, 17,* 229–234.

Van Houton, R., & Doleys, D. M. (1983). Are social reprimands effective? In S. Axelrod & J. Apsche (Eds.), *The effects of punishment on human behavior* (pp. 45–70). New York: Academic Press.

Van Houton, R., Nau, P. A., MacKenzie-Keating, S., Sameoto, D., & Colavecchia, B. (1982). An analysis of some variables influencing the effectiveness of reprimands. *Journal of Applied Behavior Analysis, 15,* 65–83.

Verplanck, W. S. (1955). The control of the content of conversation: Reinforcement of statements of opinion. *Journal of Abnormal and Social Psychology, 51,* 668–676.

Wallace, I., and & Pear, J. J. (1977). Self-control techniques of famous novelists. *Journal of Applied Behavior Analysis, 10,* 515–525.

Walster, E., & Berscheid, E. (1971, June). Adrenaline makes the heart grow fonder. *Psychology Today,* 47–50, 62.

Watson, J. B. (1924/1970). *Behaviorism.* New York: Norton.

White, M. A. (1975). Natural rates of teacher approval and disapproval in the classroom. *Journal of Applied Behavior Analysis, 8,* 367–372.

Williams, B. A. (1983). Another look at contrast in multiple schedules. *Journal of the Experimental Analysis of Behavior, 39,* 345–384.

Williams, C. D. (1959). The elimination of tantrum behavior by extinction procedures. *Journal of Abnormal and Social Psychology, 59,* 269.

Williams, S. B. (1938). Resistance to extinction as a function of the number of reinforcements. *Journal of Experimental Psychology, 23,* 506–521.

Winston, A. S., & Baker, J. E. (1985). Behavior analytic studies of creativity: A critical review. *The Behavior Analyst, 8,* 191–205.

Wolf, M. M., Birnbrauer, J. S., Williams, T., & Lawler, J. (1965). A note on apparent extinction of the vomiting behavior of a retarded child. In L. P. Ullmann & L. Krasner (Eds.), *Case studies in behavior modification* (pp. 364–366). New York: Holt, Rinehart & Winston.

Wolf, M., Risley, T., & Mees, H. (1964). Application of operant conditioning procedures to the behavior problems of an autistic child. *Behavior Research and Therapy, 1,* 305–312.

Wolfe, D. A., Mendes, M. G., & Factor, D. (1984) A parent-administered program to reduce children's television viewing. *Journal of Applied Behavior Analysis, 17,* 267–272.

Wolpe, J. (1973). *The practice of behavior therapy (2nd ed.).* New York: Pergamon Press.

Wolpe, J., & Lang, P. J. (1964). A fear survey schedule for use in behavior therapy. *Behavior Research and Therapy, 2,* 27–30.

Wong, L. Y. (1995). Research on teaching: Process-product research findings and the feelings of obviousness. *Journal of Educational Psychology, 87,* 504–511.

Wong, S. E., & Woolsey, J. E. (1989). Re-establishing conversational skills in overtly psychotic, chronic schizophrenic patients. *Behavior Modification, 13* (4), 415–430.

Woods, D. W., & Miltenberger, R. G. (1995). Habit reversal: A review of applications and variations. *Journal of Behavior Therapy and Experimental Psychiatry, 26* (2), 123–131.

Wyatt, W. J. (1997). *Behavior Analysis Digest, 9* (1), 1.

Wyatt, W. J., Hawkins, R. P., & Davis, P. (1986a). Behaviorism: Are reports of its death exaggerated? *The Behavior Analyst, 9,* 101–105.

Wyatt, W. J., Hawkins, R. P., & Davis, P. (1986b). A survey of editors of behavioral journals. *TBA Newsletter, 9,* 4–6.

Yokley, J. M., & Glenwick, D. (1984). Increasing the immunization of preschool children; an evaluation of applied community interventions. *Journal of Applied Behavior Analysis, 17,* 313–325.

Name Index

Subject Index

TO THE OWNER OF THIS BOOK:

I hope that you have found *First Course in Applied Behavior Analysis* useful. So that this book can be improved in a future edition, would you take the time to complete this sheet and return it? Thank you.

School and address: ———————————————————————————

Department: ————————————————————————————————

Instructor's name: ———————————————————————————

1. What I like most about this book is: ——————————————

———————————————————————————————————————

———————————————————————————————————————

2. What I like least about this book is: —————————————

———————————————————————————————————————

———————————————————————————————————————

3. My general reaction to this book is: ——————————————

———————————————————————————————————————

4. The name of the course in which I used this book is: ——————

———————————————————————————————————————

5. Were all of the chapters of the book assigned for you to read? —————

    If not, which ones weren't? ———————————————————

6. In the space below, or on a separate sheet of paper, please write specific suggestions for improving this book and anything else you'd care to share about your experience in using the book.

———————————————————————————————————————

———————————————————————————————————————

———————————————————————————————————————

———————————————————————————————————————

———————————————————————————————————————

Optional:

Your name: _____   Date: _____

May Brooks/Cole quote you, either in promotion for *First Course in Applied Behavior Analysis,* or in future publishing ventures?

Yes: _____ No:_____

Sincerely,

Paul Chance